LAURA GILPIN

Frontispiece. LAURA GILPIN. *Clarence H. White. Platinum print, c. 1916–1917. Collection of Lewis Allen.*

LAURA GILPIN

An Enduring Grace

MARTHA A. SANDWEISS

AMON CARTER MUSEUM
FORT WORTH, TEXAS

This book was produced in conjunction with
"*An Enduring Grace: The Photographs of Laura Gilpin*,"
an exhibition organized by the Amon Carter Museum
and exhibited at the Amon Carter Museum, January 24–
April 13, 1986; the IBM Gallery in New York City,
July 22–August 30, 1986; the Colorado Historical Society,
Denver, November 11, 1986–January 11, 1987; the Saint
Louis Art Museum, February 10–March 29, 1987; the
Museum of Fine Arts, Santa Fe, New Mexico, July 24–
September 20, 1987; and the Center for Creative Photog-
raphy, Tucson, Arizona, December, 1987–January, 1988.

This book has been published with assistance from the
Henry Luce Foundation, Inc.

International Standard Book Number: 0–88360–077–3
Library of Congress Catalog Card Number: 85–081521

Contents

Preface

It has been my good fortune to be curator of photographs at the Amon Carter Museum in Fort Worth, Texas, since May 1979. By the time I arrived, Laura Gilpin had already announced that she intended to bequeath her extensive collection of photographs, negatives, correspondence, and photographic books to the museum. I went to visit her several times in Santa Fe, and after her death in November 1979, I helped move her photographic estate to Fort Worth.

The museum's director, Jan Keene Muhlert, and its Board of Trustees have supported this project from the beginning. In 1984 I was given a four-month sabbatical from my museum responsibilities to pursue research and writing full time. Financial support for this leave came from the museum and from a generous grant from the Henry Luce Fund for Scholarship in American Art, which awarded money to the museum to help underwrite the costs of cataloguing and researching the materials in the Gilpin bequest. The staff of the museum has been of great assistance. I am particularly indebted to Milan Hughston, associate librarian, who compiled a chronological bibliography of Gilpin's career and helped me with numerous reference queries, and to Assistant Director Ron Tyler, who gave helpful comments on an earlier version of this manuscript.

The staff of the museum's photography department has helped with this project in many ways. Annabel Ross deftly catalogued nearly twenty thousand of Laura Gilpin's negatives, while Lisa Fukui catalogued the prints from the Gilpin estate and helped with numerous research queries. With funds provided by the Luce Foundation grant, Zoe Zimmerman, Dan Bartow, Patricia Chisholm, and Bill Kirby made contact prints from the Gilpin negatives. This archive of study prints has been of great assistance to me in my research and should prove to be a valuable resource to other scholars. Jessamyn Cartwright, who has labeled and filed these study prints while handling a myriad of other departmental chores, deserves recognition for her efforts, as does Carol Roark, the assistant curator of photographs. While I was absorbed in this project, Carol helped manage the department's affairs so that I could focus on Laura Gilpin. Additional help for the Gilpin project has come from museum staff members Carol Byars, Linda Lorenz, Mary Kennedy McCabe, Beth Taylor Muskat, and Rynda White.

I knew Laura Gilpin only briefly, but one of the great pleasures of working on this project has been the opportunity to meet and get to know her many friends, some of whom I now count among my own. Gerald Richardson, Mary Peck, Richard Wilder, Richard Rudisill, and Margaret Schoonover have been of particular help, and I hope they'll find that the portrait sketched in this book bears some resemblance to the woman they knew far better than I. Richard Rudisill also gave careful readings of earlier drafts of this manuscript, and my writing has benefited from his assistance.

Numerous other friends of Laura Gilpin from Santa Fe, Colorado Springs, the Navajo Reservation and elsewhere shared reminiscences with me and I thank them all for their time and generosity. I want particularly to acknowledge the assistance of Louis Allen, C. F. Bieber, Audrie Bobb, Jim Bones, Edith Brann, F. Martin Brown, Hazel Brown, Sina Brush, Moris Burge, Eleanor Caponigro, Peggy Pond Church, William Clift, Anita Da, Angie Deale, Tom Dickerson, Nora Fisher, Beverly Gile, Lillian Gish, Johnie Guero, Una Hanbury, Helen Jackson, Barbara Jeager, Fred Jim, Corky Jones, Dave Jones, Edith Kennedy, Ernest Knee, George Kubler, Marjorie Lambert, Fred Mang,

Faith Bemis Meem, John Gaw Meem, Beaumont Newhall, Anne Noggle, Georgia O'Keeffe, James Orr, Rain Parrish, Juanita Peña, Tony Peña, Eliot Porter, Charlene Reeves, Elizabeth Richardson, Paula Rodriguez, Phil Shultz, Marka Stewart, Betty Toulouse, Helen Shugg Webb, Myron Wood, and Persis Wood.

Additional assistance for this project has come from Ansel Adams, John Collier, Jr., Therese Heyman, William Homer, María Martínez, Nathan Simon, Ralph Steiner, Karl Struss, Willard Van Dyke, and Maynard P. White, Jr. I also want to thank Alfred Bush, who gave me access to the papers of the Association on American Indian Affairs; Peter Bunnell, who kindly allowed me to see the Clarence H. White Collection at The Art Museum, Princeton University; and Rutherford Witthus, who acted as guide to the Fisher Architectural Records Collection in Denver. My research took me to numerous other collections of Laura Gilpin's photographs, and for their assistance I want to single out Eric Paddock, Colorado Historical Society; Terence Pitts and James Enyeart, Center for Creative Photography; Will Wroth, Colorado Springs Fine Arts Center; and Jerald Maddox, Prints and Photographs Division, Library of Congress.

I also want to acknowledge the assistance of Laura Gilpin's cousins, Lewis Allen and Kenneth Gilpin, Jr., both of whom have been cooperative and generous supporters of my research ever since the Gilpin photographic estate arrived at the Amon Carter Museum.

For permission to quote from their interviews with Laura Gilpin, I want to thank Jon Burris, Eleanor Caponigro, Arthur Ollman and Rosella Stern, and Margaret Schoonover. For permission to quote from the letters of Brenda Putnam and Herbert Putnam, thanks go to Desmond O'Hara. My appreciation is also extended to the many others who have granted permission for me to quote from the manuscript material in the Gilpin Collection at the museum or graciously answered my research queries.

A slightly different draft of this manuscript was submitted in 1985 as my doctoral dissertation to the History Department at Yale University. My advisor, Howard Lamar, gave numerous helpful readings of the manuscript, as did Ann Fabian. Paula Tyler was a careful proofreader.

My thanks go last, but certainly not least, to my husband, Robert Horowitz, who has a good eye for pictures and shares my interest in photography and the Southwest. He has helped with this project in many ways and his presence has made the writing of this book a much more pleasant task.

Introduction: Laura Gilpin and the American Southwest

Laura Gilpin photographed the American Southwest for more than sixty years, documenting its people, its landscape, and its ancient ruins. She was born in 1891 and first experimented with a camera as a child. After studying photography in New York in 1916–1917, she returned to her native Colorado Springs to begin her professional photographic career. Although commercial jobs supported her, her real love was for the out-of-doors. She began exploring Colorado and New Mexico on camping trips in the early 1920s and even in her eighties – ignoring the physical infirmities of age – she would camp overnight to be near a place she wanted to photograph. The vast empty stretches of the southwestern desert did not deter her. She thought nothing of driving several hundred miles to make one image of a Navajo ceremony or making a long flight in a small plane to see a particular mountain peak. She was a strong, stocky woman, five feet seven inches tall, with clear blue eyes, wavy sand-colored hair that later turned a brilliant white, and a hearty laugh that suggested boundless energy. She was self-reliant and strong-willed, but a streak of eastern gentility tempered her quintessentially western independence, and an appreciation for traditional values lent a formality to her adventuresome life and extended to her work. Although her record of southwestern life was compiled over sixty years, her photographs are less about change than about the timeless and enduring qualities of the land and its people.

Through four major books, *The Pueblos: A Camera Chronicle* (1941), *Temples in Yucatan: A Camera Chronicle of Chichen Itza* (1948), *The Rio Grande: River of Destiny* (1949), and *The Enduring Navaho* (1968), Laura Gilpin established herself as an important commentator on the cultural geography of the Southwest and the culture of two of its native peoples.[1] A study of her life and work provides an opportunity to add to the growing body of work about women in the West, for while recent studies have paid much attention to the first generation of westering women and their response to the land, relatively little has been said about the reactions of their daughters who were native-born westerners.[2] Similarly, while the authors of these texts have examined literary records for clues to the ways in which women's responses to the western landscape might differ from men's, little use has been made of the visual records left behind by women artists. An examination of Gilpin's work hints of the possible value of such research, for even her landscape photographs explore the relationship between people and the land, an approach that suggests parallels with the writings of western women who, far more than their male counterparts, have traditionally described the western landscape in terms of its potential to sustain domestic life.[3] A study of Laura Gilpin's life also sheds light on the changing fashions of twentieth-century American photography, the problems of being a member of the photographic profession, and a period of southwestern history in which Americans discovered the rich heritage and seeming romance of their Indian past.

Laura Gilpin created her own niche in the literary and photographic world. A contemporary of Mary Austin, Mabel Dodge Luhan, and Willa Cather, she was unique among women chronicling the Southwest because she found her voice in the medium of photography and in the conjunction of photographs and text. Among the women who were her photographic colleagues, she was unique because she pursued landscape photography, a field pioneered and traditionally practiced by men. Even among the men who photographed the southwestern landscape, she stood out because her primary interest in the land was as an environment that shaped human activity – a point of view that distinguished her from nineteenth-century photographer-explorers, such as William Henry Jackson or Timothy O'Sullivan, or from her contemporary Ansel Adams, who photographed the West as a place of inviolate, pristine beauty. Finally, Laura Gilpin stood apart from many other photographers of southwestern Indian life because for more than fifty years she pursued this interest on her own with a keen empathy for her subjects, impelled not by scientific curiosity but by humane concerns.

Laura's work was closely linked to a personal search. Seeking a kind of peacefulness that her own family did not provide, she wanted to feel a part of a historical continuum and a spiritual tradition that transcended the realities of a day-to-day life always fraught with financial worries. Like many other writers and artists of her generation, she sought solace in the ancient traditions of the Southwest. In 1946 she moved from Colorado to New Mexico, a place she had photographed for twenty-five years, where she could feel "the deep roots of long past centuries." "Once this is imbedded in one's consciousness," she wrote, "other parts of the country seem shallow by comparison. Here one has time to think, to give time to the ripening of expression. To me this all adds up to a richer life, a life where essentials are cast aside, and the genuine has a chance to emerge."[4]

Laura had always felt a keen sense of place and a strong link to the western landscape of her childhood, but as she grew older she also began to feel a strong kinship with her Indian subjects. Her earliest photographs of Pueblo Indians are informed by a vision of loss, an outsider's romantic sense of the past glories of Pueblo culture; her later photographs of the Pueblo and Navajo people are informed by a vision of endurance, an insider's awareness of the persisting strains of native culture that link the past and present.

Particularly among the Navajo, whom she came to know better than her closer Pueblo neighbors, Laura found evidence of strong family ties, a keen sense of history and tradition, a spiritual feeling for the land, and an an aura of peacefulness. Sensing a strong identity between her own attitudes and those of the Navajo and projecting her feelings about her own life on to theirs, she perceived a direct connection between the hardship of their lives and their ability to create art. "Perhaps it is the long years of outdoor life, the deprivation, and the hardships they have endured that have produced such vitality in their art. Perhaps through the necessity of their lives come the strengths and ideas for their bold and beautiful designs."[5]

Laura's own life was also one of hardship, but she became adept at transforming privation into privilege. "I've learned a lot from doing things I didn't always want to do," she said. Delays in her book projects, necessitated by her need to earn money, seemed to make her books better. Long decades spent working with little recognition from the photographic community helped her "stick to [her] own way of seeing." Commercial jobs, executed with the same care and skill she expended on her personal work, enabled her to do the things she was "very moved to do." "Sometimes," she said, "work is the greatest thing one can do, that is, to keep on working when things get rough."[6] Laura Gilpin's work, like the Navajo's, came through the necessities of her life and drew its inspiration from the southwestern landscape.

Discovering Photography, 1891-1916

Laura Gilpin was born on April 22, 1891, in a home in Austin Bluffs, Colorado, just north of Colorado Springs, in country that her grandfather's cousin, the area's first territorial governor, William Gilpin, said had "all the natural gifts which human society needs, or may demand for the most complete development." Her parents had come from their Horse Creek ranch, some sixty-five miles away on the flat eastern Colorado plains, to await the birth of their first child. While Frank Gilpin waited, he planted saplings along the treeless bluff, and when Laura's birth seemed imminent he drove his horse and buggy to town in the middle of night to fetch a doctor.[1]

To Frank and Emma Gilpin, both recent immigrants from the East, the West meant different things. While Frank thought of it as a place where he could fashion a new life for himself, Emma considered it a spot where she could re-create the genteel life of eastern society. Their native-born daughter would eventually come to see the West in a very different way; not as a blank tableau but as a land with a rich history and tradition of its own.

Frank Gilpin was born on September 17, 1862, the youngest of three sons of Bernard Gilpin, Sr., a prominent Baltimore Quaker and pharmaceuticals manufacturer. Frank's eldest brother, Henry, inherited the family business, and when Frank was eighteen, he moved to Colorado to join his middle brother, Bernard, Jr., who had gone west six years before as a surveyor and had remained behind to become a cattle rancher. Transformed almost immediately by the vast, empty spaces of eastern Colorado and the evocative romance of the cowboy myth, Frank put away the dark, tight-fitting suits he had worn to Quaker meetings back home and adopted the garb of a western wrangler. He was, Laura recalled later, an "instant cowboy" and soon the champion calf roper of Colorado.[2]

At first this new life held splendid promise. By 1884, the Maryland Land and Cattle Company was flourishing, with Bernard as president and Frank as secretary. Frank shared a home with Bernard and his wife, Mary, on a five-thousand-acre ranch on Kettle Creek in El Paso County, ten miles northeast of Colorado Springs, and assisted with the management of the ranch. The *Denver Daily News* noted at the time that Bernard Gilpin was "one of the large number of young men who have acquired fortunes by careful attention to stock raising. Coming to Colorado less than ten years ago, he has by his own labor amassed something like $100,000, which . . . returns to him annually about $30,000." The Gilpins had two thousand head of cattle, scores of horses, and a home that was as fine as a "city dwelling." The assets of the company were chiefly Bernard's, but it must have seemed to Frank that wealth and success were within his own grasp, too.[3]

Yet the success of the Maryland Land and Cattle Company was short-lived. A severe winter in 1885–1886 destroyed fully half the cattle on the Colorado plains. This harsh weather, coupled with falling stock prices caused by an oversupply of cattle from other markets and the growth of large centralized buying operations, forced the company into reorganization. In later years, when his family asked to go to Kettle Creek to see the site of his old ranch, Frank always refused, reluctant, perhaps, to revisit the spot where he first realized that the myth and promise of the West might be at odds with the realities of western life.[4]

Following the disastrous winter the Maryland Land and Cattle Company was refinanced as the Sanborn Livestock Company, with Bernard Gilpin, Jr., holding

998 shares of stock and Frank holding just one (a Peter Tenis held the remaining one). Frank moved to a ranch on Horse Creek, sixty-five miles east of Colorado Springs and ran cattle marked with the "1/2" brand, signifying his and Bernard's joint ownership of the livestock. In the late 1880s, his distant relative William Henry Jackson, whose photographs for the Hayden Surveys of the 1870s were among the first views made of the Colorado Rockies, visited the 1/2 Ranch to make a series of photographs illustrating Colorado ranch life. He photographed the snug two-story frame house and documented the steps involved in cattle roundups and branding. Frank Gilpin posed for Jackson as the archetypal cowboy, sitting astride his horse dressed in well-worn working clothes that suggest he was a member of the ranch crew. Only a photograph of his bedroom reveals that Frank had not shed all the trappings of his former life. Hanging on the wall above his bed, scattered among family photographs, cheap prints illustrating cowboy life, and a loaded cartridge belt, appear a violin and a set of polo mallets. The violin and polo mallets represented what he had given up when he moved west and symbolized what he hoped Emma Miller would give up in order to marry him.[5]

Emma Gosler Miller grew up in St. Louis, where her father worked for a family retailing firm, but her family came from Sandy Spring, Maryland, not far from Baltimore, and it seems probable that Frank Gilpin met her there. On occasional trips between Colorado and Maryland, Frank would stop to see Emma in St. Louis, much to her pleasure. "Frank Gilpin was *evidently* more impressed with his visit to you than to me . . . ," she lamented to a cousin back in Maryland in February 1885. "I'm green with envy."[6]

Emma Miller was an exceptionally ambitious and energetic woman who preferred intellectual pursuits to the constant round of card parties and high society luncheons to which she was invited. She confided to a friend, "Doesn't it make you feel badly to see a girl you know and like very much, just give up her whole life and being for society when she could be something so much more nobler? It does me." Emma taught Sunday School (though she thought the students quite dull), belonged to a young ladies' Shakespeare Club, and sang in a choral group. When Mark Twain and

George Washington Cable came through St. Louis on speaking tours, she went to hear their lectures. She was much taken with Cable, and when he sat next to her in church, she wrote a friend, "I could not possibly help it, I shook hands with him and told him how much I enjoyed 'Dr. Sevier' and that I wanted to speak to its author. He asked me my name and talked quite a little while with me. *Mother says it was very bad for me to have done such a thing* but I did it before I thought and I am very glad I did."[7]

Sometime before the summer of 1887, Emma moved with her parents to Chicago and it was there that Frank Gilpin proposed to her in August 1887, "after so many years of hoping," he wrote, "which I sometimes thought was idle and sometimes not." On the train back to Colorado Springs after Emma's acceptance of his proposal, Frank wrote her a long letter, which set the uncertain tone for their married life. Addressing Emma with the familiar Quaker "thees" and "thous," Frank wrote:

How will thy father take it when he finds that I am probably worth nothing? Thee is the one thing Emma that life for me is worth living whether it be in wealth or poverty but [how?] I lose sight in asking thee to join me in a life of uncertainty. Does thee believe that thy life with me as a poor man of such I am to be would be happier than with any one else with wealth? Leaving all my own feelings aside that has been the one great question that I have turned over and over in my mind for several years. . . . I am afraid that it has always been my way to fear the future. So far I have made my living. . . . Oh Emma if it was only next spring and I was at some permanent occupation how happy I would be. It's this dreadful uncertainty that disturbs me so much.[8]

On April 23, 1890, Frank, twenty-seven, and Emma, who had just turned twenty-eight, were married in Chicago, and Emma left her engaging urban world to live with her new husband at the 1/2 Ranch. This rustic ranch on the bleak plains of eastern Colorado must have seemed to her tantalizingly close yet disappointingly far from the glittering social world of Colorado Springs, the "little London" of the West.[9] Certainly, the differences between Frank's home and her parents' house would have made her aware of the great differences between her and her husband. While she enjoyed art and literature and the company of friends, he was an adventurer who loved the outdoors and the physical challenge of frontier life. His extravagant dreams of success and frequently changing jobs would prove to be a continual strain for Emma, who wanted to lead a quiet, refined life among a community of like-minded people.

Within a year after Laura's birth in the spring of 1891, Frank and Emma moved from the Horse Creek ranch to Perry Park in the mountains above Colorado Springs. While Frank managed cattle, Emma cared for Laura and prepared for the birth of a second child. A son, John, was born on May 10, 1892. But he died just five months later of an illness that Laura later speculated was an allergy to his mother's milk. The family quickly moved away to an old log house in nearby Manitou Park, where Frank ran cattle and managed a summer hotel and Emma – still despondent over her son's death – hired a German governess to take charge of Laura's care. Laura soon became bilingual, and more than eighty years later she could still recall her "fräulein's" methodical drawing lessons and scary bedtime stories drawn from Wagner's *Ring Cycle*, a story she envisioned as set in the Rockies.[10]

Frank's venture at Manitou Park, like his efforts at Perry Park and the Horse Creek ranch, was short-lived. In early 1896 he let Laura's governess go and moved his family into the town of Colorado Springs, a socially conscious resort community and mining center, where a good name and family connections could almost compensate for a lack of wealth. Although they had little money, the Gilpins were accepted as one of the town's "good families" because former territorial governor William Gilpin was a cousin of Frank's father and because Frank's ranching experience suggested that they should have the status of a fine old pioneer family. Frank soon got involved in mining and began commuting on the Short Line Railroad to Cripple Creek, where he managed "The Lillie" mine for the William A. Otis Company. From Baltimore, his father confided in Emma that he was concerned about his son's seeming inability to hold a job. "I am very anxious about him all the time," he wrote, noting that his change of jobs was "a risk and a quantitude of work and worry."[11]

Laura later recalled her early days in Colorado Springs with much pleasure. There were always pet

GILPIN FAMILY. *Unknown photographer. Gelatin silver print, c. 1901. Collection of Kenneth Gilpin, Jr., Boyce, Virginia.*

rabbits in the backyard and many dogs, including a large Great Dane for neighborhood children to ride and another dog her father had trained to retrieve fish. With Anne Parrish, her best friend from the private Ferris School, she would often visit Gen. William Jackson Palmer, founder of the Denver and Rio Grande Railroad and the town of Colorado Springs, who lived in a castlelike home at the edge of town. The three of them would go on long walks together and sometimes go horseback riding. "I was less than ten," Laura recalled many years later, "and as we rode, he would point to plants, trees and wild life, citing their names. He taught me to know the outdoors, and especially to love it. At Christmas he always gave me a nice book. In fact, an influential one and the one I loved the best was *Hunting Wild Animals With a Camera*." To General Palmer, she attributed her life-long fascination with physical geography.[12]

On July 24, 1899, when Laura was eight, Emma gave birth to another son, Francis Gilpin, Jr. Frank continued to commute to Cripple Creek until the following spring, when he took a job in town with William A. Otis's mining brokerage firm. Two years later he decided to move to Durango, Mexico, to manage a mine. Emma joined her husband there after several months, "wrenching" herself away from her "dear chicks," whom she left in the care of Mr. and Mrs. William Stark, directors of Laura's school. From

LAURA GILPIN. *Unknown photographer. Gelatin silver print,*
c. 1903. Collection of Kenneth Gilpin, Jr., Boyce, Virginia.

her small adobe house in Guanacevi, Emma wrote to
a friend, "Now I am here I wonder how Mr. Gilpin
ever got on without me, for I flatter myself that life is
certainly more endurable with me here." The people
were "very picturesque looking," but they were a
"degenerate race" with deplorable work habits, which
were a constant source of frustration to an "energetic
American." Even the governor of Durango, who
came to dinner with his wife, had appallingly bad
table manners. Emma remained in Mexico for nearly
a year, and every week she received a dutifully typed
letter from Laura formally signed "yours truly."[13]

In 1903, for her twelfth birthday, Laura received a
Brownie camera and for Christmas her mother and
father (who had remained alone in Mexico) gave her
a developing tank. Laura took her camera with her to
St. Louis the next year when she went to visit the

great Louisiana Purchase Exposition, a sprawling
1,142-acre collection of beaux-arts buildings, lagoons,
and carnival midways, which stretched along the
western edge of the city. She went to the fair every
other day for a month and a half, acting as a guide and
companion to her mother's best friend and the woman
for whom she had been named, Laura Perry. Laura
Perry was blind, and it was her young companion's
task to describe to her everything that she saw. From
describing and interpreting all of the visual stimuli of
the fair, Laura Gilpin said later, she learned the powers
and pleasures of observation that kindled her serious
interest in photography.[14]

With her Brownie camera, Laura made snapshots
of the fair's imposing architecture, but what fascinated
her most were the Igorots, a small band of Philippine
natives who had set up a village along "the Pike."
Despite swarms of tourists, the Igorots were attempting to live by their traditional ways and to follow
their traditional diet, which, to the delight and horror
of local children, was reputed to include fresh dog
meat. Laura came often to watch life in the recon-
structed village and to photograph its scantily clad
inhabitants. Her mother may have been repelled by
the people she met in Mexico, but these even more
exotic people only intrigued Laura. This, she said later,
is where she first got her interest in native peoples.[15]

Emma remained ambitious for her children despite
Frank's shifting fortunes. In 1905 she took Laura, fourteen, and Francis, six, to New York and arranged for
a portrait sitting with Gertrude Käsebier, a member
of Alfred Stieglitz's influential Photo-Secession group.
Käsebier's artistic and expressive style of portraiture
had had a profound influence on the more formal
fashions of nineteenth-century portrait photography.
Emma had seen some pictures she had made of friends
and, ever interested in maintaining her old ties to the
world of culture, commissioned Käsebier to make
portraits of her and her children. A portrait session
with the foremost woman photographer of the day
left a deep impression on Laura. Years later, when she
decided to study photography, she turned to Käsebier
for advice and at Käsebier's suggestion moved to New
York to study at the Clarence H. White School.[16]

In another move that bespoke Emma's social aspirations, Laura was sent east in the fall of 1905 to attend

the Baldwin School in Bryn Mawr, Pennsylvania, a school that for some years had been a popular choice for Colorado Springs parents eager to give their daughters an eastern education. Enrolling as a member of the class of 1909, Laura signed up for the "general course" designed for girls not planning to attend college. Only five other students in the school that year came from west of the Mississippi River, and Laura felt acutely aware of her special status as a westerner, proclaiming her identity by wearing cowboy outfits to school parties and balls. As in Colorado Springs where her family name accorded her a status not consistent with the Gilpin's uncertain financial fortunes, in boarding school she seemed to be part of a group to which she did not quite have a right to belong.[17]

Whether she felt out of place or was simply ill-prepared, Laura did poorly her first year in school. She sang in the glee club and performed in the school's piano recital. But, except in music, her marks were poor and when she returned the next year, she was grouped with younger students in the class of 1910. She continued to sing in the glee club, was elected class secretary, and played for her class basketball team and the school hockey team. Her grades improved and she received merit grades in algebra and English grammar. Jane L. Brownell, head of the school, wrote to Mrs. Gilpin, "She is doing good, strong, intelligent work in every subject, and is taking her stand as one of the strongest girls in her class. . . . We feel that Laura's general influence in her class and in the school is always for good. We can depend upon her in every way and I am more than pleased with her development this year."[18]

But the following year, in the fall of 1907, Laura transferred to Rosemary Hall School in Greenwich, Connecticut, where she was placed back with the class of 1909. Again, she became an active member of the glee club, one of the school's main activities, and at the end of her first year there was elected to the school's top athletic post, captain of the field hockey team. However, sometime toward the end of her first year, Laura developed a severe double mastoid infection and went home to Colorado Springs for treatment. When she returned to school in the fall of 1908, she not only had to wear a football helmet during hockey games to protect the healing wounds on her head but

EMMA, FRANCIS, AND FRANK GILPIN AT THEIR BROADMOOR HOME. *Unknown photographer. Gelatin silver print, c. 1906. Collection of Kenneth Gilpin, Jr., Boyce, Virginia.*

also had to repeat the fifth form because she had missed so much school. Although a school yearbook described Laura as a "rather gay" girl with a cheerful disposition, Laura herself felt "out of her niche" when she returned to school. Repeating a grade, she recalled later, "was emotionally very bad for me." After her second year at Rosemary Hall she went back to Colorado Springs, and she never completed the additional year of work she needed for a high school diploma.[19]

A family portrait made while Laura was away at boarding school underscores her parents' vastly differing notions of what life in Colorado should be, at once suggesting Frank's fascination with the masculine, out-of-doors culture of the West and Emma's continuing sense of the West as a place to which one must import culture. Thus, it suggests the sources for Laura's own confusion about her place in Colorado Springs and her place as a westerner in the elite world of an eastern boarding school. The Gilpins posed for the photograph in their rented home in Broadmoor, a fashionable residential area around a big hotel just outside Colorado Springs. Frank and Emma Gilpin are seated at a tea table set with an elegant silver tea service, probably brought west by Emma. Emma wears a dark dress with an elegant lace collar and is seated in a high-backed wicker chair, gesturing as if she is about to pour some tea. Her son, Francis, wears a fashionable sailor suit and sits near her with an open book on his lap. Frank Gilpin sits off to the side dressed in a suit and high riding boots. Family photographs by Gertrude Käsebier, a framed print of William Shakespeare, and an upright piano suggest Emma's taste. A Saltillo blanket, a souvenir of Frank's time in Mexico, hangs over the rustic stone fireplace with a large deer head mounted prominently in its center. This and a leather camp stool by the hearth suggest Frank's very different vision of the West.

Despite her eastern education, Laura had a reputation among her Colorado Springs friends as an adventuresome girl who, like her father, liked to try new things. She starred in the impromptu games of field hockey that sprang up in her friends' front yards, was one of the first girls in town to learn how to drive a car, and earned recognition for her mechanical prowess with automobile engines. Few of her friends could have been surprised when, during her summers home from school, Laura began experimenting with Autochromes, an early color photographic process. In the summer of 1908, less than a year after the Autochrome plates devised by the Lumière brothers in France were first marketed in America, Laura and two Colorado Springs friends, Alfred Curtis and Gladys McConnell, obtained a box of the plates and taught themselves how to use them. The plates were sheets of glass coated with minute starch grains dyed red, green, and blue. The starch grains were distributed evenly over the plates and coated with a light-sensitive emulsion. Exposure was made through the back of the plate, and after development the negative was turned into a positive by a reversal method. It could then be viewed as a transparency reproducing the colors of the original scene. Laura worked with her friends in a crude home-made darkroom, following the directions that came in the box, and had extraordinary success. Although she had probably not seen any other Autochromes, she seemed to have an intuitive understanding of how to use the grainy, pointillist quality of the image to best advantage. She made dreamy, romantic portraits of herself and her friends, carefully staged to make best use of the plates' soft, warm colors. For a self-portrait, Laura posed outdoors in a dark, lacy dress that evoked the ideal of late nineteenth-century beauty (plate 3). She asked a friend wearing a dark blue suit to sit on a porch railing, then photographed her against

a backdrop of white posts and snowy lawns to accentuate her graceful silhouette (plate 4). She photographed another friend in a summer garden, positioning her so that the black-and-white stripes of her skirt would be framed by the rich green color of climbing vines and the pink of morning glories.[20]

As Laura experimented with photography, she also began to devote more time to music. At boarding school she had become entranced with the violin, and when she returned to Colorado Springs, she began studying with concert violinist Louis Persinger, later to become an instructor at Juilliard. Although she enjoyed her lessons she always refused her mother's entreaties to perform for guests.[21]

Determined that Laura have the social talents she had valued in her youth, Emma Gilpin took her nineteen-year-old daughter to Boston in the fall of 1910 to study at the New England Conservatory of Music. As a hedge against the financial uncertainty of her own life, she insisted that Laura enroll in outside courses in shorthand and accounting. Emma remained for a few months as Laura began her classes, then returned to Colorado.[22]

At the conservatory, Laura studied violin with instructor Eugene Gruenberg and received a grade of "C" for her first term of study, a mediocre mark that meant she could not join the conservatory's orchestra of advanced students. Nonetheless, this was the beginning of a life-long passion for music, an interest shared by many other successful photographers. Laura perceived numerous connections between the arts of music and photography, and from her study of musical structure she derived a metaphorical vocabulary for her study of visual imagery. "One may well compare photography with music," she wrote later. "Photography uses waves of light, composed and harmonized to express an idea. Music uses waves of sound for the same purpose. Unless sound waves are arranged to fit a pattern which contains a basic idea and which is expressed through pattern, line, harmony, and tone values, they have no meaning and are merely a confusion of sound. The same is true of photography, even to the terms employed."[23]

After just six months in Boston, Laura was summoned home by her parents. In the early winter of 1911, after several years of trying to get by as a mining

broker and investment counselor, Frank Gilpin decided to leave Colorado Springs and move his family
to an 1,800-acre ranch in Austin, Colorado, on the
western slope near the town of Delta. There was no
money for Laura to remain in Boston. "I certainly
hope that your dreams of life on your father's ranch
may come true," a friend wrote her when she left.
From the refined life of a Boston conservatory student,
the twenty-year-old girl plunged into life on the
Figure 4 cattle ranch, a cluster of shaded frame buildings set in the scrubby, arid land at the base of the
western side of the Rocky Mountains. A player piano
in the corner of the ranch house replaced the elegant
instruments of the conservatory, and souvenirs of
Frank's western trips cluttered the walls. Hanging over
a bookshelf crowded with books, family photographs,
candles, and glass vases, was a large framed photogravure of one of Edward S. Curtis's best known

FIGURE 4 RANCH HOUSE, AUSTIN, COLORADO. *Unknown
photographer. Gelatin silver print, c. 1912–1915. Amon Carter Museum.*

images – a photograph of seven Navajo horsemen
crossing the valley floor of Canyon de Chelly. As
Laura became increasingly interested in photography,
in the Navajo, and in the history and geology of
Canyon de Chelly, she repeatedly cited the important
influence of this print.[24]

Laura determined to make the best of her shift in
fortunes. While her friends had coming-out parties in
Colorado Springs, she threw herself into the business
of raising poultry. She purchased turkey chicks, built
all of her own pens, developed a special feed, took a
correspondence class in poultry dressing, and, with her
newly acquired accounting skills, kept the books for

LAURA GILPIN AT HER POULTRY FARM, AUSTIN,
COLORADO. *Unknown photographer. Gelatin silver print,
c. 1912–1915. Amon Carter Museum.*

her own business as well as for her father's ranching
concerns. She worked in long skirts and fashionable
sailor blouses that ill-befitted her job, but she gave in
to practicality with high leather boots to negotiate the
mud.[25]

Her turkey business was phenomenally successful.
In 1913, a Denver newspaper reported on her aston-
ishing success in a story called "Society Girl Raises
400 Turkeys" and noted that she was in town buying
a wardrobe for a winter trip to New York and Boston
with the proceeds of her enterprise.[26] Unlike her
parents, Laura saw no irreconcilable conflict between
the West and the East. With money earned on her
father's western ranch she could visit the eastern world
of culture to which her mother had introduced her.

Moreover, Laura did not associate artistic pursuits
only with urban eastern life. Working alone in Delta,
whenever she could steal time away from her poultry
business, she mastered the art of the Autochrome.
Some of her pictures were pleasant views of predictable
subjects: her chickens, the poultry pens, her younger
brother. Some, however, merit consideration with
the Autochromes made by Alfred Stieglitz, Karl
Struss, and other well-established photographers working in New York. The richest and most surprising is
a still life of locally grown peaches, which with its
formal composition, dramatic lighting, and rich color-
ing is resonant of a French still life painting (plate 2).
The peaches are in a basket that sits on a white cloth

and are bathed in a soft, warm light that makes them glow against an indistinct, dark backdrop. The peach fuzz seems almost palpable, although the limp green leaves spilling out of the basket suggest this luxuriance will be short-lived. Laura made another fine Autochrome of her friend Gladys McConnell Fowler during a return visit to Colorado Springs (plate 1). In the picture, Fowler sits in a sunroom that is flooded with rosy light. Dressed in a pink lace dress, she looks tenderly at the infant son she holds on her lap and basks in a warm, maternal glow. The composition of the picture is similar to Gertrude Käsebier's photograph *The Manger* and alludes to a long tradition of madonna figures, a fact of which Laura was probably unaware.[27]

In mid-1915, the Gilpin family returned to Colorado Springs. Heavy irrigation in the peach orchards on neighboring land had created a drainage problem for the Figure 4 Ranch, making it difficult to grow enough alfalfa for cattle feed. Frank Gilpin and his two partners sold the ranch, and he returned to town to start over again.[28]

When Laura sold her turkey operation from the ranch, after unsuccessfully trying to transfer it to land near the family's new residence, she had earned close to $10,000, more money than she would have at one time for the next sixty years. Some of it she saved and used later to finance her photographic studies in New York. However, she lent most of the money, some $9,000, to her father in 1916. Over the next few years he repaid only one-third of it. She said later that this made her mother furious; Emma did not want Frank's failings to interfere with her ambitions for Laura. But Frank merely believed that as he had done for Laura, she should do for him, and he began increasingly to rely on his daughter for his material and emotional well-being.[29]

In the fall of 1915, not long after the family's return to town, Laura went to California as a traveling companion for a friend of her mother, much as she had gone to St. Louis eleven years before. At the Louisiana Purchase Exposition she had discovered native cultures; at the Panama-Pacific Exposition in San Francisco and the Panama-California Exposition in San Diego, she discovered art. "There was practically no art interest in Colorado Springs in those early days," she recalled later. "I remember Harvey Young

CLOISTER AT THE SAN DIEGO EXPOSITION. *Laura Gilpin. Gelatin silver print, 1915. Amon Carter Museum.*

was the only painter in town and I don't think there was a sculptor. I knew NOTHING about sculpture." But in California she became fascinated with the sculpture around the fairgrounds and made negative after negative of the outdoor work, an experience she would later call the beginning of her serious interest in art and photography. She also photographed the architecture of the fairs, and a picture of the Cloister at the San Diego Exposition became her first prize-winning photograph in a monthly competition sponsored by *American Photography* magazine in May 1916.[30] As photographic subjects, architecture and sculpture attracted her for the same reasons. The solid forms modulated light in interesting ways and were still, obliging subjects for her camera.

Exhibitions at the two fairs introduced Laura to many of the themes and subjects that would fascinate her throughout her life, including aviation, southwestern Indian culture, and photography. She photographed a skywriter "who was one of the first ones to do skywriting. He wrote his own name, Art Smith, and I was fascinated and I photographed him." She probably saw Jesse Nusbaum's elaborate re-creation of a Pueblo Indian village at the San Diego exposition's "Painted Desert," replete with pueblo-style architecture and imported Indians, including the potters Julián and María Martínez from San Ildefonso Pueblo, who would later become her close friends. In San Diego she might also have seen paintings of southwestern Indians by Santa Fe painter Gerald Cassidy. At the San Francisco Palace of Fine Arts she could have seen sculpture by Brenda Putnam, who a year later would become her roommate and closest friend. In San Francisco Laura might also have seen a photography exhibition, although over the vehement protests of photographers across the country photography was classified as a liberal art rather than a fine art, as had been the case at the St. Louis Fair in 1904.[31]

While in California, Laura renewed her acquaintance with a remarkable woman whose husband was a friend of her father. Anne Simon was forty-five years old, an accomplished musician, a poet, and a critic, with a deep interest in European modernism, particularly the work of the Italian futurist poet Marinetti and the French "unaministes," who explored the relationship between the individual and the collective transcendent consciousness. As a child she had shown musical talent, and by the age of fifteen she was studying voice, violin, and piano. She later studied in London, Denmark, and Germany and acquired what one critic called "a sensitive adjustment and application of pianistic touch responsive to the subtler emotions." She was an active concert performer and worked with her husband, Otto, in the Motet Choral Society of Washington, D.C., where they made their home. She was also exceptionally well-read and familiar with the writings of Maeterlinck, Pater, Matisse, and Emerson. She filled her private journal with lists of words that

ANNE SIMON. *Bachrach studio. Modern gelatin silver print from copy negative made by Laura Gilpin, 1916. Amon Carter Museum.*

had a particular resonance and magic for her, with insightful analyses of contemporary writers and artists, and with ruminations on the nature of the human spirit.[32]

Mrs. Simon was a "very charming and very inspiring kind of woman," Laura recalled. "I mean she was the kind you just idolized. I did anyway." Indeed, although Laura was twenty-four years old, she developed an intense, adolescent crush on this talented older woman, showering her with letters, flowers, and other gifts of affection. Anne Simon reciprocated with gifts, warm notes of affection and encouragement, and offers to assist Laura with her music and her studies of art and literature. After several months of correspondence, Simon impetuously sent Laura a telegram asking her to come to Washington to be her housekeeper in exchange for a nominal salary and free harmony lessons. "Need you at once," she wrote. Almost immediately, she wrote back apologizing for proposing a situation that would have been too confining for Laura, and the two of them began to plan for the Simons to visit Colorado Springs the following summer. There was an intense correspondence through the fall and winter of 1915, which continued until the summer of 1916 when Anne Simon and her husband made their much anticipated trip west.[33]

The letters reveal Anne Simon to be a warm, inspiring person, encouraging and nurturing of others' talents, who would generously share her own interests in art and insights into human behavior. Describing her later, a newspaper reporter noted, ". . . her friends say that her personality was the most important thing about her. In her twenty summers abroad she absorbed the progressive tendencies of many people, and discarded other traditions. She had the power to arouse others to action and to awaken a desire for complete fulfillment. She had a large number of friends, men as well as women, who went to her beautiful studio because they found there direct and undeniable inspiration." Anne Simon clearly had an affection for Laura, but there is nothing in her letters to suggest that her warm interest and affection were any different from the attention she showered on her other friends, particularly those who showed some evidence of artistic talent. "Saddened on earth," as her husband said, by her inability to bear a child, she gave freely of her love to those around her.[34]

In Anne Simon, Laura found the world of culture, gentility, and spiritual refinement that she had glimpsed in her mother, in her eastern schools, and in the society whirl of Colorado Springs. Like Emma Gilpin, Mrs. Simon had high ambitions for Laura, and Laura derived a great feeling of well-being from her close association with the success, talent, and otherworldly spirituality this older woman seemed to represent.

Anne Simon believed that great art grew not from simple observation but from the human imagination, "the world beyond our senses." What she sought to cultivate in Laura was this extrasensory world. In an entry in her journal in 1912, she had written, "Artists speak of wanting and striving 'to set free' the 'soul' in a work of art, etc. I feel that way about human beings, too – I so often wish that I were fine enough, big enough, able enough, to be able to show some people how to unlock, unloosen, set the soul free." What she tried to teach Laura was that she could control her own destiny; her talents and desires should not be contained by her family or her immediate surroundings. "Nothing is able to harm a man except himself," Anne Simon wrote in her journal. "Nothing should be able to rob a man. What a man really has is what is in him. What is outside him is a matter of no importance."[35]

In the summer of 1916 the Simons made their long-planned visit to Colorado Springs. Anne performed in a series of concerts that Laura arranged and managed. Then, with no warning whatsoever, she suffered a cerebral hemorrhage and within a day, on August 5, she was dead. For Laura, it was a terrible blow. Shortly after the body had been sent back to Washington for burial, Laura went to the Grand Canyon in search of solitude and solace. She took her camera with her, and working from the rim of the canyon she made some Autochromes and a view in black and white of the canyon's sculptural formations, which won a prize the following month in an *American Photography* competition. But photography alone could not bring her the comfort she sought. On August 10, she sat on the canyon rim and began a new journal:

Tonight as I sat gazing out into the mystery of the Canyon in the glory of the moonlight I found my first great comfort. Away across that vast space, I could see you. You were holding out your arms to me, smiling and urging me forward. And all at once I could see the Canyon as my life before me, with its valleys and shadows and its peaks crowned with sunlight. I could barely perceive the great height beyond which was Eternity and you were waiting there.

Until now, I have not known where to turn, but know I want to go on, I want to climb some of those sunlight peaks. The valleys and shadows will come in their turn, but the road is ever up, up to my soul's rest and to you.

To you my Beloved Anne I dedicate all that will ever be written in this little diary. In it I shall put down all the real things in my life. The thoughts, impressions, and worth while things. You have awakened my spirit. My life, my spiritual life, I owe to you. I know your spirit will guide my way. You will be my Guardian Angel. I shall strive henceforth to think real things, do real things, and to "know my own soul." I will follow the wonderful example you have set and when that great day comes when my spirit joins yours, I can say "I have not lived in vain" and that will show the very great and deep love that fills my soul.

For the rest of her life, Laura would seek emotional

solace from the vast western landscape that she associated with the spiritualism of Anne Simon, and through her photographs she would try to capture the spiritual presence of the physical world.[36]

Within a month of Anne Simon's death, Laura resolved to follow the impulses of her own soul and to do something "real." She decided to become a photographer, and after corresponding with Gertrude Käsebier, who advised her that the Clarence H. White School in New York would be the best, indeed the only, place to study, she began making arrangements to enroll.[37]

She was a self-taught amateur with a limited portfolio of work, chiefly black-and-white prints she had printed and developed in makeshift attic darkrooms with a rudimentary knowledge of techniques gained from an employee at the local camera store. Even so, her two prize-winning photographs and, more important, her Autochromes suggest that she had an innate talent for photographic composition and creative expression. Similarly, although her knowledge of art and art history was limited and self-acquired, she seemed to have an intuitive feeling for the subject. Colorado Springs boasted several amateur art groups and an art school run by Thomas and Anne Parrish, parents of her friend Anne, but there was no art museum in town. What little Laura knew about art she had acquired from Anne Simon, from her self-enforced regimen of study at the San Diego and San Francisco expositions, and from books. Of particular interest, she recalled later, were her "Uncle Bernie's" books on Mayan art and architecture and a friend's books on oriental art. "He had two big books of Japanese reproductions of Chinese paintings," she recalled. "I used to go over there and pore over those things. The oriental has affected me all of my life."[38]

With the savings from her poultry business she could pay her own way to New York, and she went with the blessings of her parents. "My mother was pretty wonderful," she said later. "She wanted me to do what I wanted to do. There were no restraints

because I was a young girl. She let me go to New York on my own when I was in my twenties. I don't think that was easy for her but I went. She was always behind me."[39] Indeed, Emma was always ambitious for her daughter, eager for Laura to live out her own childhood dreams, which had been thwarted when she married Frank Gilpin and left the cosmopolitan world of St. Louis and Chicago for the vicissitudes of life in Colorado.

It was as much the passion and dedication of Anne Simon as the encouraging support of her mother that facilitated Laura's move to New York. And Laura immediately sought out someone whom Anne had often spoken to her about – Brenda Putnam, a pianist and sculptor living and working in New York City. Otto Simon, who became an ardent correspondent with Laura following his wife's death, echoed Anne's enthusiasm for Brenda and suggested to Laura that if she were going to New York she should write to Brenda for assistance in finding a place to live. In August, shortly after Anne's death, Laura wrote to Brenda and Brenda's reply told her she had found a true soul mate. Speaking of Anne, Brenda wrote, "Her spirit has always been so close to mine, bringing out all that was worthiest in me, and helping me to reach out always for higher and finer ideals." "It will be a great comfort," she told Laura, "to be able to speak of her sometimes, and to feel that you, too, are being watched over by the same spirit that is so close to me." She told Laura of a vacancy in the apartment she shared with several other women and invited her to come join them while she studied at the Clarence H. White School.[40]

Thus Laura moved to New York in October 1916 and met Brenda Putnam. In many regards, her friendship with Brenda would prove as important to her subsequent career as would her formal photographic studies. If it was Anne Simon who taught Laura the great emotional power and spiritual resonance of art, it was Brenda Putnam who taught her what it really meant to be a working artist.

Becoming an Artist, 1916–1918

Laura arrived in New York in October 1916 and moved in with Brenda Putnam and her roommates, violinist Edith Rubel and painter Jean Walker. They shared an apartment in the Rutland, at 256 West 57th Street, which was overseen by a Mrs. Miller, whom Brenda described as "a dear, motherly sort of person of about fifty." For her corner bedroom with a fireplace, Laura paid $10 per week plus an additional $2.50–$3.00 toward the communal marketing fund.[1]

The apartment had a busy, intensely creative atmosphere. Edith Rubel practiced her violin in the apartment every day and kept up a busy concert schedule. Brenda left for her sculpture studio early in the morning and worked there until dinnertime. In the evenings she came home to practice for her performances as the pianist for the Edith Rubel Trio. The art these intense young women pursued was not the almost inexplicable, spiritual force that Laura aspired to understand through her friendship with Anne Simon. It was a part of everyday life that necessitated long hours of work and financial sacrifice. From these women, particularly from Brenda, Laura learned the meaning of working hard to be an artist.

Born in Minneapolis in 1889, Brenda Putnam was the daughter of Herbert Putnam, the Librarian of Congress from 1899 to 1939, and through her mother's family was related to Harriet Beecher Stowe. At the age of twelve, when she announced her intention of becoming a sculptor, her father bought her clay and tools and turned his den over to her for use as a workshop. She studied sculpture under Mary E. Moore and Bela L. Pratt in Boston from 1905 to 1907, and in 1908 she moved to New York to study at the Art Students League. There she worked for two years as a pupil of James Earle Fraser. By 1916, when she met Laura, Brenda was set up in her own studio doing

occasional teaching and working to support herself through commissioned garden pieces, fountains, plaques, and portrait busts (plates 9, 18).[2]

She was a small person whose stature belied her physical strength and tough spirit. She described herself to Laura as "a small person in *brown*, 5 foot nothing, with *dutch-cut hair* (!), and a big nose. *And* a grin." Unlike Laura, she had an acute sense of the added difficulties of being a woman artist in a man's world. Laura practiced an art that was not yet old enough to have an elaborate system of schools and apprenticeships and required no great physical strength. She had never encountered any particular discrimination against herself as a photographer. In fact, she would soon discover that the majority of students in her class at the Clarence H. White School were women and that White, himself, took pride in the success of the women he taught and actively promoted professional photography as a suitable vocation for women. Brenda's experience had been different. "Most women are weak in technique," she said. "But it is not entirely our fault. A man can go into the studio of some great sculptor. He serves his apprenticeship. He learns what no school teaches, drapery, lettering, columning. But women are not accepted by men as apprentices. Women get in the way! So we must teach ourselves."[3]

By the end of the first school year they spent together, Laura had developed a strong attachment to Brenda, transferring to her the feelings she had once had toward their mutual friend, Anne Simon. She sent Brenda flowers and seemed to idolize her for her talents and her fierce devotion to her work. "Don't put me up on a pedestal," Brenda wrote to Laura while they were apart for the summer. "My feet are clay, of the earth, earthy, and if you haven't found

BRENDA PUTNAM WORKING ON A PORTRAIT BUST OF
LAURA GILPIN. *Laura Gilpin. Modern gelatin silver print from
nitrate negative, 1921. Amon Carter Museum.*

that out yet, you will soon enough."[4]

Brenda discouraged Laura's devotion but accepted her friendship. For the next fifty years each would serve as the other's finest critic and keenest supporter. In their letters they would share ideas about art, the creative process, and the difficulties of being an artist – ideas they could share with no one else. On Laura's visits to New York and Brenda's trips to Colorado, they would work together: Laura studying sculpture with Brenda and photographing her work in order to learn about form and the modeling properties of light, and Brenda studying Laura's classically composed pictures to learn about artistic style. Brenda would teach Laura: "There is no form without shadow." In like manner, Laura would give Brenda a new style of composition. Brenda had been trained that "a work of art should have *action* and *expression*." "How far astray these standards have led me," she confessed to Laura. "*You* were one of the first good influences on me, you know, with your sense of the purely decorative and your instinctive leaning toward the passive and permanently beautiful."[5]

For the decades that Laura worked in relative isolation in Colorado and New Mexico, Brenda functioned as her touchstone, keeping her aware of new shows, new ideas, and new developments in the world of art. Her cosmopolitan career remained a constant reminder to Laura of what her own life might have been like had she stayed in the East.

In October 1916, Laura enrolled in a 28-week course of study at the Clarence H. White School, newly settled into expanded quarters at 122 East 17th Street. She was probably unaware of the politics of the New York photography world. However, Clarence White was a leading figure in the movement to establish alternatives to the ideas and institutions promulgated by Alfred Stieglitz, the country's foremost proponent of photography as a fine art. By enrolling at White's school, Laura allied herself with a particular set of ideas about photography and the photographic profession.[6]

Clarence White opened his school in New York in the autumn of 1914, as an extension of the summer school he had operated in Seguinland, Maine, since 1910. The school had a practical philosophy. White wanted to instruct his students in the art of photography and to give them a skill by which they could earn a living. He announced that the school "is founded as an institution for teaching the science and art of photography and for the training of its students for the vocation of photographer." Painter Max Weber would give lectures on art "intended to acquaint the student with the principles of art appreciation and to enable him to use his medium for expressing his aesthetic sense." Photographer Paul Anderson would instruct the student "in the chemistry of photography and the laws which govern lenses and their employment."[7]

White's school was a key part of a deliberately crafted alternative to Alfred Stieglitz's Photo-Secession movement, the other major force in the New York photography world. Almost single-handedly, Stieglitz had won for photography in America status as a legitimate art. In 1902, unable to assure that his own high standards for selection could be maintained through the Camera Club of New York, whose journal *Camera Notes* he edited, Stieglitz broke away to form his own group of photographers, which he called the "Photo-Secession." Through the group exhibitions and particularly through the group's exquisitely printed publication *Camera Work*, Stieglitz promoted photography as a fine art and established standards to distinguish serious professional workers from mere camera amateurs.[8]

White was once an associate of Stieglitz. A book-keeper and self-taught amateur photographer from Newark, Ohio, he came to Stieglitz's attention when he exhibited work in the Philadelphia Salon of 1898. He was twenty-eight years old and had a flair for softly lit, carefully posed portraits that echoed the aestheticism of James McNeill Whistler. Stieglitz arranged a one-man show for White at the New York Camera Club in 1899, and in 1902 he accepted him as a founding member of the elite Photo-Secession group. White moved to New York in 1906 and a year later was hired to teach photography by Arthur Wesley Dow, chairman of the Art Department at Teachers College, Columbia University.[9]

In 1912, following a long simmering dispute precipitated by what White perceived as Stieglitz's high-handed manner in organizing the International Exhibition of Pictorial Photography for the Albright Art Gallery in Buffalo in 1910, White made a decisive break with his former mentor. With other disaffected members of the Photo-Secession, including Gertrude Käsebier and Karl Struss, all disturbed by Stieglitz's autocratic manner and increasingly narrow definition of artistic photography, White began to promote a broader and more democratic notion of pictorial photography. White and his colleagues wanted to promote pictorial photography for both artistic and commercial purposes, to encourage the education of well-intentioned amateurs, and to facilitate the reproduction and exhibition of fine examples of the photographic art. They carried out these aims through several institutions: the journal *Platinum Print: A Journal of Personal Expression*, founded in 1913 and later published under the name *Photo = Graphic Art* until 1917; the Clarence H. White School of Photography; the Pictorial Photographers of America, an organization founded in 1915; and the Art Center, founded in 1921, a place where the PPA could hold photography exhibits alongside exhibits of illustration and graphic arts.[10]

The journal *Platinum Print*, like Stieglitz's *Camera Work*, was produced with great care for printing and design and contained articles about photography, reviews of recent shows, and essays about design and modern art. However, in frank acknowledgment of photography's commercial potential – an idea abhor-rent to Stieglitz – it also included columns on the art of printing so that commercial photographers "may not fall victim into the hands of a printer who has less of taste and more of greed in him." Its chief difference from *Camera Work* was in editorial tone. *Platinum Print* lacked the preachy didactic tone of Stieglitz's publication. Rather than encouraging the elitism of a select few, it sought "the establishment of a bond of understanding and common feeling among its readers and contributors. It will not be the embodiment of arrogance, but expressive of the simplicity and truth that are attributes of right conduct and frankness."[11]

With a similar display of democratic intent, the Pictorial Photographers of America created an organization that was open to all interested parties and that encouraged the cooperation and affiliation of local camera clubs across the country; in organization it was diametrically opposed to Stieglitz's elite centralized group, which had itself begun as an alternative to the system of camera clubs that welcomed amateur workers. Still, both the journal and the organization promoted high photographic standards. A 1914 editorial in *Platinum Print* lamented the stale convention of much camera club photography and proclaimed that amateurs must be "uplifted" before they can call themselves pictorialists.[12]

Unlike Stieglitz, White believed that photography could be taught, in a rational and programmatic manner. Though he agreed with Stieglitz that photographers must invest their work with emotional feeling, he nonetheless believed that students could be *taught* to make good photographs. His pedagogical techniques and his interest in the commercial application of photography derived largely from his Columbia colleague, Arthur Wesley Dow.

Dow revolutionized the teaching of art in America in 1899 when he published *Composition*, a book that proposed that students learn to create art not by imitating the works of past masters but by studying the abstract principles of composition. From his study of Japanese art and his work with Boston orientalist Ernest Fenallosa, Dow had concluded that there should be no distinction between major and minor arts or between artists and artisans. For the fine arts as well as the practical arts, he preached the idea of harmonious "space filling," a theory of composition based on

CLASS AT CLARENCE H. WHITE SCHOOL. *(Clarence White standing at left; Laura Gilpin at center with coat over arm). Attributed to Clarence H. White. Platinum print, c. 1916–1917. Amon Carter Museum.*

the utilization of the bare elements of line, "notan" (the massing of patterns of light and dark as in Japanese prints), and color. Dow's theories were compatible with White's own thinking about photographic composition, for in his portraits, White paid great attention to light and to background spaces as integral parts of his composition. Dow's emphasis on "space-filling" merely gave a name to something White already understood.[13]

From Dow, White developed a coherent theory of photography that emphasized the necessity for good design, did not discriminate between "art" photography and photography done for commercial purposes, and embraced the notion that photography – like any other art – could be taught. These ideas became the basis for the curriculum at the Clarence H. White School. Indeed, White selected a quote from Dow to use on his school brochures: "The painter need not always paint with brushes – he can paint with light itself. Modern photography has brought light under control and made it as truly art material as pigment or clay. The photographer has demonstrated that his work need not be mechanical imitation. He can control the quality of his lines, the massing of his tones and the harmony of his gradations. He can eliminate detail, keeping only the significant. More than this, he can reveal the secrets of personality. What is this but Art?" Laura Gilpin and the Pictorial Photographers

of America adopted this same defense of photography as a fine art in publications of their own.[14]

White also adopted Dow's pedagogical strategy, which was based on the design project method, a graded series of design assignments. Max Weber, who studied with Dow at Pratt Institute in 1898–1900, described Dow's teaching technique:

[Dow] would come into class and make an unbounded drawing of trees and hills, or perhaps a winding road against the sky. Then he would ask the class to copy the drawing freely and enclose it in a rectangle, to make a horizontal picture or a vertical, as they chose, and to make whatever changes necessary to fit the drawing to the frame which they had selected, to balance the drawing by making less foreground, or more sky, to change the masses and what not. He would then criticize the studies, emphasizing good design. Later the students would make similar studies in several colors, always giving first consideration to splendid organization and distribution of light and dark masses.

At the Clarence H. White School, both Weber and White taught their classes by a similar method, assigning students to create designs in which representation would be subordinated to the overall pattern and organization of the image.[15]

Laura's basic course at the Clarence H. White School included three main areas of study. White's classes in "the art of photography," four mornings and two afternoons a week, addressed topics ranging from the selection of a camera and the construction of a darkroom to night photography and color printing. Max Weber covered "art appreciation and design" in two weekly sessions: one, an illustrated lecture "in analysis of the fundamental principles underlying the important creations in ancient and modern plastic arts"; the other, a critique session of students' design problems with "stress laid upon the cultivation of taste and personality, and power to create and discern." In four weekly classes in "technique of photography," Paul Lewis Anderson covered topics from the theory of lens construction to the chemistry of developers and alternative printing methods.[16]

"I quickly and enthusiastically say after all these years," Laura said in 1977, "that [Clarence White] was one of the greatest teachers I have ever known in any field. His enthusiasm, his interest in his students and his help in every possible way and his example without his insisting anyone do things like his own work made him an outstanding teacher in my opinion." She found him a "marvelous" teacher who pulled together the school's programs in the weekly print criticisms he conducted. Students would bring in fadeable red proofs of the design problems they had worked on during the week "and he would criticize them and show us what could have been improved . . . he was wonderful that way."[17]

White's colleagues and students all spoke similarly of his unassuming but effective manner of teaching. Dorothea Lange, who studied with White at Columbia in 1917, recalled him as a "gentle," "sweet," and inarticulate man who never "mentioned technique once, how it's done, or short cuts, or photographic manipulations. It was to him a natural instrument and I suppose he approached it something like a musical instrument which you do the best you can with when it's in your hand." White's low-key, self-effacing manner notwithstanding, he did have firm ideas about photography. As his colleague Walter Hervey wrote, "We recall that modest and tentative way he had of saying, 'I almost think,' about matters of which, by some inward monitor, he was absolutely sure and for which he was ready to fight as one fights for a principle."[18]

Painter Max Weber was a more dynamic teacher with a well-articulated philosophy of art and a keen interest in the connections between photography and modern abstract painting. His lectures on art appreciation and design, Laura said, were "a very important part of my education."[19]

Born in Bialystok, Russia, in 1881, Weber emigrated to New York with his parents ten years later. In 1898 he enrolled at the Pratt Institute, where his teacher Arthur Wesley Dow had a profound influence on his theories of art and composition, forcing him to pay attention to viewing and sensation rather than imitation and copying. Weber taught art for several years after graduating from Pratt in 1900, and in 1905 he went to Paris. There, he was deeply impressed by the work of Gauguin, Cézanne, Picasso, and Matisse, and by the primitive art he studied in museums. When he returned to America in early 1909, he was among the first to bring to this country an understanding of the artistic revolution going on in Paris. His exposure to modernism was apparent in his own paintings, and Stieglitz was sufficiently impressed with Weber's work to include him in a group show in 1910 and to give him a one-man exhibition in 1911. Weber's understanding of modern European painting, Stieglitz conceded, was "helpful in a way of clarifying [his] own ideas."[20]

White invited Weber to teach first at his summer school in Maine and subsequently at his New York school, on the basis of his training with Dow as well as his European background and his exhibition record. Weber recalled that White "asked me to take charge of the art, such as composition and design, and I said, 'To really pursue the life of an artist, you must know the history of art.'" Accordingly, Weber arranged for art history to become an integral part of the school's curriculum. Even as he championed modernism, he emphasized the study of "the antiques" as a way of better understanding the art of the present. In his lectures on art appreciation, he stressed the spiritual qualities of great art, something Laura had aspired to understand through her friendship with Anne Simon. "Art is nothing if it does not stir or kindle the art consciousness in a people," Weber taught. All great art "oozes personal expression"; even modern art with its emphasis on abstract forms should exude emotion.[21]

Laura recalled, "Both Mr. White and Max Weber

would give us design problems like taking three objects and making one of first importance, one of second, and one of third. This sounds simple, but it isn't. White against white, and dark against dark, a problem in rectangles." With the 8″ x 10″ view cameras they used in all classroom assignments, students were also asked to compose still lifes with circular or angular compositions, to photograph landscapes in horizontal and vertical formats, to compose portraits under a variety of lighting situations.[22]

Weber stressed the importance of lighting, cropping, and viewpoint in photographic work and, like his mentor, Dow, emphasized the idea of "the filling of space." With his emphasis on photography as "a flat space art" just like drawing, painting, or printing, Weber provided a way for his students to consider the relationships between photography and modern painting, two arts that involved the same principles of design. "In our choice and elimination lies the very character of our personality, the very quality of our taste and expression," Weber wrote. The artist's "mind is his screen. He may shift objects, he may choose his position, he may vary the spaces between movable objects, and finally he may vary the proportion and size of the rectangle bounding the picture or print."[23]

Photographers also had to face problems particular to their medium, and Weber encouraged his students to fight against the temptation to abandon good style and composition to the allure of a particular subject. Accordingly, he assigned design problems in abstraction. A group of his students' photographs exhibited at the Royal Photographic Society show in London in 1915 earned the admiration of British photographer Alvin Langdon Coburn, an early practitioner of non-objective photography. The students' images, Coburn wrote, "were groups of objects photographed because of their shape and color value, with no thought of their sentimental associations. . . . The idea was to be as abstract as it is possible to be with the camera." Another group of design abstractions by Weber's students appeared in *Photo = Graphic Art* in the summer of 1916. The images were "made from a choice of objects in which representation is abandoned so that the design or composition of the light and dark areas, their shape, quantity and position, their gradation and

tone, become of themselves rectangles of pictorial and abstract satisfaction."[24]

These photographs were published several months before Alfred Stieglitz reproduced the forceful, semi-abstract photographs of newcomer Paul Strand in the last two issues of *Camera Work*. Strand's photographs emphasizing form and design over pictorial representation have been credited with marking the beginning of a reorientation in photographic aesthetics and a return to the traditions of straight, unmanipulated photography. But the students at the Clarence H. White School were working along similar lines, if somewhat less successfully than the masterful Strand. Unlike him, they continued to use conventional framing and point of view in composing their images, so that although they focused on pattern they never escaped a clear and literal reference to their subject matter. Still, their design compositions offer ample evidence that Weber encouraged his students at the Clarence H. White School to explore the connections between photography and modern painting, a connection minimized by Stieglitz and Strand in order to stress the unique qualities of photography. The school was not simply a bastion for the dying strains of picturesque photography, as some of its critics attempted to portray it.[25]

Not all of Weber's students appreciated his constant emphasis on art history, the principles of modern painting, and the basic elements of composition. The Clarence H. White School class of 1916 complained to White through a duly elected representative that Weber's lessons often seemed irrelevant. They asked "that if possible Mr. Weber plan his student's work so that it will apply more directly to photography." But Laura always considered her lessons with Weber to be "invaluable" for their emphasis on the basics of design. "There is no creative thing," she said, "whether it be writing, art, painting, architecture, or music that does not have structure and design. It just does not stand up without it."[26]

The third of the instructors at the Clarence H. White School during the 1916–1917 school year was Paul L. Anderson, an electrical engineer and accomplished pictorial photographer who gave classes in photographic processes and techniques and much admired Laura's work. Nearly twenty-five years later he recalled her as one of the few pupils in the school who "really had something." Anderson's own theories of composition were more conservative than Weber's, but the lessons learned in his class could be applied to any way of seeing. From Anderson, Laura learned about cameras and lenses, and in his classes she learned how to handcoat platinum and palladium photographic papers and to print in such combination techniques as gum-platinum. There she also acquired her life-long passion for the rich velvety blacks, wide tonal range, and archival stability of platinum paper, which she found perfectly suited to the effects she sought to convey in her pictures.[27]

Laura used platinum printing papers almost exclusively through the 1930s. Eastman Kodak stopped manufacturing the material in the United States in 1916; when her supply was exhausted, Laura placed monthly orders for commercially prepared papers from the Platinotype Company in England through Ira Martin, an active pictorial photographer and staff photographer for the Frick Collection. Later, after 1932, when Paul Strand persuaded the Platinotype Company to make a double-coated platinum stock on Japine paper, Laura ordered this specially made paper for herself directly from London. She, Strand, Martin, and Stieglitz were the company's chief American customers. Throughout this period, she continued to make hand-coated platinum paper for special prints and commissions, and after the British paper company discontinued the manufacture of platinum paper altogether in 1937, she continued to make platinum prints by hand into the 1970s, helping to preserve a dying art that has seen a comeback only in the last few years.[28]

Following the 1916–1917 school year, Laura returned to Colorado Springs for the summer to manage a series of local concerts. In the fall of 1917 she went back to New York to do specialized advanced work in photogravure techniques with White and Bernard Horne, another Clarence H. White School alumnus from Princeton, New Jersey. Photogravure is a method of producing a photographic image in printer's ink, through a laborious process of transferring a carbon print to a specially prepared copper plate. When the unexposed gelatin of the carbon print is washed away, an image in relief is left on the plate. The plate is then etched with ferric chloride, which bites into the copper in proportion to the depth of the gelatin relief, and finally is inked and printed. British photographer Peter Henry Emerson demonstrated the capacity of this process for fine photographic prints in his *Pictures of East Anglian Life* in 1889, and Alfred Stieglitz brought the process to near perfection with the photogravure reproductions in his periodical *Camera Work*. Because film manufactured during the war had a reduced silver content, Laura and her colleagues had difficulty with the photogravure process until they discovered that manufacturers had not tampered with the emulsion of X-ray film. Moreover, X-ray film was coated on both sides so that the right-left reversal incurred in transferring an image to a printing plate could be avoided.[29]

The changed silver content of film was one of the few ways in which the war in Europe impinged on Laura's world. Classes at the Clarence H. White School proceeded normally, if with fewer men. Laura and her friend Brenda did occasional volunteer work at the American Women's Hospital, and Laura confided in a friend that she would like to fly for the army and be an aerial photographer, a desire that would be partially fulfilled more than twenty-five years later during the next world war.[30]

But the war did put a damper on the broader photography scene. Chemicals used in photographic materials became scarce and more expensive to procure. Many active photographers enlisted in the service, submissions to salons were down, and many coastal areas and other spots deemed strategically significant were placed off limits to photographers. The photographic journals encouraged photographers to put their skills to good use by photographing soldiers and by making arrangements with their local YMCAs.[31] Stieglitz's *Camera Work* ceased publication in 1917, as did *Photo=Graphic Art*, the journal so closely affiliated with the Clarence H. White School.

For Laura, her time in New York was nonetheless a time of heady freedom, experimentation, and work. She studied Brenda's sculpture, kept up a busy concert-going schedule with her roommates, followed the art and photography exhibitions at New York's museums and galleries, and considered ways she could earn a living as a photographer. She met the photog-

SNOWSTORM, CENTRAL PARK, NEW YORK. *Laura Gilpin.*
Platinum print, 1917. Amon Carter Museum.

raphers who passed through White's school; Doris
Ulmann, for example, gave occasional presentations.
But, as New York photographer Karl Struss later
recalled, "We were all so engrossed in learning this
beautiful art that social activities were nil." Her photography, her association with Brenda's work, and
her "music-hungry soul" kept her from even thinking
about social issues, Laura said later. She recalled "Mr.
White showing us the wonderful work of [Lewis]
Hine's done at Ellis Island," but she felt "too shy and
frightened of people to have done such work at that
time."[32]

Laura's New York pictures suggest that she, like
White, had little interest in the city as a subject for
her work. Her photographs of Washington Square
and Central Park are soft-focus images more notable
for their overall pattern of design and emotional
expressiveness than for the information they convey

about city life (plate 5). Like White, Laura was more
interested in photographing the lasting, essential
aspect of a subject than in catching the more fleeting
or temporal image, in recording the emotion felt
upon viewing a scene rather than recording the
objective or literal appearance of the subject.

Only one of her student photographs alludes to any
of the city's temporal concerns. *Recruiting Scene* (1917),
a pin-hole photograph, shows a crowd gathered on
a New York street in a composition resonant of the
city views made by Karl Struss, Alvin Langdon Coburn, and others experimenting with unusual aerial
perspectives in their work (plate 8).[33] Laura made the
photograph from an overhead perspective, flattening
the picture plane and framing the image to accentuate
the angular patterns of the buildings and streets. The
tiny, blurred white faces of the people in the crowd
seem more like impressionist brush strokes than photographic renderings, and only the photograph's title
reveals that it is an image dealing with topical concerns.

Laura shared many of White's ideas about aesthetics,
and her early portraits, made in informal settings with
strong natural backlighting, owe a debt to his work.
But her pictures still differed from his in important
ways. White sometimes transformed his portraits
into allegorical images with costumed subjects and
symbolic titles. From the start, Laura's portraits were
straightforward and revealing images of particular
people, not allusive storytelling pictures, and thus
more closely related to the emerging taste for straight,
"honest" photography than to the allegorical lyricism
of her older teacher.

Her first widely exhibited and published photograph was *The Prelude* (1917), a publicity picture of
the Edith Rubel Trio with Brenda Putnam at the
piano (plate 6). Laura created interest in what might
have been a boring picture of three performers on
stage by controlling the light and boldly dividing
the background space to focus attention on the women.
She used a standing lamp to cast an intimate light
and raised the lid on the grand piano to create a dark
backdrop for the cellist. The platinum print epito-
mized Laura's interest in photography as an expressive
art with commercial potential. It hung at an exhibition of the Colorado Springs Fine Arts Society in
April 1917 and was subsequently selected for inclusion

in the Pictorial Photographers of America's annual touring exhibition in 1917–1918. After it was reproduced in the final issue of *Photo = Graphic Art* in October 1917, Laura's instructor Paul Anderson asked to include it in his illustrated text on the fine art of photography.[34]

In style, *The Prelude* resembles the soft-focus, softly printed platinum works of White and other practitioners of turn-of-the-century pictorialism. But Laura generally eschewed the hand manipulation of the negative and print that was often associated with this style of work, and she never regarded the soft-focus style as anything more than a means of conveying a particular emotion. It was not an end in itself. A few of her early photographs were manipulated with hand work, but from the start, Laura was essentially a "straight" photographer, composing her photographs on the ground glass and printing exactly what she captured on her negatives.[35] Laura did work with soft-focus Struss Pictorial and Pinkham and Smith lenses, like White preferring the soft edges and hazy atmosphere seen through these lenses to the sharply focused, seemingly less photogenic world seen through an anastigmatic lens. But even during her time in New York she was experimenting with a different way of seeing. She frequently practiced photography on Brenda's sculpture "and in some respects," she recalled, "was getting away from soft-focus right then and there," stopping down her soft-focus lens to get a clearer image of the pieces.[36] Eventually she would abandon her soft-focus lenses altogether and adopt a new more sharp-edged approach for her photographs of the southwestern landscape.

Just a few months after returning to the Clarence H. White School in the fall of 1917 to do her "postgraduate" study in photogravure, Laura fell victim to the great influenza epidemic of 1918. When she was well enough to travel, she returned to Colorado Springs and was put to bed with a heart lesion. At first, she said, she thought "the end of time" had come because she was prevented from working. After a six-month convalescence she resumed her photographic work, but her formal study of the craft was over.[37]

Her instructors had constantly emphasized the importance of her training. "Chance," White had often said, "is a poor photographer." Laura left White's

school with a strong sense of the overriding importance of design, a keen interest in art history, a set of technical skills, a strategy for approaching photographic problems adapted from the design project method, and a respect for the field of commercial as well as "fine arts" photography. White was a leader in artistic photographic illustration recognized for his "study of photography in relation to advertising and its infinite possibilities."[38] From him and from typographer and designer Frederick Goudy, a frequent contributor to Pictorial Photographers of America publications, Laura had also acquired a fascination with printing, book illustration, and book design.

In the East, Laura acquired her skills; in the West, she found her subject. None of her New York work seems as emphatically hers as the work she did back in Colorado during the summer between her years at the Clarence H. White School and after her recovery from the flu. There she made luminous platinum and palladium landscape pictures, delicate images that reveal her fine printing technique and her continuing fascination with the spiritual atmosphere of the landscape, an interest she had first acquired from Anne Simon. The large, ghostly rock formations of the Garden of the Gods loom out from mist-shrouded backgrounds; the prairies of Colorado sprawl under low horizon lines and big, cloud-filled skies (plates 13, 14, 17). The compositions rely on the careful massing and juxtaposition of large areas of form, what Max Weber called "the filling of space." Few of these landscapes have human figures or other forms to indicate scale. *The Prairie* (1917), a picture made to illustrate a poem, does include a wind-swept figure (plate 11). But the figure's tiny scale and indistinct features only underscore Laura's overriding interest in atmosphere rather than detailed description. "I studied in New York and did quite a bit of work there," she recalled many years later, "but I'm a westerner, and I didn't want to run that rat race to earn money." Moreover, she also said, "I'm definitely a westerner and I just have to be in the mountain country. It's where I belong." Thus Laura returned home and began to photograph the place she knew best, with a sure and intuitive feel for the bright light and open spaces of the land where she had been raised.[39]

Establishing a Career, 1918–1930

When Laura returned to Colorado Springs with the flu in early 1918, her mother sought nursing help and hired Elizabeth Forster, a registered nurse who had just left the local Visiting Nurse Association. This proved to be the beginning of a friendship between Laura and Betsy that would soon become the central and most important relationship in either woman's life – a relationship that would last more than fifty years.

A thin, frail-looking woman, with considerable physical strength and a tough, dry wit, Betsy Forster was five years older than Laura. She was born in 1886 at Friendfield, her family's rice plantation near George-town, South Carolina. After selling the plantation in the mid-1890s, the Forster family moved around the South following the assignments of Betsy's father, Charles, a civil engineer and bridge designer for the Union Pacific Railroad Company. When Charles Forster died in 1906, Betsy's older brother, Alexius, became head of the family and the entire family moved to Baltimore where he worked as a physician in a tuberculosis clinic at Johns Hopkins University. In Baltimore, Betsy decided that she, too, wanted to pursue a career in health care. She studied public health nursing at Johns Hopkins and in 1912 graduated from the nursing program at Union Memorial Hospital. Later that year she, along with her mother and her sisters, followed Alexius to Colorado Springs where he had accepted a job as resident director of the Crag-mor Sanitorium. In 1913 Betsy joined the Colorado Springs Visiting Nurse Association and worked for the group until February 1918, when she was let go for lack of funds; she then went into private nursing.[1]

Betsy nursed Laura through the spring and summer of 1918. "When it comes to telling you what I think and how I feel for what you have done for Laura I am unable to express it at all," Mrs. Gilpin wrote to her following Laura's recovery. "It is the kind of thing that cannot be at all weighed in dollars and cents, but you know how I thank you for it."[2]

During the long hours they spent together, Betsy and Laura discovered that they shared a common interest in music, literature, and camping and a dedi-cation to their work. They were both self-directed women accustomed to supporting themselves and bearing much of the responsibility for supporting their families. Yet, while each was independent, neither had a solitary temperament. In the other, each sensed the presence of a supportive and understanding friend, accepting of her family obligations and professional aspirations. In a very short time, Betsy became the most important person in Laura's life, while Laura became Betsy's closest and dearest friend.

In the fall of 1918 Betsy accepted a Red Cross posi-tion that took her away from Colorado Springs until September 1919, when she returned to become super-visor of the Visiting Nurse Association. She quickly resumed her place in Laura's life, providing Laura with a friendship that was unencumbered by the expectations of Emma Gilpin or the frustrations and disappointments of Frank. Frank and Emma, in fact, embraced Betsy as one of their own, welcoming her at family birthday and Christmas celebrations and expecting her for visits even when Laura was out of town. While both Laura and Betsy continued to live with their own families, they became a familiar couple at Colorado Springs concerts and social events and companions for weekend visits to the Gilpin family cabin at Woodland Park and longer camping trips throughout the Southwest. With Brenda Putnam, Laura continued to share her feelings about art. But with Betsy, who returned her affections as Anne Simon

ELIZABETH FORSTER. *Laura Gilpin. Modern gelatin silver print from glass plate negative, 1918. Amon Carter Museum.*

and Brenda could not, Laura began to share every other aspect of her life.[3]

Betsy, like Brenda, offered support to Laura in her photographic career. But Laura's almost puritanical devotion to work derived not so much from her friends as from her parents, who saw in her the chance to redeem the disappointments of their own lives. Emma and Frank Gilpin's lives were falling farther and farther away from the ideal they had envisioned for themselves when they moved west. Frank could not find his seam of gold; and because her home life seemed so unsteady and her financial well-being so precarious, Emma could not re-create the world of gay parties and sophisticated conversation she had left behind in the Midwest. Frank hoped that Laura would find the steady income that had always eluded him; Emma hoped she would find the sense of accomplishment and self-fulfillment that had escaped her.

"My mother was the one who always wanted me to be independent," Laura recalled more than fifty years after her mother's death. "She was a remarkable woman and she was all for my doing what I wanted to do. In 1916 for a girl to go off on her own was not the usual thing, but whatever I wanted to do she was for; she was right behind me. She was wonderful – the more that I think of her the stronger I feel that."[4]

As a couple, Frank and Emma Gilpin evoked a certain gentle pity from their friends, who allowed them to retain their sense of gentility as members of the pioneer "Gilpin" clan. Occasionally, money would be given to them in a way that would allow them to maintain their pride, in the form of a repair job for Frank or a portrait commission for Laura, and they were permitted to remain members of the town's "social set." Frank, once an active polo player at the Cheyenne Mountain Country Club, was becoming more of a fixture at the club's bar than on the playing field. Still, he remained an enormously likeable fellow, admired by his friends with the kind of secret admiration those with settled lives often feel for those who live on the edge between wild failure and boundless success. Emma kept busy in the town's benevolent associations as an active member of the Visiting Nurse Association, the Colorado Springs Music Club, the Red Cross, and the Girl Scouts. It was noted that she would never accept presidencies of organizations even though she "accepted a great amount of responsibility in them." She was a large, heavyset woman whose friends recalled her as an understanding woman with a sweet, loving spirit and a commanding personality. Perhaps because she never quite felt a part of the social world of Colorado Springs herself, she was especially gracious to newcomers and able to make them feel at home.[5]

Frank and Emma focused their hopes on Laura rather than her brother, because Francis showed no signs of settling down. A handsome, gregarious youth, he too had gone east to prep school. He enrolled in the mining engineering course at Yale as a member of the class of 1919, and after a stint in the campus ROTC he enlisted in the army in the fall of 1917. He served just three months before being discharged for health reasons, and although he returned to Yale he never graduated. Like his father, he was eternally

GILPIN FAMILY. *Laura Gilpin. Modern gelatin silver print from glass plate negative, 1921. Amon Carter Museum.*

optimistic about the possibility of making a quick fortune in the oil-and-gas business but perpetually impatient and always unlucky. To Emma and even to Frank, his wanderlust must have seemed uncomfortably familiar.[6]

Thus, as Laura began her photographic career in 1918, she had the solid support of her parents. For subject matter she relied on what was familiar and close at hand in Colorado Springs; portrait subjects and local landscapes. Her platinum prints of views made in the nearby Garden of the Gods, a scenic rock formation that had long attracted photographers and tourists, were exhibited by the Colorado Springs Fine Arts Society in the summer of 1919. At the time, Laura was vacationing in Nova Scotia, but the pictures she made there were not as successful as the views she had made of the more familiar Colorado landscape (plate 7).[7]

The Broadmoor Art Academy opened in Colorado Springs in the fall of 1919, and Laura soon joined the circle of artists and craftsmen affiliated with the school. During the winter term muralist Robert Reid and others taught classes in painting, design, interior decoration, and crafts; during the summer John F. Carlson came to teach landscape painting. The school's curriculum stressed design and interior decoration and owed much to the teachings of Arthur Wesley Dow, whose emphasis on composition and the practical arts was much in vogue in art schools across the

country. Thus, in a town that had always been more interested in collecting art than in supporting the efforts of contemporary artists, Laura suddenly had a community of professional colleagues whose theories of design and art instruction were much the same as hers. She produced illustrated photographic brochures advertising the Broadmoor Art Academy programs and made portraits of the resident instructors in exchange for a painting or an etching. She moved her studio to the school and in the spring of 1921 joined the academy staff as the first and only instructor in photography. Most of her students were veterans attending school courtesy of various government vocational programs. Disabled veterans, she told friends, "are fairly camping on my doorstep for work."[8]

Portraits became the mainstay of her business. She photographed friends and distinguished visitors who passed through town and began to earn commissions from Colorado Springs families who found her carefully printed platinum pictures a pleasing and less expensive alternative to portrait paintings (plate 10). Her portraits were posed to create pleasing design patterns, but they were rarely stiff. Relying on soft, natural lighting, Laura tried to evoke the essential spirit of her sitters. In a portrait of Irish poet Padraic Colum (1919), for example, Laura captured the writer's nervous energy and otherworldly stare in a delicate platinum print that evoked the romance of his art (plate 12). To improve her portrait skills, Laura spent the winter of 1920–1921 in New York studying portrait sculpture with her friend Brenda. "It was wonderful," she recalled, "because you can learn just as much working on a clay head as you can with a live person, only you don't have to deal with the personality." When she returned home, she paid more attention to lighting and modeling in her portrait compositions. For a portrait of Margaret Carlson (1921), wife of the Broadmoor instructor, Laura used drapery much as a sculptor might to both conceal and reveal form while creating interesting patterns of light and shadow (plate 23). Carlson sits on a stool with her legs twisted to her right, her upper torso to her left. A shawl is draped across her shoulders to emphasize the placement of her arms; her right hand lies in her lap; her left hand is cocked back with her

LANDSCAPE CLASS, BROADMOOR ART ACADEMY.
Laura Gilpin. Platinum print, 1920. Amon Carter Museum.

hand balanced on her hip. The graceful flowing lines of the shawl and the sitter's full skirt accentuate the posture of her body, while a broad-rimmed hat creates deep modeling shadows on her face. Laura considered even her commercial portraits to be works of art and submitted them along with her landscapes to photographic shows and competitions.[9]

In 1920 she exhibited prints in a photographic salon in Copenhagen and had three photographs accepted into the International Exhibition at the London Salon of Photography. The following year she had a one-woman exhibition of sixty-one landscapes and portraits at the Broadmoor Art Academy, the Museum of New Mexico, and the Denver Public Library, where Denver Art Museum Director George William Eggers praised the photographs as "distinguished for their beauty of design and composition" and pointed out Laura's obvious debt to her photographic mentors. "Her message is decidedly her own," Eggers wrote, "but its clarity of expression is enhanced by that intelligence in light and dark arrangement, and that control of line and form, which comes from an appreciative study of oriental art, particularly from the Japanese as revealed to us first by Fenellosa and Dow and subsequently developed by Gertrude Käsebier, Alice Boughton and Clarence H. White in the field of photography."[10]

While Laura did submit still lifes and portraits to competitive photographic exhibitions, her chief success came with her western landscapes. A soft, ghostly image of the Garden of the Gods won honorable mention in the Wanamaker exhibition in Philadelphia in 1921, and three of her four pictures accepted at the London Salon of Photography that year were views of the prairies and rock formations around Colorado Springs, all carefully printed in platinum or palladium.[11] Thus Laura presented herself as a regional photographer who drew her inspiration and subject matter from the distinctive landscape around her home.

This affinity for the western landscape had several sources: her Colorado childhood and the easy accessibility of the prairies and mountains. But in the early 1920s Laura began to develop a more articulate theory about the meaning of regionalism and regional art, which gave her a different kind of interest in the landscape. On a trip to Durango with her father in the summer of 1921, she stopped in Santa Fe and visited the Museum of New Mexico, an institution founded in 1909 that interpreted regional culture through broad-ranging exhibitions of art, historical materials, and archaeological artifacts. Laura was deeply impressed by the museum's comprehensive approach to southwestern culture; it had labs for scientists as well as studios for artists. The museum's pueblo-style architecture seemed well adapted to its surroundings and she found "the paintings as a whole give an impression of strength, vigor, and masterly design, proving unquestionably that these New Mexico painters have produced a new and virile school of American art." Although Colorado Springs lacked the nearby Indian settlements that provided the motifs for much of the Taos and Santa Fe art, Laura said, "We have a superb landscape that can hardly be equaled and there is every reason to think that we can create here a great school of landscape painting. . . . Is there a finer way in which we can show our appreciation of Colorado than by helping to perpetuate its beauties on the walls of our future museum and homes?" The Broadmoor Art Academy, she thought, should become the center for this new local art movement.[12]

Laura expanded her notion of regional art and architecture as an expressive form of local boosterism when she went to Europe in 1922. As she studied the unfamiliar art and architecture of England and France, she began to think about art objects as historical artifacts with a documentary value. This had a profound impact on her subsequent career, reorienting her interest toward the material artifacts of prehistoric and historic Indian life in her own Southwest.

Laura saved for her trip to Europe "like all get out" and managed to scrape together $1,000, half of it borrowed from a family friend in Colorado Springs, which would permit her to live on a budget of five dollars a day. In late April 1922, after promising her mother and Betsy that she would write long letters to them both, she with Brenda boarded the *RMS Mauretania* for the crossing to Southampton. An unflattering passport photograph shows Laura to have been a heavyset but youthful looking woman of thirty-one, with blunt-cut dark blonde hair and clear blue eyes.[13]

Before they even left the pier, a portentous accident occurred. As Laura leaned over the deck to get a good look at the crowds, she dropped her soft-focus Pinkham and Smith lens into the water. "For one agonized moment, I felt as though I were dead or something," she wrote Betsy. "I got out my hated anastigmatic lens and decided I was meant to learn to use it and would find it best for what I want to do with my prints." She had just enough time before the boat sailed to order a new Pinkham and Smith lens to be sent to her in London. The new lens caught up with her in a few weeks but proved to have a flare. Still, Laura used the sharp-focus lens as little as possible, preferring to stop down her new lens to minimize the effects of the flare, a process which resulted in a sharper image. Although she had experimented with stopping down soft-focus lenses to photograph Brenda's sculpture, this, she later remarked, "was when I realized that the sharp image was what I wanted."[14]

Laura and Brenda landed at Southampton on May Day. After side trips to Winchester, Romsey Abbey, and Netley Abbey (which Laura thought "simply heaven" even though the photographs made with her "hated anastigmatic lens" did not turn out), they continued on to London and settled into a hotel just across the street from the British Museum.[15]

Disquieting news reached Laura there. A note from Betsy reported that doctors concurred with Mrs. Gilpin's feeling that the family should move back to a farm for the sake of Frank's emotional well-being. Laura quickly sent a note of encouragement to her mother, revealing that at the age of thirty-one she still saw her place as with her family, even though there was little chance she could support herself as a photographer on a remote Colorado ranch. "I do hope that just the right thing will present itself and that we can settle down somewhere for good," she wrote.[16]

With great doubts about where her future lay, Laura determined to make the best of her time in London. She and Brenda spent most of their days in museums and galleries, where they set up critical problems for themselves, taking notes on their favorite paintings and then comparing their notes at home. At the British Museum, Laura, who had always had a strong interest in family history, looked up all of the Gilpins listed in the card catalogue, then wandered with Brenda through the galleries. They spent several mornings in the Print Room "pouring over original drawings by Blake, Michael Angelo, Bellini's sketchbook, etc." While Brenda studied Michaelangelo, Laura focused on the work of Blake. Years later she said, "I think this is one of the places that probably jelled things for me because one of the things I admired about Blake was the fact that he wrote everything, printed everything, and bound it and published it. I think that got me thinking in terms of producing things like that."[17]

Everywhere she went she applied the critical notions she had acquired from Max Weber's art appreciation classes, analyzing paintings for their composition, emotive spirit, and use of light. "Am I too critical?" she asked Betsy. "Perhaps so, but then how am I to learn if I'm not, and if I don't continually search out the good and know why it's good, and the bad and know why it's bad?"[18]

With a letter of introduction from Clarence White, Laura introduced herself to J. Dudley Johnston, head of the pictorial branch of London's Royal Photographic Society, who gave her a tour of the RPS facilities and offered her use of the society's darkrooms. Several weeks later she went to a lecture with him at the society "on a subject I don't much believe in . . . softening a print made from a negative taken with an anastigmatic lens." Through Johnston, Laura was able to see much of the photographic work being done in London. But so far, she reported to her family in late May, "I haven't seen anything to fill me with awe."[19]

When Laura returned to London in early September, after a stay in France, she found that three of her own prints had been accepted into the London Salon of Photography, and she attended a private viewing of the show on September 1. There was "very little *real* stuff," she noted. She was "inclined to think that by far the best work is being done in the good old U.S.A." When she went to see the annual show at the Royal Photographic Society, Laura "saw nothing that could compare with Clarence White, Mrs. Käsebier, or Stieglitz, and a few others. . . . The general tendency is towards huge prints. I am not convinced by them. They are as yet crude and often done without knowledge of proportion. However, this will come."[20]

Constantly aware of being an American in Europe, Laura compared Turner to the American painter Winslow Homer; Constable to John Twachtman. After a few weeks in England she wrote home, "The more I see of the rest of the world, the gladder I am that I am not only American, but a Westerner. I look for the greatest art the world has yet produced to come from the West." Still later, writing from France on Bastille Day, she patriotically noted, "The best work of the present time is in America, without question to my mind, and I hope we are just entering on a new Golden Age."[21]

In France, Laura and Brenda divided their time between the countryside and Paris, where Laura bought a vest pocket camera to make record shots of possible subjects for her view camera. She was drawn most to the "delicate and subtle" drama of Mont-Saint Michel and to the timeless and romantic beauty of Chartres, which helped her to crystallize her thoughts about the connections between art and history. After visiting the cathedral at Chartres she wrote in her journal, "The romance of the old West vanished so fast and so few ever did anything with it. Does it make you realize the importance of Art, and how the main knowledge of history is thru Art alone." Later, when she visited the Bodleian Library at Oxford and saw an early globe on which Santa Fe was the

only identified spot in the vast *terra incognita* of the American West, she realized that her corner of the Southwest had an especially rich history that demanded documentation.[22]

In late September 1922, Laura and Brenda sailed for home. "I haven't much to show for my summer," Laura wrote, "a half dozen things, maybe a few more, are all the exhibition prints I shall have, but there is much in my head that needs to be worked out."[23]

Indeed, only a few exhibition prints resulted from her trip. The most successful included a photograph of sardine boats in the harbor of the French village of Concarneau, shot from an overhead point of view that flattened the picture plane and emphasized the geometric patterns of the composition; and a print made in the dimly lit interior of Chartres Cathedral (plates 29, 30). The platinum print of the church nave has an aura of hushed stillness and, with its emphasis on architectural forms illuminated with soft natural light, it is reminiscent of Frederick Evans's English cathedral views.

The greatest impact of the trip was on Laura's subsequent photographic work. Through her necessary experiments with stopping down her damaged lens, she came away with an increased respect for the merits of clear, sharp-focus photography. Her encounter with the work of William Blake renewed her interest in making photographic books. Her study of paintings sharpened her knowledge of art history and her critical facilities. Most important, though, Laura returned home with a strong sense of herself as a peculiarly *American* and *western American* person, a clear-cut self-image that put to rest any lingering doubts about the richness of western culture she might have picked up from her mother. And she began to think about how she could document the culture of her native Southwest by photographing the art and artifacts of its earliest inhabitants.

During Laura's absence, Betsy carefully saved all of her letters and postcards for a neatly prepared journal and handled her friend's business affairs. She mailed prints off to photographic exhibitions and collected reviews of Laura's work. A critic for *Camera Craft*, the chief West Coast photographic journal, had noted of Laura's one-person show in San Francisco in July to November 1922, "The photographs are unusually attractive for their beauty of design and composition and especially for the depth of tonal quality." The show was "unique," she thought, "in that the work of one person is so comprehensive as to subject-matter and is treated with such a variety of effects and with fidelity to the particular inspiration of each theme. In technique it embraces the several schools of Pictorial Photography; the more clearly defined pictures, the charming soft focus lens work, which in her pictures is always held within bounds and never allowed to become an affectation; and the more pronounced modeling, the culmination of the latest idea in pictorial photography."[24]

When Laura returned to Colorado Springs, she resumed her portrait work and her busy exhibition schedule. In 1923 she had prints accepted into the annual exhibitions of the London Salon of Photography and the Royal Photographic Society, and she showed work in pictorial photography salons in Buffalo, Pittsburgh, Colorado Springs, San Francisco, Toronto, Seattle, and New York, where her platinum print of the eastern Colorado prairies, *Sunlight and Silence*, exhibited in the International Salon of the Pictorial Photographers of America, was singled out for special praise. The image had nearly all the characteristic features of her early landscape work: a dramatically low horizon to emphasize the vast space of the vista, big clouds to give interest to the sky, atmospheric lighting to lend drama to the picture, and subtly rendered grey tones to give the image a delicate quality (plate 13). The picture showed a landscape extending 110 miles from foreground to background, yet Laura had a talent for making even large, sweeping vistas seem quiet and intimate. The critic for the *New York Evening World* noted, "The Western country is pictured with an infinite grasp and the distance is expressed in a noteworthy way. The vegetation, as well as the plains, and the cloud-flecked sky, are splendidly featured."[25]

As Colorado Springs newspapers carried news of her triumphs, Laura began to get more lucrative commercial assignments at home. She was hired to provide photographs for two promotional brochures: *The Nutrition School Camp* and *Winning Health in the Pikes Peak Region*, both published in 1923. She made all new photographs for the camp book, and for the

larger, more elaborate health brochure she used some landscapes she had already made. The local newspapers noted that the chamber of commerce's *Winning Health* brochure was the finest publication ever issued in their city, with "23 illustrations, every one of them worthy of framing." The pictures are an artful combination of descriptive views and atmospheric scenes that give the impression of a restful spot conducive to languorous good health.[26]

In the fall of 1923, Laura began work on a publication of her own to advertise all of her commercial services: portrait work, illustrations, copy work, custom-made family albums, group and interior views, and Christmas cards with half-tone reproductions of selected portraits or landscapes. Customers could arrange for a studio sitting and three platinum portraits for $35.00; a sitting in the home was $15.00 extra.[27]

More ambitious than a mere advertising circular, *Some Thoughts on Portraiture* was a handsomely designed and printed brochure that set forth Laura's philosophy of portrait photography. Laura conceded that most portraits were unappealing because few photographers had studied art. But she was well schooled in the art of photography and with cooperation from her sitters could produce a photograph with "all the beautiful qualities of an etching or any of the graphic arts." She wanted an interpretation of a personality, not just a record of a face. "The photographer must know his sitter," she wrote, "must make him feel at ease, find out his likes and dislikes, and win his co-operation, understanding, and interest instead of his antagonism, in order to find that personality which he wishes to interpret." Gertrude Käsebier, to whom Laura sent a copy of her brochure, thought the publication quite a good idea. Not only did it promote Laura's business but also its text gave some valuable information about the art of portraiture. "People as a rule are so woefully ignorant of the necessity of intelligent cooperation at a sitting," Käsebier wrote.[28]

After printing her brochure Laura returned to New York to prepare for a one-person show to be held in January 1924, under the auspices of the Pictorial Photographers of America. The exhibition was to be mounted at the Art Center, a prestigious exhibition spot for photographers and graphic artists. Problems from home, however, followed her east. In December she received a note from her father. Frank had begun spending more and more time making hand-crafted furniture and was starting to think about making that his livelihood. As he considered the possibility of earning his living by making fine reproductions of Federal- and Spanish Colonial-style furniture, he pinned his hopes on the support and collaboration of his daughter. "I have not had the heart to write lately," Frank wrote. "The days have all been so blue and hard that I have found it difficult to get thru and I cannot see much sunshine ahead. I have been feeling pretty well and things at home have been very smooth and pleasant except for this I don't know what I should have done. I have been thinking seriously of the shop as a livelihood and if nothing else develops soon will have to turn to that. I wish I could spend Christmas with you as I miss your always cheery and bright support. Perhaps when you return we can find some place together where we can work and I will get back some of my pep." He apologized for writing such a "blue" letter but said he just had to talk to somebody and closed by telling Laura all was really fine, so she "need not hurry back on our account."[29]

Laura stayed in New York and mounted her exhibition at the Art Center where it drew high praise from local critics. The *New York Herald* proclaimed her first "one man" show in New York "delightful" and called attention to her views of the prairies, "which give most successfully the sense of the vastness of the plains." The *New York Sun*'s critic thought her landscapes of the Garden of the Gods remarkable for the "startling arrangements of light, such as etchers use in delineating strong sunlight." "Others have done similar things in the past," the critic noted, "but the thing that tinges this exhibition with glory is the fact that all the prints have been made from unretouched negatives and that her photographic equipment contains no high priced lenses or other expensive apparatus."[30]

Emboldened by these favorable notices, Laura wrote short notes to Alfred Stieglitz and Paul Strand inviting them to view her work. Laura had visited Stieglitz's gallery and had been much impressed by his photographic portraits of Georgia O'Keeffe on display at the Anderson Gallery in 1921. But she was terrified

of him and never showed him any of her work. She suspected that he and Edward Steichen did not like women photographers, with the possible exception of Mrs. Käsebier. Stieglitz thanked Laura for her invitation to her show and said he would try to see it, but, he added archly, "I dislike *Exhibitions* intensely. 'Exhibitions' have been so cheapened. There is a lack of standards everywhere. Few *know* what standards are."[31]

Strand, whom Laura always called her favorite photographer, replied coolly to her invitation. "I dropped in at the Art Center the other day," he wrote. "Between occidentalized Chinese paintings, commercial American photomechanical work and a wall of mushy still-life, truly 'pictorial' photographs, I found it difficult to see your work. In some of the things I liked what you were trying to do."[32]

Changing meanings of the word *pictorial* left Laura's work hard to categorize. When Stieglitz began his campaign to have photography accepted as a fine art, he called atmosphere, or *tone*, one of the chief qualities that distinguished a fine picture from a mere photograph. By the early 1920s, however, Stieglitz had begun to champion a more sharp-focus, straight, unmanipulated kind of photography, such as that practiced by the young Paul Strand, which did not embrace the more atmospheric, hand-worked, scenic views made by many who called themselves pictorialists. Pictorialism, a word Stieglitz had once invoked, increasingly was associated only with the work of White, Käsebier, and other supporters of the Pictorial Photographers of America.[33]

The PPA had never found "straight" unmanipulated photography inimical to the effects they sought to achieve. As early as 1914, Edward Dickson, editor of *Platinum Print*, the pictorial journal that eventually became the official organ for the PPA, had praised "straight photography" as photography "founded on the retention of true photographic quality, fidelity to the basic principles of proper selection, and the possession of the spirit characterizing those who work for the joy it affords." Stieglitz, Strand, and other practitioners of what the PPA referred to as the "new," or "modern," school of photography, however, were redefining straight photography. An unmanipulated negative and an unretouched print were no longer enough to qualify a photograph as "straight." The photographs had to be made with a sharp-focus lens, certain subjects–such as extreme close-ups or boldly cropped industrial views–were more acceptable than others, and glossy gelatin silver printing papers were preferable to the flat or textured platinum papers favored by more traditional photographers.[34]

The prevailing confusion as to just what pictorial photography was, was reflected in an introduction to comments by prominent photographers published in a 1923 text, *Principles of Pictorial Photography*. The book's editor, John Wallace Gillies, noted:
In the Pictorial section of photography one can make almost any kind of statement he please, and some will nod sagely, "Yes" and others will disagree with great heat. It is right or wrong as it happens to strike the other fellow. There is nothing absolute, nothing settled. It is an art, or not an art as we please to have it. Stieglitz at present makes his pictures sharp and is ready to tell everybody that a fuzzy picture is not the thing. Clarence White likes his pictures softer, and has held to that view, which speaks well for his first opinion. Steichen made them fuzzy years ago, and now cannot get them sharp enough. So what are we to think? Each one has something to say and each statement is different.[35]

The varied response to Laura's work reflected this general confusion. Even as New York critics praised it for its straight, unmanipulated, and therefore up-to-date style, Paul Strand hedged because it seemed too "soft-focus" and therefore in the pictorial style he thought outmoded. At the same time, Ralph Steiner, a former Clarence White student who had become involved in advertising photography and professed to hate pictorial photography, lauded Laura's photographs because they did not seem pictorial at all. "I want to tell you that I think you have some pictures which must be admitted to the small group of really worthwhile photographs that have been done," he wrote to Laura asking for a print of her landscape known as *Sunlight and Silence* or *Spirit of the Prairie*. "I really do think very little that has been done of late is worth a lot. You see, I hate pictorialism and will not belong to the P P A for that reason. There is too much that is shallow."[36]

Gertrude Käsebier remained Laura's most ardent professional supporter. From the time she moved to

GERTRUDE KÄSEBIER. *Unknown photographer. Platinum print, n.d. Amon Carter Museum.*

New York to study at the Clarence H. White School, Laura had kept up a lively correspondence with the older photographer, sending frequent gifts, letters, and prints for critique. When she was in New York, she would often stop by to visit, for Käsebier found it increasingly difficult to get out herself. Through Laura, Brenda Putnam met Käsebier, and in Laura's absence she would stop by to talk about her sculpture projects and tell Käsebier of Laura's latest accomplishments.

Käsebier had been the most successful woman photographer of her time. After marrying a New York businessman and raising three children, in 1874 she enrolled in an art course at Pratt Institute and studied with Arthur Wesley Dow. Subsequently, she took up photography in her mid-thirties in order to take pictures of her family. After earning much acclaim for the naturalistic style of her portraits, which broke with the convention of nineteenth-century photographic portraiture by using many of the conventions of symbolist painting, she was accepted by Stieglitz as a founding member of the Photo-Secession in 1902.

She resigned from the Photo-Secession in 1912 and four years later became one of the founding members of the PPA.[37]

Käsebier's own upbringing made her particularly sympathetic to Laura and her work. Born in 1852 in a log cabin on the Iowa frontier, she moved to Colorado with her Quaker parents as a young girl. From 1860 to 1864 she lived in Eureka Gulch, one of the few white children in a raw, new gold mining town. There she developed her lifelong fascination with Indians, a fascination reflected in the sympathetic portraits she later made of the Indians from Buffalo Bill's Wild West show who visited her New York studio in 1898 or 1899. In 1864, after her father's death, Käsebier moved with her family to New York and later enrolled in the Moravian Seminary for Young Ladies in Bethlehem, Pennsylvania. Like Laura, she had an upbringing that was at once western and eastern.[38]

Your photographs are "doubly precious to me because of the years of my childhood which were spent amidst such surroundings," she wrote to Laura after seeing some of her Colorado landscapes. Laura's gifts of Christmas wreaths and pine cones triggered memories of "the vast altitudes and spaces" that appealed to her "in an unforgettable way."[39]

Despite an age difference of nearly forty years, Käsebier embraced Laura as a colleague who shared her passion for photography. "Comradeship in a common interest is very rare," she wrote her in 1919. "There are so few who make a life work of it and nothing else counts in the long run," she later told her. "I feel that you are on your way to succeed with your work and wish you the fullest accomplishment." There is nothing in the world, she said, so satisfying as having work that you love to do.[40]

"It made her so happy to hear from you," Brenda wrote to Laura after visiting Mrs. Käsebier. "You are one of the few people she admires absolutely and without reservation, and she's so lonely now it is touching to see how much it means to her to hear from you." Mrs. Käsebier, she reported, "just about worships you."[41]

Käsebier effusively praised Laura's work for its honesty and the "bigness" of its conception. She lauded her writing for its "dignity, simplicity and charm" and enthused over some winter scenes that Laura had sent to her. "How they did refresh me. They are just like your dear self in simplicity and truth. Truly photography is a wonderful medium to those who can understand."[42]

By the mid-1920s, Gertrude Käsebier was no longer a major presence in the New York photography world – in part because she was no longer an active photographer and exhibitor, and in part because the allegorical portraits for which she was best known seemed out of step with the work currently being shown in galleries. She, herself, was disappointed with much contemporary work and disenchanted with even the Pictorial Photographers of America, of which she was an honorary vice-president. The changes taking place in photography bewildered her. In 1926 when she served on the jury for the PPA's annual salon exhibition, she complained to Laura about the general lowering of the standards for judging and about the plethora of advertising photography that simply had no appeal. Betraying her continuing taste for one of the fashions of earlier pictorial photography, she wrote, "I put up a fight for artistic titles but think it fell flat. So that's that and if I ever hear from [the PPA] again is uncertain."[43]

Her disenchantment with photography and her growing awareness of her own age and frailty were evident in the advice she gave Laura. "There will come a time when you must call a halt, nature demands her toll, and the sooner you realize it the better. It is a great privilege to have work to do that we love to do but we must not waste our forces. Make haste slowly."[44]

In New York, Laura also kept up with her former teacher Clarence White. She sat for a portrait by White, exchanged prints with him, consulted with him on the techniques of photogravure, and became a friend and confidante of his wife, Jane Felix White. When the Clarence H. White School fell on hard times in 1921, Laura made a modest cash contribution to a group of friends and alumni seeking to find new quarters for the school. In the winter of 1922, when White and this alumni group had a falling out over the financial viability of the reorganized school, she managed, with considerable diplomatic aplomb, to remain friends with White and with her former classmates whose efforts to help he had repudiated. Thus it was not surprising that after Clarence White's sudden death in Mexico on July 8, 1925, Jane Felix White turned to Laura for guidance and support. "Mr. White was always very proud of your work," she told her.[45]

Laura went to New York in the fall of 1925 and, while helping to arrange for the publication of a memorial volume of White's pictures, she began to help Mrs. White select a group of her husband's photographs to submit for sale to the Library of Congress.[46] She wrote to Herbert Putnam, Librarian of Congress and father of her friend Brenda, encouraging him to consider White's work for the library's department of prints and photographs. Acting on Laura's suggestion, Putnam acquired a set of White's prints, probably the first photographs acquired for the collection for their aesthetic value rather than their documentary significance. Thus, through her friendship with the Putnam family, Laura was instrumental in changing the collecting focus of the Library of Congress collection, helping to orient it toward fine contemporary work. She subsequently played a role in placing a group of Käsebier prints in the collection, which in turn attracted prints from photographer F. Holland Day and others.[47]

On her visits to New York, Laura never photographed the city, which had not interested her as a subject even in her student days. Instead, she made photographs of Brenda's sculpture and on occasion did portrait studies. Her most ambitious, made in 1925, was a series of portraits of pianist Harold Bauer, whom she had met in Brenda's studio. Laura photographed him playing five different pieces of classical music, attempting in each picture to capture the mood of the performer as well as the spirit of the music. As he plays Bach, Bauer appears absorbed in the technical intricacies of the piece. As he plays Schumann, he appears transported by the music's lyricism. Brenda, who presented a portfolio of palladium prints of the pictures to Bauer, reported that "the Beethoven" made him cry.[48]

Despite her success in New York, Laura could not shake off her worries about her family. In the fall of 1925, Emma wrote to her daughter in New York that she hoped Laura could "put some courage back" into her father, for she no longer knew how to do it.

HAROLD BAUER PLAYING BEETHOVEN. *Laura Gilpin. Palladium print, 1925. Amon Carter Museum.*

"Your father is what is worrying me greatly," she confided. Summarizing a problem that had been going on for years she wrote: "Many of us could sit down and say something is gone out of [us?] but it isn't right to do it, but to buck up, and try to get at something, anything that will make a living. It is a queer complex that he has. It's always somebody else's fault things go wrong. It isn't the right way to look at our failure. . . . I know his letters just kill me, and I can never admire him, for he never sees my point of view about anything. I hate to worry you children about such things but I don't see, unless he gets some hold on himself, what is going to become of him or me – or us."[49]

Her parents' difficulties gave Laura a sense of urgency about finding a permanent spot for herself in the Southwest. In the fall of 1924, instead of going to New York, she went on a camping trip through southern Colorado and New Mexico with her two closest friends, Betsy Forster and Brenda Putnam. It was her first opportunity to study the American Southwest as she had studied Europe two years before, paying particular attention to the connections between history and art. She took her cameras with her, uncertain as to just what artifacts she would find to document.[50]

The three women left Colorado Springs in September in an open Dodge loaded down with camping supplies, three of Laura's cameras (a Graflex, a view camera, and a Vippick), and an ammonia gun to ward off coyotes. Laura was the chief car mechanic, Betsy cooked and did the laundry, and Brenda – the least experienced camper – spent her spare time writing, sketching, and collecting insects.[51]

They went first to Mesa Verde, where park supervisor Jesse Nusbaum and his wife, Aileen, introduced them to the history of the Anasazi ruins. It was Laura's first glimpse of the ancient cliff dwellings and they impressed her much as they had impressed writer Willa Cather – as fabulous sculptures by a brilliant and long-gone race of people. "Far above me," Cather wrote in *The Professor's House* (1925), "a thousand feet or so, set in a great cavern in the face of the cliff, I saw a little city of stone, asleep. It was as still as sculpture – and something like that. It all hung together, seemed to have a kind of composition: pale little houses of stone nestling close to one another, perched on top of each other, with flat roofs, narrow windows, straight walls, and in the middle of the group, a round tower . . . that held all the jumble of towers together and made them mean something."[52]

Laura photographed the structures as sculptural forms, getting up early to work in the morning light before tourists arrived to mar her photographs (plates 87, 89). The strong light made the ruined stone dwellings stand out against the darker cliff walls stained black by thousands of years of dripping water. But her photographs were not merely studies in pattern and form, as were the photographs Paul Strand made at Mesa Verde two years later. Laura wanted to evoke the strong sense of history and romance that she felt in the presence of the ancient cliff dwellings, for the stone houses symbolized an ancient culture just as the cathedrals she had seen in Europe revealed the genius of a past age. As in her portraits or her early Colorado landscapes, she wanted to express the *spirit* of her subject. Thus, in her photographs she emphasized the

way the buildings were built into caves high up cliff walls in order to suggest the difficult and precarious nature of the cliff dwellers' lives.[53]

Sensing that Cather's feelings about Mesa Verde were probably similar to her own, Laura approached the writer indirectly a few years later to inquire whether she would be interested in a photographically illustrated edition of *The Professor's House*. Cather's hero, Tom Outland, had lamented his inability to convey the grandeur of the site with photographs. "We had only a small Kodak, and these pictures didn't make much show, – looked, indeed, like grubby little 'dobe ruins such as one can find almost anywhere. They gave no idea of the beauty and vastness of the setting." But Laura never met the writer and did not get an opportunity to compensate for Tom Outland's photographic shortcomings.[54]

From Mesa Verde, Laura and her companions drove south past Shiprock, a formation she would often return to photograph, to Gallup and Zuni. There Laura bargained with a young woman who consented to pose for three exposures for fifty cents, one of the few times she ever paid an Indian subject. Brenda noted that "this girl did not have the usual white moccasin-legging that most of the women wear, so Laura took her from the knees up." This approach to the Zuni woman characterized Laura's early photographs of the Pueblos; though she would not distort the truth as she found it, she did not always reveal it fully. By framing her picture carefully, she could convey just the desired impression of picturesque traditionalism, an impression of how things *used* and perhaps *ought* to be. It was a vision informed by a sense of loss for an imagined golden age. Like Edward S. Curtis, who wanted to capture an image of the Indian "as he moved about before he ever saw a pale face," or Frederick Monsen, who wanted to show what the "earliest Americans were like before they were disturbed by the influences of the white man," Laura wanted to create a timeless image of Pueblo life, which belied the realities of historical change. Indeed, her early ideas about the Southwest, she told Brenda, had been influenced by the writings of Kirk Munroe, a distant relation of Brenda who wrote romantic juvenile fiction about the West. In her journal of the trip Brenda noted that these books "inspired

[Laura] with a romantic love of the West that colors her whole life even now."[55]

From Zuni they went to Laguna Pueblo, where Laura tried to photograph the fiesta activities and the buildings without including the cars that seemed to be everywhere (plates 84, 86). Then they continued north to San Ildefonso where they visited the potter Julián Martínez, and to Taos where Laura visited with two mainstays of the local artists' colony, painters Victor Higgins and Bert Greer Phillips. Phillips introduced her to an experienced young model from Taos Pueblo and lent her some of his studio props – a feathered head dress, beaded moccasins, a deer-skin quiver and bow – with which to adorn the young man. Nonetheless, Laura photographed her model, Juan, wrapped in a simple white sheet against an adobe wall. She shared the painters' interest in local subject matter but did not share their decorative and highly colored style of image making or their penchant for elaborate props. Her taste was still for the simple, classical composition she had learned to appreciate at the Clarence H. White School.[56]

When Laura returned to Mesa Verde in 1925 to photograph the summer pageant that Aileen Nusbaum staged amid the ruins, she made pictures that were even more romantic than those made on her previous trip. The drama was staged by firelight and moonlight in the ancient cliff dwellings. Navajo Indians worked as actors, mainly because the Pueblo descendents of the original Anasazi inhabitants lived inconveniently far away and feared the spirits that they thought lived in the ruins. Laura's purpose in photographing there was twofold. In the first concrete expression of the documentary interests that would occupy her for the rest of her life and in language that echoes the words of artists from George Catlin to Edward Curtis, she explained that "the life, the customs, the very types which the play represents are passing away with a speed that frightens one. Quite aside from my photographer's interest in its scenes, I am eager to add one more bit of accurate pictorial information about these Indians to the pitifully small amount we possess."[57] Laura's photographs, made during scenes especially staged for her, reflect the aura of mystery and the romantic setting that Aileen Nusbaum created and show more about Nusbaum's no-

HOUSE OF THE CLIFF DWELLER, MESA VERDE, COLORADO. *Laura Gilpin. Platinum print, 1925. Amon Carter Museum.*

tions of Indian life than about actual Indian customs. As Laura became increasingly well informed about Indian affairs, these soft-focus pictures of Navajo actors posing in the supposed costumes of their would-be ancestors became a source of embarrassment. It was not only the style of the photographs that bothered her but also the idea that she had photographed the Indians purely as *types*, without any regard for their individual character. In these pictures and in many of her Pueblo portraits the subjects are typically gazing off to the side, avoiding eye contact with the photographer. Thus they remain mystery-shrouded symbols rather than particular people.

After these trips Laura became increasingly interested in doing big projects with southwestern themes. Renewing her interest in the photogravure process she had studied in New York, she began planning a series of gravures of some of the images she had made on her recent southwestern trips. With books borrowed

SQUARE HOUSE TOWER, MESA VERDE, COLORADO.
Laura Gilpin. Photogravure, 1925. Amon Carter Museum.

from Clarence White's widow and White's old printing press, which she purchased from his family, she issued *Photographs of the Southwest by Laura Gilpin* in 1927. The folio included four beautifully printed gravures of images made at Laguna Pueblo and Mesa Verde, each printed with the soft, delicate tones of her platinum work. Laura marketed the suite for ten dollars per portfolio, or three dollars per print, but found little interest in the work.[58]

Even as she worked on the gravures, she began working on a series of photographically illustrated books that she hoped might prove more profitable. The idea of photographic illustration had fascinated Laura since her days at the Clarence H. White School, and, since seeing Blake's books at the British Museum, she had wanted to try her hand at producing a book, from start to finish. After her trips through the Southwest, she at last had a subject in mind. On September 1, 1925, she established the Gilpin Publishing Com-

pany, a corporation financed by the sale of $3,000 in stock purchased by her and a few friends. The following year, she produced the company's first major publication, *The Pikes Peak Region*.[59]

Subtitled "Reproductions from a Series of Photographs by Laura Gilpin," *The Pikes Peak Region* is an elaborately prepared fifteen-page brochure that Laura wrote, illustrated, and designed herself. The booklet is sewn and bound in a heavy blue paper with a specially commissioned woodcut design on the cover and has a simple design. The first five pages combine horizontal photographs with half pages of text; the last eleven pages feature reproductions of vertical images, one to a page. The firm that made the halftone plates is identified as the Beck Engraving Company, a firm Laura had often used in New York; the printer was the Dentan Printing Company of Colorado Springs, a small family firm that allowed Laura to come into the press room to oversee her own jobs. But nowhere does Laura indicate that she is the author of the text. She liked to think of her publications as being "authored by the illustrator," emphasizing that the photographs, not the text, were primary.[60]

Laura explained her theory of book design in language derived directly from her design and composition lessons at the Clarence H. White School: "The arrangement of a printed page requires the same principles of art as any other design. Arrangement of masses, balance, proportion, suitability of material, very carefully related margins: these are the components of the printer's Art." Each detail, she said, must be "a harmonious part of a united whole."[61]

The Pikes Peak Region suggests the theme that would be developed and refined through all of her subsequent publications – the idea that every region has its own peculiar history, geography, and almost inexplicable spirit of place that profoundly affects cultural development. But the text of the booklet is promotional, obviously aimed at the growing number of adventurous motorists attracted to Colorado Springs since the opening of the Pikes Peak Automobile Road in 1916. Laura writes of the "mystic spell of moonlight" in the Garden of the Gods, the "veritable wonderland of vitreous icicles and waterfalls" at the Cave of the Winds, the roads that rise "magnificently," and the houses that "glisten like jewels in the sun."[62]

In later books she would promote less and explain more as she developed confidence in her skills as a writer and refined her ideas about cultural regionalism.

The photographs in the Pikes Peak book were a combination of old and new images. Some had been used as illustrations three years before in the chamber of commerce's health brochure, some had been exhibited in photographic salons, and at least one derived from a commercial job. They were a mixture of atmospheric, soft-focus views made shortly after Laura's return to Colorado, which reveal her continuing interest in the flat, decorative forms of Japanese prints, and sharp-focus vistas, which reflect her changing approach to photographic style (plates 34, 36).

Laura hoped the booklet would be the first of many on southwestern sites that she could produce herself and market to tourists through the Fred Harvey Company. But sales of the booklet were only fair, perhaps because it sold for the relatively high price of one dollar and was too elegant to be a useful travel guide.[63] Sheets of tissue carefully tipped in between the pages of halftone reproductions made the book impractical for quick reference in a moving car. It better served Laura's interest in producing fine work than the needs of the tourists she hoped would buy it.

In late 1926, Laura lost her studio at the Broadmoor Art Academy, moved her darkroom to her home, and began work on a new booklet about Mesa Verde. She wanted the photographs and text to address three areas: the landscape and geology of the region, the ruins, and the culture of the Anasazi Indians who once inhabited them. This progression from a study of the land to a study of cultural artifacts to a study of human culture would become the structure for her subsequent books on the Pueblos and the Navajos.

As she realized the ambitiousness of her undertaking, Laura became discouraged. Brenda Putnam sympathized with her feelings of discouragement and dissatisfaction but thought she was probably being too hard on herself. In the spring of 1927, when Laura was feeling most discouraged, Brenda wrote, "I think you and I, as well as some others I could mention, suffer, in a way, from knowing and appreciating so much of the art achievements of bygone days and peoples. It leads us, unconsciously, when we take

stock of our output, to balance it, not against *one* other artist's achievements, but against that of a *group* of artists. If you stop and analyze each man's output for a period equal to our creative one, we find we've been pretty busy after all. Try it – when you're downhearted."[64]

Mesa Verde National Park proved to be a handsome companion piece to the Pikes Peak booklet. It had a similar format, although, having learned from her previous mistake, Laura omitted the tissue interleafing. And, again, she credited her engraver and printer without indicating that she had written the text. Her photographs of atmospheric vistas, ancient ruins, and Navajo Indians performing in the Mesa Verde historical pageant accompany a text that suggests the awesome romance of the region. Laura writes of the "proud majesty" and "impressive dignity" of the area; the "stately cedars" and "majestic canyon." She concludes, "it must always be with a sense of romance gathered about a forgotten people, as well as with appreciation of the country itself, that one remembers the Mesa Verde." But Laura's brief text goes beyond this effusive romanticism to anticipate the themes that would become important in her subsequent work.[65]

It introduces the idea of an ancient and genuinely romantic *American* past rooted in the American landscape. For Laura, as for many of the artists who fled to Santa Fe and Taos in the 1910s and 1920s and for writers, such as Mary Austin, who found a new validation of American life in the southwestern landscape, the discovery of this American past bestowed a new legitimacy on American life. No longer did America seem a raw, new nation. With the discovery of her Indian past she had a history seemingly as old and rich as Europe's. Laura called Mesa Verde's spectacular cliff dwellings "a living monument to a forgotten race" and added, "The atmosphere of antiquity which emanates from these age-old ruins takes possession of all who behold them."[66]

The text of *Mesa Verde National Park* draws from the disciplines of history, anthropology, and archaeology, an approach that characterizes Laura's later writings. Yet, as in her later book on the Pueblos, Laura combines this interest in didactic information with a photographic style that emphasizes her continuing interest in the spiritual resonance of the southwestern landscape and the romantic allure of Indian culture. The varied subject matter of her photographs – including landscapes, ruins, the "pueblo pageant," and a photograph of a study room in the Mesa Verde Museum – underscores her interest in presenting an interpretation of Anasazi life that is at once objective and personal.

Mesa Verde National Park can be seen as the culmination of years of work, the first project to pull together all of Laura's diverse interests in photography, photographic illustration, book design, the southwestern landscape, and the cultural history of the American West. The booklet was a way for her to reconcile her divergent interests in the East and the West: her mother's world of art and cultured gentility and her father's world of open spaces and adventure. By creating books on regional subjects she could integrate the formal concerns, technical skills, and design interests that she had acquired in New York with her love of the West and her sense of herself as a westerner.

Laura had accommodated herself to life in the West as her mother never could. When Emma Gilpin died of complications of Bright's disease in Colorado Springs in August 1927, she still felt out of place in a state she had lived in for thirty-seven years.[67] Laura did not share this discomfort; her father had given her an affection for the western landscape. Yet Emma had given her something equally important – an exposure to the arts, a spirit of independence, and support for an eastern education. With these gifts Laura was able to get the skills she needed to give creative expression to her feelings about the land.

After Emma's death, Laura assumed an even greater role in caring for her father, whose spirits had improved with the success of his furniture business. Working with an architect in New York, who provided him with measured drawings of furniture in the American period rooms at the Metropolitan Museum, he had begun to make exquisite reproductions of early American pieces. He incorporated F. Gilpin, Inc., as a furniture manufacturing concern in January 1927 and by 1928 was listing his sole occupation as custom furniture and cabinet maker. An art critic in Denver called him "an old master in the wilderness" and wrote, "Frank Gilpin has the same

love for his metier that animated those amazing artists of the Renaissance who did not care how much time they put into the making of a table, or any other object of daily use – if only it was perfect when it was finally finished."[68]

Laura supported his new endeavor, hopeful that at last he might have have found a lasting career. "How much I see your hand in all this, Laurie dear," Brenda Putnam wrote. "The daughter furthering and encouraging the art of the father. One often hears of the reverse, but your case *is* rather charmingly unique, you know." Laura photographed Frank's furniture for promotional purposes, designed and produced his advertising brochures, and had a permanent exhibition space in the expanded workshop and display space he opened in July 1929. The business promised some success. In 1927, F. Gilpin, Inc., did close to $10,000 worth of business and the following year its sales doubled. Frank was working three men "constantly." He netted an income of $2,219 and was sure he could expand even more if only he were not strapped for capital and had more time to travel to solicit new business. In addition to his reproductions of furniture from the Met, he was doing "Spanish Indian" pieces for which he solicited decorative ideas from Santa Fe painter Eugenie Shonnard, furniture repair, and special custom-built items. For P. B. Stewart of Colorado Springs he fashioned from wood "a specially built auto body . . . containing all the modern conveniences and up-to-date wrinkles beloved by auto campers on hunting or fishing trips." In 1930, he imported antique mahogany beams from Santo Domingo, certified to have been from an early-sixteenth-century house, to build an elaborate Federal-style highboy. For a time, things looked bright. With Laura keeping house for him and contributing to the household expenses, Frank finally seemed to be settling down to a job at which he had a chance to succeed.[69]

Laura, too, had found a way to use her artistic talents for commercial ends. Although her publishing ventures never proved very lucrative, her portrait business was steady and she continued to receive commissions to photograph Colorado Springs hospitals and schools for promotional brochures.[70] In early 1926, George William Eggers helped her get in touch with Arthur A. Fisher, who with his brother

William was a senior partner of Fisher and Fisher, a prominent Denver architectural firm that specialized in elaborately detailed and richly decorated renaissance-revival style commercial and residential structures. Hearing that the Fishers might be interested in having a photographer document their new buildings, Laura wrote to Arthur Fisher explaining her philosophy of commercial work. "In executing any commission," she wrote, "it is always my endeavor to furnish prints of as high a quality as those I make for exhibition. There is no question as to the worth of [platinum paper], first as to beauty, second as to quality, and third as to permanence." As to her photographic style, she wrote, "I believe in detail, but it must be properly handled so that it does not obtrude itself and hinder an interpretation of the spirit of the subject." Her approach to photographing the Fishers' buildings would be similar to the way she photographed the ruins at Mesa Verde. "Many enter the field of photography with the impulse to record a scene," she wrote some years later in an article on the photography of historical architecture. "They often fail to realize that what they wish to do is to record the emotion felt upon viewing that scene, and consequently a mere record photograph in no way reflects that emotion."[71]

The Fishers were impressed by the architectural photographs Laura made for the Colorado Springs Day Nursery, and they found Laura's expressive photographic style in perfect concert with their own philosophy of architecture, which emphasized the mood and spirit of buildings and made frequent allusions to historical styles. "I believe, as you say," Arthur Fisher wrote to Laura, "that we can have lack of harshness without losing the detail too much. We want the most beautiful photographs that we can obtain." Laura received a series of well-paying commissions to photograph the Fishers' Denver buildings: the Denver Polo Club, Morey Junior High School, the Midland Building, the Security Building, the Colorado National Bank, the Voorhies Memorial, and numerous other residential and institutional structures. And the Fishers, concurring with her desire to make her commercial prints of the same high quality as her exhibition work, paid her to make prints in platinum and to submit the prints on the mounts of her choosing.[72]

SECURITY BUILDING, DENVER, COLORADO. *Laura Gilpin. (Photographed for Fisher and Fisher). Platinum print, 1927. Amon Carter Museum.*

Laura continued to work for the Fishers into the early 1930s, but most of her work for them was done in 1926 and 1927 while she was working on her own photographic books. Her workspaces were often haphazard. In late 1927 she confessed to the Fishers, "I feel very badly that I am so long in finishing your prints. The truth of the matter is that my working facilities are so poor that I spoiled a whole group of them and must do them over again. . . . The making of the masks is a very careful job. My working quarters here has been the bathroom floor, and after I got a whole lot done, I found that the masks were crooked."[73]

Her work for Fisher and Fisher culminated in 1929 with the publication of a portfolio of engraved plates of her architectural pictures. Laura supervised the design and production of *A Monograph of the Work of*

William E. Fisher, Arthur A. Fisher, Architects, and George William Eggers contributed a foreword. Eggers wrote that in the Fishers' buildings "the traditional elements bend to the modern conditions without losing their historical continuity, as the old Spanish hauteur bent, without breaking, to the life of plains and pueblos."[74] Laura's carefully lighted photographs of the Fishers' buildings conveyed the architects' desired illusion that their new buildings, while efficient, had the grace and stately presence of older structures. It was the *spirit* of the buildings, rather than the detail, that appealed to both the photographer and her clients.

Despite her geographical isolation and her increasing load of local commissions, Laura remained active in the national and international photography world. In 1929 she exhibited prints in photographic exhibitions in Buffalo, Los Angeles, Pittsburgh, New York, and Edinburgh, Scotland, and won the yearly print competition sponsored by the Pictorial Photographers of America's new publication, *Light and Shade*. As a western photographer and regional vice-president of the PPA, she was invited to serve on the jury for the group's Third International Salon in New York City. The jury included pictorial photographers Oscar C. Reiter and Louis Boucher, advertising photographer Robert Waida, print dealer J. B. Neumann, and two photographers whose work clearly marked them as photographers of the so-called new school of photography, Anton Bruehl and painter-photographer Charles Sheeler. The jurors' selection aroused the ire of many PPA members, who thought them entirely too sympathetic to the new trends in photography that favored glossy prints, abstract designs, and industrial subjects over the more picturesque views that had been accepted into previous PPA exhibitions. Laura defended the jurors' selections against the complaints of pictorialists who decried the lack of sentimental subjects and heavily manipulated prints. "May I add the hope," she wrote, "that American photographers are thinking more seriously as to just what photography is and can do as an art medium and that the days of imitating other mediums will soon be gone, and that photography will stand only for itself." The rhetoric of her retort echoes the words of Alfred Stieglitz and fore-

shadows the language of the Group f/64, organized in 1932 around the principle that photographs should do what they do best and not aspire to any of the conventions of painting.[75]

In 1930 a fifty-print exhibition of Laura's work opened at the Milwaukee Art Institute in March and traveled to Baltimore and to Reading, Pennsylvania. Another group of prints was exhibited at the Honolulu Academy of Arts; still another went on view at the Herron Art Institute in Indianapolis. In May, Laura was elected an Associate of the Royal Photographic Society of Great Britain.[76]

That spring Herbert Putnam, the Librarian of Congress whom she had helped to educate about the merits of fine art photography, asked her to submit a group of photographs for purchase. Laura agonized over the selection and enlisted the aid of Brenda Putnam and Gertrude Käsebier. She sent a set of prints to Brenda in New York and asked her to consult with Mrs. Käsebier to select the ones to be submitted. "Mrs. K. fairly *wept* over them, she loved 'em so," Brenda reported. "She was in perfect agony of mind when I told her you evidently wanted us to *select* the best ones for the Library of Congress. 'They're *all* so wonderful,' she sighed, 'How *can* one choose'. . . . 'Tell her how I *love* 'em – how proud I am of her. I can't write. *You* tell her,' stammers Mrs. K. 'They make mine look like dirt!'" Putnam bought sixteen of Laura's prints and immediately placed them on display in an exhibition with the work of her two mentors, Clarence White and Gertrude Käsebier. The pictures were all platinum prints and represented a wide range of Laura's work. There were two landscapes, a portrait of Harold Bauer, two views of the cathedral at Chartres, several still lifes, a picture of Betsy doing bedside nursing, and a selection of pictures from Mesa Verde and the New Mexico pueblos (plates 32, 85). We regard the photographs as a beginning," Putnam wrote, "and count on your submitting 'on approval' others as you may produce them which you think especially noteworthy." It was a signal honor for someone whose photographic career was only twelve years old.[77]

Meeting the Navajo, 1930–1933

In 1930, after attending a poorly illustrated slide lecture in Colorado Springs on Mexican archaeological sites, Laura decided to make lantern slides of her own to prove that informative illustrations could be made visually pleasing.[1] She also hoped slide sets of south-western archaeological sites and contemporary Pueblo life might prove to be a commercially successful outlet for her pictures.

In the fall of 1930 she and Betsy Forster loaded an old, much-traveled Buick with camping supplies and drove southwest from Colorado Springs toward the north rim of the Grand Canyon (plate 48). They drove through southern Utah, where Laura made numerous photographs of Bryce Canyon's fantastic rock towers. She worked from the rim of the canyon, shooting down into the rock formations as the setting sun illuminated the tops of the rocks. The pictures have no horizon line and no recognizable objects to give a sense of scale. The rock towers rise from the dark in luminous, castle-like splendor (plates 49, 52). From Bryce Canyon, Laura and Betsy continued south to the Grand Canyon and then headed east. For her slide set, Laura wanted to photograph the cliff dwell-ings of Betatakin, accessible only by a long pack trip from Kayenta, Arizona (plate 94). She and Betsy rode into the ruins and then drove south toward Chinle for their first view of Canyon de Chelly. On the lonely drive between Kayenta and Chinle, they shared an experience that changed their lives. About twenty miles north of Chinle in a remote area of the Navajo Reservation with nothing visible for fifty miles around, they ran out of gas.[2]

After a night spent in bedrolls under a starry sky, Laura set off in search of help or gasoline, and Betsy remained behind to guard the car. "From what, I don't quite know!" Laura wondered later. Writing

more than thirty years after the incident, she recalled: "How well I remember my thoughts as I trudged along, recalling every vivid tale I had ever heard of a similar experience. How mortified I was at having lost my way. I remember meeting a Navaho man and a little boy in a wagon, coming out of a wash. I tried to talk to them but they spoke no English. I pointed in the direction of Chinle, indicating that I would pay them to take me there, but the man shook his head; then, reaching for something under a canvas in the wagon bed, he handed me three cool, delicious peaches."[3] After hiking two and a half hours, Laura reached Frazier's trading post, bought some gas, and rode back to her car with the trader's wife.

"I remember imagining how worried you must have been over my long absence," Laura later wrote to Betsy. "Never will I forget topping a gentle rise in the undulating desert and seeing the lonely car com-pletely surrounded by *Navaho Indians*, like a swarm of bees about a honeysuckle. When we arrived, there you were in the midst of the gathering, happily playing cards with your visitors!"[4] The Navajo had arrived, two or three at a time, seemingly from nowhere to see what the trouble was and to offer help to the white woman in the stranded automobile.

With the gas from the trading post, Laura and Betsy continued on to Canyon de Chelly, a spot long familiar to Laura from the Edward Curtis photogra-vure of Navajo horsemen that hung in her family house. They went down into the canyon and traveled as far as the White House ruins in a horse-pulled wagon. Laura set up her 8″ x 10″ camera and as her first exposure did "the same old shot that everybody has done from [Timothy] O'Sullivan down," then moved around to the other side of the ruins and photographed them again (plate 61).[5]

ELIZABETH FORSTER *Laura Gilpin. Modern gelatin silver print from nitrate negative, n.d. Amon Carter Museum.*

Neither Laura nor Betsy could forget the warm impression made by the friendly curiosity and kind help offered by the Navajo they had unexpectedly encountered on their trip. For Betsy the encounter was especially well timed. She was growing bored with the repetition and tedium of the job she had held with the Visiting Nurse Association for seventeen years. In the summer of 1931 she went camping with Laura in Yellowstone National Park and when she returned she learned that the New Mexico Association on Indian Affairs was looking for a field nurse to send to the Navajo community of Red Rock, Arizona. She applied for the position. Impressed by her combination of nursing experience and familiarity with the Southwest, the association offered her the job. Betsy quickly accepted, despite her family's disapproval and their predictions that the job would have no future, for, at heart, she was an adventurer. For years she had read

Greek myths to her young nieces, trying to inspire them with tales of fearless heroines. In the fall of 1931, she packed her belongings and moved to the tiny trading settlement of Red Rock, thirty-five miles southwest of Shiprock in the northeastern section of the Navajo Reservation, to begin a new adventure of her own, providing health care to the Indians.[6]

For the next eighteen months, Laura was her frequent visitor. Accepted in Red Rock as "a friend of the nurse," she took advantage of the Navajo's growing regard for Betsy to make a warm and empathetic photographic record of a small Navajo community in the years just before widespread federal intervention, a world war, and reorganized tribal government began to alter the long-established way of life. The people of Red Rock lived in a world poised at the edge between the old ways and the new. Horse-drawn wagons were more prevalent than automobiles; electricity and indoor plumbing were almost nonexistent. Few Navajo, save those who had returned home from boarding school, were proficient in English. The economy still revolved around the traditional livelihoods of sheepherding and weaving.[7]

Betsy's employer, the New Mexico Association on Indian Affairs, was affiliated with the larger Eastern Association on Indian Affairs in New York. It had been founded in Santa Fe in 1922 with the purpose of representing the political interests of the Pueblo Indians, but it had expanded in purpose to become a support group for the more ambitious Indian welfare programs of the federal government, with the intent of assisting "the Indian Bureau in making reforms and improvements first, by cooperating with it, and second, by the actual, positive demonstration of the worth and feasibility of a given method or procedure."[8]

Early on, in addition to working with the Pueblo Indians on land disputes and crafts projects, the New Mexico Association got involved in the Indian Bureau's health-care programs. In the early 1920s, these programs centered on regional hospitals staffed with government doctors and nurses. Field work was carried out by "field matrons," unsupervised, nonmedical personnel who did everything from home economics education to bedside nursing. Because the quality of this field work was inconsistent, in 1924 the

Indian Service dispatched two Red Cross nurses to field positions to see whether they would be more effective than field matrons. The New Mexico Association on Indian Affairs, consistent with its policy of supporting experimental field programs that would aid Indian welfare, dispatched its own nurse to work with an Indian Service doctor at the Northern Pueblos in 1924, and sent its first nurse to the Navajo Reservation, to the community of Nava, in 1928. In 1931, at the explicit request of the federal government, the association began to search for another nurse to send to Red Rock. The Presbyterian Church mission hospital there had recently closed, and the federal government had assumed control of the old hospital building. Government officials approached the New Mexico Association with a proposal for an experimental field outpost that would be served by a private field nurse working in cooperation with the Indian Service medical officials at the regional hospital in Shiprock. The association accepted the challenge and Betsy got the job.[9]

In mid-September 1931, Laura and Betsy made a brief scouting trip to see Red Rock and the abandoned mission hospital that would become Betsy's home and to meet the missionary, the trader, and the handful of Navajo settled in the tiny community. In late October, Betsy packed a trunk with warm clothes, a radio, a game of checkers, and a much-loved copy of Willa Cather's *Death Comes for the Archbishop* – the story of a nineteenth-century priest who came to work among the Spanish and Indian peoples of the Southwest – and left Colorado Springs in her old Chevy, leaving Laura behind. She gamely settled in the old mission hospital just north of the Red Rock Trading Post (plate 80). She had two tiny rooms in the long, low adobe building with no cook stove and only a small heating stove for warmth.[10]

Betsy's intuitive understanding of Navajo ways, her acceptance of unfamiliar Navajo customs, her quick sense of humor, her hard work, and her unfailing devotion to her Navajo friends earned her the name *Asdzáá Báhózhóní*, the Happy, or Contented, One.[11] Only by understanding her accepting relationship with the Navajo can one understand how Laura came to acquire her own interest in the Navajo people and to take photographs that depict the Navajo not as anthropological specimens or curiosities but as friends. Through Betsy, she was accorded a rare glimpse of the Navajo world and was accepted in Red Rock as a woman who could be trusted to understand at least a few of the secrets of Navajo life.

The key to Betsy's success in Red Rock was that she was never presumptuous or condescending in her dealings with the Navajo. She could barely conceal her dislike of the local missionary, who regarded his parishioners as childlike people in need of discipline and enlightenment and who, at every opportunity, tried to tag along on her home visits with a Bible in hand. Betsy herself was prepared to learn from Navajo ways, but she never presumed a right to know them. She questioned certain Navajo practices, but she also laughed at the strangeness of some of her "civilized" customs that seemed so inappropriate in the Navajo world. She believed in the efficacy of much of her own medicine, but she remained open to the teachings of Navajo medicine men and to the enormous healing power that faith in traditional healing practices seemed to have in the Navajo community. She never overestimated her ability to make profound changes in a long-established way of life.

Indeed, she counted her acceptance by the local medicine men as one of the key factors to her warm welcome and her success in Red Rock. After a year she reported to her employers:

When I came here . . . I soon realized that the Navajos hereabouts expected to find me antagonistic to their religious customs and were slow to consult me about illness until the medicine man had failed to help, but gradually they are showing more confidence in my good will and often notify me that they are having a sing and invite me to attend. Sometimes I am invited to practice medicine with the medicine man, sometimes am asked to wait the conclusion of the sing so as to be on hand to take the patient to the hospital. I am surprised and gratified to find my medicine men friendly and often cooperative. One of them tells me with a serious twinkle that he is glad to have me attend his sings and see good medicine practiced.[12]

She intuitively understood her Navajo friends' wry, joking humor, and she had an enormous capacity to laugh at herself. When a Navajo man named Killed-a-White-Man challenged her refusal to give him some cough medicine by asking "why she doesn't have the things a nurse is supposed to have," Betsy stood behind a chair and pretended to tremble and shake. Through her interpreter, she asked her patient if he had ever killed a white woman. He broke into peals of laughter and from then on was one of Betsy's good friends.[13]

Betsy worked hard. In one busy month she treated 225 patients in her dispensary, made thirty-four visits to hogans, and drove fourteen patients to the hospital in Shiprock.[14] And her role in Red Rock was not limited to nursing. She coached a basketball team, assisted with funerals, dispensed personal and legal advice, organized Christmas parties, and presided over a small home that was periodically a community social center, a soup kitchen, and a clothing distribution point. She was never lonely and almost never alone.

Laura made at least five trips to visit Betsy in Red Rock, driving down from Colorado Springs with her 8″ x 10″ camera and tripod packed in the back of her car. Her typical work outfit included khaki trousers, work shirts, sturdy shoes, and a "disreputable old Stetson" to shade her camera lens. She hoped to make artfully composed photographs of Navajo life that she could use in exhibitions, publications, or lantern-slide sets. She approached her subjects with courtesy and treated them with respect, offering either to pay or to give them a copy of their photograph. Always, she said, the Navajo took the picture.[15]

She worked in a slow, deliberate, and collaborative manner with her Navajo subjects, as dictated by her demeanor and her cumbersome equipment. Thus, she created a body of work that differs from her own previous work with the Pueblos as well as from most previous photography of the Navajo, because it is at once direct and honest, yet respectful and empathetic. Most of the romantic mystery of her early Pueblo work is gone, replaced by an understanding portrayal of daily life. Her vision of loss has disappeared, to be replaced by a fascination with the culture that remains. The work draws from the best traditions of previous photographs of the Navajo. She never lent props to her subjects, as Edward Curtis did, or took snapshots without consent, as Frederick Monsen liked to do with his Kodak camera. Laura combined the studied artistry of Curtis with the straightforward descriptiveness of Monsen and thus surpassed them both as an artful chronicler of Navajo life.[16]

"Gradually," Laura recalled, "I was learning the customs of the Navaho and some of the simple things one must or must not do . . . . There are good omens as well as bad, and the white man is usually excused for not knowing these customs, but better relationships may be had if the stranger takes the trouble to learn Navaho ways. Good manners and simple courtesy are very much a part of Navaho life, and there is always a right way and a wrong way to do everything."[17]

Laura accompanied Betsy on some of her home visits to traditional Navajo hogans, attended sings and dances with her, and helped out around her tiny house, which always bustled with activity. Her status was that of the nurse's friend; she took her cues from Betsy's actions and was accorded the same quiet respect given to Betsy. She understood that she and her large view camera could be an intrusive presence in Red Rock life, but her sensitivity to this allowed her to overcome much of the problem. She learned to work quietly, slowly, and as unobtrusively as possible. In spite of this deliberate working manner, or perhaps because of it, her formal portraits look unstudied. The best of them are suffused with a soft, natural light, and the sitters appear at ease.

The calm implacability with which Betsy's Indian friends accepted Laura is most evident in a photograph made inside Hardbelly's hogan (plate 74). Betsy is shown administering digitalis to the elderly man, who lies on a sheepskin blanket with his wives sitting peacefully on the floor beside him. No one acknowledges Laura's presence. The scene is lighted by sunlight filtering through the overhead smoke hole in the hogan. "Betsy proceeded with her mission while I wondered if I dared ask to make a picture," Laura wrote. "To my surprise they seemed pleased that I wanted to, which was one more evidence of their confidence in their nurse."[18] Fortunately, Hardbelly recovered from his illness, otherwise the photograph might have been blamed for his misfortune.

Laura had a similar opportunity to take advantage of her position as "the nurse's friend" when she accompanied Betsy on one of her daily trips to a hogan to dress the badly burned hands of a young girl. "The day I accompanied her I found the lovely mother

HARDBELLY'S GRANDDAUGHTER. *Laura Gilpin. Gelatin silver print, 1933. Amon Carter Museum.*

seated at her loom on the far side of the hogan," Laura recalled later. "As there was the usual blanket over the door, the only light within was from the smoke hole in the center of the roof. The beautiful overhead light accented the Oriental quality of this woman as she sat patiently while Betsy attended to the child's hands and I attempted to capture the picture I saw" (plate 75). In the picture the child looks anxious and concerned; the mother seems calm and self-contained. It is a simple and straightforward composition; the two are close together in the center of the image, bathed in a soft light that seems to shine more harshly on the loom and scattered clothes in the background. A few years later Laura submitted the picture to a book called *My Best Photograph and Why*, noting "I consider this one of my best photographs because I believe it portrays truly the individual character and the patient resignation of a member of this vanishing race." She was moving away from a stylized and romantic pictorial portrayal of Indian people, but she had not yet abandoned her fascination with the romantic myths surrounding Indian life.[19]

The generous trust with which Laura was welcomed by Betsy's Navajo friends and eventually by many of the Navajo that she met on her own is evident in all of her early Navajo portraits, and it is what distinguishes them from the work of any number of other photographers, who approached the same people with anthropological curiosity rather than human empathy. Laura wanted to document Navajo life, but to do so in a way that did not disguise her own fascination with the Navajo people or compromise her high pictorial standards. Thus, her early pictures from Red Rock fall in a category that lies somewhere between objective scientific reporting and the studied romanticism of much late-nineteenth-century western American art. They are truthful pictures composed in a simple and straightforward style, but they still reveal Laura's warm feelings toward her subjects. In a classic portrait, Betsy's friend Lilly Benally holds her infant son in a cradleboard and looks at Laura with an open gaze that reveals her trust of the photographer. Her calm, half-smiling face is surrounded by a glow of soft light that lends a beatific aura to an image that Laura often exhibited under the title *Navaho Madonna* (plate 62).

Even strangers seemed to respond to Laura and her camera with a trusting gaze. In one picture, a Navajo family of four stares at Laura from beneath the arching white sheet of their covered wagon (plate 67). Their encounter had taken place by chance as the family came over the Lukachukai Mountains toward Red Rock. The father smiles, the mother seems calm and impassive, and the two children look curiously at the photographer, but no one gives the impression of being frightened or distrustful. Fifty years after the photograph was made, the small boy in the picture still recalled his amazement at coming upon a strange white woman who used her coat as an improvised darkcloth and hid behind her odd machine.[20] For another picture, made as she and Betsy left a hogan after a nursing visit, Laura photographed a lady she did not know (plate 68). The traditionally dressed woman is shown clutching two lambs and her infant

BOY WITH SHEEP. *Laura Gilpin. Gelatin silver print, 1932. Amon Carter Museum.*

son. Her confrontation with the camera is frontal and direct, yet she appears relaxed, as if interrupted in mid-speech. Her square-headed son gazes at Laura with a solemn, wide-eyed stare and as compelling and arresting a face as any she ever photographed.

As much as Laura enjoyed making photographs, her photography was never so important as the adventure and excitement of sharing something of Navajo life. She would rush down from Colorado Springs on short notice to attend a ceremony (which might or might not be taking place), stopping in Red Rock to fill her car with curious friends of Betsy. In late fall of 1932, she and Betsy came upon a Fire Dance. They set up camp near the dance and, with delight, watched the preparations from afar. "We were afraid we might displease our host if we approached . . . . It never occurred to us that we might have asked to see the ceremony, and that possibly we might have been invited to watch," Laura wrote.[21]

In April 1933 Betsy lost her job in Red Rock when, in the midst of the Great Depression, the New Mexico Association on Indian Affairs could no longer raise the funds to meet its payroll. In addition, the local Indian Bureau superintendent in Red Rock, E. R. McCray, had made it clear that he did not wish to work with Betsy any longer. He appropriated her dispensary as a dining room, made free use of her interpreter, and announced that the building she lived in would be remodeled as a day school. At the root of his quarrels with her was a fundamental disagreement over the value of traditional Navajo medicine. Betsy worked hand in hand with the local medicine men, while McCray and many of the doctors at the Shiprock hospital saw the healers as impediments to the efficient modernization of life on the Navajo Reservation. NMAIA officials explored with the new Indian commissioner, John Collier, the possibility of finding a different field position for Betsy where local government officials would be more supportive of her work, but continuing financial difficulties forced them to abandon the idea of sending her back into the field. In April, when Betsy left Red Rock to return to Colorado Springs, she left field nursing work among the Navajo behind for good.[22]

Laura went to Red Rock to help Betsy pack for the trip home. She later wrote, "I can relive that final morning when six of your best friends arrived, watching our every act, then suddenly, solemnly, and without warning, stood, bowed their heads, and wept in unison." Betsy's Navajo neighbor, Francis Nakai, wrote a moving plea to Oliver LaFarge, director of the Eastern Association on Indian Affairs. "Some of the Navajos didnt hardly believe yet when she left Red Rocks to stay home. Miss Elizabeth Forster done all she could with her work in every way among us people whom Navajos all like her." He asked LaFarge to send her back and to build her "a House to stay in so she will be Independent."[23]

On a vacation trip in 1934, Laura and Betsy passed through Red Rock to visit old friends. Hearing that a friend known to them only as the Ute Woman was ill, they drove out toward her summer shelter. After parking their car and setting out on foot across a wash toward her home, they saw a figure hurrying toward them. "She had recognized our old car," Laura wrote, "and when we met, her arms went around Betsy's neck and she cried and cried."[24] After their visit, Laura and Betsy stopped at the closest trad-

MRS. FRANCIS NAKAI. *Laura Gilpin. Platinum print, 1932. Amon Carter Museum.*

ing post and made arrangements for staples to be sent to the Ute Woman as soon as possible. They continued on their vacation trip to the Grand Canyon but stopped again to see the Ute Woman on their way back to Colorado. Laura photographed her in her summer shelter, sitting on a dirt floor with all her possessions clustered about her (plate 64). After that, although their experiences with the Navajo remained deeply important to them both, Laura and Betsy did not return for sixteen years.

While Laura's Navajo photographs have their greatest value as a body of work documenting forty years of change in Navajo life, these early photographs, made between 1931 and 1934, have their own particular merit. Documenting life in a small corner of the Navajo world, they provide a valuable visual record of a people overlooked by the great photographic surveys of the federal government's Farm Security Administration. Like the photographs made by Dorothea Lange, Walker Evans, Russell Lee, or any of the other photographers who worked under Roy Stryker to compile a photographic record of American life during the Great Depression, Laura's Navajo photographs document a particular people and their way of life.[25] They present us with the faces of the Navajo people, the interiors of Navajo homes, the physical landscape of the Navajo community, and the ceremonies and rituals of Navajo life. The Navajo world was more unfamiliar to Laura than the world of rural white America was to the FSA photographers who documented it. But Laura brought an enormous personal empathy to her work and overcame much of the handicap of this unfamiliarity as she discovered that the Navajo people had a strong sense of tradition and a keen love of the southwestern landscape, much as she did.

Other white women, particularly traders' wives who lived on the Navajo Reservation for a long period of time, knew more about Navajo home and ceremonial life, but the few who used cameras were at best amateur photographers who produced snapshots of record.[26] The power of Laura's record of Navajo life owes as much to her formal photographic training and experience as to the knowledge of Navajo life she acquired from Betsy.

Indeed, although Laura's straightforward views of Navajo life differ markedly from her earlier soft-focus photographs, they still reflect her training at the Clarence H. White School. They betray her yearning for the beautiful and well-ordered landscape, her preference for portraits that capture the essential spirit of a person rather than a fleeting gesture. These portraits are typically illuminated with a soft, gentle light and composed so that the sitters are framed in the center of the image, gazing at the photographer. If

Laura's photographs reveal the material poverty of the Navajo world or make a political statement, it is only by accident; what she wanted to show was the beauty and dignity of the people she met in Red Rock. Any publication or slide lecture she created with her photographs would be personal and subjective. In this respect, her work invites comparison less with the work of the FSA photographers than with the photographs of another Clarence White student, Doris Ulmann, who photographed the traditional people of the Appalachian highlands during the 1920s and 1930s.[27] Ulmann made carefully posed portraits of people who seemed to exemplify a particular beauty and strength of character. She worked, as Laura did, with a large-format view camera, which compelled her to rely on the cooperation of her subjects. Her aim was to make fine photographs; the documentary value of her pictures was incidental.

Laura's early Navajo photographs now have a documentary value she did not intend for them to have. She did not set out to document a disappearing way of life, as Edward Curtis had done, or to create a sociological record of contemporary life, as Stryker would soon be urging his photographers to do. Yet her photographs make up a highly subjective and personal record of Navajo life that, with time, has acquired the weight of a historical document. Her presence can be sensed in nearly every photograph and one is aware that she recorded what she *felt* as well as what she *saw*. The empathetic feelings that existed between her and her subjects add to the emotional impact and import of her work and in no way detract from its value as an extraordinary document of Navajo life.

The Depression Years, 1931–1941

Laura's work with the Navajo was one of the few bright spots in her life during the early 1930s when simply earning a living forced her to withdraw from most of her exhibition activities. She apologized to the secretary of the Royal Photographic Society in London for not submitting any prints for the annual exhibitions of 1932 through 1934. She had been a regular contributor for a decade but now had to stop "owing to the strenuous times of earning a livelihood." Likewise, she explained to photographer Ira Martin that she was withdrawing from the Pictorial Photographers of America monthly competitions because "earning the family living has been all I have been able to do and that has been none too easy."[1]

Frank Gilpin's furniture shop, like Laura's photographic business, suffered as the Depression lengthened. In 1931 he lost more than $4,000 on his shop; Laura encouraged him to make frames so that he could keep busy and she could frame work as a business sideline. Frank, however, dreamed of quicker fortunes in the gold fields of Montana. In May 1932, Laura confessed to a business associate, "The furniture business is very sad just now, and I must keep the photographs going."[2]

Frank left for Montana in the summer of 1932, but his quest for Montana gold quickly ended in disappointment, just as his other business ventures had. He landed in a hospital in Butte with neck pains and severe dizziness. From there he complained to Laura about lack of attention from his son, Francis, and confessed, "I have a feeling that I will not be much good for a while, if ever. I have just been hanging on because I could not go home with nothing accomplished."[3]

Although Frank's extended absence from home gave Laura a respite from her housekeeping chores, his growing depression and loss of livelihood presented her with more serious problems. More than ever, she had to work to support both her father and herself. Still, she refused to neglect her photography as a tool of creative expression and never let money become more important than her high standards or her equally high ambitions.

In 1930, while juggling trips to make images for her southwestern lantern slides, visits to Denver to record buildings for Fisher and Fisher, and commercial work in Colorado Springs, Laura decided to apply for a Guggenheim fellowship to study photogravure techniques in Scandinavia. No photographer had ever been awarded one of the prestigious Guggenheim grants, but Laura was still disappointed and depressed when she learned that her application failed without samples of her work having been submitted to the jury. After making a few inquiries in New York, Brenda Putnam reported that the few jurors who had seen Laura's work had been favorably impressed: "Even if you were not accepted it could only have been on the ground that photography was not (by these be-nighted folks) deemed a *fine art*." Later, Brenda asked her brother-in-law Eliot O'Hara, a watercolor painter and former winner of a Guggenheim grant, to talk to Henry Moe, the foundation secretary. He reported that Moe did not understand the difference between rotogravure and photogravure and could not imagine why Laura wanted to do "research work" instead of sticking to her photography, which he thought was excellent. When the process was explained he seemed "decidedly chagrined" and encouraged Laura to submit a new application the following year, which she did, again without success. Years later, she took some satisfaction in imagining that her unsuccessful applications might have opened the door for Edward Weston's Guggenheim award, the first given to a photographer, in 1937. "Dr. Moe told me that I was in the running up to the last ditch but a discussion of admitting photography ended in resignation," she wrote. "I like to flatter myself that perhaps I helped pave the way for Weston."[4]

With her Guggenheim proposal rejected, Laura focused on her lantern-slide set, the project that had led to her original meeting with the Navajo in the fall of 1930. She worked on the slide project through the spring and summer of 1931 and gave a trial showing of the slides to an archaeological conference at the Laboratory of Anthropology in Santa Fe that fall. The slides began with images of the cliff dwellings at Mesa Verde and the "pueblo" pageant that Laura photographed there in 1925. Then followed photographs of the ruins at Keet Seel, Betatakin, and Canyon de Chelly in Arizona; images of the ruins and ancient cliff dwellings at the New Mexico sites of Chaco Canyon and Frijoles; and pictures of the contemporary pueblo communities of Taos, San Ildefonso, Santa Clara, and Laguna. Jesse Nusbaum, the director of the Lab and a friend of Laura since her first trip to Mesa Verde in 1924, introduced the slides and called upon some of the distinguished archaeologists in the audience, including Kenneth Chapman and Earl Morris, to comment upon the sites where they had worked. The presentation was enthusiastically received and Nusbaum gave Laura a testimonial to use in the promotion of her work: "In selection of subjects, in photographic quality, and from the artistic standpoint, your lantern slides are in a class by themselves, seldom approached, and never excelled. The particular set shown here at the Laboratory of Anthropology merits wide distribution among the scientific and educational institutions of this country."[5]

Encouraged by this response, Laura began working on a few additional slides, including some maps, to bring the total number of slides up to seventy, and prepared an elaborate sales brochure for the set. She also started work on a "printed authentic lecture" so that the slides could be used by people not familiar with her subject. Progress was slow, as she continually had to take time away from the project to accept commercial jobs. In the late winter of 1932 she sent a draft of her lecture to Jesse Nusbaum, deferring as she often did to the weight of "expert" opinion. While she waited for his critique she made multiple copies of the slide sets, using the thiocarbamide process to make her slides. This difficult and tedious method produced slides with beautiful rich blacks and delicate blue greys. It was a process seldom used in this country, and Laura had to resort to a British technical manual for her chemical formulas. She stored her completed slide sets in elegant mahogany boxes made by her father and priced the sets at $150.[6]

In her handsomely designed and printed sales brochure *Pictorial Lantern Slides of the Southwest*, Laura proclaimed her purpose: "The selection of these slides has been made with the intention of giving a comprehensive idea of the beauty of the ancient ruins and the interest of contemporary Indian life." As with her earlier project on Mesa Verde, she was interested in the connections between historical and contemporary Indian culture and with the ways in which these cultures had adapted to a particular environment. Thus she included landscapes to illustrate the country in which the Indians were located. The brochure contained a listing of the slides and half-tone reproductions of eight of the images neatly tucked into a little pocket. The back of the brochure included testimonials from Nusbaum; F. H. Douglas, the Denver Art Museum's curator of Indian Art; H. J. Hagerman, special commissioner to negotiate with Indians for the Department of the Interior; and W. W. Postlethwaite, an archaeologist at Colorado College. As in her Mesa Verde booklet, Laura's interests cut across the disciplines of history, art, archaeology, and anthropology, but she took care to remind people that her "first consideration is the pictorial one" and that they should always remember she was a photographer and not a scientist.[7]

In the winter of 1932 as she worked on this project and kept up with production work for several illustrated commercial brochures, a market she seemed to have cornered in Colorado Springs, Laura reapplied for a Guggenheim grant. This time she requested funds to go to Yucatán to take photographs and produce another series of lantern slides, parallel to the set she had prepared on the American Southwest.

Along with a set of her first lantern slides, she submitted references from Nusbaum, Gertrude Käsebier, Librarian of Congress Herbert Putnam, architect Arthur Fisher, and George William Eggers, now director of the Worcester Art Museum. Again she was rejected. Brenda Putnam speculated that it was because the project seemed so different from the one she had submitted the year before, although she acknowledged that the proposal made sense since Laura had become increasingly interested in archaeology and in architectural form but did not want to venture too far from her father.[8]

In the spring of 1932, Laura proceeded to Yucatán anyway with a group of teachers and six boys from the Fountain Valley School in Colorado Springs, determined to make a set of lantern slides of Chichén Itzá with or without foundation support. With a 5″ x 7″ Universal view camera, purchased because her 8″ x 10″ camera seemed "too big and too expensive" for the trip, she left for Mexico in late March, traveling by ship, train, and a Model A Ford. Through the generosity of Sylvanus Morley, who was at Chichén leading a team of excavation archaeologists from the Carnegie Foundation, Laura got use of a darkroom. There, despite the extreme heat and water temperatures of 90 degrees, she developed her film. She discovered that by shortening her exposures by one-third to compensate for the humidity and heat, and using a formaldehyde bath to harden the emulsion of her prints, she could obtain satisfactory results. She later reported, "By careful handling I had little trouble and lost only two or three films out of eight or ten dozen."[9]

The ruins at Chichén Itzá were a logical choice of subject for Laura since she had a long-standing interest in architecture and sculptural form and a growing interest in cultural artifacts. In Yucatán, as at Mesa Verde and the other ancient and contemporary Navajo and Pueblo sites in the Southwest, she wanted to see how ancient life related to contemporary life. She wanted to explore the meaning of an American past to which she and her contemporaries were linked through a common landscape, cultural artifacts, and the accumulated knowledge of historical memory.

In her photographs of the ruins at Chichén Itzá, Laura strove for an effect that was at once decorative and historically evocative. "One difficulty in photographing these great temples," she wrote, "is to retain their remarkable proportions and decorations and the beautiful surface qualities of the material, and at the same time retain the austere and barbaric qualities which are also present. From the practices of their religion we know that the Mayans were a barbaric people, but they had a marvelous sense of true design." She found the landscape surrounding the temples "uninteresting," so she focused her attention on the structures themselves and the contrasting patterns formed by the dark accretions in the undercuttings of the white limestone. As the sun darted in and out of the cloud cover she raced from spot to spot, trailed by a group of schoolboys who vied for the honor of carrying her camera equipment.[10]

As always, her understanding of light was critical to her work. In some instances it was purely intuitive, as in her photograph *Steps of the Castillo, Chichén Itzá* (plate 58). Laura made the picture when she saw a dramatic ragged shadow running the length of one of the stairways of the structure. The shadow ended at the ground, where a carved serpent's head protruded from the pyramid, and thus gave the illusion of being the serpent's long, sinuous body. Not until years later did she learn that she had recorded a special shadow that appears only on the spring solstice.[11]

At other times her use of light and shadow was more carefully planned. Looking down at the north colonnade of the Court of the Thousand Columns, she was first impressed by "the beauty of repetition." Neat rows of round columns topped by square capitals stood in symmetrical order. Later Laura wrote, "One must learn how to analyze impressions and to determine how they can be interpreted into design. In the full light of mid-day these columns become isolated spots and one must imagine what the shadows could do if they were present. At sunrise the columns and their shadow unified this design and created an all over pattern which seemed to give the best impression of the colonnade."[12] Thus she made her picture at sunrise when the columns cast long dark shadows. The horizontal stripes of the shadows created a dynamic rhythm with the upright shapes of the white columns and reinforced the impression of repetition

STAIRWAY, TEMPLE OF KUKULCAN. *Laura Gilpin. Silver bromide print on Gevaluxe paper, 1932. Amon Carter Museum.*

a sense of disorder or decay in her photographs. What she conveyed instead was the beauty of the ruins and the classic simplicity of their design.

When Laura returned from Mexico in early April, she began printing her Chichén Itzá pictures on Gevaluxe paper, a new silver bromide paper made with cotton fibers. The fibers gave the paper surface a three-dimensional velvety quality. The paper was delicate and easily marred; even a fingerprint could leave a lasting blemish. Nonetheless, the paper could yield rich black tones even deeper than those of a platinum print, and these deep, heavy blacks were well suited to conveying a sense of the solidity of the stone structures of Chichén.

Laura copyrighted her photographs for inclusion in a lantern-slide set and tried, unsuccessfully, to interest Henry Luce in publishing a series of photographs on the sisal hemp industry in *Fortune*. Her primary use of the photographs was in exhibitions. During the next two years she showed the pictures at the Chappell House in Denver, the Taylor Museum in Colorado Springs, the American Museum of Natural History in New York, and the Laboratory of Anthropology in Santa Fe. In early 1934, Herbert Putnam invited her to exhibit the Yucatán work along with some of her other southwestern photographs at the Library of Congress. He subsequently purchased for $500 forty-two prints from the show, including thirty-six from the Yucatán series. In response Laura wrote Putnam, "That the Library takes so great an interest in Photography is a wonderful encouragement and stimulation, and that you consider my own personal efforts worthy of your permanent collection fills me not only with pride, but also with a new zest and desire to improve and widen my scope. I can not tell you what this encouragement means particularly in these times when it is hard to keep an even keel."[13]

After returning from Yucatán in mid-April, Laura began printing the negatives she had made there. In May she dashed down to Red Rock to visit Betsy, and in July she accepted a job photographing Alexandre Dumas's *Camille*, the inaugural production of the newly restored Central City Opera House in Central City, Colorado. There, she worked under the direction of set designer Robert Edmund Jones, an experience that was both difficult and challenging.

she had felt on first viewing the scene. The picture is lively, yet still conveys the sense of classical order that pervades her Yucatán work (plate 57).

To convey this sense of order and elegance, Laura relied on several pictorial devices. For a frontal photograph of the great stairway of the Temple of Kukulcan, she arranged six Mayan Indians in a loose diagonal pattern midway up the stairs to emphasize the scale and proportions of the pyramid. In several other photographs she dissected forms with the frame of her image in order to accentuate the outlines and edge decorations of structures (plates 53, 55). She relied on tight framing to make a marvelous view of a henequen plant that emphasizes the orderly, almost abstract, pattern of the plant's leaves (plate 59). Although much of Chichén Itzá had not yet been fully excavated when she was there, Laura did not convey

"I think of the month of July as a dream," she wrote to a friend after the production was over. "It was all such a wonderful experience for me and though I was always so pressed for time and having so many new problems to solve, it crystallized my perceptions and taught me so many things that I am grateful indeed to Bobby Jones for working me so hard." Laura had never done theatrical photography and the renovated Opera House presented special problems because it had no electrical outlets, but she approached her assignment as a series of problems to be solved, much as she had been trained to do at the Clarence H. White School, and used long exposures with a fill-in flash without a reflector to simulate stage lighting. "Theater people can hold still longer than most Anglos," she discovered, "but Indians can hold still even longer."[14]

"How *much* more interesting, intriguing, truly French and romantic are the photographs than the play itself!" Brenda Putnam wrote to Laura upon seeing a portfolio of the portraits and stage views that she submitted at the close of the play. Laura, herself, was particularly pleased with a closeup portrait of the play's star, Lillian Gish, which seemed to capture the actress's beauty and a certain sweetness of temperament (plate 39). Gish also liked the picture and was fascinated by Laura's accounts of her work with the Pueblo and Navajo Indians. She even expressed her hope that she and Laura might go on a camping trip together through Indian country. The theater producers were sufficiently pleased by Laura's pictures that they retained her as the official photographer of the summer opera for the next four seasons.[15]

Betsy came up from Red Rock to attend the closing performance of *Camille*, and after the show closed Laura rushed off to drive her back. From Red Rock she returned to Colorado Springs to print her Central City negatives, then drove to Santa Fe to show Sylvanus Morley the results of her work in Yucatán. From there she headed south to photograph the Gallup Ceremonial and returned to Red Rock to visit Betsy and continue her photographic work among the Navajo.[16] It was a busy time, but few of Laura's projects generated much income; her business acumen never matched her enthusiasm or her creative talents.

HELEN FREEMAN IN *CAMILLE*. Laura Gilpin. Platinum print, 1932. Amon Carter Museum.

News from New York suggested that Brenda's life was much the same. The Depression had affected both her sales and her commissions, and she was keeping busy by working on a slightly larger-than-life statue of Laura whose broad "Maillol back" had intrigued her for many years. The simple forms of the piece reflected her growing interest in a more symbolic sculptural style and earned her much praise. When *Midsummer* was exhibited in New York in the winter of 1933, a local critic praised its creator for her "larger imaginative grasp and a growing feeling for significant simplification." The full, languorous likeness of the unidentified sitter subsequently won a Gold Medal in an annual exhibition at the National Academy of Design but did not find a buyer for more than a decade.[17]

When Betsy returned to Colorado Springs after losing her job in Red Rock in April 1933, she too had trouble finding work. Laura encouraged her to edit the letters that she had written to family and friends and prepare a small book about her "Indian experiences" to which Laura would contribute illustrations. For several months Betsy worked on her letters and helped Laura in the darkroom, and in early 1934 she found a job with the Emergency Recovery Administration in Park County, Colorado, quickly rising to become state supervisor of the ERA's nursing program.[18] Her book project was laid aside.

Searching for a comparable source of income for herself and her father, Laura decided to try to create a rental market for her sets of southwestern lantern slides. She printed a new rental brochure aimed at school groups and other organizations to advertise her ten dollar rental price: "Increasing interest in archaeological research and contemporary Indian life of the Southwest has created a demand for illustrative matter and authentic information for public enlightenment." Unfortunately, slide rentals proved no more successful than sales, and the chief use of the slides remained Laura's own lectures. "There are times when I feel very out of things and behind the times," Laura wrote to photographer Ira Martin in New York as she struggled with her rental sets. "I do hope that I will be able to manage a trip to New York before too long."[19]

With her photographic prospects still dim, Laura went into partnership with Betsy in 1935 and organized a poultry business, similar to the one she had managed before going to study with Clarence White. The Friendfield Turkey Farm, named after the Forster family plantation in South Carolina, was located on three hundred acres of land eighteen miles outside Colorado Springs, near the Woodland Park cabin that had belonged to the Gilpin family for many years. As Laura's photographically illustrated pamphlet boasted, the farm was at an altitude of eight thousand feet with sunny pastures and cool nights, which contributed to healthy appetites and rapid growth of feathers.[20]

"Nothing has less sense than a turkey and can cause you more trouble," Laura often noted.[21] All the same, raising turkeys had proved profitable before so she turned that way again when she needed money to support herself, her father, and her photographic work.

The Friendfield Turkey Farm specialized in piñon-nut-fed gourmet turkeys for the restaurant and direct mail order trade. It proved its reputation when a wealthy European baroness, wanting to impress her Colorado Springs friends, ordered a holiday turkey from the 21 Club in New York. When the turkey arrived in Colorado Springs it was marked with a tag from the Friendfield Turkey Farm.[22]

When the ERA disbanded in 1936, Betsy moved to

LAGUNA INDIAN PUEBLO, INTERIOR OF MISSION SAN JOSE. *Laura Gilpin. Gelatin silver print, 1938. Amon Carter Museum.*

the cabin at Woodland Park to manage the farm and a growing flock of birds. Laura came up on the weekends and handled purchasing and marketing arrangements. The rest of the time she remained in the city, keeping house for her father and doing whatever photographic work came her way.[23]

In 1936 she photographed the newly built Colorado Springs Fine Arts Center for its architect, John Gaw Meem, a former associate of Fisher and Fisher and the most influential figure in the revival of traditional architectural styles in twentieth-century New Mexico. Meem made frequent use of photographers, including Ernest Knee and Ansel Adams, and although he gave his photographers free reign in composing their pictures, he often signaled his disapproval by hiring one person to rephotograph a building already done by another – a situation that inevitably led to squabbling among the artists. In 1937, Laura published a set of postcards of southwestern photographs, including work from her Navajo and Pueblo series, elegantly printed in collotype by the Meriden Gravure Company. The following year she drove through northern New Mexico at the request of the Taylor Museum, a division of the Colorado Springs Fine Arts Center, to take photographs for George Kubler's forthcoming book on the religious architecture of New Mexico, and she documented Meem's new buildings at the University of New Mexico. Slowly, as her income increased, she again began submitting prints to major national and international exhibitions.[24]

The Friendfield Turkey Farm turned a modest profit its first two years, so Laura and Betsy expanded the business in 1937 and borrowed money to expand it again in 1939. By then they were managing several thousand turkeys and Laura's unusual combination of activities attracted the attention of the press. The *Albuquerque Tribune* noted, "Miss Gilpin, in addition to taking beautiful artistic photographs of Mayan ruins, is at present engaged in raising 3000 turkeys for the market." Laura told the reporter, "You may think taking pictures is work, but wait until you call 3000 turkeys in for their evening meal." Photography and turkey farming both seemed like necessary parts of her life. Later she said, "Photography came first, and the other came to help me through."[25]

Suddenly, in 1939, Laura and Betsy's turkey business failed. They suspected they were victims of a jealous competitor and a conniving inspector who downgraded their prime turkeys to reduce their market value. They lost their stock and had to sell some of their Woodland Park land to help meet their debts. Laura borrowed $1,000 from a family friend in Colorado Springs, and Brenda Putnam sent a check to help Laura and Betsy through the hard times. Betsy moved back into town and in 1940 started a guest house for well-to-do vacationers seeking a peaceful spot in the Colorado sunshine. Laura, characteristically, turned back to her photography.[26]

She began work on four series of New Mexican photographic postcards on Chimayo, Ranchos de Taos Church, San Ildefonso, and Taos Pueblo, since her earlier postcard sets were selling well, chiefly through the Fred Harvey Company. She prepared a body of work to submit to her old friend Aileen Nusbaum, who was looking for photographs for the Work Projects Administration's New Mexico state guide. She threw herself into the activities of the Colorado Springs Fine Arts Center, serving as a member of the executive committee and art school committee.[27] And, finding time to experiment with a photographic process that was new to her, she made a few dye-transfer color prints from her color transparencies. Laura had done relatively little color work since she made her Autochromes twenty years before, but

these carefully arranged still lifes of vases and flowers indicate she had retained her eye for color and her taste for simple, classical compositions (plates 21, 22).

In early 1940, William H. Cowles, publisher of the *Spokane Spokesman-Review* and a member of a large Colorado Springs family, approached her with a proposal for a more demanding and financially lucrative project. "How glad I am it came along just when everything was blackest," Brenda wrote. Cowles wanted to compile photographic albums for all the members of his family that would be arranged chronologically, beginning with photographic copies of old family portraits and proceeding down to copies of recent family photographs. He wanted the albums to be absolutely permanent and therefore wanted Laura to prepare all the photographs on hand-coated platinum paper. He sent swatches of paper and samples of chemicals to chemists to ensure that all of the materials used would meet his archival standards. Originally, he commissioned Laura to make fourteen copies of each of 44 photographs. By the time he had completed his research on the family history, this had changed to twelve 5″ x 7″ copies of each of 139 photographs, or 1,668 hand-coated platinum prints. By summer Laura was printing ten hours a day for the Cowles job, relying on sunlight when her Cooper-Hewitt lamp broke, and pleased by the idea that she was accomplishing what seemed quite impossible. When she developed an allergy to the platinum sensitizing solution midway through the project, she wrote to her old Clarence H. White School instructor Paul Anderson to ask for advice. He replied that Clarence White was the only other person he had ever known with that problem and had little to suggest except that she continue to use a respirator and goggles.[28]

During the spring of 1940, while working on the Cowles project, Laura set up a photography department at the Colorado Springs Fine Arts Center – an institution that had offered instruction in photography only occasionally – and designed a twelve-week class for beginning and advanced photographers. It had been more than twenty years since she herself had been a photography student and her work had changed greatly since her student days at the Clarence H. White

School, but she still adhered to all of the principles and teaching techniques that she had acquired in New York. Her course prospectus declared: "All students will be given a series of problems to solve, both technical and art problems. Throughout all classes an emphasis will be laid on the knowledge and practice of composition as applied to photography." Her classes showed the clear influence of Max Weber and Clarence White; Laura found it hard to understand the new emphasis on a more technical approach to photographic work. To Paul Anderson she confessed, "Teaching makes one do a lot of thinking. With all this intense interest in the scientific aspect of photography wither Art? And I do not mean that in the controlled imitative printing mediums as I have become more and more of a purist, but it seems to me that there is so much discussion of gammas and pHs that the final result is left hanging in mid-air. Maybe I am kidding myself into believing that design is more important than to what gamma you develop your negative and that the tonal values in your print are more important than anything else."[29] Laura, herself, was a technical perfectionist, but her working method was so intuitive and deeply ingrained that she had little patience with strictly technical approaches and had trouble explaining her intuitive approach to her students.

Shortly before her classes began, Laura received a letter from Walter Frese, editor at Hastings House in New York, who wrote that he was impressed by the Gilpin photographs the company had published in the WPA New Mexico state guide and hoped she might be interested in producing a photographic book in sheet-fed gravure, possibly on Bryce Canyon, which would appeal to the tourist market. Frese was unaware that Laura had been producing photographic booklets, postcards, and slide sets for the western tourist for more than fifteen years, but the Federal Writers Guides for the western states had done so well that he was interested in publishing a series of more localized guides. She responded enthusiastically to his proposal, suggesting a book on Bryce Canyon and Zion National Park and sending along a brochure describing the images in her southwestern lantern-slide set so that Frese could see what else she had done. Frese replied that he would be most interested in a

book based on the slides, something like "The Story of the Southwest in Pictures." Laura immediately began work on a dummy of the book and sent news of her good fortune to Brenda in New York. "That *bully* letter of yours," Brenda replied, "the first really hopeful and cheery one you've been able to write for years."[30]

Laura sent a dummy of her book to Frese in March 1941, and he responded with a contract in April. The book mock-up at first included photographs of some of the Spanish settlements of northern New Mexico, but in the interest of cohesiveness, Laura replaced them with newer photographs from Acoma Pueblo that she considered to be among the best she had taken (plate 82). Later, in her preface, she explained, "The photographs contained in this volume cover a period of twenty years, commencing with the 'soft focus' period of 1921 when I made my first trip to New Mexico, through successive stages of photographic change and, I hope, progress."[31]

Working with a publisher for the first time, Laura wanted to be involved in every phase of the book's production. She followed the basic order of her slide set in arranging the sequence of the photographs. She proposed a turquoise-and-silver binding for the book, suggesting it would call attention to the importance of those two materials in the Southwest. She suggested the design and lettering for the dust jacket and created the small Pueblo-inspired motifs that punctuate the book. Production work proceeded rapidly and, although the schedule was upset by the bombing of Pearl Harbor, the first of the 3,500 copies of *The Pueblos: A Camera Chronicle* were available by Christmas 1941.[32]

The text reiterates the idea, established in her booklet on Mesa Verde and pursued in her slide lecture, of a genuinely important and romantic American past that lends American culture a richness comparable to that of the Old World: "For many of us, American History begins with Columbus and the European discovery of the so-called New World. It is only in recent years that we have begun to realize the thrilling and amazing history that the archaeologists are unfolding for us – a history 'old as Egypt.'" Such classical allusions in descriptions of the American West were a familiar feature of nineteenth-century romanticism, as such disparate artists as Benjamin West, George

Catlin, and Alfred Jacob Miller found in the American Indians evidence of the exotic grandeur and heroism more often associated with the warriors of ancient Greece and Egypt. Contemporary southwestern writers continued to find emotional resonance in the seeming connections between the classical cultures of the American Southwest and ancient Egypt, Greece, and Rome. "Why go to Greece or China, o ye of little faith?" writer and editor Harriet Monroe asked in 1920. "This South-west, which is but one chapter of our rich tradition, is our own authentic wonderland – a treasure-trove of authentic myth – profoundly significant and beautiful, guarded by ancient races practicing their ancient rites, in a region of incredible color and startling natural beauty." Even English writer D. H. Lawrence, who visited New Mexico in the early 1920s, drew comparisons between the New World and the Old. Describing the adobe homes at Taos Pueblo, he wrote, "That they don't crumble is the mystery. That these little squarish mud-heaps endure for centuries after centuries, while Greek marble tumbles asunder, and cathedrals totter, is the wonder."[33] The great antiquity of American culture made it at least as good as the culture of the great classical civilizations, but for Laura, as for many other southwestern writers, the fact that it was *American* and not derivative made it even better.

The heritage of the Pueblo Indians attracted Laura and many other writers in the period between the two world wars as a heritage of peace. Willa Cather wrote in 1929 that the cliff dwellers of Mesa Verde "developed considerably the arts of peace." Likewise, Laura found at Mesa Verde an enduring and "lasting sense of peace." At Taos, where Mary Austin sensed a deep and secret "peace and stability," Laura also felt "the peace which seems so instilled in the atmosphere."[34]

The chronological structure of Laura's book proceeds from a discussion of ancient peoples in America through a description of pueblo archaeological sites to a discussion of contemporary pueblo communities, suggesting her belief that contemporary Americans could legitimately lay claim to this ancient legacy of peace. In the same spirit of cultural possessiveness that led Mary Austin to refer to the earliest inhabitants of the American southwest as "our Ancients," Laura

writes of "this land which contains our oldest history." As Tom Outland, the hero of Willa Cather's *The Professor's House*, maintained, the relics of Mesa Verde "belonged to this country, to the state and to all the people. They belonged to boys like you and me that have no other ancestors to inherit from."[35]

Laura suggested a national obligation to help preserve Pueblo culture. Her photographs documented something of importance but, in a long tradition of pictorial chroniclers of Indian life stretching from George Catlin to Edward Curtis, she recognized that her visual record could never provide a complete and thorough documentation of traditional life. So she called upon Americans to save the disappearing oral traditions of the Pueblo Indians: "There is still a vast amount of traditional material awaiting the writer who is capable of winning the confidence of the old medicine men. It will not long remain available in its true form, for the old men are dying, and the young men, under the influence of the white man and his schooling are fast losing interest in their own folklore."[36]

In her text, and in her photographs of ancient cliff dwellings snuggled into the caves of canyon walls and contemporary pueblos massed against mountain backdrops, Laura suggests that Pueblo culture is inextricably linked to and shaped by the physical environment. "In this great southwest," she writes, "the vast landscape plays an all-important part in the lives of its people. Their architecture somewhat resembles the giant erosions of nature's carving. It is a land of contrasts, of gentleness and warmth, and fierce and raging storms; of timbered mountains and verdant valleys, and wide arid desert; of gayety and song, and cruel strife." From this environment came Pueblo culture. The colored earth became the colored adobe for Pueblo homes, and the natural forms of the landscape became the inspiration for Pueblo design. Laura writes that contemporary Pueblo artists and craftsmen "are aware of the great rhythm of nature and are keen observers of her forms. They have given us in their art a virility and beauty of design beside which much of our own becomes weak and insignificant." She sounds a theme of deep-rooted unity between the people and the environment, what Mary Austin called "the expression of the life activities of the environment," an idea that, like the themes of antiquity and peacefulness, runs through much contemporary southwestern writing.[37] She conveys this unity in photographs of the mission at Acoma echoing the forms of the great mesa on which it sits, the ruins at Betatakin safely fitted into their natural rock arch, an ancient sandal woven of yucca leaves, the great black mesa looming over San Ildefonso Pueblo. Thus Laura reiterates her point visually in a way that goes beyond literary expression.

As with the text for her lantern-slide lecture, Laura took great pains to ensure that the scientific and didactic portions of her text for *The Pueblos* would be as accurate as possible. Again she turned to her friend Jesse Nusbaum at Santa Fe's Laboratory of Anthropology to proofread and verify facts, for she wanted her text to contain the most up-to-date information on the history of the Pueblo people and the progress of recent archaeological digs. In thanks for his help, Laura dedicated her project to Nusbaum and his wife, Aileen, "whose kindly interest guided the production of this book; 1925–1941."[38]

In view of these efforts to ensure the accuracy of her text, it seems ironic that she should include in her book several photographs that give a misleading impression of Pueblo life. While she apologized to her publisher for three photographs made in the early 1920s that now seemed a bit soft-focus to her retrained eye, she staunchly defended her use of several photographs from the "Pueblo" pageant that she had photographed at Mesa Verde in 1925. She explained to her editor that the "Pueblo" Indians in the Mesa Verde photographs were actually Navajo actors, whose portraits were "used symbolically," an expression of romanticism that connects her more to such backward-looking artists as Charles M. Russell and Edward Curtis than to the sympathetic and fair chronicler of Navajo life she had already shown herself to be.[39]

A similar tendency toward generalization appears in the text when Laura strains for a crude form of cultural relativism and strays from her strictly factual account of Pueblo archaeology to discuss the personal and racial attributes of the Pueblo people. "The Indian is deeply religious, and though his beliefs may differ from ours he is certainly no less sincere than we," she writes. In other passages that now seem naïve and

OLD WOMAN OF ACOMA. *Laura Gilpin. Gelatin silver print, 1939. Amon Carter Museum.*

even unconsciously condescending, she betrays just how enmeshed she was in a tangle of ideas she did not understand. She was not an unenlightened woman; she simply reflected many of the ideas of her day regarding racial and cultural stereotypes: "In many ways the Indians are a simple and childlike people, while in other ways they are exceedingly difficult to understand. One trait which is universally found is an extraordinary dignity of bearing, even among entirely strange surroundings. Their chief desire is to be left alone and allowed to live their lives as they may choose. They are a friendly, happy people, with an excellent sense of humor unsuspected by strangers."[40]

These broad racial discussions of the Pueblo people, combined with the use of photographs in a way that is "entirely symbolic," distinguish *The Pueblos* in an important way from Laura's later book on the Navajo. The subjects in the photographs in *The Pueblos* are generalized types, while many of the characters in *The Enduring Navaho* are named and figure in the story. In this earlier text she is neither a detached and observant anthropologist nor an empathetic friend with an intuitive understanding of Indian ways as she appears to be in her book on the Navajo. Anthropologist and photographer John Collier, Jr., aptly observed that her approach to the Indians in *The Pueblos* "was through archaeology rather than sociology. This was not because Gilpin did not *feel* the Indian, but rather that the concepts and techniques for social observation were not yet in her experience."[41]

Indeed, the photographer's hand is apparent in *The Pueblos* in a way it is not in the Navajo book. In addition to the staged photographs of the "Pueblo" pageant, there are photographs of Taoseño models in white sheets provided by Laura and a carefully posed photograph of women at Acoma arranged on the steps of their homes to add a sense of scale and design to the image. The finest portraits in the book are those made at San Ildefonso Pueblo (where Laura had made good friends through the families of Tony and Juanita Peña and potters María and Julián Martínez) and a portrait of an elderly Acoma woman, made shortly before the book went to press (plates 83, 88, 92). The woman gazes calmly and directly into Laura's lens in a manner more suggestive of Laura's direct manner of working with the Navajo than of her sensitive but oblique approach to the Pueblo Indians she photographed in the 1920s and 1930s.

Similarly, the text of *The Pueblos* is suffused with a romantic sensibility as the Navajo text is not. It conveys a sense of nostalgia for the old days, a regret over what seems the inevitable destructiveness of the white people's modern ways, and the sad feeling that the two different cultures cannot coexist in a congenial manner. Writing of the traditional appearance of a woman at Laguna Pueblo, Laura notes, "Her buckskin boots give a necessary balance to her costume which is entirely destroyed when she wears high-heeled American shoes." Her comments about cultural decline often take this form as a critique of aesthetic values: "In recent years Laguna has adopted white man's methods and products in wholesale fashion, much to the regret of those who knew and appreciated the unique charm of the pueblo, for already tin roofs are replacing the old adobe ones, and many modern conveniences, which do not harmonize with the picturesque charm of the pueblo, are to be seen."[42]

In spite of her sense that these incipient dangers of modernization threaten to destroy the "picturesque charms" of pueblo life, Laura ends her text on an optimistic note. Having reviewed the long history of pueblo settlement in the Southwest, she concludes, "Above all they have endured."[43] Sheer survival, or "endurance," in the face of disruptive cultural change and hard times seemed a great accomplishment. Laura thus expressed her faith in the tenacity of the human spirit while offering little optimism about the future development of Pueblo culture.

For Laura, this emphasis on the word *endurance* had a personal meaning as well. The text for *The Pueblos* was written at the end of a long decade of hard work and financial privation, while Europe was at war. Laura had survived the bad times through hard work and a willingness to adapt to the difficulties and opportunities that came her way – even raising turkeys. Basic survival, or endurance, was as much an accomplishment for herself as for the Pueblos; persistence in the face of threatening change and privation was a virtue.

To Wichita, to Yucatán, and along the Rio Grande, 1942-1949

Within weeks of the publication of *The Pueblos: A Camera Chronicle*, Laura was looking for a new project to occupy her now that the United States was at war for, money concerns aside, she had learned that she was happiest when absorbed in a big job. Writing to Walter Frese at Hastings House, she proposed a book called *Denizens of the Desert*, based on Betsy's letters and her own pictures from the Navajo Reservation. When Frese turned this down, Laura quickly proposed a photographic book on the homefront during the war. From Colorado Springs, where Camp Carson was filling up with soldiers, she wrote, "There is a good deal going on in these parts that I should surely love to get a whack at." Frese replied that the public was in the mood for nostalgic photo books, not those of a more timely nature. Laura had ideas for a number of other books, including one on the Mayan ruins in Yucatán, but with regret she concluded that they would all have to wait until after the war. "I don't suppose it will be practical for some time to go to Yucatan again."[1]

At first, she hoped that she might be able to continue the sort of photographic work she had done before. "The war at first has made us all want to stop and go fight I think. But after all things must be kept going and the so-called cultural lines will perhaps be the hardest to keep going." She soon realized, however, that war times were, indeed, different and extraordinary. Even the tire situation, she wrote to a magazine publisher, "is going to play a hardship on Western photographers where the distances are so great and other means of transportation so few." She began to look for a way to practice photography and serve the war effort at the same time. "One thing is certain," she wrote to her brother, Francis, "if I am to continue as a photographer I shall have to set up shop in town.

With the camp in prospect there should be lots of extra work, and I am quite willing to do a lot of cheap work if necessary." She had found a possible studio space downtown and was considering renting out the home she shared with her father and moving into the studio to save money and wear and tear on her car. Betsy could share a room with her in the studio and the two of them could eat dinner together at Betsy's boarding house.[2]

Frank Gilpin, though, remained a problem. She pleaded with her brother, "If you are to be kept at the oil business and not in the army could you take him there?" If he did join the army, perhaps his wife, Edna, could move to Colorado Springs to help out with Frank at home. "Poor old Dad is very feeble at the moment," Laura reported. "He is broke, has not been able to get his car license, etc. with the result that he stays at home and is obviously not getting his usual daily drinks at the club. It becomes more and more obvious how much he has been getting as a daily dose and I am not at all sure that he *can* go without." Her patience and forbearance were nearing an end. "His irritability is very great and every time I speak almost I am told that I am criticizing or something. I do my darndest to [be] just as pleasant as possible but he expects something else and assumes it is there whether it is or not." She begged Francis to at least take their father for a visit, but her entreaties went unanswered. Brenda commiserated, "I truly feel you have carried the burden of housekeeping and caring for him beyond the limits of human endurance. They should certainly be able to relieve you now." But no help was forthcoming and she continued her search for a job. While looking for studio space she could rent, she applied for special credentials to work at Camp Carson so that she could "have access to a great deal of material that might be very saleable."[3]

Finally, in June she found a space to rent in downtown Colorado Springs. She sold the house she shared with her father, moved to town, and opened her new studio at 326 North Tejon on July 31, 1942. Applying for a preferential rating certificate from the War Production Board, which would allow her to purchase photographic materials, she stressed that she would be doing most of her work for the servicemen stationed in Colorado Springs. By November, she was doing relatively well but realized "it is a question of a very short time until no more materials will be available." She recalled another difficulty years later, noting that she "just got to the point where I just couldn't photograph another one of those boys that might not come back."[4]

For months Laura had been looking for real war work. Back in January, even as she was searching for studio space to rent in Colorado Springs, she had begun looking for something in Washington. "What I want and need is a *job*," she wrote to Tom Maloney at *U.S. Camera*. "I am quite willing to do a laboratory job, or a field job, or any kind of photographic work for which I can qualify." One of her first appeals was to Roy Stryker, former director of the Farm Security Adminstration photographic program and now director of a similar program under the Office of War Information. Stryker initially told her that there might be some part-time work for her in her region sometime in the future. Tom Maloney went to talk to Stryker on Laura's behalf and reported to her that Stryker's setup was changing and that he "will be using women more than in the past" and making more frequent use of free-lance workers. He encouraged her to apply to Stryker for a laboratory job in Washington. "Confidentially," he wrote, "your Indian book gave you a little bit of a black eye with him. The reproductions certainly did not do your pictures any justice and I think made him feel that some of the things they had taken were superior. If you send him pictures, send him some of your best Indian prints (not necessarily those with too much pictorial quality) and be sure to send him some of the Mexican and other things." Laura wrote to Stryker and sent twenty-four prints, but he turned her down because her work seemed too posed and romantic.[5]

While waiting to hear from Stryker she made other inquiries. She confided to Isabel Herdle at the Rochester Memorial Art Gallery that she did not expect a woman would "have too good a chance" at getting a government job and asked whether she knew of any museums looking for staff photographers. Laura had done work for the Taylor Museum in Colorado Springs and enjoyed doing the kind of exacting copy work required by museums: "I think too much of photography to compromise to the extent demanded by many normal outlets."[6]

She also made inquiries regarding work for the Forest Service, the National Park Service, and the American Museum of Natural History. Rejection after rejection discouraged her. To Willard Morgan, publisher of *The Complete Photographer* and husband of photographer Barbara Morgan, she wrote, "For some time I have been trying hard to get some sort of a photographic war job but so far I have succeeded only in getting turned down either because I am a woman or because I am past some ridiculous age limit. It certainly seems to me I could be of use somewhere."[7]

Empathizing with Laura's sense of frustration, Brenda Putnam wrote, "What *is* the use of sculpture these days?" She reported that she was studying geometry and mechanical drawing. "If I can only master *that*, I may be able to do my farthing's worth in an airplane factory – provided I can still pretend I'm under fifty!"[8]

Betsy, too, felt at loose ends. In August she lost her home and her livelihood when the building she had been leasing for her boarding house was sold with only thirty days' notice. She took a room in Cragmor Sanitorium, the tuberculosis treatment center in Colorado Springs directed by her brother, Alexius, and in exchange for lodging and $65 a month, she resumed nursing.[9]

In early November 1942, Laura finally got her break when the public relations director of the Boeing Company in Wichita, Kansas, offered her the position of department photographer. Laura made a quick visit to Wichita and decided to take the job, anticipating that it would be "extremely interesting and stimulating." Adding to its allure was the fact that her brother and his wife, Edna, had moved to Wichita so that Francis could take a job as assistant foreman of functional testing at Boeing, and it seemed possible that they might all share a house and the burden of looking after their father. Laura wrote to a friend, "It is being a great up-rooting to pull myself out of Colorado Springs, but with Francis and Edna also in Wichita, where we can have a house and have Dad with us, it seems much the most sensible thing to do, to say nothing of the fact that I shall be doing a very real war job." With just a few weeks' notice, she packed all her belongings, put them in storage, and drove to Kansas with gas allotted her by the Boeing Company.[10]

Frank Gilpin did not come with her to live with Francis. In fact, just before her departure he rewrote his will, making her his executrix and sole heir, cutting Francis out altogether.[11]

Laura moved in with Francis and Edna, and Frank Gilpin came out for a visit around Christmas time. It was a disastrous trip as Frank constantly harped on his son and precipitated a major row. Laura confided to the family attorney, "I wish someone could dissuade Dad from his constant reading of 'True Detective' magazine. It makes him always look for 'hidden motives' and I truly think that his attitude toward both of us is greatly influenced by this." She was incensed when the attorney reported to her that her father had asked him to intercede with her for more money. Frank wanted Laura to give him a larger share of the proceeds from the sale of their house and misrepresented the extent to which she had supported him and his debts over the past ten years. In Laura's absence, he was trying to support himself in Colorado Springs with a caretaker's job, a sinecure provided by an old family friend that allowed him to earn two dollars a day.[12]

For Laura work became a refuge from family problems. She began her job on November 24, 1942, hired to work at a rate of 95 cents an hour, replacing a photographer who had joined the military. She overlapped with him for only a few days and was then on her own as the sole public relations photographer in a plant employing 28,000 people. During the two years she spent at Boeing, she got periodic raises but her job title never changed. It was perhaps the only time in her life that her sex seemed to be a

LAURA GILPIN AT BOEING. *Unknown photographer. Gelatin silver print, c. 1942–1944. Amon Carter Museum.*

handicap and held her back. "I got raises up to the point where the next raise would have put me into the foreman class, and I don't think they would have had a lady foreman. But I didn't go there for that. I went there to work."[13]

She did work and later, as the tedium of her day-to-day duties faded from memory, she called it the most challenging and difficult work of her life. She explained her responsibilities to Willard Morgan as including "a large dose of everything under the sun from news shots, 'Cheese Cake Girls,' parties, industrial, portraits, etc. etc. all to be accomplished in nothing flat." Visiting dignitaries had to be photographed in the plant and handed finished prints before they left. Her work load was so heavy that she "never made more than one exposure simply to save the labor of having to process more." Still, she remained something of a perfectionist about the prints she turned out for publicity shots and for the company magazine, and she earned the nickname "one more print Gilpin" for her persistence in the darkroom. "I guess I have lived by that rule all my life," she recalled later. "The next time I can make a better print, and of course, that is always the case."[14]

Laura adapted readily to life in the plant. Dressed in dark trousers and sturdy shoes, she drove a three-wheeled cart around the huge factory, carrying her camera and tripod in a sidecar. Some of her friends found it hard to imagine. Lillian Gish, who had kept up with Laura since their meeting at Central City in 1932, wrote, "I cannot imagine you in an airplane factory. It seems such a waste of beautiful material. Are you happy that you made the change? I just cannot imagine anyone as creative as you, taking on the routine of machines."[15]

And, of course, the job did have its frustrations. Laura complained to Willard Morgan that the fast pace of work resulted in "constant dissatisfaction with myself and a bitter struggle to hold my own standard." Her department heads had no understanding of what was reasonable to demand of a photographer, "But I have struggled to do some subtle educating and that situation is constantly improving."[16]

Laura maintained interest in her work by thinking of her assignments as conceptual and technical problems, much like those she had enjoyed solving in her student days at the Clarence H. White School. "I was given assignments and I learned how to do them and I kept my eye and feeling alive by trying to solve some of those problems."[17]

On occasion, though, the job presented genuine excitement. Laura, who had long been fascinated with flying, was assigned to make some aerial photographs while flying in the new B–29 aircraft and to make the first aerial view of a B–29 in flight. To do this, she flew in another plane whose door had been removed and, with ropes tied around her to keep her in place and a headset through which she could direct the pilot of the B–29, she got the plane maneuvered into place and took the picture.[18]

At times, she could not resist suggesting additional projects of her own. In May 1943 she proposed to her supervisor that she be permitted to make a pictorial record of the new B–29, the "embodiment of the genius of American industry, engineering and accomplishment." The photographs could be used in advertising, in a photographic book, and in museum exhi-

bitions. She saw her first duty as one of carrying on "the necessary work, but as an artist I have another responsibility – that of interpreting and translating into plastic form the drama of the magnificent effort which is being enacted before us day after day."[19]

Laura never made her pictorial record of the B–29, but she continually tried to transform her ordinary assignments into interesting and creative problems. Once she was asked to photograph a B–29 emerging from its hangar. The apron in front of the hangar would have left a third of her photograph black, but Laura noticed that a small pool of water on the apron made an interesting reflection. She waited for rain, but after three days got impatient and asked the fire department to hose down the apron. They did and she took the photograph with the hangar outlined in the late afternoon sun, the plane dramatically backlighted from the hangar lights and reflected in the water below. She satisfied the request of her employers and her own high standards for pictorial composition at the same time with a photograph that was subsequently used in *Fortune* magazine and several photographic exhibitions and competitions.[20]

All the work she did at Boeing is technically competent, even if little of it is of aesthetic interest, but throughout her life Laura remained proud of what she accomplished there. What she was assigned to do she did well and as imaginatively as possible, and the experience proved to her that at the age of fifty she could still work as hard as ever. There was nothing precious to her about photography; commercial photography and fine arts photography had to meet the same high standards. Later in her life, when young photographers would come to solicit her advice about how to find grants to support their artistic endeavors, she was decidedly unsympathetic toward their reluctance to do commercial work.[21]

On July 7, 1943, following a seemingly minor automobile accident, Frank Gilpin died at the age of 80. He was eulogized in the Colorado Springs papers as a member of a pioneer family, an accomplished furniture maker, and an expert horseman "well known for his polo playing when the sport was young in the Pikes Peak region." Laura and Francis went home from Wichita for the funeral, but it was left to Laura alone to handle her father's busi-

A B–29 Bomber Leaving the Factory. *Laura Gilpin. Gelatin silver print, 1944. Amon Carter Museum.*

ness affairs. This was difficult, not only because she and her father had had such an attenuated relationship but also because Frank had kept much of his business to himself. "My father seldom discussed business affairs with me," Laura noted later, "so that I have been very much in the dark in winding up his affairs."[22]

With her obligations at home finally discharged, Laura went back to Wichita. In the sixteen years since her mother's death she had supported her father both financially and emotionally. Now, at the age of fifty-two, she was finally free to pursue her own interests. Although her family responsibilities had not much limited her travel, they had added to her financial burdens and had kept her tied to Colorado Springs, a place where her professional reputation was well established and her family's problems were equally well known.

After her father's funeral, Laura returned to her job at Boeing and to her outside work for a photographic partnership, Krehbiel, Page and Gilpin, Co., which handled small commercial jobs in Wichita.[23] In just a few months, though, she received news more devastating than the news of her father's death: Betsy Forster was critically ill.

Laura and Betsy had kept in close contact through-

out the war, and Laura had remained protective and solicitous of her welfare at Cragmor Sanatorium, complaining to Alexius Forster that he was exploiting his sister by forcing her to work hard with inadequate compensation. When she learned, in January 1944, that Betsy was "run-down and over-worked" she became even more concerned. It seemed that Betsy was being forced to do "three years work in under two years." Betsy found their separation especially hard to bear. Complaining of headaches and severe pain in her arms, she wrote to Laura in May, "If you think for one minute it's harder for you than for me, – well think again. I am marking time and trying to live in a state of unconsciousness until we are together again. That's why it is so hard for me to write to you. It brings all the lonesomeness to the surface."[24]

In August, Betsy's illness was diagnosed as acute encephalitis. For several weeks she was critically ill; then she developed a partial paralysis in her right side. When it was determined that she also had polio, she was removed from Cragmor and hospitalized.[25]

Laura left her job at Boeing in late November 1944 but stayed on in Wichita to teach a six-week photography course at the Wichita Art Association over the winter. By the time she returned to Colorado Springs around the beginning of March, Betsy's condition had grown worse. She had lost her lucidity and her awareness of her surroundings and was "emotional and noisy at times." After spending some time for psychiatric treatment in the Emory John Brady Hospital in Colorado Springs, she was declared legally incompetent and moved to her sister Emily's home on a farm in Nebraska. "She will never again be able to stand the slightest emotional strain," Emily Stuart wrote to Laura. Laura wanted to care for Betsy herself, and it seemed a personal rebuke to have her taken away. She wrote to Alexius Forster, "I know that I can truly say that I can quiet Betsy in the face of any disturbance more than anyone. I have done it many times and it is one reason for her reliance on me."[26]

Laura's world seemed to be crumbling around her. In April 1945, as she contemplated resuming her commercial work in Colorado Springs without either her father or her closest friend, she received news of her brother's death. Francis had died in an automobile accident in New Mexico where he was working for the Richfield Oil Company. A restless dreamer like his father, Francis died with less than $700 of personal property to his name.[27] He and Laura had never been close, and in recent years their differences had been exacerbated by Francis's unwillingness to share the burden of their father's care. Nonetheless, Francis was family and Laura had a strong sense of the importance of family ties. With him gone, she was the last of her family left, and she began to question her ties to Colorado Springs. Without Betsy, her family, or a settled career, she started to wonder why she should stay.

A month after Francis's death, in May 1945, Laura left Colorado Springs for New York. She stayed with Brenda Putnam, who confessed that the war had taken the pleasure out of her work: sculpture "has become dust in my mouth and lead in my stomach." However, after two hard years at Boeing, Laura was eager to resume outdoor photography and to reestablish a stable career in her unsettled life. She began visiting photo agencies and publishing houses looking for work, and at a luncheon meeting with the editors of the publishing house of Duell, Sloan & Pearce, she proposed a book on the story of gold in Colorado. She was well versed in the subject through her father's sporadic mining activities and familiar with the mining

town of Cripple Creek, where he had once worked. When asked if she had any other ideas for photographic books, she replied, "The Rio Grande from source to mouth." "They just jumped at it," she recalled. "We signed a contract on the spot." The contract called for the completed photographs and text for the book to be turned over to Duell, Sloan & Pearce by April 1, 1946, less than eleven months away. The firm assigned to Laura as editor Walter L. Goodwin, Jr., former director of the Rydal Press in Santa Fe, who had overseen the production of numerous regional books.[28]

The idea for the book had occurred to Laura as early as 1941 when she made a short trip to the Rio Grande Valley above Creede, Colorado. "I was impressed with the beauty of the landscape of that region," she recalled. "It suddenly occurred to me what fun it would be to follow the river, and the more I thought about it the more I realized what great changes took place in the landscape and also the variety of people and life all along the river." While she was familiar with the upper part of the river from her frequent camping trips throughout Colorado, she had never been farther south along the river than Socorro, New Mexico. She hoped to start on the upper part of the river and determine an approach and a working method for her project that she could follow on her trips to the more unfamiliar regions to the south.[29]

The book was to be a portrait of the river and the land through which it flows, with but a glimpse of the life along its shores. "The people – the Spanish Americans, the Mexicans and the Anglos – are important but are subservient to the river. The people come and go – the river flows on forever." For this reason she decided to exclude closeup portraits from the book, using only more distant contextual images of people as they lived and worked along the river. She chose to divide the river into segments so as to hunt out "the most revealing points of view as to the river and the landscape and to find the characteristic native people and the most important of their activities." From the beginning she planned for each page of the book to be a "unit of picture and text," and she wanted the book to be, first, "a fine job of photography – each separate picture – second to reveal the character of landscape, of river, and of people. Third, to create a united whole with interest that will hold throughout."[30]

She recalled later that, after her years at Boeing, a big project like this seemed especially exciting, for "during many long, tedious hours in the darkroom there in the factory I thought a great deal about the Southwest and of course with longing." She wanted to get "out of doors as completely as possible." At the outset of the project Laura wrote to Willard Morgan: "The size of my undertaking staggers me at intervals, but Boeing got me in training in several respects. I learned to take one day at a time, how to get people to pose for me when I need them, and not to be afraid to tackle any-sized job, not any kind of job."[31]

When she left New York with her contract, Laura went to Washington, D.C., to meet with representatives from the United States Army, the Pan American Union, and the Mexican embassy, to ask for help in her work along the Texas-Mexico border. The biggest problem, it seemed, would be gasoline for her ten-year-old car, which had already gone 115,000 miles. The Colorado Springs ration board agreed to allocate her gasoline to travel 650 miles per month, but she estimated that she would need fuel for 2,500 miles. Her publishers wrote to the ration board on her behalf. In the meantime, Laura wrote to her editor, Wally Goodwin, "Maybe I had better start in Texas for I hear everywhere that Texas pays absolutely no attention to the ration!"[32]

When she began the Rio Grande project in July, making a twenty-six-mile pack trip on horseback up to the source of the river, film was still hard to get. She noted later, "It was necessary to be perfectly certain that each exposure I made was worth the doing. There could be only one negative to a subject. It was more than a year before film was easier to get." After two years of working indoors she also had to readjust to the strong, clear light of Colorado and New Mexico. Photographer and writer Charles Lummis had noted fifty years before that the sunlight of "Spanish America" is "as different a thing from sunlight in New York or England, as the sky from a second-hand tin pan. It gives [the photographer] cameos of definition, wonders of detail, and a real revelation in antithesis of light and shade, vigorous without being violent." As Laura recognized, "In a

country where the sun shines brilliantly most of the time, this sunlight must be felt in the picture."[33]

These problems seemed minor, however, in comparison to the severe drought, which made it impossible for Laura to meet her April 1 deadline. A dry winter the year before had reduced the snowpack in the mountains and had left the headwaters of the Rio Grande a mere trickle. She informed her publishers, "This means of course that I shall have to wait until high water in June to get a lot of river pictures that will be necessary."[34]

As she began her field work, Laura also searched for a publisher for the book on the Mayan ruins of Yucatán, which she had wanted to do since before the war. In August she signed a contract for the book with Hastings House, the publishers of her earlier volume on the Pueblos. Her plan was to combine her work for the two projects, slipping down to Yucatán once she was in the lower Rio Grande Valley. She would stop her work on the books whenever a paying commission presented itself, since she was financing her travels with borrowed money. She hoped the two books would enhance her photographic reputation and help remove the need for studio work. She wrote to Walter Frese at Hastings House in the fall of 1945, "My situation is that I do not want to go back into the portrait business unless I have to."[35]

As she immersed herself in the photography and research for her book on the Rio Grande she made a major decision. In the fall of 1945 she moved her home to Santa Fe. She was familiar with the town, a cousin could provide her with a house to rent, and the city was convenient to the areas she wanted to photograph for her Rio Grande work. But the move had even greater significance, representing her break with the family ties and burdensome responsibilities that had kept her in Colorado Springs for so long. Describing her move many years later, she turned repeatedly to the idea that the death of her family gave her a new kind of freedom: "I had lost my father and brother during the war and I was alone."[36] Thus, at the age of fifty-four, she left a community where she was identified as a "Gilpin" for a town where she could be recognized for her own talents and achievements.

If Colorado Springs was an eastern-oriented town

based on an aristocracy of wealth, Santa Fe was a quintessentially western community based on an aristocracy of achievement, where art, talent, and good deeds – particularly associated with Indian causes – meant more than money and family reputation. Involvement in the right high-minded causes could give entry to the most interesting homes in the city. In this historically conscious town Laura could shake off the specter of her family's failures in Colorado Springs and create a new life for herself centered on her interests in southwestern archaeology, anthropology, and art – all causes supported by the Museum of New Mexico, the Laboratory of Anthropology, the Indian Arts Fund, and other local institutions.

Moreover, Santa Fe was a congenial place for Betsy and her to set up a household together. Betsy had begun to recover over the summer. In August she returned from her sister's house in Nebraska to Colorado Springs for an annulment of the court action that had declared her a mental incompetent some months before, and she took up residence at Cragmor Sanatorium. Under the directorship of her brother, Alexius, Cragmor had been deemed in 1924 "the most desireable sanatorium in the world" by the National Tuberculosis Association. In its golden days of the 1920s, the sanatorium was known as a festive spot for "wealthy lungers" who could pass their time working on the institution's fortnightly literary magazine *Ninety-Eight.Six* and attending wild parties or classical concerts. However, the Depression depleted the institution's supply of wealthy invalids, and by the mid-1940s Cragmor was a grim place full of much sicker patients. Alexius Forster's fortunes had faded with the institution's. By the close of World War II, he was a bitter and depressed man with a reputed weakness for alcohol. Thus, when Laura brought Betsy to Santa Fe to live with her in the spring of 1946, Betsy too was leaving a city where her family name had become a liability.[37]

After a close and supportive friendship of almost thirty years, the two were finally able to set up a home together. In Santa Fe, a city long tolerant of unconventional living arrangements, the fact that Laura was a photographer with a keen interest in the culture of the Southwest and Betsy was a nurse who had worked on the Navajo Reservation was of more interest to people than the fact that they were two women sharing a household.

Laura also had enough contacts in Santa Fe that she could find odd jobs that would help her scrape together enough money to continue working on her two book projects. She began to do copy work for the Laboratory of Anthropology and to build a reputation as a skilled copier of art work, among other jobs doing the copy work for Mabel Dodge Luhan's *Taos and Its Artists*. Luhan was at the center of the Taos community of artists and writers and her reputation as a manipulative and high-handed woman was not lost on Laura. On one occasion after Laura completed a long day of work at her house, Luhan invited her to stay for supper. Laura was dressed in her customary work clothes of khaki trousers and a work shirt and tried to decline, but Luhan insisted it would be a small, casual supper for which she was adequately attired. She upstaged her guest by making a grand entrance into the dining room – dressed in a green evening gown.[38] The incident exemplified the difference between the two women, both of whom devoted much time and energy to championing the cause of the Pueblo Indians. While Laura approached her Pueblo friends with self-effacing humility, Luhan typically engaged her Pueblo acquaintances with her own interests and wants foremost in mind.

Even with all her contacts in Santa Fe, for many years Laura's life remained a financial struggle. As she poured her time and money into her book projects, she got by on a net income of just a few hundred dollars a year.[39]

Her hopes were pinned on her books, and it seemed apparent that her Yucatán book would be easier to finish than her more ambitious project on the Rio Grande. Consequently, in February 1946, she and a friend from Santa Fe, Roberta Robey, drove to Mexico City. From there they flew to Yucatán and Laura spent a week working at Chichén Itzá, where several new sites had been excavated since her visit fourteen years before. As he had assisted her on her first trip by lending her his darkroom facilities, archaeologist Sylvanus Morley helped with the arrangements for this trip and later served as a fact checker for her text. From Chichén, Laura went to a nearby village to take scenes she needed for her book, which would proceed from an investigation of archaeological sites to a discussion of contemporary life. She then went to Uxmal and back to Mexico City. From there she drove to San Antonio where she developed her negatives from the Yucatán and settled in for several weeks to photograph in the Rio Grande Valley for her project on the river.[40]

As she worked on her text for *Temples in Yucatan,* Laura checked for accuracy with the recognized authorities in the field. She consulted with Bertha Dutton, curator of anthropology at the Museum of New Mexico, and with several archaeologists from the Carnegie Institution. Even then she told her editor, "I am no scientist and my endeavor is to be a sort of go-between, or interpreter between the scientist and the layman."[41]

Temples in Yucatan appeared in March 1948 and Laura was generally pleased. Only a few problems with the gravure reproductions bothered her. She wrote to her publisher that "one thing is certain, I shall never do another book unless I can be on the spot when proofs are pulled."[42] When her book on the Rio Grande went to press the following year, she spent nearly two months in New York watching every proof come off the press.

Temples in Yucatan, like *The Pueblos,* has a text that stresses history with expressive pictures of cultural artifacts. Laura intended to do two things with the book. First, she wanted to be an interpreter, or popularizer, of Mayan culture, and thus she wrote a clear and generally straightforward text, which she illustrated with maps and diagrams of Mayan calendar wheels as well as photographs of the ancient ruins. Anyone who wanted more "scientific" information could refer to her bibliography. She also wanted her book to be a tribute to the Mayan people, and she hoped her pictures would "convey, in some measure, the grandeur of their buildings with their beauty of proportion, spacing and ornamentation." But when Laura pays tribute to the people, her writing takes on the same sentimental and naïve quality that marks passages of her text on the Pueblos. The Maya, she writes, "by nature . . . are a happy people and their courteous manners are characteristic of Spanish influence." Thus, in this book, as in her earlier one, Laura speaks in two voices: as a neutral explicator of

a foreign culture and as an admiring observer of an exotic race.[43]

Her text addresses broad topics, such as the geography and plant life of the Yucatán peninsula, the workings of the Mayan calendar, the history of the Mayan people from their earliest known settlements through the Spanish conquest, Mayan religious practices, and the structure of the temple ruins. It concludes with a discussion of contemporary Indian life and photographs of the Mayan people Laura met in 1946. Thus, Laura connects classical Mayan civilization with contemporary Indian life – just as she had linked the culture of the ancient Anasazi to contemporary Indian life in the Southwest – and stresses the binding power of historical ties: "With the ever-growing store of knowledge and understanding of this unique civilization of the past we of the present are made aware of a great heritage which belongs to the Amercas." This notion of Mayan Indian culture as a heroic part of the American past not only echoed the theme of her own book on the Pueblos but also restated the ideas of John Lloyd Stephens, an American explorer who had visited the Mayan ruins more than one hundred years before. He had been as impressed with the ancient structures as she would be. "The sight of this unexpected monument put at rest once and forever all uncertainty in our minds as to the character of American antiquites, and gave us the assurance that the objects we were in search of were not only interesting as the remains of an unknown people, but were works of art as well, proving, like newly discovered historical records, that the people who once occupied the American continent were not savages."[44]

Laura stressed the monumentality of Mayan culture with illustrations of closeup views that emphasized the grand scale of the ruins and downplayed the destruction wrought by time. She further suggested the vitality of the culture with pictures of lively shadows flickering across the face of the ruins and closeup shots of the animated carvings of serpents and human figures, all pictures that give ample evidence of her talents as an architectural photographer and her intuitive skill with light. Several photographs of traditionally dressed Mayans posing in the temples suggest the continuities of Mayan history, just as Laura's earlier pictures of Indians in the ruins at Mesa Verde had emphasized cultural continuities of southwestern Indian life. Some of the pictures of people, particularly of the Mayan women, whom Laura photographed in the soft, filtered light of their stick-and-thatch homes, have the feel of her Navajo portraits (plate 60). Among both people, Laura found evidence of a dignity of bearing, great resourcefulness, and manual dexterity.

Laura dedicated her book "to my good friend Brenda Putnam who taught me to understand sculpture and form." Years before, she had learned to photograph by practicing on Brenda's sculptures and had learned from Brenda that "there is no form without shadow." For all its appropriateness, the dedication still took Brenda by surprise: "My heart just stopped beating (and then lumped up in my throat) as I read the dedication on page 4! Why darling I don't deserve it, for t'is little indeed that I can have taught *you* about form – but it makes me very proud and grateful."[45]

Critics received the book as a popular but serious exposition of Mayan culture. "One can read Miss Gilpin's text with full confidence in its accuracy," noted a critic for the *Santa Fe New Mexican*, adding that her images, too, were done with "straight, square-away shooting." "The scenes are impressive enough on their own and Miss Gilpin does not presume, by artiness, to do beyond the fact." From the anthropologists and archaeologists who knew Chichén Itzá, Laura received plaudits for the quality of her work. Paul Martin, chief curator of the Department of Anthropology at the Chicago Natural History Museum, wrote, "As an anthropologist, I am grateful that you have recorded these beautiful buildings in such a stately manner." Earl Morris of the Carnegie Institution told her, "A better range of subjects could not have been chosen and you have a phenomenal gift for seeing the photographic possibilities of any subject." Clyde Fisher at the American Museum of Natural History appreciated the text as well as the "superb" illustrations, noting that it was "very brief but informative."[46] Their praise acknowledged her success at combining photographs and text to produce an accessible and scientifically accurate account of the culture of a lost people. From the perspective of time, whoever, it is clear that her book is both accurate and sentimental. Mayan Indian culture held a romantic fascination for her that she could not conceal in either her photographs or her text. Decades after she wrote the book, Laura's photographs stand alone on their aesthetic merits as her much-praised text cannot.

While she worked with her publishers on *Temples in Yucatan*, Laura continued to spend as much time and money as possible on her Rio Grande project. Expressing her concern to her publisher, she wrote, "Every once in a while I get worried over what this job is costing me and what the return may be and this just *has* to be a book that is tops if it is in my ability to make it so." In August 1947, almost a year and a half after her initial deadline for the book and after nearly 27,000 miles of travel, including two trips traversing the entire length of the river, she mailed her photographs and text to Duell, Sloan & Pearce.[47]

She conceived of the project as a simple and dignified one and so she did not go to "'the leading citizen' in each community to find 'the best' of this and that." She gained cooperation from her sitters by offering them copies of her prints and "went about it very quietly and unostentatiously in order to get next to the simple people which is the way I see this book." Laura confessed to her editors that there were a few weak photographs, particularly in the last section of the book, where she had been frustrated by poor weather and difficulty in working on the Mexican side of the border. She noted that these photographs "were due to difficult or unfortunate conditions, and they are included because they are necessary for the story." Laura's concern for the story line of her text and the integration of image and word sometimes made her a poor editor of her own pictures, but she never allowed a picture editor to interfere with her concept of a book.[48]

When her book had not gone to press more than a year after she submitted her material, Laura decided to go back to Texas to rephotograph some of the areas along the lower Rio Grande Valley. In Brownsville in January 1949, she received dummys of the book from New York along with the news that the engraver was starting to make the plates. She was distressed by the appearance of the book and fired off a letter to New York: "I have done my best to create a work with some distinction. I *don't* want the book to look like *LOOK* or *LIFE* magazines. My whole conception of this book has been for one pic-

RIO GRANDE BEFORE A STORM. *Laura Gilpin. Gelatin silver print, 1945. Collection of Ron Tyler.*

ture with its related text *as a unit*." She sent a night letter instructing the publishers to stop the plates at once and despite a case of flu offered to go to New York to straighten things out herself. "I have too much at stake, have put in too much hard work, research, effort and money to have this hurried through now, after the manuscript has been on the shelf for a year and four months." Although she needed money, she offered to repay part of her advance if the format of the book could be adjusted to her liking. Duell, Sloan & Pearce delayed printing the book and revised the dummy. Laura rewrote her text so that it would work with the photographs on the revised dummy and, in the spring, she went to New York to oversee the printing herself. An edition of 4,500 copies of the book appeared in October 1949. Despite some imperfections in the printing, Laura was generally pleased with the 243-page book and its $6.00 retail price. "I marvel that you have done so excellent a job for such a price," she wrote her editor.[49]

Laura dedicated *The Rio Grande: River of Destiny, an Interpretation of the River, the Land, and the People* "to the memory of my mother, my father, and my brother."[50] It was an appropriate gift since the book explores many generations of change in the Southwest, with the river representing the links between the past and the present and the promise of continuing life. Laura was the last of her family, and this book was given to their memory in the spirit of a procreative gift as a means of ensuring that their name would live on.

Her book surveys what the river's greatest chronicler, Paul Horgan, called "the laminated history of the Southwest." The book is in three sections – each introduced by a historical narrative – that describe the major cultural and environmental areas through which the river flows. "The Source" follows the river's course through the mountainous country of Colorado down through the San Luis Valley to document the region's cattle, mining, and farming industries. "Midstream" charts the river's southerly flow through the state of New Mexico and includes a discussion of Pueblo Indian life and the area's Spanish heritage. "The Border" surveys the life and landscape along the Texas-Mexico border. The book includes photographs of people in the landscape, but it is essentially a book about a region where the physical landscape predominates over all else. Laura was emphatic in her concern, "What I consider really fine landscapes are very few and far between. I consider this field one of the greatest challenges and it is the principal reason I live in the west. I for one am willing to drive many miles, expose a lot of film, wait untold hours, camp out to be somewhere at sunrise, make many return trips to get what I am after."[51]

Her innate talent for photographing the western landscape in which she had been raised had been refined by training, and in an article written for *U.S. Camera* about the time her book appeared, Laura tried to explain her approach to landscape work. In the first place, one had to have an understanding of the basic elements of design and an appreciation of the way light "interprets the subject, reveals its form, explains its textures, accents its focal points." Making a photographic work of art "isn't easy," she wrote: "When one goes out to make a landscape one doesn't have the control of light as in the studio. Here it is a matter of selection, of waiting for right conditions, of changing one's point of view. More and more, this photographer has come to the conclusion that the most important thing in the landscape is the foreground. It must lead to the focal point, must be relatively *un*important, must have the right lines and forms which relate the foreground to the middle distance and the horizon, if there is one. Many good landscapes are spoiled by obtrusive or overpowering foregrounds."[52]

Laura thought *Storm from La Bajada Hill, New Mexico*, a dramatic landscape of storm clouds hovering over the mountains and mesas just west of the highway between Albuquerque and Santa Fe, was "the best thing in the book" (plate 96). Huge thunderheads dominate the sky, dwarfing the rolling, scrub-dotted terrain in the foreground. At the left edge of the picture rain falls on the Jemez Mountains; in the center bright sunlight radiates from behind the clouds. The photograph was made quickly. Laura saw light breaking through the clouds, stopped her car, hastily set up her tripod, and made two exposures, relying on her intuitive feel for New Mexico light to make her exposures correct. Ansel Adams, she thought, "would have stopped and then taken two or three meter readings and then it would have been gone . . . . That is the difference between us. To him photographic technique comes first and to me the picture comes first." The other picture in *The Rio Grande* that gave her great satisfaction was an aerial photograph of the river emptying into the Gulf of Mexico (plate 115). She waited five days for favorable weather conditions and planned her flight so that the water would be backlighted, but she could not anticipate that the waves in the Gulf would be visible in her picture and this gave her "the biggest thrill of all."[53] These sharp-focus prints suggest just how much Laura's photographic style had changed since she made her first landscape views in Colorado more than thirty years before. She had come to realize that her early soft-focus pictorial style was inadequate to the dramatic light and inherent grandeur of the western landscape because it imposed an atmospheric quality on a scene that was imbued with dramatic presence of its own.

Laura did most of her aerial photography for *The*

Rio Grande with Santa Fe pilot Charlie Boyd, who accommodated her by taking a door off his plane but was still bewildered by her demands. "That goddamned woman, she was always saying lower, lower. If she fell out she'd take pictures all the way to the ground." She loved to fly: "There's a terrific challenge about it because you never know whether you're going to come off or not." As her friend, pilot and photographer Anne Noggle has observed, Laura had all the attributes of a pilot – the same reactions, the same love of flight and the challenge of flying, the same sense of freedom when she was up in the wide open spaces of the sky. She loved the plane and the act of flying even more than the view; after she was up in the sky, she discovered the ground.[54]

Laura's enthusiasm and talent for landscape photography – a field of work she pursued for more than sixty years – set her apart from all other women photographers of her generation. Landscape photography was considered the purview of men, who had the physical stamina and financial wherewithall to travel unencumbered by the burdens of family or home. The very tradition of western American landscape photography was developed by men (including Laura's distant cousin William Henry Jackson) who worked for the government survey teams of the 1860s and 1870s and was closely tied to the idea of exploration and conquest.[55] Historically, women's photographs were oriented more toward people and social interaction than toward the open landscape. It was relatively typical that Gertrude Käsebier, Laura's older mentor and the leading woman photographer of her era, first took up photography in order to make photographs of her children and then specialized in portraiture and allegorical genre scenes. Doris Ulmann, whom Laura knew slightly during her years at the Clarence H. White School, established her reputation with her portraits of southern blacks and rural Appalachian families. In California, Laura's contemporary Anne Brigman made views of Pacific coast and mountain landscapes but usually transformed them into allegorical studies through the presence of artfully placed nudes or carefully draped figures. Another of Laura's friends, New York photographer Barbara Morgan, took landscape photographs in the Southwest in the 1920s, but when her children were born, she turned to subjects that were closer at hand and easier to reconcile with her responsibilities as a mother.[56] This, perhaps, suggests a part of what made it possible for Laura to succeed in landscape work. Although she did have family duties and responsibilities, she was not encumbered with the traditional role expectations of a wife or a mother. But of yet more importance to her career as a landscape photographer was her western upbringing. As a child in Colorado she hiked and camped, rode horses and ranched, and grew accustomed to the open spaces of the West, a landscape that has proved difficult for many photographers who lack the native's sure feeling for space and light.

It seems ironic that, even though Laura practiced an art that few women had ever pursued, her choice of craft and subject matter had been greatly influenced by her mother and her closest women friends. Emma Gilpin gave Laura the independence necessary to be an artist. Anne Simon showed her the spiritual value of art, and her sudden death in 1916 impelled Laura to dedicate herself to the life of an artist. Brenda Putnam showed Laura how to earn a living as a young artist; Gertrude Käsebier provided a model of a working photographer. Betsy Forster, in turn, introduced Laura to the Navajo and became a companion for her southwestern camping trips and photographic expeditions. Thus, while landscape photography might have been an unlikely choice of field for most women, for Laura it was a logical pursuit and an interest she could share with her friends.

Laura's pictures celebrate the intrinsic beauty of the western landscape. Yet, as she makes clear in her writings, she always regarded the landscape as part of a larger cultural environment and sensed a human presence even in the most empty vista. In *The Rio Grande* she repeatedly describes the landscape in terms of its impact on human culture: as a source of irrigation water, as a shaper of immigration and settlement patterns, as a repository of mineral wealth, as a source of food for sheep and cattle, as a provider of natural shelter for the earliest settlers and good town sites for the later ones. Even the text that accompanies *Storm from La Bajada Hill*, a photograph that reveals no signs of human habitation, notes that violent storms can wash away precious top soil and flood arroyos with dangerous rushing water. The emphasis is on a human presence: "It is thrilling, sometimes terrifying, to watch such a magnificent storm sweep over the land."[57]

On the last page of the book, above the photograph of the Rio Grande snaking into the sea as its eighteen-hundred-mile journey nears an end, Laura directly indicates her theme – humans and the environment coexist in a critical and precarious relationship. *Since the earliest-known existence of human life in the Western world, all manner of men have trod the river's banks. With his progressing knowledge and experience, man has turned these life-giving waters upon the soil, magically evoking an increasing bounty from the arid land. But through misuse of its vast drainage areas – the denuding of forest lands and the destruction of soil-binding grasses – the volume of the river has been diminished, as once generous tributaries have become parched arroyos. Will present and future generations have the vision and wisdom to correct these abuses, protect this heritage, and permit a mighty river to fulfill its highest destiny?*[58]

Laura's text is best when it addresses the history and physical geography of the region, a keen interest of hers since her childhood rambles with General Palmer. As in her books on the Pueblos and the Mayans, she becomes less objective when she writes about the people and betrays the romantic primitivism that was at the root of much contemporary southwestern literature and at the heart of her own fascination with the Southwest. She contrasts her "modern world" with the "serenely close" ancient traditional life of the Rio Grande Pueblos. When she writes of the Mexican people along the lower reaches of the river, she points out that "kindness and courtesy are two outstanding characteristics of our Mexican neighbors, and we of the high-pressure, high-speed mechanical world do well to pause and consider the Mexicans' true sense of values, and their simple dignity and happiness, the heritage of the citizens of our sister republic." The qualities Laura valued in the Pueblo and Mexican people that she photographed – dignity and happiness, graciousness and poise – were the very things she valued in herself and in her friends. She sought connections between herself and her neighbors, just as she sought links between contemporary life and the culture of the past.[59]

LIVE OAK TREE. *Laura Gilpin. Gelatin silver print, 1946. Amon Carter Museum.*

As a more ambitious project than her previous books, *The Rio Grande: River of Destiny* elicited more thoughtful criticism and reviews, this time from cultural geographers and sociologists rather than the archaeologists and anthropologists who had reviewed her earlier work. Writing in the *Arizona Quarterly,* John Brinkerhoff Jackson became the first to recognize that Laura's integrated approach to the study of the landscape and human culture could properly be termed cultural geography. He chided her for excluding photographs of the eroded and impoverished countryside along the river, noting that "Miss Gilpin's camera, like the sundial, records only the sunny hours." But he praised her discussion of the complex water problems in the river valley, calling for her book to be recognized as a serious work of geography. "The book *does* provide an extraordinary amount of up-to-date information, statistical and otherwise, on agricultural practices, the economic and social set up, and conservation policies throughout the region. It is far more than a picture book, therefore; it is a geography for adults." Although the book did not include pictures of impoverished lands, he felt her photographs were direct and honest, far more than "the romantic glimpse of a sublime view." Comparing *The Rio Grande* to the picturesque regional photography books being produced by the prolific photographer-writers Wallace Nutting and Samuel Chamberlain,

Jackson concluded that it was easy to recognize "the superiority" of Laura Gilpin's treatment.[60]

While anthropologist and photographer John Collier, Jr., also criticized Laura for her naïve handling of the economic and social problems faced by the people along the river in Texas, he too praised the book for its honesty and sincerity and lauded Laura for her labor and tenacity. He found the essence of Laura's "westerness" in the way that she dealt with the landscape. "The easterner's milieu is so often man against man in contrast to the westerner's vision of man against the mountains, man finding his way across the vast plain, the personal challenge against wilderness, time, and space." Her book was weakest (as Laura too sensed it was) when she turned to Texas where people, and not the mountain landscape, formed the backdrop for social development. "Documentation of physical geography is the function of the explorer," Collier went on, "the man who measures himself by great seas and mountains. Documentation of society is primarily the expression of the revolutionary, the man who has become oppressed by a crowded economy."[61] Physical space, not human society, had always been the measure of Laura's world.

Defending Laura against Collier's contention that she lacked "social consciousness," Brenda Putnam wrote, "I don't think its fair. Your goal has been so completely different and completely your own. Should we deplore Wagner and Chopin 'cause they worked for different results than we get from Palestrina and Buxtehude?" What Laura had captured was the very quality that had so impressed Brenda with her work thirty-five years before – "timelessness."[62]

Less critical praise came from other sources. Paul Horgan, then at work on his two-volume history of the Rio Grande, wrote, "I rejoice in your book, and find it a rich and ever so valuable handling of a topic which we both know to be a very big one." Photographer Barbara Morgan said, "It is so embracing and comprehensive and interwoven. I had supposed it would simply be a series of fine pictures, and was most impressed by the book making art you have achieved in the transitions and side lights that give it many dimensions." Oliver LaFarge, writer and activist for Indian causes, criticized some passages of purple prose but called the book "deeply satisfying and illumi-

nating." "She has not merely portrayed the river in the narrow sense of a body of water moving through an area, but has perceived and caught it in the wider sense of the heart's artery of the land, the central factor from which man and nature draw life, which forms landscapes and shapes societies."[63]

While encouraging, such praise did little to ease Laura's financial straits. In 1948, while she waited for the Rio Grande book to come out and hoped that the royalties would repay her efforts, she tried to interest magazines and picture agencies in her Kodachromes and color transparencies. Laura had experimented with color photography as early as 1908 when she got her first box of Lumière Autochrome plates. In the 1940s she again turned to color for commercial purposes although she never found it satisfactory for landscape work. As she wrote to Tom Maloney at *U.S. Camera*, "My opinion is that photographers do not know how to *use* color, do not know how to combine color, and know next to nothing about color harmony and color ideas." She proposed a series of photographic postcards of the Palace of the Governors and the Fine Arts Museum in Santa Fe, in the hopes that it might "be a start toward a self-supporting photography department" at the Museum of New Mexico. She produced sales prints of the images from her Yucatán and Rio Grande books and organized exhibitions to help stimulate sales. Opening night of an exhibition of her pictures of the Rio Grande at the Colorado Springs Fine Arts Center in November 1948 attracted more than one thousand people. Unfortunately, the book was not yet published and available for sale.[64]

In late 1947 she had again applied for a Guggenheim fellowship, this time for the book on Colorado gold that she had set aside to work on the Rio Grande. She told the committee, "My quest is increasingly 'IN QUEST OF THE PERFECT BOOK.' Photography is the main structure, [supplemented] with informative text and presented through the art of book making." When her request to the Guggenheim Foundation was turned down in the spring of 1948, she reported, "I am very philosophical about such matters for I am well schooled in disappointments." She began to think about other books she could produce – on the missions of New Mexico, on Bandelier National

Monument, on Acoma Pueblo – to bring in money, to permit her to pursue her interest in books on regional themes, and to give her the sense of purposeful well-being she always had when engaged in a major project. "Things are *dreadfully* slow and tight here," Laura confessed to photohistorian and editor Nancy Newhall in the spring of 1948, "and [this] has me somewhat apprehensive of a future for me here in Santa Fe. If I had another book to work, fine and dandy, but at the moment there seems to be nothing in sight."[65]

She peppered her publishers with ideas for new books. To Walter Frese at Hastings House she suggested something on the ancient ruins of Guatemala, or another book on the American Southwest: "I feel so strongly that this is my line, and I have been very lost without a definite project since I finished the Rio Grande."[66]

Betsy Forster, still frail and weak from polio and encephalitis, sought work in order to add to the household coffers and applied, unsuccessfully, for a position in field nursing at one of the pueblos near Santa Fe.[67] Actually she remained physically unable to work, and only with money from her family was she able to contribute to household expenses. She did some household chores, but her care was largely Laura's responsibility and increased Laura's concern over their financial problems.

Laura's struggles to earn a living never forced her to withdraw from the activities she cared about most. If Santa Fe proved to be a financially unrewarding place, it nonetheless remained an interesting town. Shortly after moving there, Laura became involved in the Indian Arts Fund, an organization founded in 1925 by a high-minded group of archaeologists, artists, and philanthropists, including Mary Austin, Mabel Dodge Luhan, Sylvanus Morley, Frederick Webb Hodge, and Amelia Elizabeth White, to preserve the finest examples of Indian arts and crafts.

Laura was elected an active member of the group in the fall of 1947 and, in the summer of 1948, was made a trustee and vice-chairman. It was a time of intense discussion over the future relationship between the fund and the privately funded Laboratory of Anthropology, with which it was affiliated, and it seemed possible that the Lab might merge with the state-supported Museum of New Mexico. Laura argued for the integrity of the Indian Arts Fund and strongly opposed any plan that would allow the fund's collection to be swallowed up in the bureaucracy of a state organization. She served as vice-chairman of the organization from 1948 to 1957 and as chairman from 1957 to 1961 and again from 1964 to 1966. In 1972, when the Indian Arts Fund collection was finally signed over to the private School of American Research, Laura was still the organization's secretary and was recognized as "the prime mover" in keeping the group on course through its long and troubled relationship with the Laboratory of Anthropology and the Museum of New Mexico.[68]

To recognize her devotion to causes like the Indian Arts Fund and her hard but financially unrewarding work on projects like *The Rio Grande*, in November 1948 a group of Laura's Santa Fe friends got together and presented her with money for the purchase of new photographic equipment. The gift was made "with enthusiasm, admiration and affection" from twenty-two people – including Elinor Gregg, a pioneer in Indian health care; architect John Gaw Meem, an active member of the Indian Arts Fund; and artist Agnes Sims – who must have seen in Laura the unselfish devotion to art and Indian causes that so many Santa Feans considered their town to be all about.[69] Laura had not shaken off her financial problems when she moved from Colorado Springs, but in Santa Fe she had found a new kind of reward – a community of people who shared her interests, recognized her talent, and wanted to help her get on with her work.

Back to the Navajo, 1950–1968

As Laura cast about for a new project, her thoughts turned repeatedly to the Navajo project that she and Betsy had begun after Betsy left Red Rock. Laura had made sporadic attempts to have Betsy's letters published with her own foreword and photographic illustrations. The manuscript, first called "Happy Hogans" then given the more dignified title "Denizens of the Desert," went from publisher to publisher without success. After *The Pueblos* appeared in 1941, Laura hoped that Hastings House might publish the Navajo book as a companion piece, but they decided to wait until after the war. During the war, she tried again with Duell, Sloan & Pearce. While the text was complete, she felt her part was not. She needed "several top notch landscapes, several more good portraits, some better sheep pictures, a squaw dance series, and a sand painting if I can manage it."[1]

Undeterred by Duell, Sloan & Pearce's initial rejection of the project, she tried again in the fall of 1947 as her Rio Grande project was drawing to a close. Now she had more ambitious plans for the book that would consider the recent changes on the reservation. She wrote to her editor at Duell, Sloan & Pearce: "It seems to me that Miss Forster's book as it stands could make a wonderful background concerning the Navaho and that we could make a trip now to the reservation, see conditions for ourselves, get material and new pictures, and end the book with an up to the minute note." The manuscript had been criticized for being too short and "this addition should make it just right." Laura thought "one trip to the reservation should bring it all up to date and would not take long."[2]

Finally, in February 1950, encouraged by the success of *The Rio Grande*, which had already sold 3,500 copies, Duell, Sloan & Pearce told Laura to proceed with her Navajo project. She responded with gratitude, "You have certainly given me a much needed shot in the arm with the news of your reaction to a Navaho book. Ever since Christmas I have been sort of moping around thoroughly dissatisfied with everything I have been doing, and all of it seeming utterly useless except to add a few pennies to my bank account." Laura already had very definite ideas about the organization of the book she intended to make. She wanted it divided into four parts to correspond to the importance of the four compass points in Navajo religion and she wanted her text to proceed from an essay on history and tradition to a discussion of the transition from the old ways to the new. She also wanted the balance of photographs in the book to be different from that in her river book: "This time the people would be the theme, and the landscape the background."[3]

She particularly wanted to ensure that Betsy would receive credit for her part in the project, for "if it hadn't been for her taking that field nursing job, I would never have gotten my early pictures, and many of her experiences were of great interest."[4] She and Betsy intended to share the adventure of this project just as they had shared the adventure of Betsy's work twenty years before. Their memories of Red Rock and their continuing interest in the Navajo people remained a strong bond in their own friendship.

In March 1950, even before receiving her $250 advance and a copy of a signed contract, Laura left with Betsy for their first visit to the reservation in many years. They returned to Red Rock for an emotional welcome from old friends. Laura reported to her editors, "The reception Betsy got was very touching, after sixteen years. Some Indians immediately began asking for medicine, or relating all their symptoms. Then we found that there has never been any

ELIZABETH FORSTER AND PAULINA BARTON'S SISTER
NEAR RED ROCK. *Laura Gilpin. Modern gelatin silver print from
safety negative, 1950. Amon Carter Museum.*

medical aid in that area since Betsy left." Many changes were evident, but what they noticed first were the improved roads that allowed them to go places where a few years before it might have been impossible. Laura also found that her interest in the Navajo had changed and deepened. As she wrote to her editors, "What has interested me is to find the differences brought about by the past 16 years not only in the country, the Indians, the agencies, but also myself in reaction to it all. There certainly is a book here to be done, and I am more convinced than ever, since this trip that it will only be a short time before most traces of the old life are gone."[5] She was almost sixty, and as she grew older she was becoming more interested in how people responded and adapted to the changes taking place around them. She wanted to photograph the new ways on the Navajo Reservation, but she also wanted to document the old life before it disappeared.

After two spring trips to the reservation, she realized that her optimism about an early completion date was misplaced. She informed her publishers that her small advance would "make it necessary for me to stop now and then to do other remunerative work" and that she would need at least two years to finish the Navajo project. She paused to do some architectural photography for John Gaw Meem and copy work for the local museums, to earn some money so that she and Betsy could keep their household going.[6]

Before returning to the reservation in July to photograph a Squaw Dance at Wide Ruins, she purchased a Kodak Medalist – soon to become a favorite camera. To her editor Wally Goodwin she reported, "And believe it or not I am (slightly) turning miniature! . . . I hope I can be strong minded enough though, NEVER to use it when I know the big camera should do the job."[7]

When Laura learned that anthropologist Clyde Kluckhohn was also working on a book about the Navajo, to be illustrated with photographs by Leonard McCombe, she worried that it might upstage her project. Before returning to the reservation in September she wrote to Kluckhohn to ask if she might come talk to him about his project. She stopped to see him on her way to Red Rock and looked at the photographs in the dummy of his book. She conceded that McCombe "has a lot of interesting sociological shots – the funeral which was in *L I F E*, a series on drunkenness and police court, one series on Ceremonial (Puberty) . . . ," but he had no landscapes and no good portraits and she was pleased when Kluckhohn encouraged her work.[8]

Time seemed to be her enemy. She needed time away from the project to earn the funds that would keep her going, but she also needed time with the Navajo to capture the old customs that were fast disappearing. She knew that the Navajo could not be rushed, and she understood that it would take time to create the friendships that would allow her to get the photographs she needed to make. At times her work seemed excruciatingly slow. In the spring of 1951, she wrote to Kluckhohn, "There have been many contributing factors to this, the chief one being the fact that it seems to take practically all my time to earn the necessary existence with so little left over that I have been badly handicapped." Her income for the year was $744.54, scarcely enough to permit her to spend the time she wanted on the reservation even though she realized "changes are coming frighteningly fast."[9]

After five trips to the reservation in 1951 she appealed for an extension of her deadline from her publishers, citing her financial straits and a severe drought, which meant there was "not a cloud in the sky in a land where normally the skies are superb and on which I count much." More important, she added, "it takes time to make friends. There are some regions where other photographers have spoiled it for me by paying very high model fees, etc. Mine come through friendship and are much more genuine as a result."[10]

It was her friendship with the people she photographed that made her work different from that of other photographers. In January 1952 she saw a copy of Kluckhohn and McCombe's new book, *Navaho Means People*. She wrote Kluckhohn praising his work, but the photographs bothered her even more than they had when she had seen them more than a year before: "They are all so grim and the Navaho just aren't. At least as I know them. There is, of course, much that is grim, but I do contend that this is the minority." In their preface to the book, Kluckhohn and Evan Vogt had attempted to meet this kind of criticism: "It is perhaps true that the difficulties of adjustment to the white man's world are overemphasized at the expense of satisfactions remaining from the aboriginal culture and the genuine rewards brought to the Navaho from our modern world. Nevertheless, the drama of this story at the moment is mainly that of clash and maladjustment, and this is what the pictures appropriately reflect." Laura described McCombe's photographs to her editor Charles Pearce, stating emphatically that hers would be nothing like them: "The Navaho are a characteristically happy people, and a people to whom the land in which they live means everything! In that book not one landscape! But my observation is that *LIFE* photographers never see landscape, nor its effect on the people, not its importance. I don't want to sound too critical of that book, but I see it all so differently."[11]

As she had done before, Laura intended to stress the connections between the physical landscape and human culture, but the vehemence of her response to McCombe's pictures suggests that she had more than a mere disagreement with his approach to photographing the Navajo. She, herself, was beginning to identify with the Navajo and their strong feeling for the land and to find great personal meaning in her friendships with Navajo people. McCombe's grim depiction of their way of life seemed almost a personal affront.

Her protective attitude toward the Navajo ran deep. In the summer of 1951, when she was at a Squaw Dance west of Shiprock, her Medalist camera disappeared from her car while she was showing some photographs to a women twenty-five yards away. She offered a $10 reward for its return and put out the word through the local grapevine. Still, it was with great reluctance that she reported the loss of her camera to the local traders, so that she could substantiate her claim to her insurance company. "I don't want to get any Navaho boy into trouble, and I am sure you will understand my 'losing it.'" She apologized for the incident as if it were her own fault. "I was working at the scene of the dance with perfect friendliness and good will of the medicine man and many Navahos whom I knew there from years past. This is the first time I ever lost anything on the reservation."[12]

In 1952 Laura made three trips to the reservation, which she financed by making photographic postcards and documenting the entire collection of the Museum of International Folk Art. She applied for a grant for her Navajo work from the Wenner-Gren Foundation in hopes that it would help her buy more time on the reservation. In her application she explained that her small publisher's advance was long gone, and that only $500 more would be hers upon publication of the book. She requested $3,000 to help cover any fees for photographing of ceremonials and to pay for several long pack trips into remote areas where she hoped to find some uncommon subjects. The board of the Indian Arts Fund gave her application a formal endorsement, with archaeologist Marjorie Lambert noting, "She is one of the rare individuals who can get along extremely well with the subjects she photographs and studies."[13]

When the grant did not come through, Laura renewed her efforts to earn money by doing commercial postcards and selling transparencies to magazines and photo agencies. She had also begun to make $2\frac{1}{4}'' \times 3\frac{1}{4}''$ color slides on her visits to the reservation, in order to put together a slide lecture – similar to the ones she had prepared with her Pueblo and Yucatán material – that might gain her some extra income. Finally, in the fall she got a break: a $2,500 grant from the Laboratory of Anthropology in Santa Fe to assist her with her work.[14]

As much as she resented the delays and intrusions

on her time caused by the need to earn a living, Laura began to find a kind of comforting virtue in the slow deliberateness of her work with the Navajo. In the spring of 1953 she told Charles Pearce that if it were not for the "ever present scramble to earn a living" she would be done with the book. "However, time has taught me much that I might have skipped and which is important in trying to present Navaho life as it is." Her work with the Navajo assumed a ceremonial character that both she and her subjects enjoyed, for she learned that the longer it took her to set up a photograph the more important the act of taking a picture seemed to the Navajo. Her work became a ritual in itself with rules, an established etiquette, and a high sense of ceremony, and her photographs reflected the quiet rapport she established with her sitters.[15]

The long period of time she was spending on the project began to work in her favor. As she observed to an acquaintance: "By far the hardest thing on this whole job has been the building up of human relations to the point where I have such permission given [to photograph ceremonials]. No one knows how long it takes to build this all up. Many of the pictures have taken two, three, and even more trips and visits to finally win through. On several I have made two and three trips of 500 miles to get one picture! Not very practical but all a necessary part of the picture as far as this book goes, and it all has to be right, no 'set ups' and as complete in the Navaho story as possible."[16]

By late 1953 the end of the project seemed within sight, and Laura anticipated that the book could be out by the following Christmas. She had made five trips to the Navajo country that year to document not just the changes in the culture as a whole, but changes in the lives of her acquaintances and friends. On one occasion, she photographed the infant son of a man she had photographed as a baby two decades before. On another trip she visited with the Nakais, close neighbors and friends of Betsy in 1931–1933, whose family she had photographed many times before. The Nakais still lived in their same small Red Rock house and now had two daughters much younger than the sons she and Betsy had known before. Their oldest son had been killed in Europe in World War II, and virtually the only object in the room in which

GROUP IN HOGAN DOOR, RED ROCK. *Laura Gilpin. Modern gelatin silver print from safety negative, 1950. Amon Carter Museum.*

they sat was the flag that had been draped over the boy's coffin at the time of his burial in France.[17] Laura photographed the family posed before the flag, an image offering eloquent testimony to the passage of time since her first visits to Red Rock (plate 116).

With the photographic part of her project nearing an end, Laura began to think about how she wanted the book designed. To her editor she explained, "I visualize a rather bold, sans ceriph [*sic*] type. There is nothing superfluous about the Navaho! It would be most in keeping. I hope you agree with me on this. That is another reason why I favor bleeds in this book. No waste. Again Navaho." She had begun to think about using some color in the book, as well. This was an idea supported by the painter Georgia O'Keeffe, who told Laura she needed at least two color plates: one to give the color of the people, the other the color of the landscape. She had also come up with a better title for her book, one that lacked the mysterious and exotic connotations of "Denizens of the Desert"– "The Enduring Navaho."[18] The new title reflected the changing nature of her interest in the Navajo. They were no longer fascinating merely because they were foreign and exotic but also because they were trying to retain the best of their old ways while adapting to the modern American world.

The letter that arrived from her friends at Duell, Sloan & Pearce in early February 1954, as she began to design the book, came as a complete surprise. Charles Pearce and Charles Duell wrote to Laura, "Facing the matter realistically, [we] have had to decide that we simply could not afford to stand the great loss which unsubsidized publication on our part would involve us in," and they canceled the contract for the Navajo book. Deeply hurt by their action, Laura replied that it was "a considerable shock and I am at a loss to understand it." Charles Duell responded meekly that the decision was a result of the firm's recent merger with Little, Brown. While it might save them from financial losses, "it has wrought mental cruelty both on us and on you." Explaining the situation to her old friend Mitchell Wilder, former director of the Colorado Springs Fine Arts Center and new head of the Abby Aldrich Rockefeller Folk Art Collection at Colonial Williamsburg, Laura wrote, "I begin to wonder if I shall endure long enough to complete this magnum opus!"[19] Her Navajo, it seemed, were not the only people who needed the strength to endure in the face of unexpected problems.

Laura immediately sent her photo dummy and outline off to the University of Oklahoma Press, stressing that she still felt enthusiastic about the project. "I want to build the last section into a positive forward looking end, which I feel so strongly is in the wind. The Navaho are an amazing people and at present are going forward by leaps and bounds." When the press responded that the book would be too expensive to produce but that the pictures might be used to illustrate a text they already had, Laura quickly refused. She would lose the $5,000 she had already invested in the book and, she said, "it would also defeat my purpose in the whole book which is to interest the layman with an authentic book without being scientific. And lastly having done three books myself, it would certainly be a come down to have this end up this way so far removed from my whole conception of the book."[20]

Laura remained determined even after "the Enduring Navaho came home to their enduring author." She explained, "I am not the least deterred from finishing the Navaho book whether it ever sees the light of day or not. It is just something I have to do." She sent the dummy of the book to her old friend and publisher Walter Frese at Hastings House and

NAVAHO SACRED MOUNTAIN OF THE EAST. *Laura Gilpin. Gelatin silver print, 1953. Amon Carter Museum.*

vowed that if he turned it down she would keep working on it and not show it to anyone else until it was finished.[21]

While waiting for Frese's decision, Laura remained busy at home. Betsy's brother, Alexius, had been critically ill and shortly after she and Betsy returned from visiting him in Colorado Springs in late March, Betsy herself became ill and had to have an eye removed. Laura canceled a planned speaking tour of the East to stay home and care for her, giving only a few local lectures with her Navajo slides. By June, she was back at work on her Navajo project in spite of a lack of financial backing. She made a flight to take aerial views of the Navajo's sacred mountains and found it a "thrilling experience" that helped her to decide that she would do the history section of her book from an aerial perspective, taking in the whole sweep of the Navajo land. "Perhaps it is my love for landscape and geography that makes me want to fly," she wrote later. "From the air one can see so clearly

A NAVAHO SUMMER HOGAN. *Laura Gilpin. Gelatin silver print, 1953. Amon Carter Museum.*

the great structures of the earth's surface, the different kinds of mountains, the sweep of contours, the age-old erosions. In the air one becomes detached and the mind goes deep into the past, thinking of Time in depth."[22]

She returned to the reservation with Betsy in September. On a visit to the Navajo Mountain area in southeastern Utah, they discovered the summer hogan of Old Lady Long Salt, a woman of ninety-four who could remember the hardships of the Long Walk back from the Navajo's forced exile to Fort Sumner, New Mexico, in 1868. Laura photographed the elderly woman in her hogan surrounded by four generations

of her female descendents who continued to go about their chores while Laura made her picture. Everyone enjoyed the visit but, as Laura noted, "we have found when visiting families such as this, that a time comes when their courtesy to us has been fulfilled, their curiosity is satisfied, and their normal work must be resumed. It is well to be sensitive to this approaching moment and to take one's leave before wearing out a welcome."[23] With her own strict sense of decorum, Laura was sensitive to the proprieties of Navajo customs.

Everywhere Laura traveled she carried a mock-up of her book with high-quality prints of her photographs. She used it as her entry into the Navajo world and would sit quietly while the Navajo studied the pictures, deciding how they would respond to her request to make a photograph. Her photographs seemed warm and unobtrusive and her manner quiet and courteous, but she also won the trust of her subjects because she was now a woman in her mid-sixties with brilliantly white hair that commanded respect in a culture that revered age.

Although it was becoming increasingly difficult for Betsy to travel, she and Laura still intended to make the Navajo work a joint venture. In the early 1930s, while Betsy was still working as a nurse in Red Rock, she was the one who paved the way for their acceptance by the Navajo people. Now it was Laura who was becoming known around the reservation, particularly outside the Red Rock area. Even so, Betsy's presence continued to give Laura's trips a special richness. In 1955, despite a rejection from Hastings House, Laura made three trips to the reservation. On a summer trip to the Red Rock area, she and Betsy came upon a group of hogans, with three older women sitting in a summer shelter nearby. Laura got out to speak to them and, finding that none of them spoke English, she returned to the car to get Betsy, hopeful that she might recognize someone she had known before. None of the Navajo women recognized Betsy and Betsy recognized none of them. Laura brought out her portfolio of photographs. When she showed the photograph made inside Hardbelly's hogan in 1932 (plate 74), the three women began speaking in a rapid flow of Navajo. Later Laura described what happened next: "I pointed to the nurse in the picture, then to Betsy standing beside me, but the oldest of the three kept shaking her head. Just then a teenage boy came to see what was happening. 'My grandmother says this is not the nurse, she had dark hair.' Betsy leaned over, taking a lock of the old lady's hair, and said, 'Tell your grandmother she did too.' Recognition broke through; the old woman stood up, put her head on Betsy's shoulder and her arms around her, and wept. After a few minutes Mrs. Hardbelly raised her head, shook herself, straightened her shoulders, and returned to the present."[24] Laura did not presume to photograph this reunion. She returned to photograph the women a few days later after they had had a chance to wash, dress, and compose themselves for the event (plate 126).

On another occasion, in a log cabin in the Lukachukai Mountains, Laura was showing her dummy to two women, neither of whom spoke English. One woman suddenly shouted, "Mamma, Mamma." Apparently, Laura had photographed the older woman's mother many years before. Without thinking twice, Laura took the print out of her book and gave it to the woman. When she then asked if she could photograph the two women and their home, they happily agreed.[25] Laura treated her subjects with respect, as she expected to be treated herself.

In the summer of 1955, Betsy developed a painful and incapacitating case of shingles. Laura patiently took over the housework that Betsy had always taken pride in doing as her contribution to the household.[26] When she went east in the fall to show her book dummy to publishers, contact photo agencies, and visit Brenda Putnam, who was now retired and living in a cottage in rural Connecticut, she drove through Nebraska and dropped Betsy off at her sister's house. Laura was unable to leave Betsy alone even for short periods of time and had no money to hire a caretaker.

Laura financed her trip by giving sixteen illustrated lectures on the Navajo, ten for pay at $50–$75 per talk. She spoke at her alma mater, the Baldwin School, and at other private schools near Philadelphia and Washington where her Navajo work had recently been exhibited at the Washington Arts Club. She drove through Rochester, New York, on her way home to visit with Minor White and with Nancy and Beaumont Newhall at the George Eastman House. There she suffered a "slipped sacroiliac" and developed acute neuritis in her right leg. She was forced to hire a driver to take her and her car back to Santa Fe, thus losing the savings she had accumulated from her lecture tour. When she picked up Betsy in Nebraska, she found her "very far from well." Still, she returned home in an upbeat mood. She explained to a friend, the trip "did a lot for my morale. I could go east and earn a good living. Even if I went for two or three months a year that might free me for other work here. In addition to all else I saw a good agent for color transparencies who kept eighteen of my best ones and I know the kind of thing they can sell. So you see it was a worthwhile trip." When she returned home she also had a literary agent to help her find a home for her "problem child," her Navajo book.[27]

Shortly after her return in early November, Laura put all of her projects on hold when she learned that the house she and Betsy shared – one of a series of rented homes they had lived in since moving to Santa Fe – was to be sold. With money borrowed from the bank and a generous loan from Anne Parrish Titzell, Laura's girlhood friend from Colorado Springs, they were finally able to buy their own house at 409 Camino del Monte Sol, in the heart of Santa Fe's old artists' district.[28]

Once they had settled in, Laura again focused on her book. The agent she retained in New York to help her place the Navajo book had found some interest in the photographs as possible illustrations for someone else's text, but this was not acceptable to Laura. "The whole point is that this book is PRIMARILY a book of vision. Otherwise the complete idea would be changed to an illustrated book by someone else. . . . The text must be written to complement the pictures and to give the information to accompany them, not as a piece of literature illustrated by pictures." When the literary agent withdrew in January 1956, Laura turned to Mitchell Wilder for help. Wilder was a long-time supporter of Laura's work. A native of Colorado Springs who became curator of the Taylor Museum for Southwestern Studies in 1935 and director of the Colorado Springs Fine Arts Center in 1945, he had a keen interest in photography and shared Laura's enthusiasm for the Spanish and Indian cultures of the Southwest. He frequently sent commercial jobs her way while she lived in Colorado Springs, the largest of which was the commission in 1938 to document New Mexico churches for George Kubler's architectural study. After her move to Santa Fe, Wilder continued his encouragement, organizing and sponsoring the first major exhibition of her Rio Grande photographs in 1948 and showing her photographs in an important exhibition of work by western photographers – including Edward Weston and Ansel Adams – that he organized in 1953. "I will not give up because of another rejection," Laura wrote in 1956. "So please, Mr. Wilder, your advice as to what I should do next."[29]

HUBERT AND FLOYD LAUGHTER. *Laura Gilpin. Gelatin silver print, 1954. Amon Carter Museum.*

While Wilder considered what to do about the book, Laura pursued various publishing leads on her own and continued to make new photographs for the project whenever she had the time and money to get away from Santa Fe. Most of her income came from commercial jobs – portraiture and copy work for the Museum of International Folk Art and the Museum of Navaho Ceremonial Art. Sales of her landscape photographs and old exhibition prints at prices ranging from $20 for an 8″ x 10″ picture to $50 for a 16″ x 20″ print were almost nonexistent. Presentations of her Navajo slide lecture, now supplemented with "sound recordings of Navaho chants and song," provided one of her few steady sources of income.[30]

The more she worked on her Navajo project, the stronger her feeling became that there might be some special bond between herself and the Navajo people. In September 1957, Laura made a trip to Canyon de Chelly with a young Navajo woman from Santa Fe, while Betsy stayed at home. Laura went first to Window Rock where she photographed the Tribal Council in session, then she and Maria Teba proceeded to Chinle, on the rim of Canyon de Chelly, to set up camp. The next day they visited the clinic at Many Farms and returned by way of the Valley Store, which Laura recognized as the old Frazier Trading Post where she had gone for gas on her fateful camping trip of 1930. They stopped for lunch and, while they were inside, one of Laura's camera cases disappeared.

Two days later, on their way to photograph at the Window Rock Fair, Laura and her companion picked up an older couple looking for a ride. She heard Maria and the woman conversing in Navajo about her missing camera case. Suddenly the woman asked Maria to tell Laura "to go around that hill where it would be quiet." As Laura told her story later, "I couldn't imagine what she wanted, but I have never failed to follow such a lead." Laura drove to an isolated spot out of view of the highway. The woman told her to stop, get out of the car, spread a rug on the ground, and get out a case similar to the one she had lost. Laura knelt down beside the woman, then to her "complete surprise" watched her begin a hand-trembling ceremony over her. For fifteen minutes, Laura watched the woman's arm and hand tremble and listened to her chant. Then the woman turned to Maria and told her in Navajo that three boys had taken the camera from Laura's car. Nothing would be hurt, she said, and two boys would return the case to the Valley Store in four days. In four days Laura returned to the store. The trader said that he did not have the case but reported that two boys had just been there asking if the case had been found. Laura thought they were probably "seeing if the coast was clear," so she left reward money and postage with the trader. Then, realizing that the boys would probably see and recognize her car, she drove away. A few days after she returned to Santa Fe, she received her camera case, its contents unharmed.[31] The incident reinforced her feeling that she had a sort of spiritual connection to the Navajo people.

Continuing her work with no prospects for publication, Laura began to revise her ideas as to how her book should be organized. At first, she had planned to end it with a section on how the Navajo were adapting to current American life, but by 1959, after almost a decade of work on the project, this no longer seemed the most important thing about the Navajo. As she explained to architect Nathaniel Owings and his wife, Margaret, long-time admirerers of her work, "I suddenly clicked and now wonder how I could have been so dumb. I have moved the 'Tradition' section to the last. . . . Tradition is still going on and is the essence of the Navaho, and of course with this section last, in completes the circle."[32] With this new emphasis on "tradition," Laura's text took on a form and tone more in keeping with her photographs, which had always stressed the timeless qualities of Navajo life. Laura now consciously recognized that what seemed most important about the Navajo was not how much they were changing but how much of their rich tradition they were able to retain, a bias apparent in her earliest pictures from the 1930s. What had come to fascinate her was how these traditions could endure in the face of so much temporal change – a theme with a logical appeal to a woman of sixty-eight who had retained her nineteenth-century manners in a world of rapidly changing values.

Laura's notebook of Navajo pictures went everywhere with her. When she went to California in June 1959 to assist Ansel Adams with one of his photographic workshops in Yosemite National Park, she took it along. While she was in California she also showed the dummy to photographer Dorothea Lange, whom she had met only once before at the First Aspen Photography Conference in Aspen, Colorado, in 1951. Lange, who had received much recognition for her warm and dignified portraits of the poor and homeless during the 1930s, gave "great encouragement" to the Navajo project and bolstered Laura's faith in her work. So did Imogen Cunningham, who, at seventy-six, was the only significant woman photographer still working who could claim to have been at her craft any longer than Laura. They had never met before, but when Laura wrote to arrange their meeting, she said, "I have such a strong feeling that you and I see very much eye to eye." Oblivious of her own accomplishments, she was in awe of Cunningham's and approached her with characteristic deference. "Please do not go to a lot of trouble on my account. I live a lonely photographic life here in Santa Fe. I do see Eliot Porter occasionally, and Ansel storms through every so often, otherwise I plug along in my old fashioned way."[33] Self-contained and doggedly persistent, she continued the work on her book alone. The Navajo project had become a familiar part of her day-to-day life. Although Laura never lived on the Navajo Reservation for an extended period of time, as an earlier chronicler, Frank Hamilton Cushing, had lived at Zuñi Pueblo, she nonetheless had lived with the Navajo – in her own fashion – for a long time.

By 1960 nearly half of Laura's gross income of $901.94 came from presentations of her slide lectures. Additional income came from small commercial jobs, including portraits, Christmas cards, and a photo essay on Georgia O'Keeffe's home for *House Beautiful*. Any paying job was difficult to refuse, and in the winter of 1960 she accepted a job for the Museum of International Folk Art that took her back to Yucatán for nearly two months to photograph the land, the people, and the Mayan architecture. The museum director, William Friedman, promised her an air-conditioned darkroom, time for herself at Uxmal and Chichén Itzá, and the right to use her work in whatever way she wished after the museum's show was mounted. With just three weeks' notice, she hired a woman to stay with Betsy and prepared to leave. She had never abandoned the idea of a companion book to *Temples in Yucatan* on the ruins at Uxmal and thought this might be a splendid opportunity to get the work done while having her expenses paid and earning $500 a month. But, as she told a friend, the trip "turned into a nightmare," even though she was able to get a good series of black-and-white architectural shots at Uxmal and augment her series of 2¼″ x 3¼″ color slides of the various sites throughout the peninsula. She and Friedman did not get along, the food and accommodations were poor, she was often left for days with no assignments, the promised darkroom never materialized, and travel was done in a 1924 Ford rather than the helicopter that Friedman had promised. Christmas was a "miserable lonely day," with no one to talk to. When she returned to Santa Fe, she had difficulty getting paid for her work, and the following year, when Friedman left the museum, he took with him many of the Polaroids that she made on the trip. Laura wrote to Ansel Adams, "Never have I gotten into a project with higher hopes or greater enthusiasm, and the whole miserable business has taken a lot out of me."[34]

There were taxing problems at home as well, as Laura learned it was difficult to leave Betsy in the care of anyone else. A few weeks after Laura's departure, Betsy wrote to her sister Emily that she was

MAKING CAST SILVER, PINE SPRINGS, ARIZONA. *Laura Gilpin. Gelatin silver print, 1950. Amon Carter Museum.*

"determined" to get rid of her caretaker. She called and begged Emily to come rescue her, then in humiliation wrote back to apologize. Her caretaker wrote to Emily Stuart in mid-January complaining of Betsy's "mental deterioration" and her inability to manage such everyday chores as keeping track of the checks she wrote, telling Stuart that she must come and take care of her sister herself.[35]

When Laura returned home, she resumed taking care of Betsy, making every effort to involve her in her daily activities. When she went to photograph at San Ildefonso Pueblo, she took Betsy along and let her lie quietly in the back of the station wagon while she went about her work. When guests would come by their house, Laura would introduce her companion with a dignified graciousness – "This is Miss Forster, please excuse her that she does not rise" – and include her in the conversation as a matter of course.[36]

The frequency of Laura's trips to the Navajo Reservation slowed, in part because of Betsy, in part because

NAVAHO SHEPHERD BOY. *Laura Gilpin. Gelatin silver print, 1950. Amon Carter Museum.*

she was strapped for money and still had no assurance that she would ever have any financial reward for her Navajo project. Laura continued to do portrait jobs and copy work for the Santa Fe museums and continued, in her available time, to go to concerts and to speak out for the Indian Arts Fund, of which she was now chairman. She and Betsy lived very modestly even with the help of small checks sent by Betsy's family. In 1962 Laura reported a net loss on her income tax form of more than $350.[37] Only continuing support for her project from the Navajo people and her own deep sense that the work was truly important kept her going.

In the spring of 1963 when prospects seemed bleak, Mitchell Wilder came to visit. He was now the director of the Amon Carter Museum in Fort Worth, Texas, a new and rapidly expanding museum of American art with a particular emphasis on the American West and an ambitious exhibitions and publications program. He picked up the dummy of Laura's Navajo book and took it to show Frank Wardlaw, director of the University of Texas Press, a press that, like the museum, specialized in regional projects. Wardlaw quickly responded to Laura, "I don't think there is any doubt about our being able to swing it." She had at last found two backers who shared her interest in explicating regional culture through art. Immediately she regained her enthusiasm for the project and wrote Wardlaw asking for "a decision as to page size, type face and type size, so that I can plan a lot of the text to fit the pages properly. I am interested in the entire product and I want to do everything I am capable of to make this a beautiful book."[38] At the age of seventy-two, she began to transform her outline into a text and to schedule a few last trips to the reservation for some final photographs.

With the end of her project in sight, Laura's energy seemed unbounded. Even when she was laid up with gout, she took advantage of the time to write. As with her earlier books, she took pains to assure that the information she gave would be accurate. Although she remained in awe of scientific expertise, her long and intimate involvement with the Navajo had given her the courage to trust some of her own ideas. She wrote Wilder, "The amount of research for what seems a simple text seems very great. But I have to *know* I am right in what I am writing about. I have found some sad discrepancies among AUTHORITIES! Several that differ with my own experience, so have gone back to the Navaho for the answer."[39] She was no longer writing as an outsider, as she had when she approached Pueblo history or the religious practices of the Mayan Indians. She now had her own intuitive and direct understanding of the Navajo.

The writing of the text, like the making of the photographs, went slowly because Laura still had to interrupt her work to accept commercial jobs. She had taken over Betsy's share of the house payments and had sadly begun to look into the possibility of moving her to a nursing home, but that was a step she seemed reluctant to take while she was still engaged in the Navajo project. The project belonged as much to Betsy as to herself, and Laura wanted her there to share in every aspect of it. Laura wrote to Betsy's sister in the spring of 1964, "The Navaho book is nearly finished and it will be a great relief to me when it is done. Then I can go after work of other kinds. This book means a great deal to both of us in many ways, but it has also meant great sacrifices. How well it will pay off remains to be seen, but its value in other ways will be great."[40] The book would be a tribute to her long friendship with Betsy and a validation of all the hardships they had withstood to bring the book about. Just as she had given *The Rio Grande* to her parents and brother, so she intended to give this book to Betsy, as an ongoing and living tribute to the family that they had been together.

In 1964 Laura and Betsy made one of their last trips together to Red Rock. They learned that their friend Francis Nakai had died the previous winter and went to visit his widow and daughters. "Mrs. Francis burst into tears when she saw us," Laura wrote, "and it took Betsy quite a while to quiet and comfort her. . . . As we drove away, Betsy had them all smiling and happy." For Betsy it was an especially nostalgic visit. The old concrete hospital building that had been her home and clinic thirty years before was gone; sturdy young trees grew around the new day-school building. As Laura recalled in her book, "Though she said nothing, I was sure that Betsy's mind was filled with thoughts of her many friends and the work she had done during those years of her nursing service here in Red Rock, a service meaning more to her than anything she had ever done." The former patients she encountered all gave her "a heart-warming welcome." "As we have found so often," Laura observed, "once an Indian has learned to trust a person, the bond is lasting."[41]

As she worked on her text, Laura had to sell some of her jewelry to meet her day-to-day expenses. There was no margin for comfort. When she sustained $200 damages in an automobile accident, she had to cancel a long-planned trip to the reservation to photograph some specially made sand paintings in order "to earn the money to come over again." Still, she persisted with her work. Finally, in April 1966, she sent a sixty-pound package of text and reproduction photographs to Frank Wardlaw in Austin. With real satisfaction and much understatement, she wrote, "I am happy to tell you that *The Enduring Navaho* is on its way to you." It was sixteen years since she had begun what was intended as a one- or two-year project, but she did not really regret the delay. Later she said, "I think my book is a better book because it took that long. And I learned that much more about what I had to do. I don't think you can grasp those kinds of things in a hurry."[42]

Her friends agreed. In a community of high-minded

people quietly working to promote the Indian cause, Laura's sacrifices had not gone unnoticed. A few months after she mailed her book to the press, Laura received a note from Elinor Gregg, an old Santa Fe friend who had played a key role in establishing the nursing program of the Indian Health Service. Writing on behalf of a group of Laura's friends, Gregg explained that they would like to help relieve Laura of "some of the financial strain and worry that is caused by illness." She wrote, "We have taken the liberty of making this possible by depositing some money in your name as a tribute to all you have done for the Indians in this part of the world. . . . You have their confidence and affection far and wide, both the Pueblos and the Navahos, and Betsy shares in this." She continued that the contributors hoped that Laura would use the money to hire someone to look after Betsy and to help alleviate the pressure of her monthly mortgage payments. She concluded, "If you will accept this money from your friends who appreciate all you have done for the Indians and who would like to have you able to continue to do so much, you will make us all happy."[43]

A further tribute came a few months later from the Indian Arts and Crafts Board, a division of the Department of the Interior devoted to the promotion of Indian arts, which awarded Laura a Certificate of Appreciation for her photographs that have "eloquently preserved a record of a people's cultural transition from a period of awesome isolation to their forceful entry into the mainstream of contemporary life."[44]

By the summer of 1966, Laura was on crutches because of an arthritic hip joint that she blamed on her years of carrying around a heavy large-format camera and tripod. She could work no more than a few hours a day in her darkroom, yet she wanted to get back to the reservation to get some better aerial views of the Navajo's four sacred mountains. She was at once anxious to see the book completed but reluctant for her *raison d'être* to be finished. She may have remembered the tremendous letdown that followed the completion of her other big projects, none of which had been as absorbing as this one. She may also have feared that finishing the book, in which she had worked so hard to keep Betsy involved, could mean that her ailing companion might finally slip away. She determined to lose weight in preparation for a possible hip operation so that she could continue her work, writing to photohistorian Beaumont Newhall, "I welcome this ordeal, for it means I will be able to walk again, and, God willing, do some of the work I still have planned to do." She felt that she was no good as she was, and she had no intention of being on crutches for the rest of her life. Moreover, her handicap made it even more difficult for her to earn her living.[45]

While she waited impatiently for the book to appear, Laura worked in her darkroom, printing photographs for the large exhibition of Navajo images that Mitchell Wilder had planned at the Amon Carter Museum to celebrate the publication of her book. The work kept her busy but unable to pursue the commercial jobs that would bring in the money she needed.

Finally, on November 2, 1968, eighteen and a half years after she had begun the book, Laura received her advance copy of *The Enduring Navaho*. "It is hard to realize that eighteen years of work and planning on my part have finally reached completion," she wrote to her publisher. "It is a good thing that I am so busy getting ready for exhibitions or I would be lost with nothing to do."[46] For almost two decades, the book had been her life and now it was done.

The Enduring Navaho, *1968*

Laura dedicated her book to "Elizabeth Warham Forster, R.N." "Dear Betsy," she wrote. "This is as much your book as mine. Not only have you shared completely in the making of it, but also you have taught me to understand the Navaho People." The book was Laura's gift of thanks in appreciation of Betsy's work: " . . . my visits revealed the work you were doing, your understanding, your patience, your kindness, and your generosity, for you literally gave of your substance as well as your knowledge and nursing skill." It was also a gift of thanks for the world to which Betsy had introduced her, a world that provided her with abundant subject matter for her most compelling work. Even more it was a gift of thanks for all that Betsy had given to her in a personal way. "As a tribute to our long and happy friendship," Laura wrote, "this is your book." It was the offspring of their fifty-year companionship and, like any parents, Laura and Betsy hoped that their happily launched child would be able to support them in their old age.[1]

The Enduring Navaho was a 279-page book of text and illustrations, which Laura designed to be "a unity of picture and word (always the picture first) which would flow easily" and not be merely an "illustrated" text. The text, with no pretense of "a scientific or an ethnologic approach," was designed for the layperson.[2]

Laura divided the book into four parts to symbolize the importance of the four compass points in Navajo culture, and began her text in a forthright manner: "To understand the Navaho People, even in small measure, it is essential to know at least some part of their symbolic ritual."[3] Thus, the first section of the book, "The Navaho World," begins with a narrative of the creation myth, which expresses the deep bonds between contemporary Navaho life and religion and between the Navaho people and their land – the essence

of the deep-rooted peacefulness, timelessness, and seeming unity of Navajo life that attracted Laura. The myth is followed by a historical and geographical overview of the Navajo people (the Dinéh) and their land related from an aerial perspective as Laura flies over the reservation photographing the four sacred mountains. The text focuses on the seeming continuities of Navajo culture and the physical features of reservation life that remain unmoved by temporal change; the photographs of sacred Navajo mountains emphasize the unchanging constants of the Navajo world.

Into this religious tradition and physical setting Laura places the Navajo people: "Moving about in loneliness, though never lonely, in dignity and happiness, with song in their hearts and on their lips, in harmony with the great forces of nature, are the Dinéh – People of the Earth."[4] With photographic portraits and an anecdotal text, adapted in large part from the letters Betsy had prepared for publication three decades before, she then introduces the reader to the people that she and Betsy met in Red Rock in the early 1930s.

Next, with her broad picture of the Navajo world complete, Laura portrays the economy of Navajo life. Her photographs and text in "The Way of the People" cover the physical structure of Navajo homes, the trading post economy, the business of sheep raising and farming, and the traditional and modern crafts of weaving, silversmithing, pottery, basketry, and painting. In the third section she discusses "The Coming Way," as exemplified by the tribal government and the medical, legal, and educational institutions of the Navajo tribe. Laura concludes with "The Enduring Way," an explanation of Navajo tradition and ceremonialism. To critics who suggested that the book would be more effective as an anthropological text if it concluded with a discussion of contemporary life, Laura responded: "Ceremonialism still goes on and holds the tribe together. Having the modern section last is too much of a let down, and as this is not intended to be an anthropological work, artistically, the climax must be the Ceremonial section."[5]

The writing in the book is lean and spare in the long narrative passages of historical description and the factual accounts of industries and tribal organizations. When Laura turns to stories about the experiences she and Betsy shared with the Navajo people, her style becomes more poetic and infused with the sentiment she felt toward the Navajo people. This split in the text echoes the disparate tones of Laura's Pueblo and Yucatán books, both of which have spare passages of objective narrative mixed with more effusive descriptions of her exotic subjects. But while the sentiment in Laura's earlier books seems naïve and uninformed, the sentiment in *The Enduring Navaho* grows from personal experience and has the ring of authenticity.

The pictures in the book, like the textual passages, are divided between those that merely aid the narrative and those invested with more personal feeling. Made between 1931 and 1964, the pictures balance images of people and activities that Laura sought out with images of chance encounters; people and places she knew well are shown with people and places she had only just met. Pictorially, the best portraits are of people she knew or of traditional Navajo who appealed to her interest in the past; the weakest portraits are of people specifically photographed for inclusion in the book because they represent a particular profession or tribal office. Thus, the strongest portraits are generally of Betsy's old Red Rock friends – the Nakais, the Kellywoods, the Benallys – and the people Laura met in her travels around Red Rock (plates 62, 72, 76, 78, 116).[8] Laura photographed these people because she was drawn to their faces and these photographs have a relaxed, unstudied look that is missing in the pictures Laura made later to serve specifically as book illustrations.

Thus, in the text and in the photographs, the book attempts to do two things: to convey a warm, personal account of one Anglo woman's experiences with the

NAVAHO TWINS. *Laura Gilpin. Gelatin silver print, 1954. Amon Carter Museum.*

Navajo people and to give a systematic overview of the changes in Navajo life and culture in the mid-twentieth century. The warmth and affection that make the personal passages so strong are what make the more descriptive passages seem somewhat naïve. Still, Laura's strong personal voice is what makes the book succeed as a whole. As she herself recognized, it was a popular account of Navajo life, not an anthropological text.

Photographically, *The Enduring Navaho* is a book about people, just as *The Rio Grande* is essentially a book of landscapes. Nonetheless, Laura considered the Navajo people an inextricable part of the land in which they lived and impossible to portray without photographs of their natural and human worlds. Her pictures of the interior of the old Red Rock Trading Post, of the Long Salt summer hogan, and of the silversmith at work in his home evoke a strong sense of the slow and peaceful rhythms of traditional Navajo life (plates 63, 80). Her photograph *A Chance Meeting*, an image of two shepherds who have met, seemingly by chance, on the vast sprawling desert under a dramatic stormy sky, suggests the intimate connection between the people and the landscape that is a central concern of all her books (plate 125).

The very title of her book, "The *Enduring* Navaho," is the key to Laura's interpretation of the Navajo people. The Edward Curtis photogravure that had hung over the mantle in her childhood home also depicted a Navajo subject – a group of Navajo horse-men in Canyon de Chelly. But the Indians that Curtis called the "Vanishing Race" were Laura's "Enduring Navajo." Where he had a romantic's fascination with traditions that were disappearing and a sense of inevitable loss, Laura had a deep interest in the traditions that persevered and a profound faith that Navajo culture could survive in the modern world: "I cannot believe that the old ways will really be lost. Another generation will want to know all those things that their grandparents can tell them, and I am sure that there will always be some who can do so, and that a new interest in their traditional past will come. . . . We can but hope that those essential qualities that are the birthright of the Dinéh will never be lost."[6] Curtis looked for what was gone; Laura sought out what was left. She focused on what had survived rather than what was being destroyed.

Her interest in the traditional ways of life explains, in part, why the section of the book dealing with Navajo life in the 1930s is more insightful than the sections that describe life on the reservation after the Second World War. The strength of the earlier section is also attributable to the special entry that Laura had into Navajo life in the 1930s and, above all, to the increasing complexity of life in the Navajo community. Federal money, the development of native oil and gas industries, and the presence of an increasing number of Navajo who had studied or worked off the reservation had profoundly changed Navajo life, even in the small community of Red Rock, which Laura knew so well.[7] Her old Navajo friends could not act as competent guides to this new and rapidly changing world.

The theme of cultural endurance and adaptation had fascinated Laura ever since she wrote her book on the Pueblo Indians. "Above all they have endured," she wrote then, implying that the Pueblos had survived in the face of great changes in the outside world. Their endurance was an act of sheer physical survival; just getting by was an achievement worthy of note. But the "endurance" of the Navajo people was much more. It was an endurance of culture. It was not sheer physical persistence, but a graceful accommodation of the best of the old ways to the best of the new. It was a way of adapting to change while remaining in touch with one's deepest cultural beliefs. Laura wrote that the Pueblos "*have* endured." She concluded her Navajo book with the more forward looking faith that the Navajo "*will* endure."[8]

This change in her use of the word "endure" suggests Laura's own resiliency. With increasing age, the demands she made on herself grew greater. As she grew older, she was no longer content to accept mere physical survival as an appropriate or even adequate way to get along in the world. What made the "endurance" of the Navajo people so admirable was their ability to adapt to new ways with a remarkable grace while retaining the best of their traditional beliefs. In her mid-seventies, Laura was attempting that same graceful accommodation to the turbulent 1960s. As she retained her strong sense of Victorian propriety, privacy, and manners, she kept up with current events, the exploration of space, and the latest developments in cameras and photography. Like the Navajo she wrote about, she wanted to embrace the new while remaining true to the old.

The theme of adaptability is reiterated throughout *The Enduring Navaho*. In reviewing the Navajo economy, Laura acknowledges that the change from subsistence to commercial productivity is great, "but here, once more, the native adaptability of the Navaho will serve him in good stead." The young people she singles out for discussion are praised because they provide "a superlative example of the Navaho ability to learn new ways and a new kind of life, yet retain the best of traditional ways."[9] She concludes her book with a section on ceremonialism because ritualism and a continuing belief in the old traditions seem the key to the future of the Navajo people.

Laura's sense of identification with the Navajo was never so profound that she adopted native dress, presumed a casual familiarity with her Navajo friends, or purported to understand all the intricacies of the Navajo religion and world view. Still she perceived her book as done "entirely from the Indian viewpoint."[10] In spite of her modesty and her strong sense of decorum about her relationships with the Navajo, she did not think this a presumptuous claim. She simply felt she was presenting the Navajo as they would want to present themselves.

In her text, Laura ascribes to the Navajo the personal qualities she valued herself. "Through all runs a vein of kindliness, inherent good manners, and a special quality for which it is difficult to find the right word. Perhaps integrated personality is the attribute, for there is a 'oneness' about these people." She writes of the importance of the family to the Navajo people, of their strong feelings for the land, "the strength and beauty to be derived from closeness to the elements." She finds their law courts, like them, to be "quiet, reserved, sincere, and dignified." She speaks of their intense loyalty to those they have come to trust. She writes of their "dignity and happiness," qualities that "spring from their vital traditional faith, faith in nature, faith in themselves as a part of nature, faith in their place in the universe." She writes of their instinctive and extraordinary sense of design, speculating whether it is the hardship of their lives that has produced such vitality in their art.[11]

To Laura, the Navajo people seemed to have a stoic ability to withstand hardships, a strong sense of place and history, a loyalty to family and friends, a dignified independence and self-sufficiency. They thus represented many of the qualities Laura wanted to find in her own family, and she minimized one aspect of Navajo life that was uncomfortably familiar to her – alcoholism. Laura's hesitation to discuss the alcohol problem on the Navajo Reservation was a measure of her reluctance to dwell on the alcoholism of her father and her brother. To those who criticized her for ignoring the alcohol problem she replied, "I know how the Navaho feel about it. To me no one seems to have portrayed the very fine Navaho dignity. The alcohol problem is bad, so is ours! Why should we pick on them any more than ourselves." Aside from a portrait of a tribal policeman, the only photograph in her book alluding to the problems of social disorder shows the proceedings in a courtroom in Tuba City

(plate 117). In a spare room with a concrete floor, rough hewn wooden benches, and a bare light bulb hanging overhead, a Navajo judge looks sternly at a young defendant sitting in front of him. A copy of Gilbert Stuart's unfinished portrait of George Washington hangs on the wall. It is a picture not so much about crime as about justice. Similarly, Laura deals with politics but not political factionalism, the economy of Navajo culture but not the dire poverty, the hope for improved educational facilities but not the problems of illiteracy. The noted photographer and anthropologist John Collier, Jr., observed, "A photographer as a visual anthropologist is a fieldworker who OBSERVES METHODOLOGICALLY. He can have a closed heart and still accomplish RESEARCH. Such a specialist could NEVER have produced The Enduring Navaho, for this is a work of LOVE not ANALYSIS."[12]

Laura filled her personal journal with brief quotations and clippings that confirm how close her personal values were to the behavior she ascribed to the Navajo. She wrote that her own creed was, "All that matters is how I behave and how I take what happens to me." She believed in the necessity of accepting life's burdens with grace and stoic self-control, much as she thought the Navajo did. "Possess your emotions, don't let them possess you," she wrote in her notebook at one point. Elsewhere she noted, "genius is nothing but an uncommon aptitude for patience."[13] It is hard to know whether she came to appreciate these values because they seemed strong and admirable in the Navajo or she came to appreciate the Navajo because she realized that they possessed the values she already prized.

As Laura's interest in music went back to her girlhood, it is not surprising that she should be fascinated by the importance of music in traditional Navajo culture, or that she should close her book on this note: "Song and singing are the very essence of Navaho being, and as long as the Navaho keep singing, their tradition will endure." Into her journal she copied a quote that reiterated her own continuing fascination with music, "You must always believe that Life is as extraordinary as music says it is."[14]

Laura was a modest person, confident of her work but hesitant to call attention to herself or her achieve-

MEETING IN A HOGAN, COUNSELOR, NEW MEXICO. *Laura Gilpin. Gelatin silver print, 1953. Amon Carter Museum.*

ments. As she wrote in her journal, "A related atom is the building stone of nature. A lone human being is a destroyer of values; a related human being is the builder of individual and social peace." This credo for her own behavior might almost be an anthropologist's characterization of Navajo beliefs and the traditional Navajo reluctance to be singled out for personal recognition, and it reiterates Laura's profound sense of identification with the Navajo people.[15]

Praise was heaped upon her for her achievement in *The Enduring Navaho*. The National Cowboy Hall of Fame and Western Heritage Center named it outstanding western nonfiction book of the year. Ansel Adams sent "CONGRATULATIONS, PAEONS, PRAISE, ACCOLADES, WHEES AND CHEERIOWS!!" Photographer Paul Strand, whom Laura knew only

slightly but whom she always admired above all her contemporaries, wrote a lengthy appreciation of her work, praising the "warmth and true humanity which it communicates on every page." Like most critics of the book, he sensed immediately the love exchanged between Laura and her subjects unimpeded by the lens of her camera. "The 'Enduring Navaho' have, through you, an enduring book which reflects their spirit as it needed to be recorded, truly and without patronizing or sentimentality. Clearly it is a life work, this book of yours, which like all true things will live, through the years, a monument to your love and understanding of these people."[16]

Nothing pleased Laura more, however, than the praise from her Navajo friends. Ned Hatathli, executive vice-president of the Navajo Community College,

TYING A TSIIYÉÉL. *Laura Gilpin. Gelatin silver print, 1954. Amon Carter Museum.*

wrote her, "We think it is 'The Book' of all Navajo books [that have] ever been published. . . . We shall treasure it from now on." The book reviewer for the *Navaho Times*, noting that the book might well be called "The Endearing Navaho," commented, "A book like this is nostalgic; it makes one homesick for the ways of twenty years ago, but brings a feeling of

pride for the development of the Navajos to their present status. Still, it is pleasant to scan the earlier pictures and say 'I remember.'" Laura wrote to a Navajo friend, "I have been very much touched and delighted over the way these Navaho People whom I have seen, have liked the book. This means more than anything to me."[17]

Finished in Beauty, 1969-1979

Laura's gift to Betsy, her book-length tribute to their friendship and their shared adventures with the Navajo, was made just in time. Betsy's health was becoming increasingly frail; she could not walk and at times only Laura could understand her speech. Working on crutches and suffering from a bad back herself, Laura strained to keep up with her own photographic work and to take care of her companion, washing and dressing her every day. She seemed unwilling to let go of Betsy and relinquish what had been the most important personal relationship of her life. Brenda Putnam, too, was in frail health. Dwindling use of the muscles in her arm made it impossible to draw or sketch or even to write. All around her, Laura saw the debilitating effects of old age.[1]

Royalties from *The Enduring Navaho* and a check for the sale of a large group of prints to the Center of Art for Indian America helped improve her finances. From 1968 to 1969, her income climbed from just over $1,600 to nearly $5,500, a figure that included more than $500 for the sale of "art prints" to the general public. It was a staggering loss, however, when the large exhibition of Navajo pictures that she had printed for exhibition at the Amon Carter Museum and a subsequent nationwide tour was lost in transit from one site to another in the fall of 1969. The insurance settlement could not compensate for the canceled exhibits with their potential for book sales or buy her the time to go back and redo all of the darkroom work that had been involved in preparing the show. A case of pneumonia in the winter of 1969–70 was one further blow. From the oxygen tent where she was recovering, Laura acknowledged the news that she had been selected to receive an honorary doctorate from the University of New Mexico. In a hand-written note to the university

president, she called the news "the best possible medicine I could have." "I am very humble and very proud . . . ," she wrote; proud, especially, because she had never finished high school. As requested, she sent a photograph to the university for publicity use, but she sent a "working picture," since it seemed "more suitable to me than a formal one." By now her life seemed inseparable from her work.[2]

"As a photographer, she has demonstrated for over fifty years that her art draws its expressive power from her compassionate attunement to her chosen subjects and her honest respect for her medium," read the citation delivered to Laura along with a Doctor of Humane Letters degree. "She is one of the pioneers in the recognition of photography as a fine art; she stands as the world's foremost master of the exquisite lost photographic art of platinum printing; and she illustrates vitally her innate conviction that aesthetic statements are enriched and made stronger when they answer humane concerns."[3]

Invigorated by the receipt of her degree in June 1970 and heartened that she was back to using just one crutch, which made her "naturally a tripod," Laura applied to the Guggenheim Foundation for a fourth time. She wanted funds to do the photographic book she had long contemplated on Canyon de Chelly, a gorge of spectacular rock formations and Anasazi ruins still inhabited and farmed by the Navajo. Writing to Ansel Adams to request a letter of recommendation, Laura observed, "I am 79, but still have, God willing, a few more years of production ahead of me. One thing has happened to me, I have lost a lot of inhibitions! And I certainly will go after all this with a lot of experience behind me." In addition to working in the canyon "at each season of the year to try once more to produce the kind of book that is always hanging out in front of me," she wanted to make new photographs along the lower Rio Grande for a revised edition of *The Rio Grande*. She told Adams that if she had a grant, "I think I could accomplish the two books within a two year period."[4]

Her application for a Guggenheim grant was turned down, but commercial jobs continued to come in and for the first time a New York gallery – the Witkin Gallery – showed interest in her work. Dozens of young photographers were ringing her doorbell, interested to see her work and more eager to get her approval and advice.[5]

Even as Laura's reputation grew stronger, Betsy was slipping away. In the fall of 1971, Laura was forced to place her in a nursing home. With her own bad back and hip she could no longer lift her companion in and out of bed. "It is all very sad and grim," she wrote to Mitchell Wilder. She visited Betsy every day to help feed her her meals, and quickly turned back to her work for solace. Only a few weeks after placing Betsy in the home, Laura contacted the University of Texas Press to sound out its interest in her Canyon de Chelly project, which she was now "more determined than ever to do" despite her rejection from the Guggenheim Foundation. "The problems of old age are very great," she wrote to director Frank Wardlaw. "Now I am alone and need to get busy on a major project."[6]

On New Years Day 1972, Betsy Forster died of respiratory and heart failure and the complications of Parkinson's disease. Laura wrote the obituary for the local paper. She noted simply that Miss Forster resided with "her friend Laura Gilpin," a quiet understatement of Laura's role as a devoted and loving companion.[7] For almost half the time of their fifty-four-year life together, Laura had borne the burden of Betsy's care.

Betsy's sister wrote to Laura from Nebraska, "It must be of untold comfort to know that you did everything possible for a human being to do to ease her suffering. I have never known of greater or more unselfish devotion than you showed her through all."[8]

Laura asked that tributes in Betsy's memory be sent to the Navajo Community College at Chinle. "As she was a great reader and lover of books herself," Laura wrote to Ned Hatathli at the college, "I think that books for the College library would be what would please her the most. Her years as a nurse at Red Rock meant more to her than any work she ever did, and I know you know how closely we worked together to produce my book."[9]

With Betsy's death, Laura experienced both a profound loss and a sense of release. "From this hour, freedom!" she typed in her journal, quoting from Walt Whitman's *Song of the Open Road*. "From this hour I ordain myself loos'd of limits and imaginary lines, / Going where I list, my own master, total and absolute." She understood the gift of freedom she had been given, because she had earned it. With her freedom came a choice between "stoicism or self pity, work or weeping." As she had always done, and as she presumed the Navajo would do as well, she chose the path of stoicism. "Sometimes work is the greatest thing one can do," she said; "that is to keep on working when things get tough." In the very letters in which she announced Betsy's death to her friends and associates, Laura announced her intention to begin working on her new Canyon de Chelly book, and she considered returning to Yucatán to get a more complete series of photographs of the ruins at Uxmal, Labná, and Sayil.[10] Through her work she intended to assault the dark shadows of age, loss, and depression.

A few days after Betsy's death, she enrolled in a class on photographic history taught by Santa Fe photohistorian Richard Rudisill. She went to learn, not to teach, despite the fact that her own professional career spanned fifty-five years and she knew many of the key figures in the history of twentieth-century American photography. Never boasting of her own accomplishments, Laura startled the instructor and his class when she mentioned that she knew William Henry Jackson, the great pioneer of nineteenth-century American western photography. His second wife was her father's cousin. When they met in 1933, when Jackson was ninety, Laura had showed him some of her Navajo work and discussed the problems of photographing in the West. Laura told him that she admired his work but wondered why he had photographed the West without any people in it. She recalled that he told her, "It seems funny to me now, but when I was in that country in the earlier days, I was just interested in the landscape and the ruins and didn't pay any attention to the people."[11]

In March the School of American Research awarded Laura a $12,000 grant to prepare a photographic book on Canyon de Chelly to be delivered in two years. She immediately began preparations for the project. Making no concessions to her age, she secured permission from the director of the park at the canyon to camp on the canyon floor. To dealer Lee Witkin, who was encouraging her to make a return visit to New York, Laura wrote that she was excited about the Canyon de Chelly project: "I only hope my advanced age and some incapacity will see me through. Somehow tackling this job seems much easier to think about than a trip to New York. I don't know how I would manage the city traffic." She hoped that the canyon book would be an "extension of the *Enduring Navaho*," and she wrote her Navajo friends of her plans, adding "it will be wonderful to be back in the country I love so dearly."[12]

The project on Canyon de Chelly was a logical sequel to her previous books. *The Rio Grande* had explored the relationship between humans and the physical environment in a vast area of the Southwest. *The Enduring Navaho* had explored these connections within a single ethnic group in a narrowly delineated geographical area. Now, in a book about one canyon and the handful of Navajo families that maintained summer homes there, Laura wanted to explore these issues in a more limited and personal way.

If the Canyon de Chelly project was pursued with any less energy than Laura's earlier work, it was less because of her age and physical infirmities than because of the demands placed upon her by her increasing celebrity. Since the Depression, when she had been forced to curtail her exhibition activities, she had mainly worked alone. She had carved a place for herself in the world of southwestern archaeology and anthropology and had earned recognition from a wider community through her books, but recognition had been slow in coming from the photographic community, in large part because Laura was not aggressive about celebrating her own accomplishments. For her, as for the Navajo, that would be unseemly boasting.

In the early 1970s, more and more strangers came by her home in Santa Fe to see her photographs. Occasionally, too, there were Navajo visitors looking for a place to spend the night. Laura put up her

AIR SHOT OF CANYON DE CHELLY, ARIZONA. *Laura Gilpin. Gelatin silver print, 1972. Amon Carter Museum.*

Navajo guests, overlooking the breach of proper etiquette involved in their unexpected arrival as she would be reluctant to do with other guests. She rarely refused to talk with visitors because she enjoyed sharing her enthusiasm for photography and was flattered by their interest and because, with Betsy gone, she enjoyed company. When dealer Lee Witkin paid a visit in June 1972 and took a large number of photographs, including many early platinum prints, back to New York for an exhibition at his gallery, he initiated the long-overdue rediscovery of her work. Laura was genuinely pleased and flattered by his attention, particularly by his interest in the platinum prints that had lain for decades in her bureau drawer: "It was simply great to have you come all the way here to see me and go over so much of my 'stuff.' Of course I am so very pleased that you wanted some of the platinums and others and I hope you find a market for them."[13]

Laura tried to balance the demands of her new book project with the demands and pleasures of her emerging celebrity. She made two trips to Canyon de Chelly in the summer and fall of 1972, using a copy of *The Enduring Navaho* as her introduction to the Navajo living in the canyon that she had not yet met. As always, she worked quietly, deliberately, and patiently. The success of her book and her increasing recognition in the world of photography had not interfered with the gentle, joking rapport she had with her Navajo subjects.

On one trip to the canyon, Laura described to a Navajo companion the experience she had had with the hand trembler some years earlier, when her camera case had been stolen while she was working on *The Enduring Navaho*. The woman led her to the home of Mary Brown on the rim of Canyon de Chelly. Mary Brown was the very woman who had helped Laura many years before. She looked up and recognized Laura instantly. Without hesitation, she asked, "Did you get your case back?" Nonplused, Laura managed to reply, "Yes, that's the reason I came – to thank you." Brown had developed a sharp pain in her shoulder after her husband's recent death and could no longer weave. On a later trip to the canyon, Laura invited Santa Fe physician Audrie Bobb to come with her to visit Brown and try to alleviate her shoulder pain. Laura brought a side of mutton to present to Mary Brown as a gift and Bobb arrived with ice. After some stretches and an ice massage, Mary Brown's shoulder pain was cured.[14]

Laura moved easily between the quiet Navajo world and the increasingly active world of American photography. In the spring of 1973, she made her first trip to New York in eighteen years. She toured the retrospective exhibition of the work of Paul Strand at the Metropolitan Museum with Strand and his wife, Hazel, talked shop with Barbara Morgan, and visited Witkin's gallery. She marveled that he could actually sell her platinum prints and wondered at all the changes that had taken place in the photographic world since she had studied in New York at the Clarence H. White School. She wrote to her old friend Ansel Adams, "How suddenly attitudes and understandings can change place. Now Photography is IT. And everything is buzzing. More and more photographers are coming to New Mexico. Those of us who think back to the 1916s and on, can too well

remember the attitude of institutions as well as the general public who used to say 'Oh, it's just a photograph.'" In the winter of 1973–74, Witkin gave Laura a one-person show and sold forty of her pictures at prices of up to $250 for the old platinum prints. For her this was a source of amusement as much as pride.[15]

Encouraged by the reception of her old platinum work in New York, Laura decided to apply yet again for a Guggenheim fellowship, despite the fact that it had eluded her four times before over a period of forty years. In the fall of 1974 she sat down with a spirited recording of Beethoven's Ninth Symphony on her stereo and wrote a grant proposal requesting $12,000 to make hand-coated platinum prints. Her application was successful. "I can't think of a better way to taper off one's life," she said, "than to settle down to hand-coated platinums." At a party held in her honor near Santa Fe with a group of other Guggenheim award winners present – including photographers Paul Caponigro, Eliot Porter, William Clift, and Edward Ranney – photohistorian Beaumont Newhall introduced Laura as the newest and youngest of the select lot.[16]

Suddenly, in addition to the demands of her two big projects, there was a flurry of requests for reproductions and exhibitions, talk of a monograph, and requests from film makers. A retrospective exhibition at the Museum of New Mexico's Museum of Fine Arts over the winter of 1974–75 brought Laura new recognition in her hometown and resulted in an onslaught of photo orders, which she was hard pressed to meet. The prints for the exhibition, selected by Laura with assistance from photographers Anne Noggle and William Clift, spanned her career from her early experiments with Autochrome plates to her most recent work in Canyon de Chelly. Finding it hard to believe that people could be interested in the pictures she had made so long ago, Laura spoke up against including her early platinum prints. Her associates outvoted her, so she carefully reprinted many of her silver prints, trying to match the softness and broad tonal range of her platinum work, in order to make the show as fine and consistent as possible.[17]

Ansel Adams wrote in the brief statement he contributed to the exhibition catalogue, "I make no pretense of evaluating Laura or her work from a high critical or scholarly level. As with all great people of this world, one is impressed with the simplicity, the aura of sympathy and understanding. Add to this a determined twinkle, a gregarious intensity and personal glow which seems to come from stored-up shining light on mesas, canyon, vast skies and thunder clouds, Navahos and piñon trees – all this is part of Laura Gilpin, one of the most important photographers of our time." "You've done it from the heart and as it is," painter Georgia O'Keeffe told Laura after she saw the show.[18]

Increasingly, it became difficult for Laura to steal time away from Santa Fe to go out to the canyon; it was difficult for her to refuse those who came wanting to talk and visit. As an old friend remarked, fame didn't change her, it just covered her up. Some of her friends were annoyed with her lack of progress on her new project; only a few understood just how lonely she was without Betsy or her old friend Brenda Putnam, who died in a nursing home in the fall of 1975.[19] An independent worker, Laura was still a woman who craved close companionship.

Laura planned to photograph the canyon during all seasons of the year in black and white as well as color, but, as she had learned in her previous book projects, the weather was not always reliable. A trip in April 1975 to photograph the leaves coming out was unsuccessful because there was "so much water running in the canyon it was impossible to get there."[20]

She was beginning to find that the Navajo who lived in or near the canyon wanted to collaborate with her in the making of her book. Photographer William Clift, who accompanied her on a ten-day trip to the canyon in 1975, found, "The Navaho who lived in the Canyon all knew and liked her. One woman, Annie Yazzie, heard we would be coming and without saying a word had her sheep all around the hogan and her loom set out for Laura to photograph. They wanted to do all they could to help her to document them and their way of life."[21]

On another trip to the canyon in the fall of 1975 to photograph the turning leaves, Laura again found the canyon residents to be willing collaborators in her project. Having worked on the book for several years, she now had a photographic dummy that she carried to show to the people she hoped to photo-

CANYON DE CHELLY, ARIZONA. *Laura Gilpin. Gelatin silver print, 1964. Amon Carter Museum.*

graph. A woman from the National Park Service recognized a photograph of a friend's mother and called her friend over to see it. When the woman arrived she confirmed that Laura's photographs of a weaver near Mummy Cave were photographs of her mother and said they were the only photographs of her that had ever been made. Laura immediately took the photographs out of her binder and presented them to the woman. Two days later the woman telephoned Laura and invited her to her home, offering to ride with her to act as her guide. When Laura arrived at the Draper Farm, a beautiful spot on the canyon floor that she had often photographed from the rim, she found that a feast was being staged entirely for her benefit. A family of about thirty people was busy preparing a huge meal of roast mutton and freshly roasted cornmeal tortillas. Laura was invited not only to eat but to photograph it all.[22]

"It was a Navaho gift," she said of that day. "That

was a day I'll never forget because it just summed it all up. . . . It was just that I was accepted by them, I think, as much as anything else – as somebody that understood them." Through all the years that she was working on *The Enduring Navaho*, Laura had longed to be accepted as one of them: "I did that book from *their* point of view. That's the whole point. They see the difference. . . . They like it and I don't care about any other part of it."[23] However, she had never been made to feel so much a part of a Navajo family. She had never felt her affection for the Navajo people so fully returned. The day at the Draper Farm filled a deep longing for a sense of connection to a family, a place, and a rich historical tradition.

Many circumstances of her life had conspired to produce this deep sense of identification with the Navajo people. Her wandering childhood helped her appreciate their profound sense of place. Her Colorado upbringing gave her an understanding of their deep affection for the land. Her friendship with Anne Simon gave her insight into the power of spiritualism in Navajo life. The financial difficulties of her own life helped her understand the traditional Navajo culture of scarcity. Her family's ambiguous social standing in status-conscious Colorado Springs made her appreciate the Navajo's nonjudgmental acceptance of those they embraced as friends. Her devotion to the care of her father and her companion, Betsy, led her to admire the Navajo devotion to those within their extended family units. Her studies with Max Weber and Brenda Putnam led her to appreciate the beauty and design of Indian art. Her sense of herself as the last of her family sharpened her interest in tradition and gave an edge of urgency to her efforts to document traditional culture.

She said later of her day at the Draper Farm, "It was a very important episode in my life. I know that and I just treasure the memory of it."[24]

On a trip to San Francisco in the spring of 1976 to attend an opening of an exhibition of her work at the Focus Gallery, Laura visited with Imogen Cunningham. Cunningham, ninety-three, was at work on a book of portraits of elderly people called "Over Ninety." Laura, a mere eighty-five, wrote to her, "I think that for the only time in my life (for a few minutes) [I wished] I were older instead of younger,

so that I could be one of the '90 and Over.' Anyway, I think we both thoroughly enjoy ourselves and our many contacts and activities and I am glad I am a photographer." Cunningham responded gracefully, "I feel that you are not really old yet, but I am." A few months later Cunningham died, and Laura realized with a jolt that she was now "the senior photographer of our line of work." She wrote to a friend, "Is there another that you know of 85 or over? If you do, please let me know."[25]

After years of working in relative obscurity, she relished her new status as a senior photographer. In June 1976, with financial aid from a cousin, she opened a small work space and gallery in the front of her house. It was the first display area she had had since she had shared exhibition space in her father's furniture studio, and it gave her ample opportunity to show her work to visitors. She fell far behind on her print orders; even though she now had a part-time darkroom assistant she liked to supervise all of the work. She never managed to begin the platinum-printing project for which she had received her Guggenheim grant, and she never began the portfolio of prints she had promised to produce for Lee Witkin's gallery. For the first time in her life she began turning down sales orders and requests for exhibitions. She made two trips to Canyon de Chelly in 1976 but never assembled the prints for the book she had promised to the School of American Research in 1974. She explained her situation to the administrators of her Guggenheim grant, "I find that at my age I have not got the staying power I used to have and it is very hard for me to realize that I cannot get as much done in a day as I used to do."[26]

Her work schedule slackened as she took pleasure in her increasing celebrity. In 1974 the governor of New Mexico awarded her one of the First Annual Awards for Excellence in the Arts, an honor she shared with three people she had worked with and photographed, painter Georgia O'Keeffe, architect John Gaw Meem, and potter María Martínez. The governor of Colorado awarded her the Governor's Award in the Arts and Humanities in 1977, noting "she is living testimony of the courage it took for a young woman in the arts, daring to break down the masculine barriers of the profession to emerge as one of the most

AT THE DRAPER FARM. *Laura Gilpin. Gelatin silver print, 1975.*
Amon Carter Museum.

sensitive photographic historians of the American
Native Indian." Colorado College, in her native
Colorado Springs, awarded her her second honorary
doctorate in the spring of 1979. Museums and galleries
showed a growing interest in her work.[27]

Through it all Laura remained a modest woman,
and her burgeoning reputation did little to change
her day-to-day life, aside from bringing her more
visitors and creating a new market for her fine prints,
which freed her from the burdens of commercial
work. She continued to attend concerts, remained an
alert and critical follower of Santa Fe's museum and
gallery exhibitions, and kept herself informed about
contemporary Indian affairs and new photographic
technology. She was unfailingly kind and generous
to young photographers and had a talent for putting
them at ease by confiding in them about her own
photographic mistakes.[28]

She seemed surprised and amused to be cast in the
role of a mentor to young photographers. Laura told
them, "Get busy and earn your own living first, then
you can do the other things which you're very moved
to do. . . . I've learned a lot from doing things I didn't

always want to do." For young women she had no
special advice. She told one aspiring photographer,
"You ask how hard is it for a woman to become a
pro. My answer is it is just as difficult as it is for a man."
When a reporter from *Ms. Magazine* came to her
home, Laura answered her questions politely, though
she knew neither the magazine nor the reporter. After-
ward she recalled the last question was, "What do
you think of women's lib?" Her reply was, "I don't
think about it at all." She was amused to discover
later that her interviewer was Gloria Steinem, about
whom she was completely unaware. After Steinem's
article appeared, Laura dropped her a note. "I am
pleased that you say I have a compassionate eye and
that I am a professional. I do hope that I am both."[29]

To her friends, Laura seemed an "ordinary human
being experiencing life as fully as she could." She
appeared "unspoiled" and without artifice, "very
alive to other peoples' interests," and able to give
freely of her love to those around her. "She was
always a kind of breath of fresh air," said Ansel Adams.
"Even when she was going around with crutches she
seemed like she was going to start outdoing Pavlova."
Her friends recalled her absolute unwillingness to let
her physical infirmities slow her down and the delight
she took in cooking a steak in an open fireplace as
her cowboy-father had always done. Dynamic as she
was, she invariably impressed people with her manners
as "a real lady."[30]

Toward the end of her life, Laura was often inter-
viewed about her life and work.[31] She presented
herself as an inner-directed loner pursuing her work
with a quiet determination, despite long spells of
financial hardship and little recognition. She rarely
failed to tell the stories of her trip to the St. Louis
World's Fair in 1904, her studies with Clarence White
and Max Weber, or her first meeting with the Navajo
in 1930. She scarcely mentioned her difficulties with
her family, her financial problems, or the active exhibition career she gave up during the Depression. A
woman of western toughness and eastern gentility,
she was willing to talk about her adventures but
reluctant to speak about her accomplishments or her
misfortunes. She alone knew the personal cost of her
achievements and wished that to remain a private
matter.

She had developed her approach to the southwestern landscape and her photographic style alone. Once she left the Clarence H. White School and returned home to Colorado, no single photographer had a profound influence on her work. On her own she moved away from the soft-focus style and romanticism of her early work to the sharply focused vision of her later work. She had "a highly individualistic eye," Ansel Adams said. "I don't have any sense that she was influenced except by the land itself."[32]

With her "highly individualistic eye," Laura created a thoroughly personal image of the American Southwest as a historical landscape. Her parents, like many western settlers, had seen the land as an empty stage upon which they could invent new roles for themselves. But Laura perceived it as an ever-changing set upon which hundreds of years of human activity had already been enacted. Instead of creating a new life for herself in the West, she wanted to connect herself to the people and cultures that had passed there before her. Through her photography she explored the marks that the land had made on the people and the marks the people had made on the land. In doing so, she explored her own relationship to the place where she lived and created a photographic record of a region that gives equal emphasis to physical geography and human culture. Like the writer Mary Austin, she was interested in the "pattern of established adjustments between the within and the without of man" in the vast stretches of the American Southwest.[33]

She never pretended that her craft was neutral or objective. As John Collier, Jr., himself an anthropologist and photographer, saw, "Laura was a photographer in the grand tradition and a profound humanist, which is often the case with fine photographers. Her winning point was that she never let photography as a craft come between Laura and the Navajos. . . . Laura's accomplishment remains her extreme emotional bridge between her subject and herself THROUGH the lens of her camera."[34] Laura abandoned the romanticism of her earliest photographs of Pueblo Indians, but she never became embarrassed or afraid to convey feeling in her photographs. She came to understand the difference between sentimentality and sentiment and thus created a record of Indian life that bridges the gap between Curtis's nostalgia for a vanishing race and modern work that aspires to a more objective and documentary view of Indian culture.

Such writers as Mary Austin and Mabel Dodge Luhan shared Laura's interest in the native American people of the Southwest and the cultural influences of the physical environment. In emotional prose they conveyed their feelings *toward* the exotic people of the Southwest. Laura had neither their writing skill nor their ego. In her photographs and texts, particularly in *The Enduring Navaho*, she conveyed the feeling that existed *between* her and her Indian subjects; using photography she could not conceal how her subjects regarded her. Their frank, open gazes seem to signal their acceptance of this white woman. Laura took pride in this, for she knew that the Navajo would not cooperate with anyone they perceived as patronizing.[35]

Laura felt comfortable in the out-of-doors from the time she was a young girl – unlike many women who immigrated to the West she did not have to be defeated by the land before she could admit to its beauties.[36] She moved and worked with an intuitive understanding of the slow rhythms of the landscape, and her work is informed by a sensitivity to the passage of time. Her photographs of the ruins at Chichén Itzá and Mesa Verde explore the effect of time on the artifacts of lost cultures. Her Pueblo and Navajo books consider the persistence of cultural traits through time. Her book on the Rio Grande explores the changes in a river through centuries of human use.

She could work quickly but she would not be rushed. A portrait of a Navajo woman or a particular quality of light on a mesa top might take many trips to capture. She spent forty-eight years photographing the Navajo people, and she was still working on her Canyon de Chelly project when she died. No other photographer has devoted so much time to the documentation of an American Indian tribe, and no one else so thoroughly documented Navajo or Pueblo life during the mid-twentieth century. Laura began to photograph the Pueblo and Navajo people during the 1920s and 1930s, before New Deal programs and a world war greatly changed Indian life, when respectful and well-intentioned outsiders were relatively rare and were welcomed at the pueblos and on the Navajo Reservation.[37] Most of her closest friendships with Navajo and Pueblo people were made then. Her friends grew old along with her and gave her a continuing link to the traditional ways, which were increasingly difficult for outsiders to see as the reservation communities adopted more and more of the material trappings of the outside world.

Laura Gilpin's work has been too little known to have had a deep impact on writers, on popular images of the Southwest, or on many other photographers outside her small circle of friends. But it deserves further recognition for its consummate technique, its value as a historical record, its contribution to the humane tradition of photography, and its suggestion that photography has its greatest value as an expressive and documentary medium when it is informed by compassion and personal concerns.

Laura's life also merits attention for what it reveals about her tenacity of spirit and devotion to her craft. For sixteen years she took care of her father, for twenty-six years she devoted herself to the care of Betsy Forster, and the whole time she struggled to make a living. Through it all she never lost her interest in the art of photography. She executed paying commissions with the same care she gave to her own projects, and she made great financial sacrifices to produce the books she committed herself to do. With her unselfish devotion to her work she impressed other people, who worked with many fewer handicaps. "You have been [the Indians'] friend more than most of us and could represent us all," wrote Elinor Gregg on behalf of some of Laura's Santa Fe friends. "This is what we would all like to have done for them. Your photography has been a 'modus operandi' that has reached their lives and few of us have made the effort to be as kind and understanding of them as you have."[38]

Laura made her last photographic trip in September 1979. The year before she had announced that she intended to leave her photographic estate to the Amon Carter Museum in Fort Worth, Texas, where her long-time friend Mitchell Wilder was building a major collection of American photography. When a film crew from the museum arrived in Santa Fe to make a documentary about her long career, Laura wanted to work outside even though she was confined to a wheelchair. The crew made arrangements for

LAURA GILPIN AT WORK. *Fred Mang, Jr. Gelatin silver print, 1971. Amon Carter Museum.*

her to make a trip in a small plane up over the Rio Grande Valley with one of the pilots she had worked with for many years. They drove her to the airport, carefully lifted her out of her wheelchair, and awkwardly folded her into the tiny plane. As the plane lifted off the runway all of her physical infirmities were forgotten. Laura laughed her hearty laugh, opened the window by her seat, and leaned out the window to begin making pictures as she had always done. When she came home she happily told friends that she had seen something new to photograph.[39]

Two months later, on November 30, 1979, she died of heart failure at the age of 88.[40]

A memorial service was held at the School of American Research in Santa Fe in a room crowded with photographers, old Navajo and Pueblo friends, and other friends and admirers representing many walks of life. The most fitting eulogy came from Laura's own book, *The Enduring Navaho* – it was a chant from the Navajo Nightway ceremonial:

> In Beauty (happily) I walk
> With Beauty before me I walk
> With Beauty behind me I walk
> With Beauty above me I walk
> With Beauty all around me I walk
> It is finished in Beauty.[41]

Plates

1: *Gladys McConnell Fowler and Son George*   Autochrome, 1914

2: *Still Life with Peaches*   Autochrome, 1912

3: *Self-Portrait*   Autochrome, c. 1912

4: *Portrait*   Autochrome, 1910

5: *Washington Square, New York* Platinum print, 1916

6:   *The Prelude*   Platinum print, 1917

7:   *Sailboat Race, Nova Scotia*   Platinum print, 1919

8: *Recruiting Scene, New York City*   Platinum print, 1917

9:   *Brenda Putnam and Marble Cutters, New York*   Platinum print, 1917

10:   *Edith Farnsworth*   Platinum print, 1917

11:   *The Prairie*   Platinum print, 1917

12:   *Padraic Colum*   Platinum print, 1919

13 : *The Spirit of the Prairie* Platinum print, 1921

14:   *Cathedral Spires*   Platinum print, 1919

15: *Snow Coral* Platinum print, 1924

16:   *Sunrise on the Desert*   Platinum print, 1921

17:   *Ghost Rock, Garden of the Gods, Colorado*   Platinum print, 1919

18: *Brenda Putnam* Platinum print, 1921

19:   *Betsy's Aspens*   Platinum print, 1921

20: *Emma Miller Gilpin* Autochrome, c. 1912

23:   *Margaret Carlson*   Platinum print, 1921

24: *The Babe*   Platinum print, 1927

25: *The Flower Garden* Platinum print, 1927

26: *Barbara Mayor* Platinum print, 1923

27: *Farnsworth-Hazlehurst Wedding, Colorado Springs, Colorado*   Platinum print, 1926

28:   *George William Eggers*   Platinum print, 1926

29: *Fishermen at Concarneau, France* Platinum print, 1922

30: *Interior of Chartres Cathedral*   Platinum print, 1922

31: *Chartres Cathedral* Platinum print, 1922

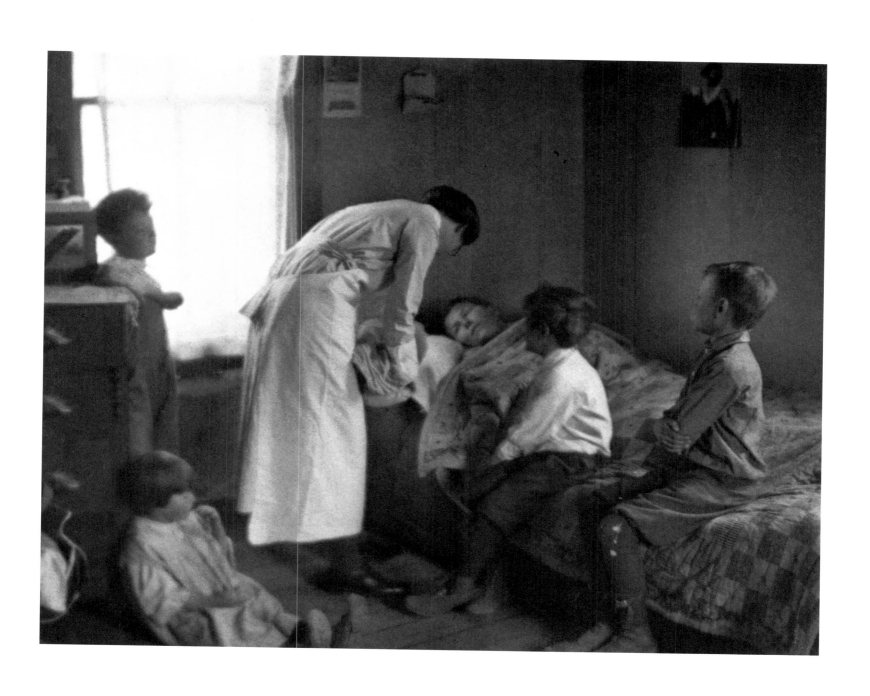

32: *A Visiting Nurse*   Platinum print, 1924

33: *Grace Church, Colorado Springs*   Platinum print, 1928

34:   *Corley Road Tunnel*   Platinum print, 1925

35: *A Problem for Students to Make a Still Life of a Pair of Scissors, Two Books, and a Ball of String*   Platinum print, 1930

38:   *Model in Fortuny Gown*   Platinum print, 1925

39:   *Lillian Gish in* Camille, *Central City, Colorado*   Platinum print, 1932

40: *Mrs. Hendrie* Platinum print, 1930

41: *U.S. Supreme Court Justice McReynolds* Platinum print, 1934

42: *Joy Krebbs*   Platinum print, 1930

43: *Hubbard Phelps, Los Alamos School, New Mexico* Platinum print, 1933

44: *Louisa Graham*   Platinum print, 1936

47: *Narcissus* Platinum print, 1928

48: *Sunrise, Grand Canyon* Platinum print, 1930

49: *Bryce Canyon* Platinum print, 1930

50: *Colorado Sand Dunes*   Platinum print, c. 1946

51: *Zion Canyon* Platinum print, 1930

52: *Bryce Canyon, no. 2*   Platinum print, 1930

53: *Sunburst, the Castillo, Chichén Itzá*   Silver bromide print on Gevaluxe paper, 1932

54:   *Temple of the Warriors, Chichén Itzá*   Silver bromide print on Gevaluxe paper, 1932

55: *Temple of the Warriors from the Castillo, Chichén Itzá* Silver bromide print on Gevaluxe paper, 1932

56: *Top Platform of the Castillo, Chichén Itzá*   Silver bromide print on Gevaluxe paper, 1932

57: *North Colonnade, Chichén Itzá*   Silver bromide print on Gevaluxe paper, 1932

58: *Steps of the Castillo, Chichén Itzá*   Silver bromide print on Gevaluxe paper, 1932

59: *Sisal Plant, Yucatán*   Platinum print, 1932

60: *Maya Women, Yucatán*   Gelatin silver print, 1932

61:   *Casa Blanca, Canyon de Chelly*   Platinum print, 1930

62: *Navaho Madonna*   Gelatin silver print, 1932

63:   *A Navaho Silversmith*   Gelatin silver print, 1934

64:   *The Ute Woman*   Silver bromide print on Gevaluxe paper, 1934

65: *Shepherds of the Desert*   Gelatin silver print, 1934

66: *Sunrise from Lukachukai Mountains, Arizona*   Gelatin silver print, 1934

67: *Navaho Covered Wagon*   Gelatin silver print, 1934

68:   *Navaho Woman, Child, and Lambs*   Platinum print, 1932

69: *Shiprock, New Mexico*   Gelatin silver print, 1932

70:   *Setah Begay, Navaho Medicine Man*   Platinum print, 1932

71:   *The Little Medicine Man*   Platinum print, 1932

72:   *Ethel Kellywood*   Silver bromide print on Gevaluxe paper, 1932

73: *Navaho Weaver* Platinum print, 1933

74: *Hardbelly's Hogan*   Gelatin silver print, 1932

75: *Navaho Woman and Child in Hogan*   Gelatin silver print, 1932

76:   *Timothy Kellywood and His Family*   Gelatin silver print, 1932

77: *Shiprock from the North Rim of Mesa Verde*   Platinum print, 1926

78: *Mrs. Francis Nakai and Son* Platinum print, 1932

79: *Navaho Family under Tree*   Gelatin silver print, 1932

80: *Red Rock Trading Post, Arizona*   Gelatin silver print, 1932

81: *Navahos by Firelight*   Silver bromide print on Gevaluxe paper, 1933

82:   *Water Hole, Acoma, New Mexico*   Gelatin silver print, 1939

83: *San Ildefonso Potters* Platinum print, 1925

84:   *Laguna Pueblo Mission, New Mexico*   Platinum print, 1924

85: *Taos Ovens, New Mexico* Platinum print, 1926

86: *The Gate, Laguna, New Mexico* Platinum print, 1924

87: *Round Tower, Cliff Palace, Mesa Verde, Colorado*   Hand-coated platinum print, 1925

88: *Grandmother and Child, San Ildefonso Pueblo, New Mexico*   Platinum print, 1925

89: *Balcony House, Mesa Verde, Colorado*   Platinum print, 1924

90:   *Chaco Canyon, Pueblo Bonito*   Platinum print, 1931

91: *Pueblo Bonito, Chaco Canyon, New Mexico* Platinum print, 1931

92:   *At the San Ildefonso Pueblo, New Mexico*   Platinum print, 1927

93:   *Tony Peña, San Ildefonso Pueblo, New Mexico*   Gelatin silver print, 1945

94: *Cliff Dwellings of Betatakin, Arizona*   Gelatin silver print, 1930

95: *Governor, Taos Pueblo, New Mexico* Gelatin silver print, 1971

96:   *Storm from La Bajada Hill, New Mexico*   Gelatin silver print, 1946

97: *Church at Picuris Pueblo, New Mexico*   Gelatin silver print, 1963

98: *A Campo Santo*   Gelatin silver print, 1961

99: *Near Rinconada* Gelatin silver print, 1946

100:   *Door at Ranchos de Taos Church*   Gelatin silver print, 1947

101: *Georgia O'Keeffe* Gelatin silver print, 1953

102: *Santo, San José de Chama*   Gelatin silver print, 1938

103: *Near Chimayo, New Mexico*   Gelatin silver print, 1948

104:   *Tommy Dickerson with Chicken*   Gelatin silver print, 1944

105: *New Mexico Santo*   Gelatin silver print, 1957

106:   *Peter Goodwin*   Gelatin silver print, 1960

107: *White Sands, New Mexico, no. 3* Gelatin silver print, 1947

108: *The Friendly People of Cerralvo, Mexico* Gelatin silver print, 1949

109: *Near the Old Comanche Trail, Big Bend National Park* Gelatin silver print, 1946

110: *South Park, Colorado* Gelatin silver print, 1941

111: *Rabbit Ear Pass, Colorado*   Gelatin silver print, 1937

112:   *Paradise Valley, near the Big Bend, Texas*   Gelatin silver print, 1946

113:   *White Sands, New Mexico*   Gelatin silver print, 1945

114: *Sotol Plant*   Gelatin silver print, 1946

115: *Rio Grande Yields Its Surplus to the Sea* Gelatin silver print, 1947

116: *A Navaho Family*   Gelatin silver print, 1950

117: *A Navaho Court* Gelatin silver print, 1954

118: *Classroom at Crystal with a Navaho Teacher*   Gelatin silver print, 1954

119: *Hubert and Floyd Laughter, Betatakin, Arizona*   Gelatin silver print, 1954

120: *Irene Yazzie, Pine Springs, Arizona* Gelatin silver print, 1952

121: *Navaho Grandmother*   Gelatin silver print, 1951

122: *Modern Medicine Man, Goldtooth Begay, Round Rock, Arizona*   Gelatin silver print, 1951

123:   *Florence at Long Salt Hogan*   Gelatin silver print, 1953

124:   *Big and Little Shiprock, New Mexico*   Gelatin silver print, 1951

125: *A Chance Meeting in the Desert*   Gelatin silver print, 1950

126: *Mrs. Hardbelly* Gelatin silver print, 1953

Checklist of the Exhibition

In the given dimensions, height precedes width.

1: *Gladys McConnell Fowler and Son George*
Autochrome, 1914
7 × 5″ (17.8 × 12.7 cm.)
Amon Carter Museum 79.146/9

2: *Still Life with Peaches*
Autochrome, 1912
3 × 5⅛″ (7.6 × 13.0 cm.)
Amon Carter Museum 79.146/50

3: *Self-Portrait*
Autochrome, c. 1912
5½ × 3¼″ (14.0 × 8.2 cm.)
Amon Carter Museum 79.146/37

4: *Portrait*
Autochrome, 1910
5½ × 3¼″ (14.0 × 8.2 cm.)
Amon Carter Museum 79.146/31

5: *Washington Square, New York*
Platinum print, 1916
8 × 6″ (20.4 × 15.4 cm.)
Amon Carter Museum 79.95/33

6: *The Prelude*
Platinum print, 1917
6⅛ × 7¹³⁄₁₆″ (15.6 × 19.8 cm.)
Amon Carter Museum 79.95/87

7: *Sailboat Race, Nova Scotia*
Platinum print, 1919
3⁹⁄₁₆ × 4½″ (9.0 × 11.5 cm.)
Amon Carter Museum 79.129/3

8: *Recruiting Scene, New York City*
Platinum print, 1917
7⅞ × 5¹¹⁄₁₆″ (20.0 × 14.4 cm.)
Amon Carter Museum 79.95/45

9: *Brenda Putnam and Marble Cutters, New York*
Platinum print, 1917
8 × 5¹⁵⁄₁₆″ (20.3 × 15.1 cm.)
Amon Carter Museum 79.102/1

10: *Edith Farnsworth*
Platinum print, 1917
8 × 5¹⁵⁄₁₆″ (20.3 × 15.0 cm.)
Amon Carter Museum 79.95/44

11: *The Prairie*
Platinum print, 1917
5⅞ × 7⅝″ (14.9 × 19.3 cm.)
Amon Carter Museum 79.119/8

12: *Padraic Colum*
Platinum print, 1919
8⅛ × 6³⁄₁₆″ (20.6 × 15.7 cm.)
Amon Carter Museum 79.130/930

13: *The Spirit of the Prairie*
Platinum print, 1921
7⁵⁄₁₆ × 9⅜″ (18.6 × 23.8 cm.)
Amon Carter Museum 77.64/2

14: *Cathedral Spires*
Platinum print, 1919
9⁷⁄₁₆ × 7½″ (23.9 × 19.1 cm.)
Center for Creative Photography 77:023:002

15: *Snow Coral*
Platinum print, 1924
9⁹⁄₁₆ × 7⅝″ (24.2 × 19.3 cm.)
Center for Creative Photography 77:023:015

16: *Sunrise on the Desert*
Platinum print, 1921
7¾ × 9¼″ (19.6 × 23.5 cm.)
Amon Carter Museum 79.95/59

17: *Ghost Rock, Garden of the Gods, Colorado*
Platinum print, 1919
9½ × 7½″ (24.1 × 19.1 cm.)
Amon Carter Museum 79.95/66

18: *Brenda Putnam*
Platinum print, 1921
8¹³⁄₁₆ × 7″ (22.4 × 17.7 cm.)
Amon Carter Museum 79.44/8

19: *Betsy's Aspens*
Platinum print, 1921
4¾ × 3¹³⁄₁₆″ (12.0 × 9.7 cm.)
Amon Carter Museum 79.141/28

20: *Emma Miller Gilpin*
Autochrome, c. 1912
5½ × 3¼″ (14.0 × 8.2 cm.)
Amon Carter Museum 79.146/45

21: *Three Ceramic Pots*
Dye-transfer print, 1941
9 × 7⅜″ (22.8 × 18.7 cm.)
Amon Carter Museum 79.149/1

22: *Apple Blossoms*
Dye-transfer print, 1941
9⅜ × 7⅝″ (23.8 × 19.4 cm.)
Amon Carter Museum 79.149/2

23: *Margaret Carlson*
Platinum print, 1921
9⅝ × 7¹¹⁄₁₆″ (24.4 × 19.4 cm.)
Amon Carter Museum 79.95/86

24: *The Babe*
Platinum print, 1927
9⁷⁄₁₆ × 7⅛″ (24.0 × 18.1 cm.)
Mr. Jerry Richardson

25: *The Flower Garden*
Platinum print, 1927
9⁹⁄₁₆ × 7¹¹⁄₁₆″ (24.3 × 19.5 cm.)
Amon Carter Museum 79.95/76

26: *Barbara Mayor*
Platinum print, 1923
9½ × 7½″ (24.1 × 19.0 cm.)
Amon Carter Museum 79.130/558

27: *Farnsworth-Hazlehurst Wedding,*
Colorado Springs, Colorado
Platinum print, 1926
7⅝ × 9½″ (19.4 × 24.2 cm.)
Amon Carter Museum 79.130/97

28: *George William Eggers*
Platinum print, 1926
4¹³⁄₁₆ × 5½″ (12.3 × 14.0 cm.)
Amon Carter Museum 79.130/79

29: *Fishermen at Concarneau, France*
Platinum print, 1922
12¼ × 9¾″ (31.1 × 24.7 cm.)
Amon Carter Museum 78.92/11

30: *Interior of Chartres Cathedral*
Platinum print, 1922
9½ × 7¼″ (24.1 × 18.2 cm.)
Amon Carter Museum 79.44/1

31: *Chartres Cathedral*
Platinum print, 1922
9⁷⁄₁₆ × 7¼″ (24.0 × 18.4 cm.)
Amon Carter Museum 79.114/11

32: *A Visiting Nurse*
Platinum print, 1924
7⅝ × 9¾″ (19.4 × 24.5 cm.)
Amon Carter Museum 79.95/62

33: *Corley Road Tunnel*
Platinum print, 1925
9⅝ × 7⅝″ (24.4 × 19.4 cm.)
Amon Carter Museum 78.84/11

34: *Grace Church, Colorado Springs*
Platinum print, 1928
9⁹⁄₁₆ × 7½″ (24.2 × 19.1 cm.)
Amon Carter Museum 78.84/27

35: *A Problem for Students to Make a Still Life of*
a Pair of Scissors, Two Books, and a Ball of String
Platinum print, 1930
9⁹⁄₁₆ × 7⅝″ (24.2 × 19.3 cm.)
Center for Creative Photography 77:023:024

36: *Cave of the Winds*
Platinum print, 1925
9½ × 7½″ (24.0 × 18.9 cm.)
Amon Carter Museum 78.84/21

37: *Roses in Vase*
Platinum print, 1928
9⁷⁄₁₆ × 7⁹⁄₁₆″ (23.9 × 19.2 cm.)
Center for Creative Photography 77:023:010

38: *Model in Fortuny Gown*
Platinum print, 1925
7⁹⁄₁₆ × 9¹¹⁄₁₆″ (19.2 × 24.5 cm.)
Amon Carter Museum 79.130/5

39: *Lillian Gish in* Camille, *Central City, Colorado*
Platinum print, 1932
9⅝ × 7¾″ (24.5 × 19.6 cm.)
Amon Carter Museum 79.140/2

40: *Mrs. Hendrie*
Platinum print, 1930
9½ × 7¾″ (24.1 × 19.6 cm.)
Amon Carter Museum 79.130/13

41: *U.S. Supreme Court Justice McReynolds*
Platinum print, 1934
9½ × 7⅝″ (24.2 × 19.3 cm.)
Amon Carter Museum 79.95/48

42: *Joy Krebbs*
Platinum print, 1930
9⁹⁄₁₆ × 7⁹⁄₁₆″ (24.3 × 19.2 cm.)
Amon Carter Museum 79.130/191

43: *Hubbard Phelps, Los Alamos School, New Mexico*
Platinum print, 1933
$9\frac{9}{16} \times 7\frac{5}{8}''$ (24.3 × 19.3 cm.)
Amon Carter Museum 79.130/657

44: *Louisa Graham*
Platinum print, 1936
$9\frac{3}{4} \times 7\frac{5}{8}''$ (24.7 × 19.4 cm.)
Amon Carter Museum 79.95/50

45: *White Iris*
Silver bromide print on Gevaluxe paper, 1926
$13\frac{7}{8} \times 11''$ (35.2 × 28.0 cm.)
Amon Carter Museum 79.141/23

46: *Rain Drops on Lupin Leaves*
Platinum print, c. 1931
$4\frac{3}{4} \times 6\frac{5}{8}''$ (11.8 × 16.8 cm.)
Amon Carter Museum 78.92/18

47: *Narcissus*
Platinum print, 1928
$9\frac{9}{16} \times 7\frac{5}{8}''$ (24.2 × 19.4 cm.)
Amon Carter Museum 79.95/84

48: *Sunrise, Grand Canyon*
Platinum print, 1930
$7\frac{3}{4} \times 9\frac{5}{8}''$ (19.7 × 24.4 cm.)
Amon Carter Museum 76.158/2

49: *Bryce Canyon*
Platinum print, 1930
$9\frac{1}{2} \times 7\frac{9}{16}''$ (24.1 × 19.2 cm.)
Amon Carter Museum 80.35/18

50: *Colorado Sand Dunes*
Platinum print, c. 1946
$7\frac{9}{16} \times 9\frac{1}{2}''$ (19.1 × 24.2 cm.)
Amon Carter Museum 79.44/3

51: *Zion Canyon*
Platinum print, 1930
$9\frac{1}{2} \times 7\frac{9}{16}''$ (24.1 × 19.2 cm.)
Private Collection

52: *Bryce Canyon, no. 2*
Platinum print, 1930
$7\frac{11}{16} \times 9\frac{9}{16}''$ (19.5 × 24.2 cm.)
Amon Carter Museum 76.158/1

53: *Sunburst, the Castillo, Chichén Itzá*
Silver bromide print on Gevaluxe paper, 1932
$14 \times 10''$ (35.6 × 25.2 cm.)
Amon Carter Museum 79.95/13

54: *Temple of the Warriors, Chichén Itzá*
Silver bromide print on Gevaluxe paper, 1932
$10\frac{3}{16} \times 14''$ (25.9 × 35.6 cm.)
Amon Carter Museum 79.145/95

55: *Temple of the Warriors from the Castillo, Chichén Itzá*
Silver bromide print on Gevaluxe paper, 1932
$13\frac{7}{8} \times 10\frac{1}{4}''$ (35.2 × 26.0 cm.)
Amon Carter Museum 79.145/94

56: *Top Platform of the Castillo, Chichén Itzá*
Silver bromide print on Gevaluxe paper, 1932
$12\frac{1}{8} \times 8\frac{1}{2}''$ (30.8 × 21.6 cm.)
Amon Carter Museum 79.145/99

57: *North Colonnade, Chichén Itzá*
Silver bromide print on Gevaluxe paper, 1932
$10\frac{1}{4} \times 14''$ (26.0 × 35.6 cm.)
Amon Carter Museum 79.95/91

58: *Steps of the Castillo, Chichén Itzá*
Silver bromide print on Gevaluxe paper, 1932
$14 \times 10\frac{1}{2}''$ (35.6 × 26.6 cm.)
Amon Carter Museum 64.130

59: *Sisal Plant, Yucatán*
Platinum print, 1932
$6\frac{9}{16} \times 4\frac{5}{8}''$ (16.7 × 11.7 cm.)
Center for Creative Photography 77:023:019

60: *Maya Women, Yucatán*
Gelatin silver print, negative 1932, print later
$9\frac{3}{4} \times 7\frac{1}{2}''$ (24.7 × 19.0 cm.)
Amon Carter Museum 79.95/65

61: *Casa Blanca, Canyon de Chelly*
Platinum print, 1930
$9\frac{5}{16} \times 7\frac{7}{16}''$ (23.7 × 18.7 cm.)
Prints and Photographs Division, Library of
Congress Mph 6489 A39

62: *Navaho Madonna*
Gelatin silver print, negative 1932, print later
$13 \times 10\frac{3}{4}''$ (33.0 × 27.3 cm.)
Dr. and Mrs. Joseph L. Horowitz

63: *A Navaho Silversmith*
Gelatin silver print, 1934
$13\frac{5}{8} \times 10\frac{1}{16}''$ (34.6 × 25.5 cm.)
Private Collection

64: *The Ute Woman*
Silver bromide print on Gevaluxe paper, 1934
$12\frac{1}{2} \times 10\frac{1}{16}''$ (31.8 × 25.5 cm.)
Private Collection

65: *Shepherds of the Desert*
Gelatin silver print, negative 1934, print later
$10\frac{9}{16} \times 13\frac{3}{8}''$ (26.8 × 33.9 cm.)
Amon Carter Museum 79.95/18

66: *Sunrise from Lukachukai Mountains, Arizona*
Gelatin silver print, negative 1934, print later
$10\frac{1}{2} \times 13\frac{1}{4}''$ (26.7 × 33.6 cm.)
Amon Carter Museum 79.95/19

67: *Navaho Covered Wagon*
Gelatin silver print, negative 1934, print later
13¾ × 10¹³⁄₁₆″ (35.0 × 27.4 cm.)
Amon Carter Museum 79.95/98

68: *Navaho Woman, Child, and Lambs*
Platinum print, 1932
13⅜ × 10½″ (34.0 × 26.7 cm.)
Amon Carter Museum 79.95/90

69: *Shiprock, New Mexico*
Gelatin silver print, negative 1932, print later
9¹³⁄₁₆ × 13⁷⁄₁₆″ (24.9 × 34.1 cm.)
Amon Carter Museum 79.128/392

70: *Setah Begay, Navaho Medicine Man*
Platinum print, 1932
9½ × 7½″ (24.0 × 19.0 cm.)
Amon Carter Museum 79.95/31

71: *The Little Medicine Man*
Platinum print, 1932
9½ × 7½″ (24.1 × 19.1 cm.)
Center for Creative Photography 77:023:003

72: *Ethel Kellywood*
Silver bromide print on Gevaluxe paper, 1932
9½ × 7⁹⁄₁₆″ (24.0 × 19.2 cm.)
Mr. Jerry Richardson

73: *Navaho Weaver*
Platinum print, 1933
13⅜ × 9⅝″ (34.0 × 24.4 cm.)
Amon Carter Museum 79.95/8

74: *Hardbelly's Hogan*
Gelatin silver print, negative 1932, print later
10⅝ × 13½″ (27.1 × 34.2 cm.)
Amon Carter Museum 79.95/100

75: *Navaho Woman and Child in Hogan*
Gelatin silver print, negative 1932, print later
9½ × 7⁵⁄₁₆″ (24.0 × 18.5 cm.)
Amon Carter Museum 79.95/25

76: *Timothy Kellywood and His Family*
Gelatin silver print, 1932
9⁷⁄₁₆ × 7½″ (24.0 × 19.0 cm.)
Amon Carter Museum 79.128/258

77: *Shiprock from the North Rim of Mesa Verde*
Platinum print, 1926
4⁵⁄₁₆ × 6¼″ (11.5 × 15.9 cm.)
Christopher M. Harte and W. Amon Burton, Jr.

78: *Mrs. Francis Nakai and Son*
Platinum print, 1932
9⁷⁄₁₆ × 7⅜″ (23.9 × 18.7 cm.)
Christopher M. Harte and W. Amon Burton, Jr.

79: *Navaho Family under Tree*
Gelatin silver print, 1932
6½ × 4⅝″ (16.5 × 11.7 cm.)
Amon Carter Museum 78.92/1

80: *Red Rock Trading Post, Arizona*
Gelatin silver print, 1932
7½ × 9⅜″ (19.0 × 23.7 cm.)
Amon Carter Museum 79.95/88

81: *Navahos by Firelight*
Silver bromide print on Gevaluxe paper, 1933
9⁹⁄₁₆ × 7½″ (24.3 × 19.1 cm.)
Private Collection

82: *Water Hole, Acoma, New Mexico*
Gelatin silver print, 1939
13⅝ × 10¾″ (34.5 × 27.2 cm.)
Amon Carter Museum 80.35/12

83: *San Ildefonso Potters*
Platinum print, 1925
9⁷⁄₁₆ × 7⅜″ (24.0 × 18.7 cm.)
Center for Creative Photography 79:098:002

84: *Laguna Pueblo Mission, New Mexico*
Platinum print, 1924
9¼ × 7⅜″ (23.5 × 18.7 cm.)
Amon Carter Museum 79.95/51

85: *Taos Ovens, New Mexico*
Platinum print, 1926
8¾ × 6¾″ (22.2 × 17.2 cm.)
Amon Carter Museum 79.95/29

86: *The Gate, Laguna, New Mexico*
Platinum print, 1924
9¼ × 7⅜″ (23.5 × 18.8 cm.)
Amon Carter Museum 79.95/28

87: *Round Tower, Cliff Palace, Mesa Verde, Colorado*
Hand-coated platinum print, 1925
9⁹⁄₁₆ × 7⅝″ (24.3 × 19.4 cm.)
Amon Carter Museum 79.125/24

88: *Grandmother and Child, San Ildefonso Pueblo,
New Mexico*
Platinum print, 1925
8⅝ × 6⅝″ (21.9 × 16.8 cm.)
Amon Carter Museum 79.95/89

89: *Balcony House, Mesa Verde, Colorado*
Platinum print, 1924
9¹⁄₁₆ × 7¼″ (23.0 × 18.3 cm.)
Amon Carter Museum 79.95/61

90: *Chaco Canyon, Pueblo Bonito*
Platinum print, 1931
9⅜ × 7⁷⁄₁₆″ (23.8 × 18.9 cm.)
Center for Creative Photography 77:071:002

91: *Pueblo Bonito, Chaco Canyon, New Mexico*
Platinum print, 1931
$7\frac{1}{2} \times 9\frac{1}{2}''$ (19.0 × 24.1 cm.)
Amon Carter Museum 79.107/9

92: *At the San Ildefonso Pueblo, New Mexico*
Platinum print, 1927
$9\frac{1}{2} \times 7\frac{1}{2}''$ (24.0 × 19.0 cm.)
Amon Carter Museum 79.95/56

93: *Tony Peña, San Ildefonso Pueblo, New Mexico*
Gelatin silver print, 1945
$9\frac{11}{16} \times 7\frac{3}{4}''$ (24.6 × 19.7 cm.)
Amon Carter Museum 79.133/102

94: *Cliff Dwellings of Betatakin, Arizona*
Gelatin silver print, 1930
$13\frac{1}{2} \times 10\frac{5}{8}''$ (34.2 × 27.0 cm.)
Amon Carter Museum 79.95/4

95: *Governor, Taos Pueblo, New Mexico*
Gelatin silver print, 1971
$9\frac{5}{8} \times 7\frac{1}{2}''$ (24.3 × 19.1 cm.)
Amon Carter Museum 79.95/38

96: *Storm from La Bajada Hill, New Mexico*
Gelatin silver print, negative 1946, print later
$16\frac{1}{2} \times 20\frac{11}{16}''$ (41.8 × 52.1 cm.)
Amon Carter Museum 79.95/96

97: *Church at Picuris Pueblo, New Mexico*
Gelatin silver print, 1963
$7\frac{3}{4} \times 9\frac{13}{16}''$ (19.7 × 24.9 cm.)
Amon Carter Museum 79.95/93

98: *A Campo Santo*
Gelatin silver print, 1961
$9\frac{3}{4} \times 7\frac{7}{8}''$ (24.8 × 20.0 cm.)
Amon Carter Museum 79.95/47

99: *Near Rinconada*
Gelatin silver print, 1946
$6\frac{15}{16} \times 9\frac{7}{16}''$ (17.6 × 23.9 cm.)
Mr. Jerry Richardson

100: *Door at Ranchos de Taos Church*
Gelatin silver print, 1947
$9\frac{1}{2} \times 7\frac{5}{8}''$ (24.1 × 19.3 cm.)
Amon Carter Museum 79.95/73

101: *Georgia O'Keeffe*
Gelatin silver print, 1953
$9\frac{1}{2} \times 7\frac{7}{16}''$ (24.2 × 18.9 cm.)
Amon Carter Museum 78.92/40

102: *Santo, San José de Chama*
Gelatin silver print, negative 1938, print c. 1977
$5\frac{13}{16} \times 3\frac{3}{4}''$ (13.0 × 9.4 cm.)
Amon Carter Museum 77.88

103: *Near Chimayo, New Mexico*
Gelatin silver print, negative 1948, print later
$9\frac{1}{16} \times 13''$ (23.0 × 33.0 cm.)
Amon Carter Museum 79.123/150

104: *Tommy Dickerson with Chicken*
Gelatin silver print, 1944
$13\frac{1}{2} \times 10\frac{1}{2}''$ (34.3 × 26.6 cm.)
Amon Carter Museum 79.130/1050

105: *New Mexico Santo*
Gelatin silver print, 1957
$3\frac{7}{16} \times 4\frac{7}{16}''$ (8.7 × 11.3 cm.)
Amon Carter Museum 79.139/13

106: *Peter Goodwin*
Gelatin silver print, 1960
$9\frac{3}{8} \times 7\frac{1}{2}''$ (23.8 × 19.0 cm.)
Amon Carter Museum 79.130/986

107: *White Sands, New Mexico, no. 3*
Gelatin silver print, negative 1947, print later
$7\frac{1}{2} \times 9\frac{1}{2}''$ (19.1 × 24.0 cm.)
Amon Carter Museum 79.95/49

108: *The Friendly People of Cerralvo, Mexico*
Gelatin silver print, 1949
$9\frac{1}{4} \times 7\frac{3}{16}''$ (23.5 × 18.2 cm.)
Amon Carter Museum 79.134/6

109: *Near the Old Comanche Trail, Big Bend National Park*
Gelatin silver print, negative 1946, print 1975
$15\frac{1}{4} \times 19\frac{1}{2}''$ (38.6 × 49.2 cm.)
Amon Carter Museum 75.141/4

110: *South Park, Colorado*
Gelatin silver print, negative 1941, print later
$15 \times 18\frac{13}{16}''$ (38.0 × 47.8 cm.)
Amon Carter Museum 76.158/6

111: *Rabbit Ear Pass, Colorado*
Gelatin silver print, negative 1937, print later
$15\frac{5}{16} \times 19\frac{15}{16}''$ (38.9 × 49.0 cm.)
Amon Carter Museum 79.123/151

112: *Paradise Valley, near the Big Bend, Texas*
Gelatin silver print, negative 1946, print 1975
$15\frac{9}{16} \times 19\frac{1}{2}''$ (39.5 × 48.6 cm.)
Amon Carter Museum 74.141/2

113: *White Sands, New Mexico*
Gelatin silver print, 1945
$7\frac{5}{8} \times 9\frac{9}{16}''$ (19.4 × 24.3 cm.)
Amon Carter Museum 79.123/144

114: *Sotol Plant*
Gelatin silver print, negative 1946, print later
$9\frac{15}{16} \times 7\frac{13}{16}''$ (25.3 × 19.8 cm.)
Amon Carter Museum 79.134/4

115: *Rio Grande Yields Its Surplus to the Sea*
Gelatin silver print, 1947
6³⁄₈ × 9¹⁄₂″ (16.1 × 24.1 cm.)
Amon Carter Museum 79.134/1

116: *A Navaho Family*
Gelatin silver print, 1950
13³⁄₄ × 10³⁄₄″ (35.1 × 23.7 cm.)
Amon Carter Museum 79.95/15

117: *A Navaho Court*
Gelatin silver print, 1954
7³⁄₄ × 9⁵⁄₈″ (19.6 × 24.4 cm.)
Amon Carter Museum 78.92/42

118: *Classroom at Crystal with a Navaho Teacher*
Gelatin silver print, 1954
7³⁄₈ × 9⁷⁄₈″ (18.7 × 25.1 cm.)
Amon Carter Museum 79.128/223

119: *Hubert and Floyd Laughter, Betatakin, Arizona*
Gelatin silver print, 1954
13¹⁄₂ × 10⁷⁄₁₆″ (34.3 × 26.5 cm.)
Amon Carter Museum 79.128/400

120: *Irene Yazzie, Pine Springs, Arizona*
Gelatin silver print, 1952
13¹¹⁄₁₆ × 10³⁄₄″ (34.8 × 27.2 cm.)
Amon Carter Museum 79.128/537

121: *Navaho Grandmother*
Gelatin silver print, 1951
9⁵⁄₈ × 7⁵⁄₈″ (24.5 × 19.5 cm.)
Amon Carter Museum 79.95/69

122: *Modern Medicine Man, Goldtooth Begay,
Round Rock, Arizona*
Gelatin silver print, 1951
9³⁄₈ × 7³⁄₈″ (23.8 × 18.6 cm.)
Amon Carter Museum 79.128/273

123: *Florence at Long Salt Hogan*
Gelatin silver print, 1953
13¹¹⁄₁₆ × 10¹³⁄₁₆″ (34.7 × 27.5 cm.)
The Albuquerque Museum

124: *Big and Little Shiprock, New Mexico*
Gelatin silver print, negative 1951, print later
10¹⁄₂ × 13¹⁄₂″ (26.7 × 34.3 cm.)
Amon Carter Museum 79.95/10

125: *A Chance Meeting in the Desert*
Gelatin silver print, negative 1950, print later
13¹⁄₄ × 18³⁄₄″ (33.6 × 47.3 cm.)
Amon Carter Museum 79.95/81

126: *Mrs. Hardbelly*
Gelatin silver print, 1953
9¹³⁄₁₆ × 7¹³⁄₁₆″ (24.9 × 19.8 cm.)
Amon Carter Museum 79.128/106

Appendix
Chronological Bibliography

This bibliography is intended to serve as a record of Laura Gilpin's multifaceted career as it appeared in print throughout her long life as a photographer, writer, designer, and publisher. The extensive documentation in the bibliography was made possible because of Gilpin's tenacity in keeping almost every letter, salon catalogue, or publication that dealt with her life as a photographer. As a result, the Laura Gilpin Collection at the Amon Carter Museum is especially rich in salon catalogues, brochures, and periodicals from 1915 to 1940. The importance of the collection was further emphasized as I came to realize that many of the items were not duplicated in other collections. Therefore, it is hoped that future researchers will use this bibliography not only for research on Gilpin but also for research in the history of photography.

The arrangement of the bibliography is chronological. Each year is further subdivided by exhibitions (one-person and group); publications by, designed by, or about Laura Gilpin; and additional photographs published. Reviews and notices for each entry have been included when known. The citations are as complete as possible; brackets indicate ascribed dates or titles. An asterisk (*) indicates that an illustration by Gilpin appears in the work cited. Titles of photographs are listed as cited in the original publication. Post cards published and marketed as sets are included, but not those individually published.

MILAN R. HUGHSTON

1916
Publications
ABOUT LAURA GILPIN
"Our Competitions." *American Photography* 10 (July 1916): 397.

Additional Photographs Published
*"Our Competitions." *American Photography* 10 (November 1916): 632, *A Glimpse of the Canyon*.

1917
Exhibitions
GROUP
April 15–29:   Colorado Springs, Colo. Colorado Springs Art Society. *Spring Exhibition*. 3 prints. REVIEW: Cheney, Russell. "Critic Finds Many Pleasing Qualities in Spring Exhibition of Art Society." [Colorado Springs newspaper, April 1917].

September: Minneapolis, Minn. Minneapolis Institute of Arts. Pictorial Photographers of America. *An Exhibition of Pictorial Photography by American Artists* [Western group]. 1 print.

October: Newark, N.J. Newark Museum Association. Pictorial Photographers of America. *An Exhibition of Pictorial Photography by American Artists* [Eastern group]. 2 prints.

November: Chicago, Ill. Art Institute. PPA. *An Exhibition of Pictorial Photography by American Artists* [Western group]. 1 print.

November: New Britain, Conn. New Britain Institute. PPA. *An Exhibition of Pictorial Photography by American Artists* [Eastern group]. 2 prints.

December: St. Louis, Mo. City Art Museum. PPA. *An Exhibition of Pictorial Photography by American Artists* [Western group]. 1 print.

December 2–30:   Worcester, Mass. Worcester Art Museum. PPA. *An Exhibition of Pictorial Photography by American Artists* [Eastern group]. 2 prints.

December 18–January 12, 1918:   New York, N.Y. *Clarence H. White School Alumni Exhibition of Pictorial Photography*. 5 prints. REVIEW: "An Exhibition of Pictorial Photography." *Photographic Journal of America* 55 (February 1918): 78–79.

Additional Photographs Published
American Photography 11 (September 1917): 518, *Cloister at San Diego Exposition*.
Photo=Graphic Art 3 (October 1917): [7], *The Prelude*.
Edith Rubel Trio. [ca. 1917], cover, *The Trio*. Flyer.

1918

Exhibitions

GROUP

January: Toledo, Ohio. Museum of Art. PPA. *An Exhibition of Pictorial Photography by American Artists* [Western group]. 1 print.

January: Syracuse, N.Y. Museum of Fine Arts. PPA. *An Exhibition of Pictorial Photography by American Artists* [Eastern group]. 2 prints.

February: Detroit, Mich. Museum of Art. PPA. *An Exhibition of Pictorial Photography by American Artists* [Western group]. 1 print.

February: Buffalo, N.Y. Guild of Allied Arts. PPA. *An Exhibition of Pictorial Photography by American Artists* [Eastern group]. 2 prints.

March: Cleveland, Ohio. Cleveland Art Museum. PPA. *An Exhibition of Pictorial Photography by American Artists* [Western group]. 1 print.

March: Grand Rapids, Mich. Art Association. PPA. *An Exhibition of Pictorial Photography by American Artists* [Eastern group]. 2 prints.

April: Cincinnati, Ohio. Cincinnati Museum of Art. PPA. *An Exhibition of Pictorial Photography by American Artists* [Western group]. 1 print. REVIEW: "The Week in Art Circles." *Cincinnati Enquirer*, April 14, 1918.

[April]: New Orleans, La. Art Association. PPA. *An Exhibition of Pictorial Photography by American Artists* [Eastern group]. 2 prints.

May: [Montclair, N.J.]. PPA. *An Exhibition of Pictorial Photography by American Artists* [Western group]. 1 print.

May: Norman, Okla. University of Oklahoma. PPA. *An Exhibition of Pictorial Photography by American Artists* [Eastern group]. 2 prints.

Additional Photographs Published

*Swift, Eliza Morgan. "On the Prairie." *Scribner's Magazine* 63 (May 1918): 620, *The Prairie*.

Pictorial Photographers of America Annual Report 1918, opp. p. 11, *Still-Life [no. 1]*.

1919

Exhibitions

GROUP

July–August: Colorado Springs, Colo. Colorado Springs Art Society. *Summer Exhibition*. 5 prints. REVIEW: "Brilliant Canvases by Local Artists, Feature Exhibit in Antlers Parlor." *Colorado Springs Gazette*, July 20, 1919.

October: New York, N.Y. Camera Club of New York Galleries. [*Exhibition of Photographs of Joan of Arc Statue Photographic Competition*]. 1 print, honorable mention. REVIEW: "Joan of Arc Prize Winners." *New York Times*, October 10, 1919.

November 7–December 7: Indianapolis, Ind. Herron Art Institute. [*100 Prints from 1920 PPA Annual*]. 1 print.

December 10–January 5, 1920: Jackson, Mich. Art Association. [*100 Prints from 1920 PPA Annual*]. 1 print.

Additional Photographs Published

*Anderson, Paul L. *The Fine Art of Photography*. Philadelphia: J. B. Lippincott Co., 1919, opp. p. 168, *The Prelude*.

*Pictorial Photographers of America. *Pictorial Photography in America, 1920*. New York: Tennant and Ward, 1919, p. 47, *The Marble Cutters*.

1920

Exhibitions

GROUP

January 3–31: Los Angeles, Calif. Gallery of Fine and Applied Arts. Museum of History, Science and Art. Camera Pictorialists of Los Angeles. *Third International Photographic Salon*. 6 prints. REVIEW: Kales, Arthur F. "The Third Los Angeles Salon." *Photo-Era* 44 (April 1920): 167–174.

January 10–February 1: Portland, Oreg. Art Museum. *An Exhibition of Pictorial Photography under the Auspices of The Pictorial Photographers of America*. 4 prints.

January 15–30: Boston, Mass. Boston Society of Arts. [*100 Prints from 1920 PPA Annual*]. 1 print.

February 5–27: Rochester, N.Y. Mechanics' Institute. [*100 Prints from 1920 PPA Annual*]. 1 print.

March 11–28: Elmira, N.Y. Arnot Art Gallery. [*100 Prints from 1920 PPA Annual*]. 1 print.

April 5–21: Dubuque, Iowa. Art Association. *An Exhibition of Pictorial Photography by American Artists* [PPA traveling salon]. 4 prints.

April 13–28: New Bedford, Mass. [*100 Prints from 1920 PPA Annual*]. 1 print.

May 9–June 1: Charlottesville, Va. University of Virginia. [*100 Prints from 1920 PPA Annual*]. 1 print.

May 22–June 6: Colorado Springs, Colo. Broadmoor Art Academy. Perkins Hall. *Spring Exhibition*. 6 prints.

June 1–30: Colorado Springs, Colo. [Broadmoor Art Academy]. *An Exhibition of Pictorial Photography by American Artists* [PPA traveling salon]. 4 prints.

July 15–August 1: Denver, Colo. Art Association. *An Exhibition of Pictorial Photography by American Artists* [PPA traveling salon]. 4 prints. REVIEW: *"Photographers' Art

Collection Here." [Denver newspaper, July–August 1920], *Brenda Putnam.*

August 20–28: [Milwaukee, Wis.]. [Milwaukee Art Institute.] *An Exhibition of Pictorial Photography by American Artists* [PPA traveling salon]. 4 prints.

August 25–September 10: Copenhagen, Denmark. Copenhagen Photographic Amateur Club. *Exhibition 1920.* American Section. Collected under the auspices of PPA. 6 prints.

September 11–October 9: London, England. London Salon of Photography. *International Exhibition.* 3 prints. REVIEWS: *Tilney, F. C. "Some Pictures of the Year." *Photograms of the Year 1920.* London: Iliffe & Sons, 1921, p. 30, pl. 53, *The Prairie.* § *Tilney, F. C. "The London Exhibitions." *American Photography* 14 (December 1920): 657–668, 671, *The Prairie.*

Publications

ABOUT LAURA GILPIN
BY LAURA GILPIN
Portraiture by Photography. [Colorado Springs: published by the author, ca. 1920], [p. 1], *Margaret Carlson.* Brochure.

DESIGNED BY LAURA GILPIN
Portraiture by Photography.

ABOUT LAURA GILPIN
"Miss Gilpin Finds Inspiration in Art Museum of New Mexicans." *Colorado Springs Gazette,* July 4, 1920.

Additional Photographs Published

*Russell, C. P. "Artistic Settings for Photographs." *Printer's Ink Monthly,* January 1920, p. 51, *The Prelude.*
Broadmoor Art Academy, Colorado Springs, Colorado. Colorado Springs, [1920]. 4-pt. folding brochure, 5 illus.
*Mortimer, F. J., ed. *Photograms of the Year 1920.* London: Iliffe & Sons, 1921, p. 30, pl. 53, *The Prairie.*

1921

Exhibitions

ONE-PERSON
March 16–26: New York, N.Y. Clarence H. White School. *Exhibition of Photographs by Laura Gilpin.* REVIEW: "Exhibitions at the School." *Clarence H. White School of Photography Bulletin of the Alumni,* June 1921, [p. 4].

April: Los Angeles, Calif. Southern California Camera Club. [*Exhibition of Photographs by Laura Gilpin*]. 30 prints: portraits, still lifes, Southwest scenes.

August 1–15: Colorado Springs, Colo. Broadmoor Art Academy. *An Exhibition of Photographs by Laura Gilpin.* 61 prints; portraits, still lifes, Southwest scenes. REVIEWS: "Notes of the Broadmoor Art Academy." *Colorado Springs*

Gazette, August 7, 1921. § "Gilpin Exhibit Interesting Group of Photographs." *Colorado Springs Telegraph,* August 7, 1921.

[October]: Santa Fe, N.M. Museum of New Mexico. Art Museum. *An Exhibition of Photographs by Laura Gilpin.* 61 prints: portraits, still lifes, Southwest scenes. REVIEW: "Gilpin Art Photographs at Museum." *Santa Fe New Mexican,* October 15, 1921.

November: Denver, Colo. Denver Public Library. Denver Art Association. *Exhibition of Photographs Opening November 1, 1921.* 61 prints: portraits, still lifes, Southwest scenes. REVIEWS: Valle, M. R. F. "Art Association to Give Private View of Interesting Group of Photographs." *Rocky Mountain News,* October 30, 1921. § Valle, M. R. F. "Art Notes." *Rocky Mountain News,* November 6, 1921. § "Laura Gilpin Photographs Create Sensation in Denver." *Colorado Springs* [*Telegraph*], November 13, 1921. § Valle, M. R. F. "New Movement in Art to Remain." *Rocky Mountain News,* November 20, 1921. § [Eggers, George William]. "The Art of Laura Gilpin." *Allied Arts,* no. 2 (December 1921): xvii.

GROUP
January 4–31: Los Angeles, Calif. Gallery of Fine and Applied Arts. Museum of History, Science and Art. Camera Pictorialists of Los Angeles. *Fourth International Photographic Salon.* 3 prints.

March 7–26: Philadelphia, Pa. John Wanamaker. *Fifteenth Annual Exhibition of Photographs.* 4 prints; *In the Garden of the Gods* wins honorable mention.

May 1–22: Baltimore, Md. Peabody Gallery. Photographic Guild of Baltimore. *Exhibition of the Nineteen Hundred & Twenty-One Portfolio.* 10 prints. REVIEWS: "Artists and Their Work." *Baltimore News,* May 8, 1921. § Yardley, Elizabeth F. "News and Reviews of Art Events." *Baltimore American,* May 8, 1921. § *Baltimore Evening Sun,* May 10, 1921. § *"Examples of Photographic Art on View in Baltimore." *Baltimore American,* [May 1921], *The Prelude.*

September 10–October 8: London, England. London Salon of Photography. *International Exhibition.* 4 prints.

October 31–November 30: New York, N.Y. Art Center. *Pictorial Photographers of America Exhibition* [on the occasion of the opening of the building of the Art Center]. 2 prints.

December 13, 1921–January 2: Los Angeles, Calif. Los Angeles Museum. Camera Pictorialists of Los Angeles. *Fifth International Photographic Salon.* 1 print.

n.d.: New York, N.Y. Clarence H. White School of Photography. *Exhibition of Photographs by Alumni.* 3 prints.

Publications

ABOUT LAURA GILPIN

"Activities of the Alumni." *Clarence H. White School of Photography Bulletin of the Alumni*, June 1921, [p. 2].

Additional Photographs Published

*The Broadmoor Art Academy. *Colorado Springs, Colorado. 1921–1922.* New York: William Edwin Rudge, [1921]. 16 pp., 8 illus.
*Pictorial Photography in America, 1921. New York: Pictorial Photographers of America, 1921, p. 31, *Summer Portrait.*

1922

Exhibitions

ONE-PERSON

January–February: Ypsilanti, Mich. Normal Gallery. *An Exhibition of Photographs by Laura Gilpin.* 50 prints: portraits, still lifes, Southwest scenes. REVIEW: "Photography as an Art Proved by Normal Exhibit." [Ypsilanti newspaper, February 1922].

March: San Diego, Calif. Fine Arts Gallery. *An Exhibition of Photographs by Laura Gilpin.* 50 prints: portraits, still lifes, Southwest scenes. REVIEWS: "Unusual Photograph Exhibit Opens in Balboa Park Today." *San Diego Union*, March 1, 1922. § *Sun Dial* 1, no. 26 (March 23, 1922): cover, *Summer Portrait.* § "Pictorial Photographs on Exhibition." [San Diego newspaper, March 1922]. § "Unusual Treat to Friends of Art." [San Diego newspaper, March 1922].

May: Oakland, Calif. Art Gallery. *An Exhibition of Photographs by Laura Gilpin.* 50 prints: portraits, still lifes, Southwest scenes.

[June]: Stanford, Calif. University Art Museum. [*An Exhibition of Photographs by Laura Gilpin*]. 50 prints: portraits, still lifes, Southwest scenes.

July 28–November: San Francisco, Calif. Museum of Art. *An Exhibition of Photographs by Laura Gilpin.* 50 prints: portraits, still lifes, Southwest scenes.

GROUP

January–May 1923: American Federation of Arts circulated 162 prints from the PPA exhibition (October–November 1921) at the New York Art Center to Corvallis, Oreg.; Emporia, Kans.; College Station, Tex.; Greeley, Colo.; Muncie, Ind.; Washington, D.C.; Oxford, Ohio; Peoria, Ill.; Sioux Falls, S.D.; Birmingham, Ala.; Albany, N.Y. 2 prints.

January 28–February 28: Buffalo, N.Y. Albright Art Gallery. Buffalo Camera Club. *Third National Salon of Pictorial Photography.* 3 prints.

March 1–31: Pittsburgh, Pa. Carnegie Institute. Photographic Section, Academy of Science and Art of Pittsburgh. *Ninth Annual Pittsburgh Salon of Photography.* 1 print.

April 23–May 7: Colorado Springs, Colo. Broadmoor Art Academy. Perkins Hall. *Spring Exhibition by Active Members Association.* 5 prints.

May 20–June 18: San Francisco, Calif. Palace of Fine Arts. Pictorial Photographic Society of San Francisco. *First Annual International Exhibition of Pictorial Photography.* 4 prints.

September 9–October 7: London, England. London Salon of Photography. *International Exhibition.* 3 prints.

November 20–December 11: Los Angeles, Calif. Los Angeles Museum. Camera Pictorialists of Los Angeles. *Sixth International Salon of Photography.* 3 prints.

December 28–January 12, 1923: New York, N.Y. Art Center. Pictorial Photographers of America. [*Exhibition of Prints from PPA Annual, 1922*]. 1 print. REVIEW: "[PPA Exhibition]." *American Magazine of Art* 14 (February 1923): 71.

Publications

ABOUT LAURA GILPIN

*Sauter, Mary G. "Laura Gilpin's Work." *Camera Craft* 29 (September 1922): 419–421. 4 illus.
"Laura Gilpin Honored." *Colorado Springs Evening Telegraph*, September 2, 1922.

Additional Photographs Published

*The Broadmoor Art Academy, *Colorado Springs, Colorado, 1922.* Colorado Springs: Dentan Printing Co., 1922. 14 pp., 6 illus.
*Mortimer, F. J., ed. *Photograms of the Year, 1922.* London: Iliffe & Sons, 1923, pl. 63, *The Prelude.*
*Pictorial Photography in America, 1922. New York: Pictorial Photographers of America, 1922, p. 87, *The Moon of the Red Gods.*

1923

Exhibitions

GROUP

March: Portland, Maine. Society of Art. *Prize Winning Prints in the Third Annual Competition Organized by American Photography.* 2 prints.

March 2–31: Pittsburgh, Pa. Carnegie Institute. Photographic Section, Academy of Science and Art of Pittsburgh. *Tenth Annual Pittsburgh Salon of Photography.* 2 prints.

March 10–April 2: Buffalo, N.Y. Albright Art Gallery. Buffalo Camera Club. *Fourth Annual Salon of Pictorial Photography.* 3 prints.

[April–May]: Springfield, Mass. Public Library. *Prize Winning Prints in the Third Annual Competition Organized by American Photography*. 2 prints.

[April–May]: New York, N.Y. Camera Club of New York. *Prize Winning Prints in the Third Annual Competition Organized by American Photography*. 2 prints.

April 15–29: Colorado Springs, Colo. Broadmoor Art Academy. Perkins Hall. *Annual Exhibition by Professional Members*. 7 prints.

April 21–28: New York, N.Y. Grand Central Palace. *First International Photographic Arts and Crafts Exposition*. 4 prints.

[May]: Boston, Mass. Y.M.C.U. Camera Club. *Prize Winning Prints in the Third Annual Competition Organized by American Photography*. 2 prints.

May 3–31: New York, N.Y. Art Center. *International Salon of the Pictorial Photographers of America*. 3 prints. REVIEWS: "International Camera Salon at the Art Centre." *New York Evening World*, May 29, 1923. § *Mason, Joseph R. "The Camera Contest at the International Salon." *Shadowland* 8 (July 1923): 64, *Sardine Fishers*.

[June]: New York, N.Y. Clarence H. White School of Photography. *Exhibit of Photographs by Alumni*. 3 prints.

June: Colorado Springs, Colo. Broadmoor Art Academy. *Prize Winning Prints in the Third Annual Competition Organized by American Photography*. 2 prints.

June: Pueblo, Colo. McClelland Library. *Prize Winning Prints in the Third Annual Competition Organized by American Photography*. 2 prints.

June: Denver, Colo. Art Association. *Prize Winning Prints in the Third Annual Competition Organized by American Photography*. 2 prints.

July–August: San Diego, Calif. Y.M.C.A. *Prize Winning Prints in the Third Annual Competition Organized by American Photography*. 2 prints.

July–August: Oakland, Calif. Art Association. *Prize Winning Prints in the Third Annual Competition Organized by American Photography*. 2 prints.

August 25–September 8: Toronto, Canada. Toronto Camera Club. *Thirty-Second Annual Salon* [part of Canadian National Exhibition]. 8 prints.

August 31–October 7: San Francisco, Calif. [Palace of the Fine Arts]. Pictorial Photographic Society of San Francisco. *Second Annual International Exhibition of Pictorial Photography*. 2 prints.

September 8–October 6: London, England. London Salon of Photography. *International Exhibition*. 1 print.

September 17–October 27: London, England. Royal Photographic Society of Great Britain. *68th Annual Exhibition*. 1 print.

October 14–November 11: Oakland, Calif. Art Association. Pictorial Photographic Society of San Francisco. *Second Annual International Exhibition*. 2 prints.

October 15–November 5: Los Angeles, Calif. Los Angeles Museum. Camera Pictorialists of Los Angeles. *Seventh International Salon of Photography*. 1 print.

November 5–17: Seattle, Wash. *The Frederick and Nelson Fourth Annual Salon of Pictorial Photography*. 7 prints.

[December–January]: Denver, Colo. Camera Club. [Annual Exhibition]. 6 prints.

Publications

BY LAURA GILPIN

Some Thoughts on Portraiture. [Colorado Springs: published by the author, ca. 1923], cover, *Louisa Graham*. Brochure.

Additional Photographs Published

*Fisher, Theo. M. "Denver Civic Centre." *Architectural Record* 53 (March 1923): 189–201. [8] illus.

*"The Camera Contest: Looking Backward." *Shadowland* 8 (March 1923): 62, *We*; wins first prize.

*Fraprie, Frank R. "Our Third Annual Competition." *American Photography* 17 (April 1923): 223, *The Prelude*; wins fifth prize and honorable mention.

Shadowland 8 (July 1923): 41, *The Prelude*.

Shadowland 9 (September 1923): 32, *A String of Peppers*.

The Broadmoor Art Academy, 1923. Colorado Springs: Dentan Printing Co., 1923. 18 pp., 7 illus.

The Edith Rubel Trio. [ca. 1923], *The Prelude*. Circular.

*Gillies, John Wallace. *Principles of Pictorial Photography*. New York: Falk Publishing Co., 1923, p. 56, *Sunlight and Shadow*.

The Nutrition School Camp, Colorado Springs, Colorado. Colorado Springs: Glockner Sanitorium, 1923. 10 pp., 8 illus.

Winning Health in the Pikes Peak Region: Colorado Springs – Manitou. Colorado Springs: Chamber of Commerce, 1923. 18 illus. REVIEWS: "Health Book Finest Ever Issued Here." [Colorado Springs newspaper, 1923]. § "Will Interest Health Seeker." [Colorado Springs newspaper, 1923]. § *Advertisement. In *Literary Digest* 80 (January 19, 1924): 59. 3 illus. § "Health Booklet and Ads Getting Speedy Results." [Colorado Springs newspaper, January–February 1924].

1924

Exhibitions

ONE-PERSON

January 10–February 6:   New York, N.Y. Art Center. [*Exhibition of Photographs by Laura Gilpin*]. 16 prints: portraits, still lifes, Southwest scenes. REVIEWS: "Skillful Photography." *New York Sun*, January 18, 1924. § *New York Herald*, January 20, 1924.

April 1–30:   St. Louis, Mo. Art Museum. *Photographs of Colorado Scenes and Other Subjects*. 56 prints: portraits, still lifes, Southwest scenes.

[May–June]:   Baltimore, Md. Maryland Academy of Sciences. Baltimore Photographic Club. [*An Exhibition of Photographs by Laura Gilpin*]. 40 prints: portraits, still lifes, Southwest scenes. REVIEWS: Brown, Warren Wilmer. "Photographs Exhibited at Academy." *Baltimore News*, June 3, 1924. § "Photographic Exhibition by Laura Gilpin Highly Praised." [Colorado Springs newspaper, June 1924].

GROUP

March 2–31:   Pittsburgh, Pa. Carnegie Institute. Photographic Section, Academy of Science and Art of Pittsburgh. *Eleventh Annual Pittsburgh Salon of Photographic Art*. 1 print.

April 25–May 4:   London, England. Hammersmith Hampshire House Photographic Society. *Hampshire House Exhibition*. 1 print.

June 1–15:   Colorado Springs, Colo. Broadmoor Art Academy. *Annual Exhibition*. 6 prints. REVIEW: Putnam, Brenda. "'Have You Seen Exhibit?' Is Enthusiastic Question of Noted Visiting Artist." [Colorado Springs newspaper, June 1924].

August 23–September 6:   Toronto, Canada. Toronto Camera Club. *Thirty-Third Annual Salon* (part of Canadian National Exhibition). 2 prints.

September 6–October 4:   London, England. London Salon of Photography. *International Exhibition, 1924*. 1 print.

September 15–October 25:   London, England. Royal Photographic Society of Great Britain. *69th Annual Exhibition*. 2 prints. REVIEWS: *Illustrated Catalogue*, opp. p. 41, *The New Baby*. § "The Pictorial Section." *Photographic Journal* 64 (October 1924): 432.

[October]:   Denver, Colo. Denver Art Association. Denver Camera Club. [*Annual Exhibition*].

October 14–November 3:   *Los Angeles, Calif. Los Angeles Museum. Camera Pictorialists of Los Angeles. *Eighth International Salon of Photography*. 2 prints. REVIEW: *Hanna, Forman G. "The Los Angeles Salon." *Pictorialist*, December 1924, opp. p. 8, *Summer in the Garden of the Gods*.

October 31–December 7:   San Francisco, Calif. California School of Fine Arts. Pictorial Photographic Society of San Francisco. *Third Annual International Exhibition of Pictorial Photography*. 2 prints.

Publications

BY LAURA GILPIN

The Colorado Springs Day Nursery. Colorado Springs: Dentan Printing Co., 1924. 36 pp., 18 illus. REVIEW: "Book Describing Day Nursery on Sale Here." [Colorado Springs newspaper, December 1924].

DESIGNED BY LAURA GILPIN

The Colorado Springs Day Nursery.

ABOUT LAURA GILPIN

"Broadmoor Art Academy." *Colorado Springs Gazette and Telegraph*, January 20, 1924.

Additional Photographs Published

New York Art Center Bulletin 2 (January 1924): cover, *The Marble Cutters*.

DuBois Acorn: The Photographic Number (July 1924). Rochester, N.Y.: DuBois Press, 1924. 4 illus.

American Girl 7 (October 1924): 7, *Colorado Springs Girl Scouts*.

The Broadmoor Art Academy. Colorado Springs, Colorado. Colorado Springs: Dentan Printing Co., 1924. 18 pp., 6 illus.

Camera Pictures. New York: Alumni Association, Clarence H. White School of Photography, 1924, *Summer, Garden of the Gods*.

*Howe, Percy, ed. *American Annual of Photography, 1924*. New York: American Annual of Photography, 1923, p. 125, *I Will Lift Up Mine Eyes to the Hills*.

1925

Exhibitions

ONE-PERSON

n.d.:   Norman, Okla. University of Oklahoma. Department of Fine Arts. [*An Exhibition of Photographs by Laura Gilpin*]. 50 prints: portraits, still lifes, Southwest scenes.

GROUP

March 3–31:   Pittsburgh, Pa. Carnegie Institute. Photographic Section, Academy of Science and Art of Pittsburgh. *Twelfth Annual Pittsburgh Salon of Photographic Art*. 1 print. REVIEWS: Rankin, David. "Twelfth Annual Pittsburgh Salon of Photographic Art." *Pittsburgh Bulletin*, March 14, 1925. § Fraprie, Frank R. "Some Spring Picture Shows–Pittsburgh." *American Photography* 19 (June 1925): 312.

March 16–21:   New York, N.Y. Clarence H. White School of Photography. *Exhibition of Photographs by the Students and Alumni*. 4 prints.

April 1–June 1:   Fort Wayne and Indianapolis, Ind. Fort Wayne Art School and John Herron Art Institute. *Second Annual Salon of Pictorial Photography*. 4 prints.

May 10–June 24:   Colorado Springs, Colo. Broadmoor Art Academy. *Tenth Annual Exhibition*. 6 prints. REVIEW: "Annual Exhibit of Colorado Springs Artists Is Show of Charm and Beauty." [*Colorado Springs Gazette* or *Telegraph*, May 11, 1925].

May 19–June 15:   New York, N.Y. Art Center. *Second International Salon of Pictorial Photography*. 3 prints. REVIEWS: Robinson, Karl Davis. "Pictorial Photographers of America." *New York Art Center Bulletin* 3 (June 1925): 280. § Robinson, Karl Davis. "The New York Salon." *American Photography* 19 (August 1925): 432.

August 29–September 12:   Toronto, Canada. Toronto Camera Club. *Thirty-Fourth Annual Salon* [part of Canadian National Exhibition]. 3 prints.

September 12–October 10:   London, England. London Salon of Photography. *International Exhibition*. 2 prints. REVIEW: Tilney, F. C. "American Photography at the London Exhibitions." *American Photography* 19 (December 1925): 664.

September 14–October 24:   London, England. Royal Photographic Society of Great Britain. *70th Annual Exhibition*. 1 print. REVIEW: Tilney, F. C. "American Photography at the London Exhibitions." *American Photography* 19 (December 1925): 656.

October 12–31:   Seattle, Wash. *The Frederick and Nelson Sixth Annual Salon of Pictorial Photography*. 6 prints. REVIEWS: "Camera Art Opens Sixth Salon Here." *Seattle Post-Intelligencer*, October 13, 1925. § Geithman, Harriet. "Seattle's Sixth Annual Salon of Pictorial Photography." [Seattle publication, October 1925]. § "Miss Gilpin's Photo Wins $100 Award." [Colorado Springs newspaper, October–November 1925]. § *Albee, Elvira. "The Frederick and Nelson Sixth Annual Salon of Pictorial Photography." *Camera Craft* 32 (December 1925): 596, *The Visiting Nurse*.

December 19–January 10, 1926:   Turin, Italy. Nella Galleria Centrale d'Arte. Gruppo Piemontese per la Fotografia Artistica and Societa Fotografica Subalpina. *Primo Salon Italiano d'Arte Fotografica Internazionale*. 2 prints.

n.d.:   Denver, Colo. Denver Camera Club. [*Annual Exhibition*]. 10 prints.

Publications

BY LAURA GILPIN

"Exhibit of Prints at Perkins Hall Draws Interested Crowd." [*Colorado Springs Telegraph*, February 1925].

"Exhibition of Etchings Attracts Good Crowds." *Colorado Springs Telegraph*, February 22, 1925.

"More Processes Described in Intaglio Printing Here." *Colorado Springs Gazette*, February 26, 1925.

"Print Exhibit Here Will Close Today." [*Colorado Springs Telegraph*, March 1925].

"Copper Etching Is Job for Experts." [*Colorado Springs Telegraph*, March 1925].

"Few Examples of Lithography Shown at Art Exhibit Here." *Colorado Springs Gazette*, March 3, 1925.

ABOUT LAURA GILPIN

Eliot, Jean. "Festival to Make Music History." *Washington Times*, October 29, 1925.

Additional Photographs Published

New York Art Center Bulletin 3 (March 1925): 182, *The Gate*.

Ninety-Eight.Six 7 [a journal edited at Cragmor Sanitorium, Colorado Springs], March 19, 1925, cover, *Summer in the Garden of the Gods*.

Pictorial Supplement to Ninety-Eight.Six 7 (April 30, 1925). 5 illus.

*Waring, James J., M.D. "The Climate of Denver." *Municipal Facts* 8 (May–June 1925): 11, 13–14. 3 illus.

New York Times, October 18, 1925, *Frederick Jacobi*.

Theatre Magazine 42 (November 1925): 34, *Harold Bauer*.

Vogue, December 15, 1925, *Harold Bauer*.

The Broadmoor Art Academy, Colorado Springs. Colorado Springs: Dentan Printing Co., 1925. 18 pp., 7 illus.

Cragmor. Colorado Springs, Colorado. Colorado Springs: Dentan Printing Co., [1925]. 16 pp., 8 illus.

*Howe, Percy Y., ed. *American Annual of Photography, 1925*. New York: American Annual of Photography, 1924, p. 63, *Charles Eaton*.

*The Mowry Creamery Co. Colorado Springs, [1925], *Punches*. Leaflet.

1926

Exhibitions

ONE-PERSON

February 1–28:   San Francisco, Calif. California Camera Club. [*Photographs by Laura Gilpin*]. 27 prints: portraits, still lifes, Southwest scenes.

July: Santa Fe, N.M. Fine Arts Museum, Museum of New Mexico. [*Photographs by Laura Gilpin*]. 37 prints: Southwest scenes—Taos, Laguna, Mesa Verde. REVIEWS:

"Interesting and Beautiful Exhibits at State Museum." *Santa Fe New Mexican*, [July 1926]. § "Museum Events." *El Palacio* 21 (July 15, 1926): 50.

GROUP

[January]: Denver, Colo. Denver Camera Club. [*Annual Exhibition*]. 13 prints.

January 4–31: Los Angeles, Calif. Los Angeles Museum. Camera Pictorialists of Los Angeles. *Ninth International Salon of Photography*. 3 prints.

March 14–April 18: Pittsburgh, Pa. Carnegie Institute. Photographic Section, Academy of Science and Art of Pittsburgh. *Thirteenth Annual Pittsburgh Salon of Photographic Art*. 1 print.

May 16–30: Colorado Springs, Colo. Broadmoor Art Academy. *Eleventh Annual Exhibition*. 5 prints. REVIEW: "Varied Works in Show at Broadmoor Academy." [Colorado Springs newspaper, May 1926].

August 28–September 11: Toronto, Canada. Toronto Camera Club. *Thirty-Fifth Annual Salon of Photography* [part of Canadian National Exhibition]. 2 prints.

September 6–11: New Westminster, British Columbia, Canada. Royal Agricultural and Industrial Society. *Sixth Annual International Salon of Pictorial Photography*. 6 prints.

September 11–October 9: London, England. London Salon of Photography. *International Exhibition*. 2 prints.

September 13–October 9: London, England. Royal Photographic Society of Great Britain. *71st Annual Exhibition*. 1 print. REVIEWS: "Art of the Modern Photographer." *Times*, September 11, 1926. § *The Year's Photography, 1926*, the Exhibition Number of *Photographic Journal*, April [*sic*] *Blossoms*.

September 14–October 5: Portland, Oreg. Burlington House. Oregon Camera Club. *First Annual Oregon International Salon of Pictorial Photography*. 2 prints.

September 25–October 10: Antwerp, Belgium. Stedelijke Feestzaal. Koninklijke Fotografische Kring. *International Salon van Fotografische Kunst*. 5 prints.

October 17–31: San Francisco, Calif. California Palace of the Legion of Honor. Pictorial Photographic Society of San Francisco. *Fourth International Exhibition of Pictorial Photography*. 2 prints.

November 15–December 13: Los Angeles, Calif. Los Angeles Public Library. Southern California Camera Club. *Fifth Annual Western Salon of Pictorial Photography, 1926*. 1 print.

December 1–31: Washington, D.C. United States National Museum, Arts and Industries Building. *The Pictorial Section from the 71th [sic] Annual Exhibition of the Royal Photographic Society of Great Britain*. 1 print.

December 3–January 8, 1927: Glasgow, Scotland. People's Palace Museum. *The Scottish International Salon of Pictorial Photography*. 3 prints.

December 15–30: Los Angeles, Calif. Southwest Museum. Southern California Camera Club. *Fifth Annual Western Salon of Pictorial Photography, 1926*. 1 print.

Publications

BY LAURA GILPIN

*"The Dream Pictures of My People." *Art and Archaeology* 22 (July–August 1926): 12–19, 46. 9 illus.

*"The Need for Design in Photography." *American Annual of Photography* 40 (1926): 154–156; 155, *Still Life* [No. 2].

The Pikes Peak Region: Reproductions from a Series of Photographs by Laura Gilpin. Colorado Springs: Gilpin Publishing Co., 1926. 16 pp., 15 illus. REVIEWS: "Gilpin Pub. Co. Issues New Booklet." [Colorado Springs newspaper, 1926]. § "Miss Gilpin's Book Is Full of Interest." [Colorado Springs newspaper, 1926]. § *Echo* 4 (July 1926): 18.

DESIGNED BY LAURA GILPIN

The Pikes Peak Region.

ABOUT LAURA GILPIN

*Eggers, George William, ed. "News and Comment of Art World." *Rocky Mountain News*, January 3, 1926, p. 8, *Laguna Mission*.

*Adams, Mildred. "A Worker in Light." *Woman Citizen* 54 (March 1926): 10–11. 4 illus.

Additional Photographs Published

Echo 4 (February 1926): 7, *The Square Tower House*.

Echo 4 (April 1926): 14, *Christus, Chartres*.

Echo 4 (June 1926): 8, *Indian Youth*.

*"The Pikes Peak Region." *Your First Reminder* 64 (August 1926). Colorado Springs: Dentan Printing Co., 1926. 5 illus.

The Broadmoor Art Academy. Colorado Springs, 1926. Colorado Springs: Dentan Printing Co., 1926. 24 pp., 8 illus.

Edith Farnsworth's Book Shop. Colorado Springs, [1926], [*Interior*]. Handbill.

Pictorial Photography in America, Volume 4. New York: Pictorial Photographers of America, 1926, p. 59, *Square Tower House*.

1927

Exhibitions

GROUP

[January]: Denver, Colo. Denver Camera Club. [*Annual Exhibition*]. 5 prints.

January 1–31:   Los Angeles, Calif. Los Angeles Museum. Camera Pictorialists of Los Angeles. *Tenth International Salon of Photography*. 1 print.

March 26–April 19:   Liverpool, England. Walker Art Gallery. International Circle of Pictorial Photographers. *Third Annual Exhibition*. 4 prints.

April 16–May 1:   Brussels, Belgium. Musées Royaux du Cinquantenaire. *Salon International d'Art Photographique*, organized by *L'Art Photographique* and *Photographie Moderne*. 1 print.

May 29–June 12:   Colorado Springs, Colo. Broadmoor Art Academy. *Twelfth Annual Exhibition*. 5 prints.

August 27–September 10:   Toronto, Canada. Toronto Camera Club. *Thirty-Sixth Annual Salon of Photography* [part of Canadian National Exhibition]. 2 prints.

September 5–27:   New Westminster. British Columbia, Canada. Royal Agricultural and Industrial Society. *Seventh Annual International Salon of Pictorial Photography*. 7 prints; wins bronze medal.

September 8–October 3:   Warsaw, Poland. *Katalog Pierwszego Miedzynarodowego Salonu Fotografji Artystycznej w Warszawie*. 2 prints.

September 12–October 8:   London, England. Royal Photographic Society of Great Britain. *72nd Annual Exhibition*. 2 prints. REVIEWS: "The Royal Photographic Society's Exhibition: The Natural History Section." *British Journal of Photography*, September 30, 1927. § *The Year's Photography, 1927*, Exhibition Number of *Photographic Journal*, *The Frosted Tree*.

September 14–October 2:   Budapest, Hungary. *II. Nemzetközi Müvészi Fényképkiállitása*. 4 prints.

October 1–16:   Paris, France. Photo-Club of Paris and French Society of Photography. *XXIIe Salon International d'Art Photographique*. 3 prints.

October 30–November 20:   Los Angeles, Calif. Los Angeles Public Library. Los Angeles Camera Club. *All-American Photographic Salon, 1927*. 3 prints.

Publications

BY LAURA GILPIN

*"The Art of Portraiture." *Camera Portraits by Laura Gilpin*. [Colorado Springs: published by the author, 1927], cover, *Louisa Graham*.

**Furniture by Francis Gilpin, 1215 Wood Avenue, Colorado Springs*. [Colorado Springs: published by the author, 1927]. Brochure, 9 illus.

**The Mesa Verde National Park: Reproductions from a Series of Photographs by Laura Gilpin*. Colorado Springs: Gilpin Publishing Co., 1927. 20 pp., 19 illus. REVIEWS: "Books and Authors." *New York Times Book Review*,

July 24, 1927. § "Mesa Verde Pictures." *New York Times*, July 30, 1927. § "Triumphant Photography." *Echo* 5 (August 1927): 23. § Dodge, Faith. "Travlgram [*sic*]." *Gary*, [Ind.] *Post-Tribune*, August 12, 1927.

**Photographs of the Southwest by Laura Gilpin*. [Colorado Springs: published by the author, 1927]. 4 photogravures issued in folder.

DESIGNED BY LAURA GILPIN

**Camera Portraits by Laura Gilpin*.

**Furniture by Francis Gilpin, 1215 Wood Avenue, Colorado Springs*.

**The Mesa Verde National Park*.

**Photographs of the Southwest by Laura Gilpin*.

Additional Photographs Published

**First Methodist Episcopal Church, Colorado Springs. *Bulletin*, April 3, 1927, cover, [*Plains East of Colorado Springs*].

**The Broadmoor Art Academy, Colorado Springs, 1927*. Colorado Springs: Dentan Printing Co., 1927. 24 pp., 11 illus.

**Fraprie, Frank R., and E. J. Wall, eds. *American Annual of Photography, 1927*. Boston: American Photographic Publishing Co., 1926, p. 102, *Snow Coral*.

**Imperilled Monuments of Early American History*. Published by the Society for the Restoration and Preservation of the New Mexican Missions, 1927, [p. 4], *Laguna Pueblo*. REVIEW: *"Old Missions Being Preserved as Landmarks." *Rocky Mountain News*, June 19, 1927, *Laguna Pueblo*.

1928

Exhibitions

ONE-PERSON

July: Cleveland, Ohio. Cleveland Photographic Society. [*Exhibition of Photographs by Laura Gilpin*]. 65 prints: portraits, still lifes, Southwest scenes. REVIEWS: "Our Exhibit This Month." *Thru the Darkroom Door* (publication of the Cleveland Photographic Society) 3 (July 1928): [2]. § "An Exhibit by Laura Gilpin." *Thru the Darkroom Door* 3 (August 1928): [4].

August: Akron, Ohio. Portage Camera Club. [*Exhibition of Photographs by Laura Gilpin*]. 65 prints: portraits, still lifes, Southwest scenes. REVIEW: Griner, Metta K. "The Realm of Art." *Akron Sunday Times*, August 12, 1928.

September: Chicago, Ill. Chicago–Fort Dearborn Camera Club. [*Exhibition of Photographs by Laura Gilpin*]. 65 prints: portraits, still lifes, Southwest scenes.

October: Rochester, N.Y. Kodak Park Camera Club. [*Exhibition of Photographs by Laura Gilpin*]. 65 prints: portraits, still lifes, Southwest scenes.

January: Los Angeles, Calif. Los Angeles Museum. Camera Pictorialists of Los Angeles. *Eleventh International Salon of Photography*. 1 print.

March 9–27: Prague, Czechoslovakia. [*1st International Salon of Pictorial Photography at Prague*]. 1 print.

March 17–April 15: Pittsburgh, Pa. Carnegie Institute. Photographic Section, Academy of Science and Art of Pittsburgh. *Fifteenth Annual Pittsburgh Salon of Photographic Art*. 2 prints. REVIEW: *"Photographic Salon Opens." *Pittsburgh Post-Gazette*, March 19, 1928, *The Flower Garden*.

[April]: New York, N.Y. Camera Club of New York. *International Invitation Salon of 1928*. 1 print.

May 27–June 10: Colorado Springs, Colo. Broadmoor Art Academy. *Thirteenth Annual Exhibition*. 5 prints.

June 1–16: Seattle, Wash. Frederick and Nelson Auditorium. Seattle Camera Club. *Fourth International Exhibition of Pictorial Photography*. 2 prints. REVIEW: Koike, Dr. K. "Fourth Seattle International Exhibition of Pictorial Photography." *Notan* (Bulletin of the Seattle Camera Club) 50 (July 13, 1928): [2].

June 2–18: Arnhem, Netherlands. *Internationale Foto-Salon, 1928*. 3 prints.

June 23–28: Amsterdam, Netherlands. *Internationale Foto-Salon, 1928*. 3 prints.

July 15–August 15: Rotterdam, Netherlands. *Internationale Foto-Salon, 1928*. 3 prints.

August 24–September 8: Toronto, Canada. Toronto Camera Club. *Thirty-Seventh Annual Salon of Photography* [part of Canadian National Exhibition]. 1 print.

September 3–8: New Westminster, British Columbia, Canada. The Bursill Gallery. Royal Agricultural and Industrial Society. *Eighth Annual Salon of Fine Art and Pictorial Photography*. 6 prints; wins silver medal.

September 8–October 6: London, England. London Salon of Photography. *International Exhibition*. 2 prints.

September 10–October 7: San Francisco, Calif. California Palace of the Legion of Honor. Pictorial Photographic Society of San Francisco. *Fifth International Exhibition of Pictorial Photography*. 3 prints. REVIEW: *San Francisco Chronicle*, September 23, 1928.

September 17–October 13: London, England. Royal Photographic Society of Great Britain. *73rd Annual Exhibition*. 1 print. REVIEW: *Tilney, F. C. *Pictorial Photography Exhibited at the Royal Photographic Society of Great Britain, 1928: A Critical Dissertation*. London: Fountain Press, 1928, pl. 68, *Narcissus*.

October 6–21: Paris, France. Photo-Club of Paris and French Society of Photography. *XXIIIe Salon International d'Art Photographique de Paris*. 1 print.

October 19–31: Stockholm, Sweden. *Internationella Fotografiska Salongen*. 4 prints.

November 18–December 10: Los Angeles, Calif. Los Angeles Public Library. Los Angeles Camera Club. *All-American Photographic Salon*. 3 prints.

December 23–January 6, 1929: Antwerp, Belgium. [Organized by a photographic society called "Iris".] *IIe Internationaal Kerstsalon von Fotografie te Antwerpen Borgerhout*. 3 prints.

n.d.: Colorado Springs, Colo. Colorado Springs Mountain Club. *Annual Exhibition*. 5 prints; wins blue and red ribbons.

Publications

BY LAURA GILPIN

"The Fine Art of Photography." *Ninety-Eight.Six* 30 (May 24, 1928): 7.

ABOUT LAURA GILPIN

Women of the West, comp. and ed. Max Binheim. Los Angeles: Publishers Press, 1928, p. 108.

Additional Photographs Published

*First Methodist Episcopal Church, Colorado Springs. *Bulletin*, February 5, 1928, cover, *An Indian Fire Ceremony*.

*First Methodist Episcopal Church, Colorado Springs. *Bulletin*, Easter Sunday 1928, cover, *Anemone*.

*"Art in Denver." *Lookout* [from the Denver Public Library] 1 (April 1928). 4 illus.

*"Denver Architects Win Special Recognition." *Rocky Mountain News*, April 15, 1928, *Polo Club, Denver*.

The Broadmoor Art Academy, Colorado Springs, 1928. Colorado Springs: Dentan Printing Co., 1928. 24 pp., 9 illus.

*Fraprie, Frank R., and E. J. Wall, eds. *American Annual of Photography, 1928*. Boston: American Photographic Publishing Co., 1927, p. 77, *House of the Cliff Dwellers*.

The Greenwood Camp of the Girl Scouts, Colorado Springs, 1928, [*Camp*].

San Luis School. Boarding Department. Colorado Springs, Colorado. [Colorado Springs, 1928]. 12 pp., 7 illus.

1929

Exhibitions

ONE-PERSON

August: Chicago, Ill. Chicago–Fort Dearborn Camera Club. [*Exhibition of Photographs by Laura Gilpin*]. 63 prints: portraits, still lifes, Southwest scenes.

October 1–15:   Denver, Colo. Denver Artist's Guild. [*Photographs by Laura Gilpin*]. 18 prints: portraits, still lifes, Southwest scenes. REVIEW: "Has Photo Exhibit in Denver Artist's Guild." [Colorado Springs newspaper, October 11, 1929].

GROUP

January: Los Angeles, Calif. Los Angeles Museum. Camera Pictorialists of Los Angeles. *Twelfth International Salon of Photography*. 2 prints.

January 5–28:   Buffalo, N.Y. Albright Art Gallery. Buffalo Camera Club. *Tenth Annual Salon of Pictorial Photography*. 5 prints.

February 9–23:   Edinburgh, Scotland. [Edinburgh Photographic Society]. *67th Annual Open Exhibition*. 2 prints.

March 23–April 22:   Pittsburgh, Pa. Carnegie Institute. Photographic Section, Academy of Science and Art of Pittsburgh. *Sixteenth Annual Pittsburgh Salon of Photographic Art*. 1 print.

April 15–27:   New York, N.Y. Art Center. *Third International Salon of the Pictorial Photographers of America*. 3 prints. REVIEWS: "Method of Judging." *Light and Shade* 1 (April 1929): 8–9. § Martin, Ira W. "The P.P.A. Third International." *Light and Shade* 1 (May 1929): 6–7, 9. § Haz, Nicholas. "The Third International Salon of the Pictorial Photographers of America." *American Photography* 23 (July 1929): 341–344. § "The P.P.A. Salon in Retrospect" [Defense of criticism of jury]. *Light and Shade* 2 (October 1929): 6–7, 10. § Gilpin, Laura. "Correspondence . . . The Third International Salon of the Pictorial Photographers of America: In Answer to Mr. Haz." *American Photography* 23 (November 1929): 625–626.

May 1–15:   New York, N.Y. Camera Club of New York. *Second International Invitation Salon*. 1 print. REVIEW: [Haz, Nicholas]. "The Second Invitation Salon of the Camera Club, New York." *American Photography* 23 (July 1929): 344–350.

May 19–June 2:   Colorado Springs, Colo. Broadmoor Art Academy. *Fourteenth Annual Exhibition*. 5 prints; wins honorable mention. REVIEW: F.R.C. "West's Color and Strength Exemplified in Canvases at Broadmoor Exhibition." [Colorado Springs newspaper, May–June 1929].

June 6–30:   New York, N.Y. American Museum of Natural History. Camera Club of New York. *Second International Invitation Salon*. 1 print.

October 28–November 12:   Pittsburgh, Pa. Carnegie Institute. [*Photographs from Pictorial Photography in America, Volume 5*]. 1 print.

December 5–January 5, 1930:   Rochester, N.Y. Memorial Art Gallery. *First Rochester International Salon of Photog-raphy*. 3 prints. REVIEWS: Matthews, Glenn E. "The First Rochester International Salon of Photography." *American Photography* 24 (March 1930): 113–126. § Beardsley, A. H. "First Rochester International Salon of Photography." *Photo-Era Magazine* 64 (April 1930): 176–186.

Publications

BY LAURA GILPIN

"Correspondence . . . In Answer to Mr. Haz." *American Photography* 23 (November 1929): 625–626.

*A Monograph on the Work of William E. Fisher, Arthur A. Fisher, Architects. Colorado Springs: Dentan Printing Co., 1929. 29 half-tone reproductions issued in folder with a foreword by George William Eggers.

DESIGNED BY LAURA GILPIN

*A Monograph on the Work of William E. Fisher, Arthur A. Fisher, Architects.

ABOUT LAURA GILPIN

"The Cup Competition." *Light and Shade* 2 (October 1929): 7.

Additional Photographs Published

*Light and Shade 1 (January 1929): 5, *Sunrise on the Desert*.
*Light and Shade 1 (April 1929): 7, *Square Tower House*.
*American Photography 23 (July 1929): 343, *Flower Garden*.
**"The Editor's Variorum." *House Beautiful* 66 (August 1929): 141, *Narcissus*.
**Beattie, Barbara. "Preparing Your Daughter for Adolescence." *Parents Magazine* 4 (October 1929): 17, [*Girl Scout*].
**Fraprie, Frank R., and E. J. Wall, eds. *American Annual of Photography, 1929*. Boston: American Photographic Publishing Co., 1928, p. 91, *Narcissus*.
*Pictorial Photography in America, Volume 5. New York: Pictorial Photographers of America, 1929, pl. 37, *The Frosted Pine Tree*.

1930

Exhibitions

ONE-PERSON

March: Honolulu, Hawaii. Academy of Arts. [*Exhibition of Photographs by Laura Gilpin*]. 26 prints: portraits, still lifes, Southwest scenes. REVIEWS: **"Etchings and Photographs." *Honolulu Star-Bulletin*, March 15, 1930, *The Frosted Pine*. § **"Art Demonstration at the Academy by Dr. Tetsuzan Hori." [*Honolulu Advertiser*, March 16, 1930], *Hymn to the Sun*. § "Art Photographs Draw Visitors to Art Academy." *Honolulu Star-Bulletin*, March 22, 1930. § "Photographic Art." [Honolulu newspaper, March 23, 1930].

March 1–15: Milwaukee, Wis. Art Institute. Photo Pictorialists of Milwaukee. [*Fifty Prints by Laura Gilpin*]. 50 prints: portraits, still lifes, Southwest scenes. REVIEW: *Milwaukee Art Institute Bulletin* 3 (March 1930): 6.

April: Reading, Pa. Camera Club. [*Fifty Prints by Laura Gilpin*]. 50 prints: portraits, still lifes, Southwest scenes.

[April–May]: New York, N.Y. Camera Club. [*Photographs by Laura Gilpin*].

May: East Orange, N.J. Camera Club. [*Fifty Prints by Laura Gilpin*]. 50 prints: portraits, still lifes, Southwest scenes.

[May]: Washington, D.C. Library of Congress. [*Photographs by Laura Gilpin*]. 16 prints.

June: Indianapolis, Ind. Herron Art Institute. Indianapolis Camera Club. [*Photographs by Laura Gilpin*]. REVIEW: Morehouse, Lucille E. "Pictorial Photography Exhibit Includes Three Noted Artists." *Indianapolis Sunday Star*, June 8, 1930.

n.d.: Baltimore, Md. [*Fifty Prints by Laura Gilpin*]. 50 prints: portraits, still lifes, Southwest scenes.

GROUP

January: Dayton, Ohio. Art Institute. [*50 Prints from Pictorial Photography in America, Volume 5*]. 1 print.

February: St. Louis, Mo. Art Museum. [*50 Prints from Pictorial Photography in America, Volume 5*]. 1 print.

March: Denver, Colo. Art Museum. [*50 Prints from Pictorial Photography in America, Volume 5*]. 1 print. REVIEWS: Bear, Donald. "Photography as Art Seen in Collection of Pictures from New York at Museum." *Rocky Mountain News*, March 1930. § *"Calendar–Denver Art Museum." *Rocky Mountain News*, March 16, 1930, *The Frosted Pine Tree*.

May 4–18: Colorado Springs, Colo. Broadmoor Art Academy. *Fifteenth Annual Exhibition*. 5 prints.

[June]: Seattle, Wash. Art Institute. Seattle Camera Club. *Fifth International Exhibition*. 1 print.

July: Trondhjem, Norway. Trondhjems Kamera Klub. *2. Internationale Fotografiutstilling i Norge*. 6 prints.

December 4–January 4, 1931: Rochester, N.Y. Memorial Art Gallery. *Second Rochester International Salon of Photography*. 2 prints.

n.d.: Tokyo, Japan. *Sixth Annual and First International Photographic Exhibition*. 3 prints.

Publications

BY LAURA GILPIN

*With Boyd St. Clair. *A Printer's Reader: Your First Reminder*. Colorado Springs: Dentan Printing Co.,

February 1930. 43 pp., 1 illus. Booklet/calendar.
"Epilogue." *A Printer's Reader*.
"Exhibit of Prints Is Rare Treat." *Colorado Springs Gazette*, March 23, 1930.
"Exhibition of Photo Prints at Studio Room Interesting." [Colorado Springs newspaper, 1930].
"Reproductions." *A Printer's Reader*.
"Type designs." *A Printer's Reader*.

DESIGNED BY LAURA GILPIN

Glockner Sanatorium. Colorado Springs, Colorado. Colorado Springs: Dentan Printing Co., [1930]. 28 pp., 22 illus.
A Printer's Reader [with Boyd St. Clair].

Additional Photographs Published

*Evarts, Hal G. "The Lure of the Southwest." *World's Work* 59 (March 1930): 110, *Pueblo of Santa Clara*.
*"[Robert S. Gast Residence, Pueblo, Colorado]." *Architect* 14 (April 1930): 63–69. 4 illus.
Fanny Robbins' Travelogue. Colorado Springs, [1930]. 3-part folding brochure, 3 illus.
The Fountain Valley School of Colorado. [1930]. Large folding brochure, 5 illus.
The Fountain Valley School of Colorado. Opening September 1930. New York: William E. Rudge, [1930]. 22 pp., 5 illus.
Glockner Sanatorium. Colorado Springs, Colorado. Colorado Springs: Dentan Printing Co. [1930]. 28 pp., 22 illus.
San Luis School. Colorado Springs, Colorado. Colorado Springs: Dentan Printing Co. [1929–1930]. 21 pp., 5 illus.
San Luis Open Air School, 1930–1931, Announcing the New Location. [Colorado Springs, 1930]. 16 pp., 6 illus.
Visiting Nurse Association. [1930], [*Visiting Nurse*]. Bookmark.

1931
Exhibitions

ONE-PERSON

December 5–18: Colorado Springs, Colo. Broadmoor Art Academy. *Exhibition of Photographs by Laura Gilpin*. 70 prints: portraits, still lifes, Southwest and Indian scenes. REVIEWS: "Spring's Artist to Show Pictures at Academy." [Colorado Springs newspaper, December 5, 1931]. § Brown, F. Martin. "Laura Gilpin Opens Exhibition of Prints at Art Academy." *Colorado Springs Gazette*, December 6, 1931. § *S.H.M. "The Seacoast of Bohemia: The Art of Laura Gilpin." *PikeSpeaker* 1 (December 11, 1931): 16–17. 2 illus.

GROUP

January: Los Angeles, Calif. Los Angeles Museum. Camera Pictorialists of Los Angeles. *Fourteenth International*

Salon of Photography. 3 prints. REVIEW: *"Camera Art." Los Angeles Sunday Times, January 11, 1931, Potters of Santa Clara.

March 20–April 19: Pittsburgh, Pa. Carnegie Institute. Photographic Section, Academy of Science and Art of Pittsburgh. Eighteenth Annual Pittsburgh Salon of Photographic Art. 1 print.

September 12–October 10: London, England. Royal Photographic Society of Great Britain. 76th Annual Exhibition. 1 print.

December: Denver, Colo. Chapell House. Denver Camera Club. [Annual Exhibition]. REVIEW: Bear, Donald J. "The Seacoast of Bohemia: Chapell House Exhibit." Pike-Speaker 1 (December 11, 1931): 17, 27.

Publications

ABOUT LAURA GILPIN

"Await Laura Gilpin's Fiesta Photos Eagerly." Santa Fe New Mexican, [Fall 1931].

"Laura Gilpin's Southwest Photos [lantern slides] Delight Scientists." Santa Fe New Mexican, [Fall 1931].

"Our Travel Salons." Light and Shade 4 (December 1931): 9.

Additional Photographs Published

*The Sportsman 9 (January 1931): 28, Polo; wins first place in magazine's photo contest.

*Broadmoor Art Academy, 1931. 8 pp., [3] illus.

*Los Alamos Ranch School. Otowi, Sandoval County, New Mexico. Colorado Springs: Dentan Printing Co., [1931]. 34 pp., 9 illus. [designed by LG?]

*The Pictorialist [a compilation of photographs from the Fourteenth Annual International Salon of Pictorial Photography under the auspices of the Camera Pictorialists of Los Angeles]. 1931, pl. 34, Flight.

1932

Exhibitions

ONE-PERSON

July 1–30: New York, N.Y. Camera Club of New York. Exhibition of Photographs by Laura Gilpin [and 5 other women]. 20 prints: Southwest scenes.

September 19–October: Santa Fe, N.M. Laboratory of Anthropology. [Photographs of Yucatán by Laura Gilpin]. 48 prints.

October: Colorado Springs, Colo. Broadmoor Art Academy. Greenhouse Gallery. An Exhibition of Photographs of Central City by Laura Gilpin, Taken During the Production of "Camille." 44 prints.

December 4–10: Denver, Colo. Chappell House. An Exhibition of Photographs of Central City by Laura Gilpin, Taken During the Production of "Camile." 44 prints. REVIEW: *Shafroth, Janet Durrie. "Cast Photographs Shown." Rocky Mountain News, December 25, 1932, Lillian Gish.

December 10–12: Washington, D.C. Carnegie Institution. Exhibition Representing Results of Research Activities of the Carnegie Institution of Washington. Yucatán prints.

GROUP

January: Los Angeles, Calif. Camera Pictorialists of Los Angeles. Fifteenth Annual Salon of Pictorial Photography. 2 prints.

January 18–30: New York, N.Y. Art Center. Pictorial Photographers of America. Second Travel Salon, 1931–32. 3 prints.

February: Jacksonville, Fla. David Strawn Art Gallery. [Laura Gilpin, Imogen Cunningham, and Doris Ulmann].

[February–September]: PPA Second Travel Salon, 1931–32 to: Northern Illinois State Teachers College; University of Illinois; Alabama Museum; Massachusetts State College; Orange Camera Club; San Luis Obispo Library; M. H. de Young Memorial Gallery; Patterson, N.J. Public Library. 3 prints

March: Philadelphia, Pa. Pennsylvania Museum of Art, Sixty-Ninth Street Branch. First Annual Philadelphia International Salon of Photography. 3 prints.

October 18–November 5: New York, N.Y. National Alliance of Art and Industry. Exhibition of Photographs for Art and Industry. 5 prints.

Publications

BY LAURA GILPIN

*Pictorial Lantern Slides of the Southwest by Laura Gilpin. [Colorado Springs: published by the author, 1932]. Brochure, 8 illus.

DESIGNED BY LAURA GILPIN

*Colorado Springs Psychopathic Hospital. Colorado Springs: Dentan Printing Co., [1932]. 34 pp., [27] illus.

*Pictorial Lantern Slides of the Southwest by Laura Gilpin.

ABOUT LAURA GILPIN

"Distinguidos Turistas Norteamericanos en Mérida." Diario del Sureste, April 3, 1932.

"Paleontologist to Pursue Homo Sapiens' Trail Back to Pre-Pleistocene Times." Santa Fe New Mexican, September 19, 1932.

Additional Photographs Published

*Kerbey, McFall. "Colorado, a Barrier That Became a

Goal." *National Geographic* 62 (July 1932): 8, *Footprints in the Sands of a Miniature Desert.*

*"[Cast of *Camille*, Central City Opera House]." *Theatre Arts Monthly* 16 (October 1932): 850–852. 3 illus.

**The Broadmoor Art Academy, 1932, Colorado Springs, Colorado.* 12 pp., [2] illus.

**Dedication of Mary Reed Library, University of Denver, October 26, 27, 28, 1932.* Denver, 1932, p. 3, *Mrs. Verner Z. Reed.*

**The Fountain Valley School of Colorado.* Colorado Springs: Dentan Printing Co., [1932]. 30 pp., 13 illus. [designed by LG?]

**The Pictorialist* [a compilation of photographs from the Fifteenth Annual International Salon, Camera Pictorialists of Los Angeles]. 1932, pl. 43, *Sand Dunes.*

1933
Exhibitions
ONE-PERSON

January: Brooklyn, N.Y. Brooklyn Institute of Arts and Sciences. [*Exhibition of Photographs by Laura Gilpin*]. 24 prints.

December 1–15: Denver, Colo. Art Museum. Chappell House. *Photographs of the Yucatan and Southwest.* REVIEW: *Douglas, F. H. "Laura Gilpin Photographs of Chichen Itza Shown." *Rocky Mountain News*, December 10, 1933, *Temple of the Three Lintels.*

GROUP

January 3–31: Los Angeles, Calif. Los Angeles Museum. Camera Pictorialists of Los Angeles. *Sixteenth Annual International Salon of Pictorial Photography.* 3 prints.

February 4–28: San Francisco, Calif. M. H. de Young Museum. Camera Pictorialists of Los Angeles. *Sixteenth Annual International Salon of Pictorial Photography.* 3 prints.

May 6–June 26: Philadelphia, Pa. Pennsylvania Museum of Art. *Second Philadelphia International Salon of Photography.*

[June–?]: Chicago, Ill. Camera Club. *A Century of Progress International Exhibition: International Salon of Photography.* 2 prints.

Publications
BY LAURA GILPIN

**Los Alamos Ranch School. Photo Supplement, 1933.* [n.p., published for Los Alamos Ranch School, 1933]. 12 pp., 12 illus.

ABOUT LAURA GILPIN

Ormes, Manly D. *The Book of Colorado Springs.* Colorado Springs: Dentan Printing Co., 1933, p. 340.

Additional Photographs Published
*"[Set from *The Merry Widow*, Central City Opera House]." *Theatre Arts Monthly* 17 (August 1933): 586.

1934
Exhibitions
ONE-PERSON

January: New York, N.Y. American Museum of Natural History. *Photographs of the Yucatan and Southwest.* 92 prints.

February–April: Washington, D.C. Library of Congress. *Photographs of the Yucatan and Southwest.* [85] prints.
REVIEW: Mechlin, Leila. *Washington Star*, February 25, 1934.

n.d.: Bloomfield Hills, Mich. Cranbrook Academy of Art. *Photographs of the Yucatan and Southwest.*

n.d.: Colorado Springs, Colo. Taylor Museum. *An Exhibition of Photographs of the Mayan Ruins at Chichen Itza.* 47 prints.

GROUP

April 10–?: Denver, Colo. Chappell House. [*100 Print Travel Salon, Pictorial Photographers of America*].

April 21–May 6: Colorado Springs, Colo. Broadmoor Art Academy. Greenhouse Gallery. *19th Annual Exhibition by Professional Members.* 5 prints.

August 24–September 8: Toronto, Canada. Toronto Camera Club. *Forty-Third Annual Toronto Salon of Photography* [part of Canadian National Exhibition]. 3 prints.

Publications
BY LAURA GILPIN

**Pictorial Lantern Slides of the Southwest.* [Colorado Springs: published by the author, 1934]. 8 illus. Rental brochure.

DESIGNED BY LAURA GILPIN

**Pictorial Lantern Slides of the Southwest.*

**Saint Martins Chapel*, Denver. Colorado Springs: Dentan Printing Co., [1934]. 20 pp., 7 illus. REVIEW: Bear, Donald J. "Booklet Tells of Beauty of St. Martin's Chapel." *Denver News*, April 8, 1934.

Additional Photographs Published
**Fanny Robbins': The House of Delectable Sweets and Beautiful Things.* Colorado Springs, n.d. 4-part folding brochure, 5 illus.

**First Methodist Episcopal Church, Colorado Springs.* Bulletin, August 26, 1934, cover, *Colorado Springs at the Foot of Pikes Peak.*

**The Fountain Valley School of Colorado.* Colorado Springs: Dentan Printing Co., [1934]. 14 pp., 15 illus. [designed by LG?]

*Strong, William M. *Photography for Fun*. New York: Leisure League of America, 1934, *Polo*.

1935
Exhibitions
ONE-PERSON

June 1–10: Wellesley Heights, Mass. Beacon School. *Photographs of the Yucatan and Southwest*. 59 prints.

November–December: Los Angeles, Calif. Southwest Museum. *Photographs of the Yucatan and Southwest*. 83 prints.

GROUP

April 25–May 8: Madrid, Spain. Sociedad Fotográfica de Madrid. *XI Salon Internacional de Fotografía de Madrid*. 3 prints.

Publications
BY LAURA GILPIN

Friendfield Turkeys, Woodland Park, Colorado. [Colorado Springs: published by the author, ca. 1935]. 2-part folding brochure, 1 illus., [*Turkey Farm*].

DESIGNED BY LAURA GILPIN

Brownmoor School, Santa Fe, New Mexico. [1935] 24 pp., [3] illus. [designed by LG?]

Friendfield Turkeys, Woodland Park, Colorado.

San Luis Open Air School. Colorado Springs, Colorado. [n.d., post-1930] 26 pp., [16] illus. [designed by LG?]

San Luis Ranch School. Colorado Springs, Colorado. [1935] 26 pp., [23] illus. [designed by LG?]

Additional Photographs Published

Colorado Springs Fine Arts Center. 1935 Summer School. Colorado Springs, Colorado, [*Exterior, Colorado Springs Fine Arts Center*].

*Jordan, Franklin I. *Photographic Enlarging*. Rochester, N.Y.: Folmer Graflex Corp., 1935, p. 129, *Ranchos de Taos Church*.

*Luhan, Mabel Dodge. *Winter in Taos*. Denver: Sage Books, 1935, opp. p. 121, *Goat*.

*Maloney, T. J., ed. *U.S. Camera, 1935*. New York: William Morrow & Co., 1935, p. 122, *Steps of the Castillo*.

1936
Exhibitions
ONE-PERSON

January: Claremont, Calif. Scripps College. *Photographs of the Yucatan and Southwest*. [50] prints.

March: Norman, Okla. University of Oklahoma. *Photographs of the Yucatan and Southwest*. [50] prints.

April 12–June 8: Chicago, Ill. Museum of Science and Industry. *Photographs of the Yucatan and Southwest*. [81] prints.

June: Colorado Springs, Colo. Taylor Museum. [*Photographs of Navajo, Pueblo and Mesa Verde*]. 39 prints.

GROUP

April: Colorado Springs, Colo. Fine Arts Center. [*Inaugural Exhibition*]. REVIEW: *"Fine Arts Center Opening Marks New Era for Region." *Colorado Springs Gazette and Telegraph*, April 19, 1936. [3] illus.

June 6–July 4: Colorado Springs, Colo. Fine Arts Center. *Group Exhibition of Work by Professional Members*. 5 prints.

July 1–August 12: St. Louis, Mo. City Art Museum. *International Pictorial Photography*. 1 print.

September 28–October 12: New York, N.Y. Rockefeller Center, Mezzanine Galleries. *Prints from U.S. Camera Annual* [1936]. 1 print.

Publications
ABOUT LAURA GILPIN

"Indian Talk." *Louisville* [Ky.] *Herald-Post*, February 20, 1936.

Carmack, Donie. "She Pictures the Southwest." *Louisville Courier-Journal*, February 22, 1936.

"The C.M.C. Pictures." *Trail and Timberline*, no. 212 (June 1936): 61–62.

Fisher, Irene. "Somebody Told Me." *Albuquerque Tribune*, October 20, 1936.

Additional Photographs Published

*"[Donald L. Gilpin Home, Colorado Springs]." *Architecture* 73 (April 1936): 223–228. 9 illus.

*"The L. C. Phipps' Estate in Denver, Colorado." *Country Life* 70 (May 1936): 25–29. 15 illus.

*"Colorado Springs Fine Arts Center." *Architectural Forum* 65 (July 1936): 11–20. 9 illus.

*Allen, Parker B. *New Mexico: Impressions of an Eastern Visitor*. Meriden, Conn.: Columbiad Club, 1936. 4 illus.

*Maloney, T. J., ed. *U.S. Camera, 1936*. New York: William Morrow & Co., 1936, p. 41, [*Infant on Wood Floor*].

1937
Exhibitions
ONE-PERSON

February–March 15: Buffalo, N.Y. Museum of Science. *Photographs of the Yucatan and Southwest*. 47 prints.

GROUP

March 29–April 17: New York, N.Y. American Museum of Natural History. Pictorial Photographers of America.

Fourth International Salon. 4 prints. REVIEW: *"Through the Camera's Eye." Natural History* 39 (May 1937): 343–352. 2 illus.

May 16–June 13: San Francisco, Calif. Museum of Art. San Francisco Art Association and Photographic Society of San Francisco. *San Francisco Invitational Salon of International Photography.* 1 print.

[Summer]: Colorado Springs, Colo. Fine Arts Center. *Twenty-Second Annual Exhibition of the Work of Professional Members.* 5 prints.

September 11–October 9: London, England. Royal Photographic Society of Great Britain. *82nd Annual Exhibition.* 3 prints. REVIEWS: *The Year's Photography, 1937–1938.* London: Royal Photographic Society, 1937, pls. 47, 59. 2 illus. § *"A Great Monument of Mediaeval America." Illustrated London News* 101 (October 2, 1937): 557, *Castillo Steps.*

Publications

BY LAURA GILPIN

Pictorial Post Cards of the Southwest by Laura Gilpin. Set No. 1, Navajo; Set No. 2, Acoma; Set No. 3, Mesa Verde; Set No. 4, Navajo. Colorado Springs: Gilpin Publishing Co., 1937. 6 illus. in each set.

Post Cards of the Colorado Springs Fine Arts Center. Colorado Springs: Gilpin Publishing Co., 1937. [29] illus.

DESIGNED BY LAURA GILPIN

Pictorial Post Cards of the Southwest by Laura Gilpin.

Post Cards of the Colorado Springs Fine Arts Center.

Sandia School. Albuquerque, New Mexico. Colorado Springs: Dentan Printing Co., [1937]. 36 pp., 39 illus. [designed by LG?]

The Will Rogers Shrine of the Sun. Broadmoor, Colorado Springs, Colorado. Colorado Springs: Dentan Printing Co., 1937. 16 pp., 10 illus.

ABOUT LAURA GILPIN

White, Mrs. Clarence H. "Camera's Eye View of Careers." *Independent Woman* 16 (February 1937): 48.

Additional Photographs Published

Fountain Valley School of Colorado, Colorado Springs. Year Book: Class of 1937, [portraits, groups, and scenes].

Los Alamos Ranch School. Otowi, New Mexico. [1937]. 16 pp., [5] illus.

Maloney, T. J., ed. U.S. Camera, 1937. New York: William Morrow & Co., 1937, p. 168, *Temple of the Warriors from the Castillo.*

Perry-Mansfield Round-Up Camps for Girls; Club Camp for Adults and Theatre Arts School. Steamboat Springs, Colo., 1937. 26 pp.

Taylor, G. Herbert. My Best Photograph and Why. New York: Dodge Publishing Co., 1937, p. 34, *Navaho Woman and Child.*

1938

Exhibitions

ONE-PERSON

February–March 15: Santa Fe, N.M. School of American Research. *Photographs of the Yucatan and Southwest.* 65 prints sent.

GROUP

[April]: Colorado Springs, Colo. Fine Arts Center. [*Photographs from U.S. Camera, 1937*]. 1 print. REVIEW: Gilpin, Laura. "Miss Gilpin Picks Best at Camera Salon Photographic Exhibition at Arts Center." [*Colorado Springs Gazette* or *Telegraph*, April 25, 1938].

April 1–15: Denver, Colo. Denver Photographic Society. *The First Annual Rocky Mountain National Salon of Photography.* 4 prints.

April 13–28: New York, N.Y. American Museum of Natural History. Pictorial Photographers of America. *Fifth International Salon of Photography.* 5 prints.

May 24–July: Paris, France. Musée de Jeu de Paume. *Trois Siècles d'Art aux États-Unis.* American Architecture Section. 3 prints.

Publications

BY LAURA GILPIN

"Los Poblanos Ranch: The Estate of Mr. and Mrs. Albert Gallatin Simms, Albuquerque, New Mexico." Country Life 73 (March 1938): 80–85. 22 illus.

Pictorial Post Cards of the Southwest by Laura Gilpin. Set No. 5, Taos Pueblo; Set No. 6, San Ildefonso and Santa Clara Pueblos; Set No. 7, El Santuario de Chimayo; Set No. 8, Ranchos de Taos Church. Colorado Springs: Gilpin Publishing Co., 1939. 6 illus. in each set.

DESIGNED BY LAURA GILPIN

Pictorial Post Cards of the Southwest by Laura Gilpin. Set

San Luis Ranch School. Colorado Springs: Dentan Printing Co., 1938. 22 pp., [4] illus.

ABOUT LAURA GILPIN

"Laura Gilpin Opposes Photographic Gadgets." [Colorado Springs high school newspaper, January 21, 1938].

Johnston, J. Dudley. "My Experiences in America." *Photographic Journal* 78 (April 1938): 251.

Additional Photographs Published

"Chichen Itza – in Old Yucatan." Country Life 73 (February 1938). 3 illus.

James Sykes. On handbill advertising his concert at Town Hall, New York, February 20, 1938.

Country Life 73 (March 1938): 69, *Casa Blanca, Canyon de Chelly*.

*Stembridge, Jasper H. "Man's Occupations around the World, No. 11." *Pictorial Education*, August 1938, *San Ildefonso Interior*.

Perry-Mansfield Western Round-Up Camps. Steamboat Springs, Colo., 1938. 24 pp.

1939
Exhibitions
ONE-PERSON

December: Colorado Springs, Colo. Fine Arts Center. [*Photographs of the Yucatan and Southwest by Laura Gilpin*]. [75] prints: portraits, Yucatán and Southwest scenes. REVIEW: *["Photographs by Laura Gilpin."] *Colorado Springs Gazette*, December 23, 1939, *Old Woman, Acoma Pueblo*.

GROUP

February 15–March 15:   New York, N.Y. Museum of Modern Art. *Three Centuries of American Architecture*. 3 prints.

April 26–May 5:   Copenhagen, Denmark. Kunstindustrimuseet. *The Copenhagen Salon of Photography*. 3 prints.

Publications
DESIGNED BY LAURA GILPIN

Sandia School. Albuquerque, New Mexico. [1939]. 40 pp., 43 illus.

Additional Photographs Published
*"Art Center and Cheyenne Zoo Win Praises from Brenda Putnam, Noted Sculptor Visitor." [Colorado Springs newspaper, 1939], [*Brenda Putnam at Fine Arts Center*].

*"Building Types: Community Theaters." *Architectural Record* 86 (October 1939): 102, *Theatre, Colorado Springs Fine Arts Center*.

Egon Petri. In leaflet promoting his 1939 American tour.

Mesa Verde. On U.S. Post Office 4¢ commemorative stamp, National Park Series.

1940
Exhibitions
ONE-PERSON

January–February 15:   Dallas, Tex. Dallas Historical Society. *Photographs of the Yucatan and Southwest*. 112 prints sent. REVIEWS: Crocker, Elizabeth. "Yucatan Prints by L. Gilpin at State Hall." *Dallas Morning News*, January 18, 1940. § Heartsill, Graydon. "High Notes and High Lights in the World of Arts." *Dallas Times Herald*, January 29, 1940.

March 13–22:   St. Louis, Mo. Washington University, School of Architecture. *American Indians of the Southwest; Mayan Architecture of Yucatan*.

GROUP

[June 1–21]:   New York, N.Y. Photographic Society of America. *Invitation Salon, World's Fair of 1940*. 2 prints.

August 23–September 7:   Toronto, Canada. Toronto Camera Club. *Forty-Ninth Annual International Toronto Salon of Photography* [part of Canadian National Exhibition]. 2 prints.

Publications
BY LAURA GILPIN

Pictorial Post Cards of the Southwest by Laura Gilpin. Set No. 9, Canyon de Chelly. Colorado Springs: Gilpin Publishing Co., ca. 1940–1942. 6 illus.

DESIGNED BY LAURA GILPIN

Pictorial Post Cards of the Southwest by Laura Gilpin.

Additional Photographs Published
*Von Qualen, Lillian. "Horsemanship Training in the Rockies." *Rider and Driver*, February 1940. 3 illus.

*Mangravite, Peppino. "Saints and a Death Angel." *Magazine of Art* 33 (March 1940): 160–165. 8 illus.

*Valliant, George C. "Chichen Itza." *Natural History* 46 (June 1940): 9–20. 15 illus.

U.S. Camera, no. 11 (October 1940): 13, [*Monkey in Cage*].

*Campbell, Hayworth, ed. *Modern Masters of Photography: Series 1, Pictorialists*. New York: Galleon Press, [1940], *Helen Freeman as Olympe in "Camille."*

*Fergusson, Erna. *Our Southwest*. New York: A. A. Knopf, 1940, opp. pp. 194 & 230. 2 illus. REVIEW: *Woods, Katherine. *New York Times*, May 5, 1940, *Canyon de Chelly*.

*Kubler, George. *Religious Architecture of New Mexico*. Colorado Springs: Taylor Museum, 1940. 38 illus.

*Maloney, T. J., ed. *U.S. Camera, 1940*. New York: Random House, 1939, opp. pp. 191 & 193. 2 illus.

New Mexico: A Guide to the Colorful State. Comp. Writer's Program of the Work Projects Administration in the State of New Mexico. 1940. 11 illus.

1941
Exhibitions
GROUP

June 25–28:   Oakland, Calif. Hotel Leamington. Western Amateur Camera Conclave. *Second Invitational Show*. 4 prints.

Publications

BY LAURA GILPIN

*The Pueblos: A Camera Chronicle. New York: Hastings House, 1941. 124 pp., 76 illus. SELECTED REVIEWS: Ellingson, H. K. Colorado Springs Gazette, January 18, 1942. § [Tucson] Arizona Daily Star, January 18, 1942. § Mott, Harvey L. [Phoenix] Arizona Republic, January 18, 1942. § "Photographic Book of the Pueblos Is Beautiful Work." Gallup Gazette, January 22, 1942. § *Chicago Sun, January 24, 1942. 2 illus. § King, Art. "Pueblo Civilization Is as Old as Egypt." Winston-Salem Sentinel, January 25, 1942. § Stein, Herbert. "Amerika-Bilderbozen." Staats-Zeitung und Herold, January 25, 1942. § Coit, E. Architectural Record 91 (February 1942): 30. § Blanton, Ben. "Pueblo Indian Homes Pictured by Laura Gilpin." Houston Post, February 1, 1942. § Rouse, Katherine E. Monroe City [Mo.] News, February 5, 1942. § "Story of the Pueblos." Oakland [Calif.] Post-Enquirer, February 7, 1942. § Salt Lake City Deseret News, February 18, 1942. § Boyle, Lois F. El Paso Times, February 22, 1942. § "A Reader's List." New Republic, February 23, 1942. § "Life of Pueblos Shown in Photos with Good Text." Hartford [Conn.] Times, February 26, 1942. § "Pueblo Pictures." Washington Post, March 1, 1942. § "A Camera Chronicle of the Pueblos." Christian Science Monitor, March 7, 1942. § "A Picture Story of the Pueblos." St. Louis Post Dispatch, April 5, 1942. § Weston, Sam. "Pictures Magnificent." San Diego Union, April 12, 1942. § Snow, Edith A. "Our South West." Worcester Telegram, April 12, 1942. § Fisher, Clyde. "Your New Books." Natural History 49 (May 1942): 291. § Fergusson, Erna. "Dealing with the Indian." New York Herald-Tribune, November 8, 1942.

ABOUT LAURA GILPIN

Parker, Paul. "Photography Exhibit at Art Center Shows Fine Work Here." Colorado Springs Gazette and Telegraph, January 26, 1941.

Additional Photographs Published

*U.S. Camera, no. 14 (February 1941): 13, Pueblo.

*American Artist 5 (April 1941): cover, Peppino Mangravite.

*Complete Photographer 1 (October 20, 1941): ff. p. 216, Pueblo Bonito.

*Complete Photographer 2 (December 10, 1941): fol. p. 544. 2 illus.

*Maloney, T. J., ed. U.S. Camera, 1941, Volume II. New York: Duell, Sloan & Pearce, 1940, p. 180, The Water Hole.

*Rhode Island School of Design. Bulletin of the Museum of Art 29 (1941): cover, Caracol, Incense Burners.

1942

Exhibitions

ONE-PERSON

February 6–22:   Rochester, N.Y. Memorial Art Gallery. Photographs of the Yucatan and Southwest. 87 prints. REVIEWS: "New Exhibits Open This Week at Memorial, Rundel, Bevier." Rochester Democrat and Chronicle, February 1, 1942. § Croughton, Amy H. "Photographs of Southwest." Rochester Times-Union, February 13, 1942. § Herdle, Isabel C. "Gallery Shows Gilpin Photos." Rochester Democrat and Chronicle, February 15, 1942.

GROUP

February 23–May 23:   Chicago, Ill. Lakeside Press Galleries. Modern American Photography. 9 prints.

Publications

BY LAURA GILPIN

*"Historic Architecture Photography: The Southwest." Complete Photographer 6 (July 20, 1942): 1986–1995. 10 illus.

ABOUT LAURA GILPIN

"Photographer, Writer." [Boeing Plane Talk, n.d.].

Rowley, Gladys. "Reno Revue." [Reno, Nevada, newspaper, 1942].

"Wealth of Photographic Material Is Found by Girl Cameraman at Boeing's." [Wichita Eagle or Beacon, n.d.].

Additional Photographs Published

During Gilpin's tenure at Boeing, many of her photographs recording life at the plant in Wichita found their way into print. The two primary sources are Boeing Plane Talk (an in-house newsletter published at the plant) and two Wichita newspapers, the Beacon and the Eagle. These citations are not included here, but the clippings can be found in scrapbooks in the Laura Gilpin Collection at the Amon Carter Museum.

*Complete Photographer 3 (January 30, 1942): 913, Chapel Interior.

*Complete Photographer 4 (March 20, 1942): 1214, Square Tower House.

*Complete Photographer 5 (July 10, 1942): 1940, [Photographic Greeting Card].

*Complete Photographer 6 (August 20, 1942): 2186, Desert Sunrise.

*Complete Photographer 6 (September 10, 1942): opp. p. 2313, Cheyenne Mountain School.

*Complete Photographer 7 (September 20, 1942): fol. p. 2376. 2 illus.

*Complete Photographer 7 (September 30, 1942): fol. p. 2440, Desert Butte.

*Chamberlain, Samuel, ed. Fair Is Our Land. New York: Hastings House, 1942. 2 illus.

*Maloney, T. J., ed. *U.S. Camera, 1942*. New York: Duell, Sloan & Pearce, 1941, p. 176, *Dew on Foliage*.

1943
Exhibitions
ONE-PERSON

April: Wichita, Kans. Art Association. [*Photographs of the Yucatán and Southwest*].   REVIEW: "Photographic Prints Are Displayed." *Wichita Beacon*, April 11, 1943.

November 22–December 31:   Seattle, Wash. University of Washington. Henry Art Gallery. *Photographs by Laura Gilpin*. 92 prints.

GROUP

September 15–November 15:   Chicago, Ill. Field Museum of Natural History. *Lenses on Nature: First International Photographic Exhibit*. 2 prints.

Publications
ABOUT LAURA GILPIN

"Judges Selected for Photo Show." [*Wichita Beacon* or *Eagle*, August–September 1943].

Additional Photographs Published
*Arnold, Oren. "Allemande Left and Promenade All." *Woman's Day* (July 1943): 16–17. 4 illus.
*Maloney, T. J., ed. *U.S. Camera, 1943*. New York: Duell, Sloan & Pearce, 1942, p. 75, *Big Bed, Tiny Tot*.

1944
Exhibitions
GROUP

May 13–28:   Wichita, Kans. Wichita Art Museum. Wichita Photographic Society. *1944 Wichita International Salon of Photography*. 4 prints.

Publications
ABOUT LAURA GILPIN

"Public Relations Job Is One of Friendly Relations between All." *Boeing Plane Talk*, August 11, 1944.

1945
Exhibitions
ONE-PERSON

July 23–August 2:   Chautauqua, N.Y. Chautauqua Woman's Club. *Exhibition of Photographs: Navajo & Mayan*.

GROUP

March 4–18:   Wichita, Kans. Wichita Art Museum. The Wichita Photographic Society. *Second Wichita International Salon of Photography*. 4 prints (*B-29 Leaving the Factory* illus. in cat.).

April 6–30:   St. Louis, Mo. Photographic Salon Society of St. Louis. *Fifth Annual Saint Louis International Salon of Photography*. 4 prints (*The Old Saloon* illus. in cat.).   REVIEW: *Journal of the Photographic Society of America* 11 (September 1945): 299, *The Old Saloon*.

Additional Photographs Published
Fortune 31 (May 1945): 133, *B-29 Leaving the Factory*.
Journal of the Photographic Society of America 11 (November 1945): 403, *B-29 Leaving the Factory*.
*Burt, Struthers. "So You're Going Ranching!" *Saturday Evening Post* 218 (November 17, 1945): 22–23, 89–91. 6 illus.
*Collison, Thomas. *The Superfortress Is Born: The Story of the Boeing B-29*. New York: Duell, Sloan & Pearce, 1945. 9 illus., plus endpapers.
Kansans Build the Boeing B-29 and the Boeing Kaydet. Wichita, Kans: Boeing Airplane Co., Public Relations Division, 1945. [5] illus.

1946
Exhibitions
GROUP

[January]:   Cairo, Egypt. Gallery of the Friends of the Society of Art. [*Exhibit of American Photography*] organized by USIA and *U.S. Camera*. 4 prints.

February: Mérida, Mexico. Museo Arqueológico e Histórico de Yucatán. [*Photographs of the Yucatán by Laura Gilpin*].   REVIEWS: Advertisement. *Diario del Sureste*, February 16, 1949. § "Exposición de Arte Forográfico en Nuestro Museo." [Mérida, *Diario del Sureste*, February 1946].

February 17–March 3:   Wichita, Kans. Art Museum. Wichita Photographic Society. *Third Wichita International Salon of Photography*. 4 prints.   REVIEWS: "Laura Gilpin Photo Judge." [*Wichita Eagle* or *Beacon*, February 1946]. "Salon Judges at Work." [Wichita newspaper, February 1946]. § "Salon of Photography Opens Here February 17." [*Wichita Eagle* or *Beacon*, February 1946]. § "Photo Salon Opens Today." [*Wichita Eagle* or *Beacon*], February 17, 1946. § "Photo Display Is Excellent." [*Wichita Eagle* or *Beacon*], February 18, 1946.

September 29–October 20:   Omaha, Nebr. Joslyn Memorial Gallery. Omaha Camera Clubs. *1946 Omaha International Salon of Photography*. 4 prints.

Publications
ABOUT LAURA GILPIN
Memories and Records of Antoinette Bryant Hervey, 1857–1945. Privately printed by Walter L. Hervey, 1946.

1947

Exhibitions

GROUP

March 26–April 9:   St. Louis, Mo. Photographic Salon Society of St. Louis, Inc. *Seventh Annual Saint Louis International Salon of Photography.* 4 prints.

August 31–September 27:   Albuquerque, N.M. Guadalupe Gallery. *Photographs of New Mexico.*

September 28–October 20:   Omaha, Nebr. Joslyn Art Museum. Omaha Camera Clubs. *1947 2nd International Photographic Salon.* 4 prints.

Publications

BY LAURA GILPIN

*"Portrait Photography." In *Graphic Graflex Photography*, ed. Willard D. Morgan and Henry M. Lester, pp. 145–153. 8th ed. New York: Morgan and Lester, 1947. 10 illus.

ABOUT LAURA GILPIN

*"Heat and Humidity as Photographic Problems Met by Laura Gilpin." *Mallinkrodt Photo Bulletin*, no. 52 [ca. 1946–1947].

Additional Photographs Published

*Luhan, Mabel Dodge. *Taos and Its Artists*. New York: Duell, Sloan & Pearce, 1947. 48 illus.

1948

Exhibitions

ONE-PERSON

November 14–December 27:   Colorado Springs, Colo. Fine Arts Center. *Laura Gilpin: Follow the Rio Grande.* REVIEWS: "Laura Gilpin Will Discuss Rio Grande Pictures at 3:30." [*Colorado Springs Gazette* or *Telegraph*, November 1948]. § "Laura Gilpin's Rio Grande Photos on Exhibit at Center." [*Colorado Springs Gazette* or *Telegraph*], November 14, 1948. § "Gilpin Show Rates Praise in Colorado." *Santa Fe New Mexican*, December 2, 1948. § "1000 Attend Laura Gilpin Art Exhibit." *Rocky Mountain News*, November 15, 1948.

GROUP

November 1–30:   New York, N.Y. Camera Club of New York. *Second Women's Invitation Exhibition.* 4 prints.

Publications

BY LAURA GILPIN

*"Follow the Rio Grande." In *Follow the Rio Grande.* Exhibition catalogue. Colorado Springs: Colorado Springs Fine Arts Center, 1948, cover, *Rio Grande Yields Its Surplus to the Sea.*

Temples in Yucatan: A Camera Chronicle of Chichen Itza.

New York: Hastings House, 1948. 124 pp., 103 illus. SELECTED REVIEWS: McNulty, William. "Laura Gilpin's Mayan Text Expertly Done." *Santa Fe New Mexican*, April 2, 1948. § *Dallas Times Herald*, April 11, 1948, *The Caracol through a Corbel Arch.* § *New York World-Telegram*, April 12, 1948. § *"Maya Civilization Pictured in Laura Gilpin's New Book." Colorado Springs Gazette and Telegraph*, April 18, 1948, *Vista between Iglesia Walls.* § Guzman, Don. "Visitor in Mexico Comes to Respect Its Nationals." *Los Angeles Times*, April 25, 1948. § Fisher, Clyde. *Natural History* 57 (June 1948): 247. § *Popular Photography* 23 (July 1948): 155. § Tichy, Marjorie F. *El Palacio* 55 (July 1948): 209–210. § Wyse, Alexander. *Americas* 7 (July 1950): 127. § Thompson, J. Eric S. *Boletín Bibliográfico Anthropológia Americana* 13 (1951).

ABOUT LAURA GILPIN

"Light and Shadow Artist Authors Visual Narratives." [*Santa Fe New Mexican*, 1948].

Additional Photographs Published

Forest Park Guest Ranch, Albuquerque, New Mexico. 2-part folding brochure, 5 illus.
*Morgan, Willard D. *Famous Photographs.* New York: National Educational Alliance, 1948, *Square Tower House.*
North Side of the Ancient Plaza, Santa Fe. Santa Fe: Old Santa Fe Association, 1948. 20 pp., 10 illus.
*Putnam, Brenda. *The Sculptor's Way.* New York: Watson-Guptill, 1948. 10 illus.
Santa Fe Boy's Club, 1948. Brochure, 4 illus.

1949

Exhibitions

ONE-PERSON

May–June: New York, N.Y. Town Hall Club. *Photographs by Laura Gilpin.*

November 7–22:   Santa Fe, N.M. Museum of New Mexico, Fine Arts Museum. [*Photographs of the Rio Grande*]. REVIEWS: *Fuller, Harvey B. "Laura Gilpin, an Artist with a Camera." *Santa Fe New Mexican*, November 13, 1949, *Rio Grande Drops Out of the High Country.* § Morang, Alfred. "Art . . . in the News." [Santa Fe newspaper, November 1949].

December 4–January 15, 1950:   Dallas, Tex. Museum of Fine Arts. *Rio Grande: River of Destiny.* 141 prints. REVIEWS: Askew, Rual. "Two Exhibits Prove Camera Is Artistic." *Dallas Morning News*, [December 1949]. § "Authority on Rio Grande to Lecture at Art Museum." *Dallas Morning News*, December 7, 1949.

Publications

BY LAURA GILPIN

The Rio Grande: River of Destiny. New York: Duell, Sloan & Pearce, 1949. 244 pp., 229 illus. SELECTED REVIEWS: *Adlow, Dorothy. *Christian Science Monitor*, January 5, 1949, *The Rio Grande Yields Its Surplus to the Sea*. § *"Follow the Rio Grande." *Denver Post*, January 16, 1949. 5 illus. § "The Story of the Rio Grande." *Brownsville Herald*, January 26, 1949. § Allen, Betty. "Woman Writes Book about Rio Grande and Its People." *Brownsville Herald*, January 30, 1949. § *Adlow, Dorothy. *Christian Science Monitor*, April 28, 1949, *Aspens near the Rio Grande*. § News of promotional campaign. *Publishers Weekly*, September 3, 1949. § Horan, Kenneth. "Laura Gilpin Records a River in Photographs." *Dallas Times Herald*, September 11, 1949. § *New York Herald Tribune Weekly Book Review*, September 25, 1949, *Santa Elena Canyon*. § *"Scenery on Rio Grande Is Feature of New Gilpin Book." [Colorado Springs newspaper, October 1949], *Aspens near the Rio Grande*. § *Tacoma* [Wash.] *News Tribune*, October 16, 1949. § "Author Inks Copies of New Book." *Colorado Springs Free Press*, October 17, 1949. § "Majesty of Rio Grande Portrayed in New Book." *Las Cruces Sun News*, October 18, 1949. § *Bywaters, Jerry. "Rio Grande: Magic from Camera." *Dallas Morning News*, October 23, 1949, *Mission Church, Ranchos de Taos*. § McNulty, William. "Magnificent Production." *Santa Fe New Mexican*, October 23, 1949. § "Rio Grande Depicted in Photographs, Words." *Denver Post*, October 24, 1949. § Broaddus, Marian Howe. *El Paso Times*, November 6, 1949. § *La Farge, Oliver. "That Picturesque and Vital Artery, the Rio Grande." *New York Herald Tribune Book Review*, November 13, 1949, [*Indian in Cornfield*]. § Waters, Frank. *Taos* [N.M.] *El Crepusculo*, November 17, 1949. § Gannett, Lewis. "Books and Things: A River That Flows through Beauty." *New York Herald Tribune*, November 18, 1949. § Gilliam, Tom R. "Rio Grande Pictorial." *Ft. Wayne* [Ind.] *Journal-Gazette*, November 27, 1949. § Guzman, Don. "Rio Grande Traced from Its Source." *Los Angeles Times*, December 4, 1949. § Cooper, George B. "The Big River." *Hartford* [Conn.] *Courant*, December 25, 1949. § Jackson, John B. *Arizona Quarterly* 5 (Winter 1949): 368–370. § Shawver, Lona. "Southwest in Print." *Amarillo News*, [1949]. § La Farge, Oliver. "Rio Grande Gains Literary Recognition: Truly Great River and Giver of Life." [*New York Herald Tribune*, Winter 1949–50]. § Gregory, Marjorie. "The Story of a Storied River." *Cincinnati Times-Star*, January 7, 1950. § "Authored by Illustrator." *New Mexico School Review*, January 1950. § Morgan, Ruth. "From Colorado to the Gulf." *Southwest Review* 35 (Winter 1950): 71–73. § *Sabin, E. L. *Saturday Review of Literature* 33 (January 21, 1950): 12. 3 illus. § Vincent, Upshur. "Photos Depict Rio Grande from Creede to Brownsville." *Fort Worth Star-Telegram*, February 12, 1950. § Tschopik, H. T., Jr. *Natural History* 59 (June 1950): 245.

ABOUT LAURA GILPIN

Who's Who in the West. 1st ed. Chicago: A. N. Marquis Co., 1949, p. 341.

Additional Photographs Published

*"Santa Fe Handcrafts: Your City Leads the Entire Southwest." *Santa Fe New Mexican*, October 26, 1949. 2 illus.

1950

Exhibitions

ONE-PERSON

April: Austin, Tex. University of Texas. Barker Texas History Center. [*Photographs of the Rio Grande*]. 30 prints. REVIEW: "Rio Grande Photos on Exhibit Here." *Daily Texan*, June 16, 1950.

September: Santa Barbara, Calif. Museum of Art. [*Photographs of the Rio Grande*]. REVIEW: *"Rio Grande Photos Make Excellent Show." *Santa Barbara News Press*, [September 1950], *Source of the Rio Grande*.

Publications

BY LAURA GILPIN

*"Laura Gilpin's Rio Grande Country." *U.S. Camera* 13 (February 1950): 44–47. 8 illus.

ABOUT LAURA GILPIN

*Adlow, Dorothy. "[Laura Gilpin]." *Christian Science Monitor*, March 1, 1950, *Snow*.
"Photographer's Tool Is Ray of Light Says Laura Gilpin Speaking at Altrusa Dinner." *Santa Fe New Mexican*, December 12, 1950.
*Collier, John, Jr. "Laura Gilpin: Western Photographer." *New Mexico Quarterly* 20 (Winter 1950–51): 485–493, *The Prospector*.

1951

Exhibitions

ONE-PERSON

February 4–March 4:   Roswell, N.M. Museum and Art Center. [*Photographs of the Rio Grande*]. [141] prints. REVIEWS: "Photographs of Rio Grande on Show at Museum." *Roswell Record*, February 4, 1951. § "Noted Photographer Is to Lecture at Roswell Museum Monday Evening." *Roswell Record*, February 18, 1951.

February 16–March 9: Washington, D.C. Arts Club of Washington. *Pictorial Photographs and "Camera Chronicles."* [85] prints: Rio Grande and Yucatán.

November 5–December: Wichita, Kans. Art Association. [*Photographs of the Rio Grande*]. REVIEW: "Laura Gilpin Is Exhibiting Photos at Art Galleries." *Wichita Eagle*, November 11, 1951.

GROUP

December 9–January 6, 1952: Santa Fe, N.M. Museum of New Mexico, Fine Arts Museum. *5th Exhibition: Graphic Arts in New Mexico.* 2 prints.

Publications

ABOUT LAURA GILPIN

McNulty, William. "Gilpin Earns Good Review in Quarterly." *Santa Fe New Mexican*, February 18, 1951.
People and Places in Santa Fe and Taos, 1951–52. Santa Fe: C. R. Ferguson Publications, 1951, p. 23.

1952
Exhibitions

ONE-PERSON

January: Santa Fe, N.M. Under the Portal. [*Photographs of the Rio Grande, Canyon de Chelly, and Navajo*]. REVIEWS: Carr, Lorraine. "Pictorialists, Archaeologists; Writers on the Gravy Train." [*Santa Fe New Mexican*, January 1952]. § *Santa Fe New Mexican*, January 29, 1952, *Spider Rock, Canyon de Chelly*.

Additional Photographs Published

*Arizona Highways 28 (December 1952): 8–9, 23. 2 illus.
*Boyd, E. "Santos of the Southwest." *House and Garden* 102 (December 1952): 93, *Santos*.
*Santa Fe New Mexican, December 1952, *Mrs. C. Grant La Farge*.
*Santa Fe New Mexican, December 14, 1952, *Maria Martínez, Bernard Leach, Shoji Hamada, Soyetsu Yanagi*.
*King, Bernice. "Hamada's Pottery Demonstration Fascinates Audience of Artists, University Students and Laymen." *Santa Fe New Mexican*, December 19, 1952, *Shoji Hamada*.
*Santa Fe New Mexican, December 30, 1952, and January 4, 1953, *Mrs. Manuel Patrício Sánchez*.
*Morrison, Hugh. *Early American Architecture from the First Colonial Settlements to the National Period.* New York: Oxford University Press, 1952. 5 illus.
*Santa Fe Maternal Health Center. 14th Annual Report, 1951–1952. 6 illus.
*[Christmas brochure for Grand Imperial Hotel in Silverton, Colorado]. 1952. 4 illus.

1953
Exhibitions

GROUP

January 4–February 2: Santa Fe, N.M. Museum of New Mexico, Fine Arts Museum. **6th Exhibition: Graphic Arts in New Mexico.* 2 prints, 1 illus. in cat.

June 6–August 31: Colorado Springs, Colo. Fine Arts Center. *The West.* 10 prints.

June 14–July 31: Santa Fe, N.M. Museum of New Mexico, Fine Arts Museum. *A Retrospective Exhibition of Architecture of John Gaw Meem.*

October 25–[December]: Roswell, N.M. Museum and Art Center. *A Retrospective Exhibition of Architecture of John Gaw Meem.*

Publications

BY LAURA GILPIN

**"La Conquistadora." *New Mexico Sun Trails* 6 (September 1953): 21–23. 11 illus.

ABOUT LAURA GILPIN

"Gilpin to Do Navaho Photos." *Santa Fe New Mexican*, June 28, 1953.

Additional Photographs Published

**"Camera Touring New Mexico." *New Mexico Magazine* 31 (March 1953): 30, *Sanctuary at Chimayo*.
*Lambert, Marjorie F. "The San Gabriel del Yunque Helmet." *Archaeology* 6 (Summer 1953): 108, *San Gabriel del Yunque*.
*Pillsbury, Dorothy L. "New Mexico Blends World Folk Arts." *Christian Science Monitor*, September 17, 1953, *Museum of International Folk Art*.
*Museum of International Folk Art. On cover of small brochure for institution.
*Santa Fe Maternal Health Center. 15th Annual Report, 1952–1953. 5 illus.

1954
Exhibitions

GROUP

April: Roswell, N.M. Museum and Art Center. *Archbishop Lamy and Church Architecture.* [28] prints: Fray Chávez and La Conquistadora.

October 9–31: Dallas, Tex. Museum of Fine Arts. *The Fabulous West.* 3 prints.

Publications

ABOUT LAURA GILPIN

"Laura Gilpin to Be Guest on KOB-TV." *Santa Fe New Mexican*, February 28, 1954.

"Laura Gilpin Will Show Slides on Life of Navahos."
Colorado Springs Gazette-Telegraph, March 11, 1954.

Samson, Carolyn. "Laura Gilpin Started with Brownie:
Now She Carries Four Cameras." *Colorado Springs
Free Press*, March 12, 1954.

O'Connor, Ellen. "Laura Gilpin Top Photographer and
Writer on S.W. Indian Life." *Denver Post*, March 15,
1954.

"Laura Gilpin Will Present Picture Story of Navahos."
Santa Fe New Mexican, June 15, 1954.

"Miss Gilpin Flies to Reservation to Take Additional Navaho Pictures." *Santa Fe New Mexican*, June 18, 1954.

*"Laura Gilpin Presents Navaho Picture Story." *Santa Fe
New Mexican*, June 22, 1954, *Ason Kinlichine*.

"Story of Navahos Told via Slides by Laura Gilpin." *Santa
Fe New Mexican*, June 24, 1954.

Additional Photographs Published

*Charles, Kate H. "Highway Rio Grande." *Pen Magazine*,
August 1954.

**New Mexico Sun Trails* 7 (October–November 1954):
cover.

*Edar, Ursula. "Tradition and Our Heritage." *Everyday
Art*, Fall 1954. 3 illus.

*Chávez, Fray Angelico. *La Conquistadora: The Autobiog-
raphy of an Ancient Statue*. Paterson, N.J.: St. Anthony
Guild Press, 1954, frontispiece, *La Conquistadora*.

*Maloney, T. J., ed. *U.S. Camera, 1954*. New York: U.S.
Camera Publishing Corp., 1953, pp. 236–237, *Meeting
in a Hogan*. REVIEW: Dmitri, Ivan. "Emulsions of
Life." *Saturday Review* 36 (March 27, 1954): 18.

*Sprague, Marshall. "The Renaissance of Gregory Gulch."
Colorado Wonderland, 1954 special edition, p. 12, *Lillian Gish in* Camille.

1955

Exhibitions

ONE-PERSON

April 17–May 6: Washington, D.C. Arts Club of Wash-
ington. [*Photographs of the Navajo*]. 88 prints. REVIEW:
Portner, Leslie Judd. "A.U. Offers New, Young Talent."
Washington Post and Times Herald, May 1, 1955.

GROUP

February 20–March 6: Tucson, Ariz. Fine Arts Associa-
tion. *The Southwest Indian: Designer-Craftsman*. 48 prints:
Navajo and Pueblo. REVIEWS: "Tucson Displays Gilpin's
Photos." [*Santa Fe New Mexican*, February–March 1955].
§ Stanley, Byrd. "Indian Art Good by Any Standards."
Tucson Daily Citizen, February 26, 1955.

Publications

ABOUT LAURA GILPIN

McSwain, Larry. "Noted Photographer Compiles Navajo

Book." *Gallup Independent*, January 26, 1955.

"Laura Gilpin Plans LA Picture-Lecture." *Santa Fe New
Mexican*, June 5, 1955.

"Los Alamos Showing Set for Famed Navajo Photos."
Albuquerque Journal, June 17, 1955.

Additional Photographs Published

**Musical America*, February 15, 1955, *Vitya Vronsky and
Victor Babin*.

**Santa Fe New Mexican*, May 22, 1955, *Mary Cabot
Wheelwright and Kenneth Foster*.

**Landscape* 5 (Summer 1955), cover, *Sand Dunes*.

*Horgan, Paul. "Romance of the Rivers." *Coronet* 38
(June 1955): 135, *Rio Grande Yields Its Surplus to the Sea*.

*Santa Fe. Museum of International Folk Art. *The Folk
Art of Japan*. October 3–30, 1955.

**A Book about D.N.S.* [Dorothy Newkirk Stewart,
1891–1955], *Dorothy at Her Galeria Window*.

**1955 Annual Report*. Newburyport, Mass.: Towle Manu-
facturing Company.

1956

Exhibitions

ONE-PERSON

November 4–January 6, 1957: New York, N.Y. American Museum of Natural History. *The Enduring Navaho*.
47 prints. REVIEWS: "The Enduring Navaho." *Santa Fe
New Mexican*, September 16, 1956. § "Camera Notes."
New York Times, November 11, 1956.

GROUP

June 17–July 14: Santa Fe, N.M. Museum of New
Mexico, Fine Arts Museum. *First New Mexico Photographers
Exhibition*. 2 prints.

Publications

ABOUT LAURA GILPIN

*"Gilpin Home Wins First in Contest." *Santa Fe New
Mexican*, December 1956, [*Gilpin Home*].

Additional Photographs Published

*"Vast Tribal Oil Deal Kept under Wraps." *Santa Fe
New Mexican*, July 22, 1956. 2 illus.

*Dutton, Bertha. "A Brief Discussion of Chichen Itza."
El Palacio 63 (July–August 1956): 202–232. 6 illus.

*Horgan, Paul. "The Rio Grande." *Holiday* 20 (October
1956). 5 illus.

*"The Hogan to Be Re-dedicated." *Santa Fe New Mexican*,
November 18, 1956, *Mary Cabot Wheelwright*.

*Dominguez, Francisco A. *The Missions of New Mexico,
1776*. Albuquerque: University of New Mexico Press,
[1956], frontispiece, *Reredos of Our Lady of Light, 1776*.

*Keleman, Pal. *Medieval American Art*. New York: Dover
Publications, 1956. 2 illus.

1957

Exhibitions

ONE-PERSON

February 15–April 1: Rochester, N.Y. George Eastman House. [*Photographs of the Navajo*]. 95 prints. REVIEW: *Smith, Virginia Jeffrey. "Navajos' Charm Lensed." *Rochester Times-Union*, March 18, 1957, *Timothy Kellywood and Mother*.

June: Santa Fe, N.M. Laboratory of Anthropology. *The Enduring Navaho*. 104 prints. REVIEW: "Gilpin Exhibit Now on Display at Laboratory." [*Santa Fe New Mexican*, June 1957].

December: Stillwater, Okla. Oklahoma State University. Art Gallery. *The Enduring Navaho*. 104 prints. REVIEWS: "Photo Display to Open Today." *Stillwater News-Press*, December 7, 1957. § "Display of Navajo Photographs Gives Insight into Indian Culture." *Daily O'Collegian*, December 13, 1957.

GROUP

September 19–October 31: Berlin, Germany. Kongresshalle. *American Spirit*. [USIA exhibition]. 9 prints. REVIEWS: *Smith, Virginia Jeffrey. "Exhibit Goes to Berlin." *Rochester Times-Union*, August 29, 1957, *Shepherds of the Desert*. § "Laura Gilpin, Eliot Porter in Berlin Exhibit." *Santa Fe New Mexican*, September 15, 1957.

Publications

ABOUT LAURA GILPIN

"Santa Fe Warmly Praised in 'Charm' Story of State." *Santa Fe New Mexican*, September 27, 1957.

Additional Photographs Published

*El Palacio 64 (January–February 1957): cover, *Butterfly Katsina Maiden Kneeling at a Corn-Grinding Bin*.

*Lambert, Marjorie F. "A Rare Stone Hump-Backed Figurine from Pecos Pueblo, New Mexico." *El Palacio* 64 (March–April 1957): 102, *Mesa Verde Black and White Bowl*.

*Koltun, Frances. "New Mexico." *Charm*, October 1957, *Navajo Women*.

*"Christmas in Santa Fe." *Santa Fe New Mexican*, December 15, 1957, [*Gilpin Home*].

*Our Friends the Navahos. Santa Fe: Church of the Holy Faith, Young People's Fellowship, 1957. 8 illus.

*Santa Fe. Museum of New Mexico. Museum of International Folk Art. *Craftsmen of New Mexico, 1957*. 6 illus.

1958

Exhibitions

ONE-PERSON

April–May: Colorado Springs, Colo. Fine Arts Center. *The Enduring Navaho*. 80 prints. REVIEW: *Fisher, Theodore. "Ex-Springs Woman Has Top Photo Exhibit Here." *Colorado Springs Free Press*, May 5, 1958, *Shepherds of the Desert*.

July 15–August 17: Santa Fe, N.M. Museum of New Mexico, Fine Arts Museum. [*Fourteen Photographs by Laura Gilpin*. REVIEW: Bowen, Ben. "About the Arts." *Santa Fe New Mexican*, July 20, 1958.

November: Boulder, Colo. University of Colorado. [*Photographs by Laura Gilpin*]. 53 prints.

GROUP

April: Coral Gables, Fla. University of Miami. Lowe Art Museum. *Indian Art from the Collection of Alfred I. Barton*. 20 prints.

April 12–28: Essen, West Germany. Amerika Haus. *American Spirit* [USIA exhibition]. 9 prints.

June 6–22: Boston, Mass. Public Garden Arts Festival. [*Fifteen Western Photographers*]. 2 prints.

August 16–24: Munich, Germany. Amerika-Haus. *American Spirit* [USIA exhibition]. 9 prints.

[December]: Santa Fe, N.M. Museum of New Mexico, Fine Arts Museum. *1958 New Mexico Photographers Annual Exhibition*. 4 prints; *The Doorway* illus. in cat.

Additional Photographs Published

*Family Circle, March 1958, p. 33, [*Pueblo Interior*].

*Santa Fe. Museum of New Mexico. Museum of International Folk Art. *Indonesian Art*. April 7–September 1, 1958.

*Santa Fe. Museum of New Mexico. Museum of International Folk Art. *Craftsmen of New Mexico, 1958*. June 30–September 2, 1958. 9 illus.

*Santa Fe Opera Souvenir Program, Second Season 1958, [Summer].

*"Lucy Lewis of Acoma Wins Award." *Santa Fe New Mexican*, September 7, 1958, *Lucy Lewis and Kenneth Chapman*.

*New Mexico Magazine 36 (December 1958): cover, *A. O. Peabody Home*.

1959

Exhibitions

ONE-PERSON

December 9–?: San Diego, Calif. Museum of Man. [*The Enduring Navaho*].

GROUP

December: Santa Fe, N.M. [Museum of New Mexico, Fine Arts Gallery]. *New Mexico Photographers Annual Exhibition*. 4 prints; 2 illus. in cat.

n.d.: Wiesbaden, West Germany. *American Spirit* [USIA exhibition]. 9 prints.

Additional Photographs Published

*"Santa Fe Puppet Expert to Report on Festival." *Santa Fe New Mexican*, January 25, 1959, [*Marjorie McFarlin and Puppets*].

Santa Fe Scene, January 31, 1959, cover, *Bust of Witter Bynner*.

*Calendar, February 1959, Museum of International Folk Art, Santa Fe, cover, *The Gallery: School Children Sketching*.

*Calendar, May 1959, Museum of International Folk Art, Santa Fe, cover, *Morada Window*.

*Calendar, June 1959, Museum of International Folk Art, Santa Fe, cover, *Architectural Detail*.

*Clark, Merle. "Regional Show at Museum's Folk Art Unit." *El Palacio* 66 (June 1959): 101–105. 3 illus.

*Santa Fe. Museum of International Folk Art. *Craftsmen of New Mexico*, 1959. June 29–August 28, 1959. 7 illus.

*Calendar, August 1959, Museum of International Folk Art, Santa Fe, cover, [*Indian Pot*].

*Calendar, September 1959, Museum of International Folk Art, Santa Fe, cover, [*Architectural Detail*].

New Mexico Transporter, December 1959, cover, *Portal of Santa Fe Residence*.

*Boyd, E. *Popular Arts of Colonial New Mexico*. Santa Fe: Museum of International Folk Art, 1959. 7 illus.

*"Furnishing Southwest Garden Rooms." *Ortho Lawn & Garden Book*, [1959], pp. 17–18. 3 illus.

*Janson, H. W., ed. *Key Monuments of the History of Art: A Visual Survey*. New York: Harry N. Abrams, 1959, p. 366, *Temple of the Warriors*.

La Posada de Santa Fe. [1959]. Brochure. [6 illus.]

*Putnam, Brenda. "Sculpture in the Americas." In *Book of Knowledge*. New York: Grolier Society, 1959, 10: 3700, *Chac-Mool*.

1960

Exhibitions

GROUP

July 12–October 30: Kansas City, Mo. Nelson-Atkins Museum of Art. *The Art of the Navajo Silversmith, with Photographs by Laura Gilpin*. 30 prints. REVIEWS: "Navajo and Zuni Objects on Display." *Kansas City Star*, August 7, 1960. § "View of Indians." *Kansas City Star*, August 7, 1960.

Publications

BY LAURA GILPIN

*"[Comment on *The Spring at Cerralvo*]", *Southwest Review* 45 (Summer 1960): iv. 1 illus.

ABOUT LAURA GILPIN

"Top Photographer to Give Navajo Program." *Lubbock* [Tex.] *Avalanche-Journal*, November 6, 1960.

"Laura Gilpin to Lecture and Present Slides." *Taos News*, November 10, 1960.

"Laura Gilpin, Fine Arts Photographer." *Santa Fe Scene* 3 (November 12, 1960): 4–7.

"'Navajo World' to Be Presented on Thursday." [*Lubbock Avalanche-Journal*], November 13, 1960.

"Photographer to Speak in City." *Lubbock Avalanche-Journal*, November 17, 1960.

"Laura Gilpin Wows Taosenos with 'The Enduring Navajo.'" *Santa Fe New Mexican*, November 27, 1960.

Additional Photographs Published

*Santa Fe. Museum of International Folk Art. *Tibetan Life and Culture*. May 29–December 31, 1960. 15 illus.

Southwest Review 45 (Summer 1960), cover, *The Spring at Cerralvo*.

*Santa Fe. Museum of International Folk Art. *Craftsmen of New Mexico*, 1960. June 27–September 5, 1960. 10 illus.

*La Farge, Oliver. *The American Indian*. New York: Golden Press, 1960. 35 illus.

*Scully, Vincent, Jr. *Frank Lloyd Wright*. New York: Braziller, 1960, pl. 60, *Temple of Two Lintels*.

Six Costumes from Around the World. Santa Fe: Museum of International Folk Art, Mobile Unit, 1960–1961. 6 illus.

1961

Exhibitions

ONE-PERSON

August 27–September 10: Santa Fe, N.M. Three Cities of Spain. [*Photographs by Laura Gilpin*]. 22 prints.

GROUP

June–December 31: Santa Fe, N.M. Museum of International Folk Art. *Popular Arts of Yucatan*. REVIEWS: "Yucatan Exhibit Arrives Here." *Santa Fe New Mexican*, March 27, 1961. § Wadleigh, John. "About the Arts." [*Santa Fe New Mexican*, June 1961].

Publications

BY LAURA GILPIN

"Pioneer Camera." *Santa Fe New Mexican*, December 10, 1961.

ABOUT LAURA GILPIN

*Rogers, Vern. "Laura Gilpin: Artist with a Camera." *New Mexico Magazine* 39 (October 1961): 14–17, 31. 6 illus.

Bright, Robert. "About the Arts." *Santa Fe New Mexican*, October 22, 1961.

Additional Photographs Published

*"A Most Poetic Habitation." *House Beautiful* 103 (February 1961): 83–97. 5 illus.

*Olsen, Virginia. "Indian Art Today and Yesterday."
   America Illustrated 67 (October 24, 1961): 42, *María Martínez.*
New Mexico Magazine 39 (November–December 1961).
   2 illus.
*Bennett, Edna. *Nature Photography.* New York: Universal
   Photo Books, 1961, pp. 18, 70, 72. 3 illus.
*Handbill for Webb Young, trader, Santa Fe, *Church at
   Chimayo.*
*"Maya." In *Grolier Encyclopedia.* New York: Grolier
   Society, 1961, 14: 11, *Temple of the Warriors.*
Vergara Printing Company, Santa Fe. Brochure, 4 illus.

1962
Exhibitions
GROUP
January 12–February 27:   Santa Fe, N.M. Museum of
New Mexico, Fine Arts Museum. *An Exhibition of Photo-
graphs: Laura Gilpin, Eliot Porter, Todd Webb.*   REVIEWS:
Packard, Maggy. "About the Arts – Diversity in Photog-
raphy." *Santa Fe New Mexican,* [January 1962]. § "'Fine
Arts' Photograph Show Is by Three Santa Feans." *Santa
Fe New Mexican,* January 14, 1962.

Publications
ABOUT LAURA GILPIN
"Laura Gilpin to Show 'Navajo Land' Slides as Benefit for
   Tewa Center Saturday Evening at San Ildefonso."
   [*Santa Fe New Mexican,* March 4, 1962].
"Talk with Slides Slated for Arts Center Friday." *Colorado
   Springs Gazette Telegraph,* August 16, 1962.

Additional Photographs Published
*Temple, F. J. "Les Psaumes de la Creation." *L'Arc* 19
   (Summer 1962), opp. p. 70, *Navajo Women Returning
   from the Trading Post.*
Santa Fe New Mexican, September 9, 1962, *Alix Young
   Maruchess.*
Taos News, November 29, 1962, *Mrs. Griffin.*
Aperture 10 (1962): cover, *Graveyard.*
*Cammann, Schuyler. *Substance and Symbol in Chinese
   Toggles: Chinese Belt Toggles from the C. F. Bieber Collec-
   tion.* Philadelphia: University of Pennsylvania Press,
   1962.
*Carmel, James H. *Exhibition Techniques, Traveling and
   Temporary.* New York: Reinhold Pub. Corp., [1962].
   2 illus.
*Collier, John, Sr. *On the Gleaming Way.* Denver: Sage
   Books, 1962. 12 illus.

1963
Exhibitions
GROUP
May 8–29:   Tucson, Ariz. Art Center. *Invitational Photo-
graphic Show: Photographs from the Southwest.* 10 prints.

Publications
BY LAURA GILPIN
*"The Austerity of the Desert Pervades Her Home and
   Work." *House Beautiful* 105 (April 1963): 144–145, 198.
   6 illus.
*"Historic Architecture and Monument Photography."
   In *The Encyclopedia of Photography,* ed. Willard Mor-
   gan. New York: Greystone Press, 1963, 9: 1711–1716.
   5 illus.

Additional Photographs Published
*Santa Fe. Museum of International Folk Art. *Embroideries
   by Rebecca James.* May 19–September 8, 1963. 7 illus.
Pasatiempo [*Santa Fe New Mexican* Sunday magazine],
   December 22, 1963. 4 illus.
*Bolles, John S. *La Iglesia: Chichén Itzá, Yucatán.* San Fran-
   cisco, 1963, n.p., *Caracol from the Iglesia.*
*Collier, John, Sr. *From Every Zenith.* Denver: Sage Books,
   1963, cover, *John Collier.*
*De Mille, Agnes. *The Book of the Dance.* New York:
   Golden Press, 1963. 2 illus.
*"Let's Keep Our Heritage." [*Santa Fe New Mexican,*
   1963]. [4] illus.
*Robb, David M., and J. J. Garrison. *Art in the Western
   World.* 4th ed. New York: Harper & Row, 1963, p. 212,
   Acoma, San Estevan.
*Santa Fe. Museum of International Folk Art. *The First 10
   Years: 1953–1963.* 14 illus.

1964
Exhibitions
ONE-PERSON
[May]:   Sandia, N.M. Sandia Base Exhibit. [*Photographs
of the Yucatán and Navajo*]. 66 prints.

Publications
ABOUT LAURA GILPIN
*"Economic Struggle, Sacred Traditions of the Navajo
   to be Portrayed Friday by Miss Laura Gilpin in Slide
   Lecture." *Santa Fe New Mexican,* [March 1964],
   [*Timothy Kellywood and His Mother*].
"Special Event." *Southwestern Association on Indian Affairs,
   Inc.,* Quarterly, Spring 1964.

Additional Photographs Published
*James, Rebecca. "Paintings in Yarn: The Colcha Stitch."
   Woman's Day, April 1964, pp. 40–43, 91. 8 illus.

*Montague, Robert L. III, and Tony P. Wrenn. "Santa Fe Victorious." *Historic Preservation* 16 (September–October 1964): 174–177. [2] illus.
*Wallbank, T. Walter, and Arnold Schrier. *Living World History*. Chicago: Scott, Foresman and Co., 1964, p. 255, *Buffalo Robe*. [2d–5th eds., 1964, 1969, 1974, 1982].

1965

Exhibitions

ONE-PERSON

July 4–?: Sandoval, N.M. Corrales Art Association. [*Photographs by Laura Gilpin*]. 14 prints. REVIEW: "Four Photographers Exhibit in Corrales." *Albuquerque Journal*, July 4, 1965.

GROUP

January 29–April 4: Fort Worth, Tex. Amon Carter Museum. *Standing Up Country: The Canyon Lands of Utah and Arizona*. 9 prints.

Publications

BY LAURA GILPIN

*"[Statement]." *American Indian Performing Arts Exhibition*. Washington, D.C.: Gallery of American Indian Art, April 21–May 28, 1965, p. 36.

Additional Photographs Published

New Mexico Transporter, April 1965, cover, [*Dogwood Trees*].
Western Review 2 (Summer 1965): cover, *Heritage from Spain*.
*Forrest, James Taylor. *A Portrait of Lincoln*. Santa Fe: Museum of New Mexico, 1965, cover, [*Abraham Lincoln*].

1966

Exhibitions

ONE-PERSON

January: Santa Fe, N.M. Northern New Mexico Loan & Trust Company. [*Photographs by Laura Gilpin*]. 22 prints. REVIEW: "First Northern Showing Laura Gilpin Photos." *Santa Fe New Mexican*, January 23, 1966.

July: Espanola, N.M. Valley National Bank. [*Photographs by Laura Gilpin*]. 50 prints. REVIEWS: "Exhibit to Honor Santa Fe Woman." [Espanola newspaper, July 1966]. § Houle, Joyce. "Arte del Valle." [*Santa Fe New Mexican*], July 14, 1966.

November 20–December 30: Santa Fe, N.M. St. John's College. [*Photographs by Laura Gilpin*]. [35] prints. RE-VIEWS: MacGregor, John. "Laura Gilpin's Show Marks 50 Years as Photographer." *Santa Fe New Mexican*, November 27, 1966. § "St. John's College Plans to Honor Laura Gilpin." *Santa Fe New Mexican*, December 15, 1966. § [Photos of Gilpin at St. John's College reception] in *Santa Fe New Mexican*, December 20, 1966.

Additional Photographs Published

*Fort Worth. Amon Carter Museum. *Quiet Triumph: Forty Years with the Indian Arts Fund*. January 1966. 7 illus.
*"The Adventure of Art." *MD* 10 (February 1966): 198, *Arch of Maya Ruin, Yucatan*.
*Crosby, Alexander. *The Rio Grande: Life for the Desert*. Champaign, Ill.: Garrard Publishing Co., 1966. 13 illus.
*Historic Santa Fe Foundation. *Old Santa Fe Today*. Santa Fe: School of American Research, 1966. 8 illus.
*"New Mexico." In *Compton's Pictured Encyclopedia*. Chicago, 1966, 10:206, *Acoma, Sky City*.

1967

Exhibitions

GROUP

April 2–23: Santa Fe, N.M. Institute of American Indian Arts. *Powhoge: An Exhibition of Pottery and Painting from a Family in San Ildefonso Pueblo, New Mexico*. 12 illus. in cat. REVIEW: *"Maria, Popovi Da, Toni Da Show Opens Today at Institute." *Santa Fe New Mexican*, April 2, 1967. 3 illus.

May 15–June 30: Washington, D.C. Center for the Arts of Indian America. *Powhoge: An Exhibition of Pottery and Painting from a Family in San Ildefonso Pueblo, New Mexico*. 12 illus. in cat.

Publications

ABOUT LAURA GILPIN

Jennings, Mary Lou. "Photography Is a Grown-up Medium in the Art World, an Expert Says." *Albuquerque Tribune*, October 12, 1967.
*White, Jerry. "A Photographer's Photographer." *Santa Fe News*, November 23, 1967. 2 illus.

Additional Photographs Published

*Santa Fe. Museum of International Folk Art. *Fabric for Living*. March 27, 1967–January 7, 1968, cover, *Navajo Woman Spinning*.
Santa Fe New Mexican, May 7, 1967. 2 illus.
El Palacio 74 (Winter 1967): 19, *Santos*.
*Spence, William P. *Architecture: Design, Engineering, Drawing*. Bloomington, Ill.: McKnight & McKnight, 1967. 2 illus.

1968

Exhibitions

ONE-PERSON

May 27–September: Albuquerque, N.M. Museum of

Albuquerque. *Rio Grande: River of the Arid Land.* RE-
VIEWS: Alexander, Betty. "Laura Gilpin 'Paints' with a
Camera." *Albuquerque Tribune*, May 30, 1968. § "Laura
Gilpin Photos Feature at Museum." [*Albuquerque Tribune*,
May–June 1968]. § "Laura Gilpin Photos Added by
Museum." [Albuquerque newspaper, September 1968]. §
Taos News, October 24, 1968.

October 16–November 3:   Midland, Tex. Museum of the
Southwest. *Rio Grande: River of the Arid Land.* REVIEW:
"Gilpin Exhibit to Texas." *Santa Fe New Mexican*, October
13, 1968.

December 12–January 12, 1969:   Fort Worth, Tex. Amon
Carter Museum. *The Enduring Navaho.* 151 prints. RE-
VIEWS: *"Museum Will Open Exhibit on Navahos."
Fort Worth Star-Telegram, December 8, 1968, [*Old Navajo
Woman*]. § "Gilpin Has Dallas [*sic*] Show." *Santa Fe New
Mexican*, December 15, 1968.

Publications

BY LAURA GILPIN
"Photography Exhibit Found 'Provocative.'" *Santa Fe
New Mexican*, April 14, 1968.
[Review of *Navajo Wildlands* by Philip Hyde]. *El Palacio*
75 (Autumn 1968): 42–43.
**The Enduring Navaho*. Austin: University of Texas Press,
1968. 156 pp., 267 illus. § SELECTED REVIEWS:
*Bullock, Alice. "Beauty, Warmth in Gilpin's Book."
Santa Fe New Mexican, November 24, 1968, *Young
Navajo Mother*. § Hunter, Sam. "This Week's Books."
Fort Worth Press, November 24, 1968. § *Reid, Mar-
garet W. "Fine Art Distinguishes These Lasting Trea-
sures." *Wichita Falls* [Tex.] *Times*, December 1, 1968,
Navajo Weaver and Child. § "Miss Gilpin Publishes
New Book." *Colorado Springs Free-Press*, [December
3, 1968]. § Bullock, Alice. "Laura Gilpin's Beautiful
Book a Monument to Her Talent." [*Santa Fe New
Mexican*, November 1968]. § *New York Review of
Books*, December 5, 1968, *Navajo Costume of the 1880's*.
§ *Alexander, Betty. "Gilpin Book Destined to Be-
come a Classic." *Albuquerque Tribune*, December 5,
1968, [*Navajo Woman*]. § "Where Gilpin Book Is on
Sale in Albuquerque." *Albuquerque Tribune*, December
7, 1968. § "Laura Gilpin's New Book Sensitive Navajo
Study." *Albuquerque Journal*, December 15, 1968. §
*Holt, David Earl. "New Book News." *Austin Ameri-
can-Statesman*, December 15, 1968, *Navajo Weaver and
Child*. § *Atkinson, M. Jourdan. "Among the Na-
vajo." *Houston Post*, December 15, 1968, *Navajo Mother*.
§ "People of the Earth Last." *Sacramento Bee*, December
15, 1968. § "Book Briefs." *Arizona Republic*, Decem-
ber 26, 1968. § Watson, Editha L. "Book Review."
Window Rock [Ariz.] *Navajo Times*, January 9, 1969. §
Krisch, Lucille Stewart. "Twigs and Trees." *San*

Antonio Light, January 19, 1969. § *History News* 24
(February 1969): 38. § *Russell, David. "The Story
of the Navaho Is Beautiful." *Dallas Daily News Journal*,
February 3, 1969, *Summer Shelter in the Cove*. § "'En-
during Navaho' Winner in Multi-state Competition."
Santa Fe New Mexican, March 5, 1969. § Ford,
Robert E. "Emphasis on Camera Work Rather Than
Text in Writing of Tribe." *Las Cruces* [N.M.] *Sun
News*, April 20, 1969. § *Lurie, Nancy Oestreich.
"Books in Review." *Natural History* 78 (May 1969):
72–75. 2 illus. § *Hill, W. W. "Books." *El Palacio*
76 (Spring 1969): 47–48, *Navajo Woman, Child and
Lambs*. § Webb, William. "Indian Photography."
Monterey Peninsula Herald, June 7, 1969. § *Newhall,
Nancy. "The Enduring Navaho: Review of a Book
and a People." *Brighton-Pittsford* [N.Y.] *Post*, September
4, 1969, *Chance Meeting in the Desert*. § Mason, Alice S.
Utah Historical Quarterly 37 (Fall 1969): 437–438. §
Newman, Stanley. *Western Folklore* 28 (October 1969):
288–290. § Unrau, William E. *Rocky Mountain Social
Science Journal*, October 1969, p. 186. § James, Peggy.
"Abiding Interest in Navahos Lifelong Passion of
Artist." *Colorado Springs Gazette Telegraph*, November
5, 1969. § Harris, David R. *The Geographical Journal*
136, part 2 (June 1970): 282. § Brinegar, David.
[Tucson] *Arizona Daily Star*, August 2, 1970. § "Tribe
on the Increase." *Times Literary Supplement*, October
9, 1970. § Bullock, Alice. *Southwestern American Litera-
ture* 1 (January 1971): 31–32. § Halpern, Katherine S.
American Anthropologist 74 (August 1972): 993. §
Watson, Editha L. "Book Review." *Navajo Times*,
July 12, 1973.

ABOUT LAURA GILPIN
Alexander, Betty. "Laura Gilpin 'Paints' with a Camera."
Albuquerque Tribune, May 30, 1968.
Eyrich, Claire. "Navaho Life Preserved on Film by City
Visitor." *Fort Worth Star-Telegram*, December 14, 1968.

1969
Exhibitions

ONE-PERSON
February 23–June 1:   New York, N.Y. Riverside Mu-
seum. *Communication from the Reservations: Southwestern
Indian Art and Laura Gilpin's Photographs.* 75 prints: Navajo.
REVIEWS: *Coleman, A. D. "Latent Image." *Village
Voice*, March 6, 1969, *Francis Nakai and Family*. § Gruen,
John. "Art in New York: No Reservations Needed." *New
York*, March 17, 1969. § Deschin, Jacob. "Beaton's Parade
of Personalities." *New York Times*, May 11, 1969.

June–July: Lubbock, Tex. Texas Tech University. West
Texas Museum. *Rio Grande: River of the Arid Land.*

November 6–30:   Colorado Springs, Colo. Taylor Museum. [*Photographs of Indians by Laura Gilpin*]. [100] prints. REVIEW: James, Peggy. "Abiding Interest in Navahos Life-Long Passion of Artist." *Colorado Springs Gazette Telegraph*, November 5, 1969.

Publications

ABOUT LAURA GILPIN

"Additional Honor Given to Miss Laura Gilpin for Her 'Enduring Navaho.'" *Santa Fe New Mexican*, April 16, 1969.

"Western Flavor Spices Cowboy Hall's Wrangler Ceremony." *Daily Oklahoman*, April 26, 1969.

*Vestal, David. "The Enduring Laura Gilpin." *Popular Photography* 64 (June 1969): 50, *Navajo Woman, Child and Lambs*.

Additional Photographs Published

*Bathke, Alice, and Jerry Bathke. "They Call Themselves 'The People.'" *University of Chicago Magazine* 61 (March–April 1969): 2–17. 4 illus.

*Keleman, Pal. *Art of the Americas: Ancient and Hispanic*. New York: Bonanza Books, 1969, p. 245, *Interior, San Jose de Laguna, N.M.*

*Keleman, Pal. *Medieval American Art*. 3d rev. ed. New York: Dover, 1969. 2 illus.

*Owings, Nathaniel A. *The American Aesthetic*. New York: Harper and Row, 1969, p. 31, *Doorway, Pueblo Bonito*.

1970

Exhibitions

ONE-PERSON

[March–September] Cimarron, N.M. Philmont Scout Ranch. Seton Memorial Library and Museum. [*Photographs by Laura Gilpin*]. 16 prints.

December 6–February 26, 1971: Santa Fe, N.M. Institute of American Indian Arts. *A Retrospective Exhibition of Photographs by Laura Gilpin*. [300] prints. REVIEWS: *"Laura Gilpin Retrospective Opens Today in Santa Fe." *Albuquerque Journal*, December 6, 1970. 2 illus.
Kirby, V. G. "Santa Fe Art." [Santa Fe newspaper], December 10, 1970.

GROUP

August: Santa Fe, N.M. Gallery f22. *Fiesta 70: Photography Focusing on the Southwest*.

Publications

ABOUT LAURA GILPIN

"Miss Laura Gilpin Recalls the Years She Photographed." [*Santa Fe New Mexican*, February 1970].

*"Photographer Laura Gilpin Recalls Era of Lillian Gish at Central City." *Albuquerque Tribune*, February 13, 1970, *Lillian Gish by Mirror*.

Newton, Jim. "Lillian Gish Renews State Friendships." *Albuquerque Journal*, [February 17, 1970].

"We Headed toward Santa Fe." *Rough Rock News*, February 25, 1970.

Carr, Lorraine. "It Happened in S.F." [Albuquerque newspaper, April 1970].

"Laura Gilpin, Noted Photographer, Headliner in Culture Category." *Albuquerque Journal*, April 5, 1970.

"Miss Laura Gilpin Named as One of Headliners Trio." *Santa Fe New Mexican*, April 10, 1970.

"Chemist, Photographer, Linguist to be Honored." *Albuquerque Tribune*, May 15, 1970.

"U. to Present 3 Honorary Doctorates." *Albuquerque Journal*, May 18, 1970.

"University of New Mexico Will Honor Citizens with Doctorates." [Albuquerque newspaper, May–June 1970].

McCarty, Frankie. "U. Speaker Hits Sole Cause Idea." *Albuquerque Journal*, June 6, 1970.

Citation from David F. Cargo, Governor of New Mexico, appointing Laura Gilpin a Colonel, Aide-de-Camp, June 22, 1970.

Additional Photographs Published

*1970 Calendar, Mutual Building and Loan Association, Santa Fe. 6 illus.

Annual Report, Commission of Aging, Santa Fe, New Mexico. July 1, 1969–June 30, 1970, *Senior Sculptress*.

New Mexico Architecture 12 (September–October 1970): 21, 24, 34, 37. 4 illus.

*McGrath, James, and Mary Lou Denning. *Art and Indian Children: No. 1 – Pima, Papago, Apache*. Washington, D.C.: Center for Arts of Indian America, 1970, pp. 20–21. 2 illus.

A Place to Be. Reading, Mass.: Addison-Wesley Publishing Co., 1970, opp. p. 250, *Francis Nakai and Family*.

Una Hanbury. Santa Fe, n.d. Brochure/catalogue. 6 illus.

1971

Exhibitions

ONE-PERSON

May 30–June 18: Santa Fe, N.M. St. John's College. *An Exhibition of Photographs by Laura Gilpin*. 61 prints: Yucatán, Rio Grande, New Mexico. REVIEWS: "Laura Gilpin Exhibit Opens Today." *Santa Fe New Mexican*, May 30, 1971. § "Barbara Morgan and Laura Gilpin at St. John's College." *Santa Fe New Mexican*, June 6, 1971.

Publications

ABOUT LAURA GILPIN

*"Photographers Present Award to Laura Gilpin." [Colorado Springs newspaper, May 1971], *Old Lady Grey Salt*.

Citation from Bruce King, Governor of New Mexico, appointing Laura Gilpin a Colonel, Aide-de-Camp, May 3, 1971.

*"Laura Gilpin Honored in Santa Fe by IPSW." *Santa Fe New Mexican*, May 9, 1971. 4 illus.

*"Southwest Industrial Photographers Honor Laura Gilpin." *Albuquerque Journal*, [May 10, 1971], *Ason Kinlichine*.

*Waugh, Lynn. "Navajo Beauty Drawn with Light." *Christian Science Monitor*, September 13, 1971, *Navajo Weaver*.

Adams, Ansel. "An Honor for Laura Gilpin." *Friends of Photography Newsletter* 11 (November 1971).

"Noted Photographer Returns to Mesa Verde Park." *Cortez* [N.M.] *Sentinel*, November 22, 1971.

Additional Photographs Published

*1971 Calendar, Mutual Building and Loan Association, Santa Fe. 13 illus. REVIEW: *"Gilpin Photos Collected in 1971 Calendar." *Santa Fe New Mexican*, December 13, 1970, *Corndance, San Ildefonso*.

Gerontologist 2 (Spring 1971): cover, *Old Navajo Woman*.

*Soper, John. "Artist Popovi Da Remembered." *Santa Fe New Mexican*, October 24, 1971. 6 illus.

*"Christmas in Santa Fe Is a Special Time." *Santa Fe New Mexican*, November 14, 1971, *Ernest Rodriguez Home*.

*"Indian." In *World Book Encyclopedia*. Chicago: Field Enterprises Education Corp., 1971, 10: 138b, *Kachina Doll*.

*Rittenhouse, Jack D. *The Santa Fe Trail: A Historical Bibliography*. Albuquerque: University of New Mexico Press, 1971, fol. p. 56, *Santa Fe Trail near Ft. Union*.

1972

Exhibitions

GROUP

February 20–March 5:   Santa Fe, N.M. St. John's College. *A Selection of Churches and Public Buildings by John Gaw Meem, Architect.*

October 22–December 31:   Minneapolis, Minn. Walker Art Center. *American Indian Art: Form & Tradition.* 35 prints.

Publications

BY LAURA GILPIN

*"[Comment on Shiprock, New Mexico]." *Southwest Energy Study: Report of the Recreation and Aesthetics Work Group.* Santa Fe: U.S. Department of the Interior, National Park Service, Southwest Region, March 1972, appendix VI. 4 illus.

"Foreword." *The Navajo Blanket*, by Mary Hunt Kahlenberg and Anthony Berlant. Exhibition catalogue, Los Angeles County Museum of Art, 1972, p. 5.

*"In Memoriam: Popovi Da of San Ildefonso." *El Palacio* 78 (March 1972): 45, *Popovi Da*.

ABOUT LAURA GILPIN

Wilson, Maggie. "Pathways of History Lead to Discoveries." [Phoenix] *Arizona Republic*, January 29, 1972.

"Miss Laura Gilpin to Recall Reminiscenes [sic] of Navajo Life during Tuesday Night Lecture." *Santa Fe New Mexican*, February 13, 1972.

Aragon, John. "Brotherhood Awards Go to 2 from Albq, Santa Fe Woman." *Albuquerque Tribune*, [March 10, 1972].

Carr, Lorraine. "It Happened in Santa Fe." *Albuquerque Tribune*, April 12, 1972.

"Laura Gilpin and Ansel Adams." *Albuquerque Journal*, April 12, 1972.

Gregory, Wayne. "Three Praised for Their 'Exemplary Lives.'" *Albuquerque Tribune*, April 14, 1972.

Hay, Calla F. "Paso por Aqui." *Santa Fe New Mexican*, April 19, 1972.

*Kerr, Walter. "A Photographer's Light on Indian Trails." *New Mexico Magazine* 50 (May–June 1972): 6–11. 7 illus.

Additional Photographs Published

Southwestern Association on Indian Affairs, Inc., Santa Fe, Quarterly 7 (Spring 1972). 11 illus.

*"Ansel Adams Talks in Santa Fe Today." *Santa Fe New Mexican*, April 16, 1972, *Ansel Adams*.

*Bacher, Robert. "Robert Oppenheimer (1904–1967)." *Proceedings of the American Philosophical Society* 116 (August 1972). 2 illus.

*Pasadena, Calif. Art Museum. *Dorothy S. Benrimo.* November 21, 1972–February 4, 1973, *Dorothy Benrimo*.

*Blumenschein, Helen G. *Sounds and Sights of Taos Valley.* Santa Fe: Sunstone Press, 1972. [29] illus.

*Brochure for tour sponsored by the Northern Pueblos Enterprises, Inc. 1972. 2 illus.

*Donaldson, Scott. *Poet in America: Winfield Townley Scott.* Austin: University of Texas Press, 1972, fol. p. 114, *Scott Family*.

*Foster, Joseph O. *D. H. Lawrence in Taos.* Albuquerque: University of New Mexico Press, 1972, opp. p. 123, *Mabel Dodge Luhan*.

*Historic Santa Fe Foundation. *Old Santa Fe Today.* Albuquerque: University of New Mexico Press, 1972. 7 illus.

Meet the Pueblo Indians [tour brochure issued by Northern Pueblos Enterprises, Inc.]. 1972, *Tony Peña and Wife*.

*Sunset Books. *The Beautiful Southwest.* Menlo Park, Calif.: Lane Magazine and Book Company, 1972. 2 illus.

1973

Exhibitions

ONE-PERSON

October 10–December 15:   New York, N.Y. Witkin Gallery. [*Exhibition of Photographs by Laura Gilpin*]. 66 prints. REVIEWS: Hay, Calla. "Paso por Aqui." *Santa Fe New Mexican*, October 14, 1973. § Coleman, A. D. "She Studies People, He Fantasizes." *New York Times*, November 4, 1973.

GROUP

n.d.:   Albuquerque, N.M. University of New Mexico Art Museum. [*10th Anniversary Exhibition*]. 1 print.

Publications

ABOUT LAURA GILPIN

"Miss Laura Gilpin, Photographer-Author, Honored Further." *Santa Fe New Mexican*, January 28, 1973.
"Santa Fe Photographer Feted by Navajo Museum." *Navajo Times*, February 8, 1973.
"Laura Gilpin [and] Mr. and Mrs. Tony Peña." *Santa Fe New Mexican*, February 15, 1973.
"Gilpin Visits Tewa Center Children." [*Los Alamos Monitor*, February 18, 1973].
"Pop Culture Conference Set at Lawrence Ranch." *Albuquerque Journal*, February 19, 1973.
"3 Artists Featured at Taos Conference." *Santa Fe New Mexican*, February 20, 1973.
Oertl, Mary. "Enthusiasts Recall 'Old West' at Lawrence Ranch Meet." *University of New Mexico Campus News*, March 1, 1973.
"Paso por Aqui." *Santa Fe New Mexican*, May 20, 1973.
"Laura Gilpin, Nathaniel Owings, and Beaumont Newhall." *Santa Fe New Mexican*, June 10, 1973.
Daniels, Mary. "She's Recording the Roots of the Great Southwest." *Chicago Tribune*, July 1, 1973.

Additional Photographs Published

*U.S. Commission on Civil Rights. *The Southwest Indian Report*. Washington, May 1973. 10 illus.
El Palacio 79 (June 1973): 29, *Navajo Woman Wearing Bead Turquoise Necklace*.
*Daniels, Mary. "For Lady Brett of Taos, the Sun Also Sets." *Chicago Tribune*, July 22, 1973, *Lady Dorothy Brett*.
*"The Mystique of Turquoise, the Luster of Silver." *New Mexico Magazine* 51 (July–August 1973): 25–26. 2 illus.
*Portraits of the Enduring Land and Its People, Circa 1970." *Arizona Highways* 49 (August 1973): 16–33. 4 illus.
*Morrill, Claire. *A Taos Mosaic: Portrait of a New Mexico Village*. Albuquerque: University of New Mexico Press, 1973. 29 illus. REVIEW: Bullock, Alice. *Santa Fe New Mexican*, January 25, 1974.

*Owings, Nathaniel A. *The Spaces in Between: An Architect's Journey*. Boston: Houghton Mifflin, 1973. 2 illus.

1974

Exhibitions

ONE-PERSON

September–October: Farmington, N.M. San Juan County Salmon Ruins Archaeological Research Center and Library. [*Photographs by Laura Gilpin*]. 14 prints. REVIEWS: *"Camera Artists Exhibit." *Farmington Daily Times*, September 29, 1974, *Young Navajo Mother*. § "Photographer's Show at Ruins." *Farmington Daily Times*, October 13, 1974.

December 15–February 23, 1975:   Santa Fe, N.M. Museum of New Mexico, Fine Arts Museum. *Laura Gilpin Retrospective*. 100 prints. REVIEWS: *"Museum Offers Three Special Christmas Exhibitions." *Santa Fe New Mexican*, November 10, 1974, *Navajo Woman, Child and Lambs*. § *Perkins, Leroy. "State Museum's Tripledecker Is Yule Art Delight." *Albuquerque Journal*, December 15, 1974, *Picuris Church*. § *Mehalek, Jay. "Gilpin: Drawing with Light." *Santa Fe Reporter*, December 19, 1974, *Campo Santo*. § Price, Geraldine. "Laura Gilpin Photo Retrospective." *Santa Fe New Mexican*, December 29, 1974. § *Clift, William. "Laura Gilpin Retrospective." *Artweek*, February 8, 1975, p. 11. 2 illus.

Publications

BY LAURA GILPIN

*"María Martínez: Potter of San Ildefonso." *New Mexico Magazine* 52 (January 1974): 32. 2 illus.

ABOUT LAURA GILPIN

Noble, David Grant. "Laura Gilpin and Canyon de Chelly." *Santa Fe New Mexican*, March 24, 1974.
"Laura Gilpin Will Give Photographic Lecture Tonight." *Santa Fe News & Buyers Guide*, March 28, 1974.
*"Laura Gilpin Honors FAC Open House." *Colorado Springs Gazette Telegraph*, April 20, 1974, *Francis Nakai and Family*.
"Laura Gilpin to Return Home and Show-off Her Art." *Colorado Springs Sun*, April 21, 1974.
"Paso por Aqui." *Santa Fe New Mexican*, April 24, 1974.
Black, Charlotte. "Today's Laura Gilpin Still Focuses on Work." *Albuquerque Journal*, July 11, 1974.
"Vignette: Laura Gilpin, Photographer." *Santa Fean Magazine* 2 (September 1974): 6–7.
*Steinem, Gloria. "Laura Gilpin: The Compassionate Eye." *Ms.* 3 (September 1974): 59–61. 2 illus. REVIEW: Hay, Calla. "Paso por Aqui." *Santa Fe New Mexican*, August 28, 1974.
"October Proclaimed NM Arts Month." *Santa Fe New Mexican*, October 2, 1974.

Hoffman, Will. "Six Given Arts Awards." *Albuquerque Journal*, October 7, 1974.

Hillerman, Anne. "Governor's First Excellence Awards Given 6 NM Artists." *Santa Fe New Mexican*, October 7, 1974.

"N.M. Artists Honored." *Santa Fe New Mexican*, October 11, 1974.

Additional Photographs Published

*Gartler, Marion, and Marcella Benditt. *Smoke Signals*. Phoenix Reading Series. Englewood Cliffs, N.J.: Prentice-Hall, 1974. 2 illus.

*Los Alamos Historical Society. *When Los Alamos Was a Ranch School*. Los Alamos, 1974.

*McCarthy, Joseph F. X. *Record of America*. New York: Charles Scribners's Sons, 1974, 5: n.p., *San Jose Mission Church, Laguna, New Mexico*.

1975

Exhibitions

ONE-PERSON

April 1–30: Colorado Springs, Colo. Fine Arts Center. *Laura Gilpin Retrospective*. 100 prints. REVIEW: *"Gilpin Exhibit to Open at FAC." *Colorado Springs Sun*, April 4, 1975. 2 illus.

July 1–August 30: Phoenix, Ariz. Heard Museum. *Laura Gilpin Retrospective*. 100 prints.

September 10–October 6: Oklahoma City, Okla. Art Center. *Laura Gilpin Retrospective*. 100 prints.

October 15–November 30: Wichita Falls, Tex. Wichita Falls Museum and Art Center. *Laura Gilpin Retrospective*. 100 prints.

December 1–January 11, 1976: Tyler, Tex. Tyler Museum of Art. *Laura Gilpin Retrospective*. 100 prints.

GROUP

[February]: New London, Conn. Lyman Allyn Museum. *Women Look at Women*. 2 prints.

April 18–June 15: San Francisco, Calif. Museum of Art. *Women of Photography: An Historical Survey*. 5 prints. REVIEWS: Frankenstein, Alfred. "Imagery of Women." *San Francisco Chronicle*, April 27, 1975. § Mann, Margery. "Selecting Woman of Photography." *San Francisco Sunday Examiner and Chronicle*, May 25, 1975.

[May]: Providence, R.I. University of Rhode Island. *Women Look at Women*. 2 prints.

June: Washington, D.C. Smithsonian Institution. National Museum of American History. *We the People: The American People and Their Government*. 1 print.

June 22–October 6: Albuquerque, N.M. University of New Mexico. Maxwell Museum of Anthropology. *Roadrunner's Trail*. 8 prints.

June 28–July 25: New Canaan, Conn. Photographics Workshop. *Women Look at Women*. 2 prints.

August 7–October 5: Fort Worth, Tex. Amon Carter Museum. *The Big Bend: The Last Frontier of Texas*. 4 prints.

September 15–October 26: Santa Fe, N.M. Museum of New Mexico, Fine Arts Museum. *Women of Photography: An Historical Survey*. 5 prints. REVIEWS: Perkins, Leroy. "Blending Controversies: Women and Photography." *Albuquerque Journal*, [September 15, 1975]. § Koppel, Rolf. "A Complex, Exemplary Performance." *Santa Fe Reporter*, September 18, 1975. § Hamilton, John. "Photography as Art–at Long Last." *Santa Fe New Mexican*, September 21, 1975.

November 11–January 11, 1976: New Haven, Conn. Yale University Art Gallery. *Color Photography: Inventors and Innovators, 1850–1975*. 3 prints.

November 29–January 3, 1976: New York, N.Y. Sidney Janis Gallery. *Women of Photography: An Historical Survey*. 5 prints.

Publications

ABOUT LAURA GILPIN

Dravo, Andrea. "Through a Lens, from the Heart." *Santa Fe Reporter*, February 27, 1975.

Hay, Calla. "Local Photographer Selected by Guggenheim." *Santa Fe New Mexican*, April 13, 1975.

*"Laura Gilpin, Photographer." *New America: A Review* 1 (Spring 1975): 28–32. 10 illus.: Yucatán.

Koops, Sandra. "Laura Gilpin: 'First Lady' of Photography." *Santa Fe New Mexican*, July 25, 1975.

*"Laura Gilpin: Reflections." *Santa Fe Reporter*, August 14, 1975. 10 illus.

*Lindsay, Rick. "The Corner Stone: In the Beginning There Was Turquoise . . ." *Santa Fe Reporter*, August 14, 1975, *Tony Peña*.

*Ward, Bob. "Words for the Wary." *Santa Fe Reporter*, August 14, 1975, [*Indian Jewelry*].

*Seymour, Jim. "Laura Gilpin: 84 and Still Clicking in the Southwest." *Modern Photography* 39 (September 1975): 38, *Covered Wagon*.

Hillerman, Anne. "Santa Fe's Fiesta Goes on Camera." *Santa Fe New Mexican*, September 2, 1975.

*"Laura Gilpin." *Creative Camera*, no. 137 (November 1975), pp. 364, 368–371. 4 illus.

Clurman, Irene. "Lively Laura Gilpin Preparing Another Southwest Chronicle." *Rocky Mountain News*, November 16, 1975.

Hay, Calla. "Santa Fe Stars in 'W' Article." *Santa Fe New Mexican*, November 20, 1975.

*Noble, David Grant. "Laura Gilpin and Canyon de Chelly." *Exploration 1975* (Santa Fe: School of American Research), pp. 16–19. 2 illus.

Additional Photographs Published
The American Revolution Bicentennial in New Mexico. [1975], *The Rio Grande at Rinconado.*

1976
Exhibitions
ONE-PERSON

February 1–28:   Roswell, N.M. Museum and Art Center. *Laura Gilpin Retrospective.* 100 prints.   REVIEW: "Roswell Museum Exhibiting Gilpin." *Albuquerque Journal,* February 8, 1976.

March 2–27:   San Francisco, Calif. Focus Gallery. *Laura Gilpin: A 50 Print Retrospective.* 50 prints.   REVIEWS: Hay, Calla. "Gilpin Show to Open in San Francisco." [*Santa Fe New Mexican,* March 1975]. § Albright, Thomas. "Gilpin Photos at Focus." *San Francisco Chronicle,* March 16, 1976. § *Bloomfield, Arthur. "A Great Landscape Photographer." *San Francisco Examiner,* March 16, 1976, *Covered Wagon.* § *Fischer, Hal. "Laura Gilpin and John Harding." *Artweek,* March 20, 1976, *Ranchos de Taos Church.* § *"Shows We've Seen." *Popular Photography* 79 (July 1976): 13. 2 illus. § *Bloomfield, Arthur. "Photography Has Come into Its Own as an Art." *San Francisco Sunday Examiner and Chronicle,* December 26, 1976, *Old Navajo Woman.*

April 2–May 2:   Dayton, Ohio. Art Institute. *Laura Gilpin Retrospective.* 100 prints.   REVIEWS: *McCaslin, Walt. "Photographs By Gilpin Reflect Quest for 'Art.'" *Dayton Journal Herald,* April 7, 1976. 2 illus. § *Krebs, Betty Dietz. "Without Gilpin, the Gap Would Have Been Wide." *Dayton Leisure,* April 11, 1976. 4 illus.

May 20–June 15:   Newcastle, Wyo. Butler Gallery. *Laura Gilpin Retrospective.* 100 prints.

June 15–July 12:   Worland, Wyo. Gallery Mart. *Laura Gilpin Retrospective.* 100 prints.

July 12–August 12:   Wheatland, Wyo. Platte City Library. *Laura Gilpin Retrospective.* 100 prints.

September 1–26:   Kansas City, Mo. Nelson-Atkins Museum of Art. *Laura Gilpin Retrospective.* 100 prints.   REVIEW: *Hoffman, Donald. "Now's the Time for the Indians." *Kansas City Star,* [September 1976], *Francis Nakai and Family.*

October 4–30:   St. Joseph, Mo. Albrecht Museum of Art. *Laura Gilpin Retrospective.* 100 prints.

November 7–December 15:   Poughkeepsie, N.Y. Vassar College Art Gallery. *Laura Gilpin Retrospective.* 100 prints.

GROUP

January 23–31:   Los Alamos, N.M. Fuller Lodge. *Santa Fe Women.* REVIEW: Dunning, Anne. "Women's Week Events Enhanced by Art Exhibit." [Los Alamos newspaper], February 3, 1976.

February 1–June 6:   Albuquerque, N.M. Museum of Albuquerque. *Women in New Mexico.* REVIEWS: Hay, Calla. "'Women in New Mexico' Opens in the Duke City on Feb. 1." *Santa Fe New Mexican,* January 18, 1976. L'Hommedieu, Helena. "AAUW Exhibit Depicts Women's Contributions." *Albuquerque Journal,* January 23, 1976.

February 2–March 14:   Milwaukee, Wis. University of Wisconsin. Art History Galleries. *Women of Photography: An Historical Survey.* 5 prints.

April 1–30:   St. Louis, Mo. University of Missouri. *Aspects of American Photography 1976.* 6 prints; *Canyon de Chelly* illus. in cat.

April 12–May 30:   Wellesley, Mass. Wellesley College. *Women of Photography: An Historical Survey.* 5 prints.

May 25–August 13:   Santa Fe, N.M. Museum of New Mexico. Art Museum. *Masterworks from the Permanent Collection.* [2] prints.   REVIEW: "Santa Fe Art Show Breathtaking." *Albuquerque Journal,* May 23, 1976.

June 21–August 1:   West Palm Beach, Fla. Norton Gallery and School of Art. *Women of Photography: An Historical Survey.* 5 prints.

June 29–July 30:   Santa Fe, N.M. Governor's Gallery. *Art in Nuevo Mexico Circa 1776.*

August 30–October 10:   San Diego, Calif. Fine Arts Gallery. *Women of Photography: An Historical Survey.* 5 prints.

October 3–26:   Pullman, Wash. Washington State University Museum of Art. *A Temporary Possession: The Human Image in 20th Century Photography.* 2 prints.

Publications
ABOUT LAURA GILPIN

Hall, Rosanna. "Laura Gilpin: A Lifetime of Photography." *Santa Fe New Mexican,* July 1, 1976.

"Paso por Aqui." *Santa Fe New Mexican,* July 15, 1976.

*Pearl, George Clayton. "Tradition and the Individual Talent: The Architecture of John Gaw Meem as Photographed by Laura Gilpin." *El Palacio* 82 (Summer 1976): 22–35. 14 illus.

Mitchell, Linda. "New Mexico's Women Are at the Top of Photographic Profession." *Albuquerque Herald,* October 1, 1976.

Hill, Paul, and Tom Cooper. "Camera Interview: Laura Gilpin." *Camera,* no. 11 (November 1976), pp. 11, 27, 35–37.

*McCumber, David C. "Images of the Southwest: A Landmark in New Mexico Photography – Laura Gilpin." [*Los Alamos Monitor*] *Sunrise*, November 7, 1976, [*Navajo Woman*].

Konopak, John. "The Old Man and the Sky." *Santa Fe Reporter*, November 11, 1976.

"Laura Gilpin and William Clift." *Santa Fe New Mexican*, November 12, 1976.

*Rosnek, Carl, and Joseph Stacey. *Skystone and Silver: The Collector's Book of Southwest Indian Jewelry.* Englewood Cliffs, N.J.: Prentice-Hall, 1976, pp. 122–124. 5 illus.

Who's Who in American Art, 1976. New York: R. R. Bowker, 1976, p. 201.

Additional Photographs Published

Landscape Architectural Forum, June 1976, cover, p. 3. 4 illus.

*Kimbro, Harriet. "An Artist Looks at Architecture." *New Mexico Architecture* 18 (September–October 1976): 10–12. 3 illus.

1977

Exhibitions

ONE-PERSON

January 15–February 15:   Littleton, Colo. Littleton Historical Museum. *Laura Gilpin Retrospective.* 100 prints.

March 1–30:   Grand Junction, Colo. Western Colorado Center for the Arts. *Laura Gilpin Retrospective.* 100 prints.

May: Santa Fe, N.M. School of American Research. [*Photographs of the Canyon de Chelly by Laura Gilpin*]. REVIEWS: "Paso por Aqui." *Santa Fe New Mexican*, May 22, 1977. § Clark, Ann D. "SAR Exhibit Honors Gilpin." *Santa Fe New Mexican*, May 24, 1977.

May 1–30:   Blanding, Utah. Broken Arrow Center. *Laura Gilpin Retrospective.* 100 prints.

June 16–July 17:   Austin, Tex. Laguna Gloria Art Museum. *Laura Gilpin Retrospective.* 100 prints.

September 12–October 6:   Santa Fe, N.M. State Capitol. Governor's Gallery. *Laura Gilpin.* 77 prints, 2 illus. in cat. REVIEWS: "Governor Honors Gilpin." [*Santa Fe New Mexican*], September 11, 1977. § "Photographer Honored." *Santa Fe New Mexican*, September 13, 1977. § Hay, Calla. "Gallery Social Honors Laura Gilpin." *Santa Fe New Mexican*, September 15, 1977. § *Kieve, Rudolph. "Gilpin Show Offers Beauty, Sensitivity." *Santa Fe New Mexican*, September 18, 1977, [*Junction Overlook*].

November 1–30:   Phoenix, Ariz. University of Arizona. Center for Creative Photography. *Platinum Prints by Laura Gilpin.*

GROUP

May: El Paso, Tex. El Paso National Bank. [*Women's Photography Exhibit*]. REVIEWS: "Photo Exhibit by Women Set." *El Paso Herald-Post*, May 20, 1977. § *"Women's Photo Exhibit Opens at El Paso Bank." *El Paso Times*, May 22, 1977, *Basil McCormick*.

May 8–?:   Santa Fe, N.M. Elaine Horwitch Galleries. *5 Santa Fe Photographers.* REVIEWS: Beerer, Pamela. "Photographers Show Beauty, Detail." [*Albuquerque Journal*, May 1977]. § Beerer, Pamela. "Laura Gilpin Favors Platinum Prints." [*Albuquerque Journal*, May 1977]. § *Koppel, Rolf. "Santa Fe Five: Casting Diffuse Lights." *Santa Fe Reporter*, May 19, 1977, *White Iris*.

July 12–August 5:   New York, N.Y. Prakapas Gallery. *The Landscape in Photography.*

July 31–October 30:   Santa Fe, N.M. Wheelwright Museum. *Children of Changing Woman: Myth, Symbol and Navajo Women.* 3 illus. in cat.

September 9–October 14:   Boulder, Colo. University of Colorado. Fine Arts Department. *The Great West: Real/Ideal.* 3 prints, illus. in cat. REVIEW: Ross, Trudie. "Photographic Artists of Southwest Shine." *Denver Post*, April 23, 1978.

September 25–October 30:   Phoenix, Ariz. University of Arizona Museum of Art. *Photographs from the Collection of the Center for Creative Photography.* 6 prints.

October: Edinboro, Pa. Edinboro State College. *Photography: The Selected Image.* [2] prints, illus. in cat.

November: University Park, Pa. Pennsylvania State University. *Photography: The Selected Image.* [2] prints, illus. in cat.

December 13–January 27, 1978:   Santa Fe, N.M. State Capitol. Governor's Gallery. *The San Francisco de Assisi Church, Ranchos de Taos.* 1 print, illus. in cat. REVIEW: *"A Look at Ranchos Church." *Santa Fe New Mexican*, December 11, 1977, *Ranchos de Taos Church*.

Publications

ABOUT LAURA GILPIN

Bullock, Alice. "Laura Gilpin: America's Grande Dame of Photography." *Enchantment* 27 (February 1977): 4.

*Vestal, David. "Laura Gilpin: Photographer of the Southwest." *Popular Photography* 80 (February 1977): 100–105, 130–134. 6 illus.

Tryk, Sheila. "Laura Gilpin: An Image for All Time." *Dallas Times Herald Sunday Magazine*, March 20, 1977, pp. 6–11.

*Koops, Sandra. "Museum Features New Acquisitions." *Santa Fe New Mexican*, March 27, 1977, *Covered Wagon*.

Steinberg, Dave. "State's Photo Talent Looms Bright." *Albuquerque Journal*, March 31, 1977.

Hay, Calla. "Laura Gilpin Celebrates 87th [sic] Birthday." *Santa Fe New Mexican,* April 27, 1977.

Executive Order from Richard D. Lamm, Governor of Colorado, naming Laura Gilpin a recipient of Governor's Award in the Arts and Humanities, September 9, 1977.

Mills, James. "Three Honored for Contributions to Art." *Denver Post,* September 12, 1977.

"Carter Museum to Open Administrative Wing, Auditorium." *Fort Worth Star-Telegram,* October 23, 1977.

"Carter Museum Adds Sculpture, Photographs." *Dallas Times Herald,* October 24, 1977.

Peck, John. "Time Exposure." [Tucson] *Arizona Daily Star,* November 9, 1977.

Moser, Charlotte. "New Mexico: Open Land and Psychic Elbow Room." *Art News* 76 (December 1977): 74–78.

Scarborough, John. "Gilpin, 86, Shooting Fifth Book." *Houston Chronicle,* December 30, 1977.

"Laura Gilpin." *1977 Colorado Governor's Award for the Arts and Humanities.* Brochure.

Additional Photographs Published

**New Mexico Magazine*'s Collector's Calendar: *1977 Enchanted New Mexico Desk Engagement Book.* 3 illus.

**Journal Advertiser* 1 (May 4–11, 1977): cover, *Rio Grande at Rinconado.*

*"Center for Creative Photography." In *Tenth Annual Report. The Presidents Club. University of Arizona.* Tucson, October 1977, p. 11. 2 illus.

*Colorado Springs. Fine Arts Center. Taylor Museum. *Hispanic Crafts of the Southwest.* October 4–December 4, 1977, cover, *Chimayo Weaver.*

*Prairie Schooner 51 (Fall 1977): 249, *The Cliff Palace from Sun Point.*

**Vassar College Alumni Quarterly* (Winter 1977–78), *Rain Drops on Lupin Leaves.*

**Amon Carter Museum, 1961–1977.* Fort Worth, 1977, p. 36, *Bryce Canyon, No. 2.*

*Hassrick, Peter. *The Way West.* New York: Harry N. Abrams, 1977, p. 226, *Great Northern Skyline of Sangre de Cristo.*

*Keleman, Pal. *Vanishing Art of the Americas.* New York: Walker & Company, 1977. 2 illus.

*Vedder, Alan C. *Furniture of Spanish New Mexico.* Santa Fe: Sunstone Press, 1977. 8 illus.

1978

Exhibitions

ONE-PERSON

March 17–April 30:   Oklahoma City, Okla. National Cowboy Hall of Fame. *Laura Gilpin Retrospective.* 125 prints. REVIEWS: "Cowboy Hall Shows Gilpin Photographs." [unidentified newspaper, March 1978].

§ *"Photographer Achieves Long-Awaited Famed [sic]." *Sunday Oklahoman,* March 12, 1978, *Typical Navajo Posture.*

May 11–June 25:   Fort Worth, Tex. Amon Carter Museum. *Laura Gilpin Retrospective.* 125 prints. REVIEWS: Kutner, Janet. "Simplicity Marks Gilpin Show." *Dallas Morning News,* May 13, 1978. § *Nuckols, Carol. "Laura Gilpin Show Reflects a 75-year Career." *Fort Worth Star-Telegram,* May 14, 1978, *A Chance Meeting in the Desert.* § *Nuckols, Carol. "Subtle Shading Highlights Gilpin Collection at Museum." *Fort Worth Star-Telegram,* May 26, 1978. 2 illus.

October: Laramie, Wyo. University of Wyoming. Fine Arts Museum. *Laura Gilpin Retrospective.* 100 prints. REVIEWS: *Stoesz, Mike. "Laura Gilpin: A Retrospective Exhibit." *Laramie Sunday Boomerang,* October 8, 1978. 7 illus. § "Museum to Feature Gilpin Photographs." *Laramie Boomerang,* October 8, 1978. § "Gilpin's Photos Displayed at UW." [unidentified Laramie newspaper], October 11, 1978.

GROUP

July 13–September 3:   New York, N.Y. International Center of Photography. *The Great West: Real/Ideal.* 3 prints, illus. in cat.

September 23–October 22:   North Adams, Mass. North Adams State College. *The Great West: Real/Ideal.* 3 prints, illus. in cat.

October: Houston, Tex. Museum of Fine Arts. *Photography: The Selected Image.* [2] prints, illus. in cat. REVIEW: *Crossley, Mimi. "A Different View." *Houston Post,* October 8, 1978, *Navajo Woman, Child and Lambs.*

November 3–December 17:   New Orleans, La. Museum of Art. **Diverse Images: Photographs from the New Orleans Museum of Art.* [1] print, illus. in cat.

November 11–December 10:   Houston, Tex. Sharpview Nursing Center. *The Great West: Real/Ideal.* 3 prints, illus. in cat.

December 30–January 28, 1978:   Columbus, Ohio. Columbus Gallery of Fine Arts. *The Great West: Real/Ideal.* 3 prints, illus. in cat.

Publications

ABOUT LAURA GILPIN

Hall, Rosanna. "13 Outstanding New Mexico Women." *Santa Fe New Mexican,* January 15, 1978.

"Photography Group Honors Miss Gilpin." *Albuquerque Journal,* March 6, 1978.

*James, Peggy. "Laura Gilpin, Photographer: The Elusive Image Magnetized into Art." *Colorado Springs* 2 (March–April 1978): 18–27. 10 illus.

"Photographer to Donate Collection to Museum." *Fort Worth Star-Telegram,* May 12, 1978.

Marvel, Bill. "Laura Gilpin's Work Donated." *Dallas Times Herald*, May 12, 1978.

"Acquisition of Gilpin Works a First for Amon Carter Museum." *Fort Worth Star-Telegram*, May 12, 1978.

*Marvel, Bill. "Laura Gilpin Legacy a Photographic Treasury of the Southwest." *Dallas Times Herald*, May 14, 1978. 3 illus.

*Belden, Dorothy. "For 75 Years, She Froze Story of West on Film." *Wichita* [Kans.] *Eagle Beacon*, May 28, 1978. 2 illus.

Belden, Dorothy. "Gilpin Focuses on Indians, Canyons." *Fort Worth Star-Telegram*, June 16, 1978.

"Gilpin Granted National Award." *Santa Fe New Mexican*, June 29, 1978.

Belden, Dorothy. "Laura Gilpin: Portrait of the Artist as a Young Woman." *Colorado Springs Gazette Telegraph*, July 4, 1978.

Dickman, Marcy. "Gilpin Legacy to Bypass Museum of New Mexico." *Santa Fe Reporter*, September 28, 1978.

*"Camera Chronicles of Laura Gilpin." *Persimmon Hill* 8 (1978): 66–79. 9 illus.

Who's Who in American Art, 1978. New York: R. R. Bowker, 1978, p. 250.

Additional Photographs Published

*"Better Than a Thousand Words." *Outside* 1 (January 1978). 2 illus.

*[Albuquerque] *Journal Advertiser*, April 1978, *White Iris*.

Southwest Review 63 (Spring 1978): cover, *George Lopez, Cordova, N.M.*

*Cooper, Tom C. "Faces of the Land." *Arizona Highways* 54 (September 1978): 2–15. 3 illus.

*Green, Jonathan. "Photography as Popular Culture." *Journal of the University Film Association* 30 (Fall 1978): 16, *Big Bed, Tiny Tot.*

*Nabokov, Peter, ed. *Native American Testimony*. New York: Thomas Y. Crowell, 1978, p. 58, *Tonajinni (Blanca Peak)*.

*Tetreault, Mary K. *Women in America: Half of History*. Chicago: Rand McNally & Co., 1978, p. 129, *Old Navajo Woman and Baby*.

1979

Exhibitions

ONE-PERSON

May 12–September 21:   Los Alamos, N.M. Los Alamos Historical Museum. *Laura Gilpin: Ranch School Photographs.*

August–September 30:   Farmington, N.M. Civic Center. *Laura Gilpin Retrospective*. 100 prints. REVIEW: *"The Sensitive Eye of Photographer Laura Gilpin." *Farmington Daily Times*, August 26, 1979. 6 illus.

November 6–December 31:   Phoenix, Ariz. Arizona Bank Galleria. *Laura Gilpin: Platinum Prints.*

December 9–January 31, 1980:   Santa Fe, N.M. Museum of New Mexico. Fine Arts Museum. *Laura Gilpin Memorial Exhibition*. REVIEW: "Gilpin Photos on View." [*Santa Fe New Mexican*, December 1979].

GROUP

January: Washington, D.C. Library of Congress. *Women Look at Women*. 1 print.

January 25–February 28:   New York, N.Y. Whitney Museum of American Art, Downtown Branch. *Industrial Sights*. 1 print.

February–?:   Santa Fe, N.M. Armory for the Arts. *21 Photographers*. REVIEW: Fabricant, Don. "Photograph Show Has High Quality." *Santa Fe New Mexican*, February 9, 1979.

February 17–March 18:   Buffalo, N.Y. Erie Savings Bank. *The Great West: Real/Ideal*. 3 prints, illus. in cat.

March 20–May 5:   New York, N.Y. Witkin Gallery. *1969–1979*. 3 prints.

April 7–May 6:   Vermillion, S.D. University of South Dakota, W. H. Over Museum. *The Great West: Real/Ideal*. 3 prints, illus. in cat.

May 12–June 29:   Los Alamos, N.M. Fuller Lodge Art Center. *Laura Gilpin/William Clift Photographs*. 20 prints.

May 14–September 5:   Taos, N.M. Millicent Rogers Museum. *Navajo Weaving – A Survey*. 1 photo-mural.

July 29–September 7:   Santa Fe, N.M. Santa Fe Gallery of Photography. *Santa Fe: Past & Present, 1860–1979*. 6 prints, 2 illus. in cat.

August–September 3:   Dallas, Tex. Museum of Fine Arts. *Photography: The Selected Image*. [2] prints. REVIEW: Kutner, Janet. "Photograph Exhibit Frames Art Form Mastery." *Dallas Morning News*, August 15, 1979.

September 19–November 25:   New York, N.Y. Whitney Museum of American Art. *Photography Rediscovered: American Photographs, 1900–1930*. 7 prints, illus. in cat.

September 20–November 4:   New York, N.Y. International Center of Photography. *Recollections: Ten Women of Photography*. 20 prints. REVIEW: Glueck, Grace. "Art: Photography of 10 Gifted Women." *New York Times*, September 28, 1979.

September 28–October 7:   Santa Fe, N.M. Sweeney Center. Festival of the Arts. *Contemporary New Mexico Photography*. REVIEW: Dooling, Anna. "Photography As Document, and As Art." *Santa Fe Reporter*, October 4, 1979.

September 30–November 18: Colorado Springs, Colo. Fine Arts Center. *Photographs by Laura Gilpin and Ernest Knee.*

October 20–November 18: Rochester, N.Y. Lincoln First Bank. *The Great West: Real/Ideal.* 3 prints, illus. in cat.

December 22–February 4, 1980: Chicago, Ill. Art Institute. *Photography Rediscovered: American Photographs, 1900–1930.* 7 prints, illus. in cat.

Publications

ABOUT LAURA GILPIN

*Thompson, C. B. "Laura Gilpin." *Art Voices/South* 2 (January–February 1979): 23. 2 illus.

*Evans, Karen. "Laura Gilpin: A Portfolio of Photographs." *Rocky Mountain Magazine* 1 (May 1979): 72–79. 6 illus.

*Kane, Sid. "Images by Laura Gilpin." *New Mexico Craft* 1 (May–June 1979): 15–17. 3 illus.

Dillon, David. "A Mitchell Wilder Retrospective." *D Magazine* 6 (June 1979): 22.

Hoelterhoff, Manuela. "Santa Fe: A Veritable Pueblo of the Arts." *Wall Street Journal*, August 17, 1979.

*Dean, Katie. "Laura: Grand Lady of Santa Fe." *Denver Post*, October 21, 1979. 5 illus.

Dickman, Marcy. "Letter from Santa Fe." *American Photographer* 3 (November 1979): 76–79.

*Green, Stewart M. "The Skies of Laura Gilpin." *Colorado Springs Sun*, November 4, 1979, *Navajos in the Shiprock Area.*

*Coke, Van Deren. *Photography in New Mexico.* Albuquerque: University of New Mexico Press, 1979, pp. 32–33. 4 illus.

Dater, Judy. *Imogen Cunningham: A Portrait.* Boston: New York Graphic Society, 1979, pp. 66–67, 93, 101.

Hill, Paul, and Thomas Cooper. *Dialogue with Photography.* New York: Farrar, Straus, Giroux, 1979, pp. 282–292.

*Mitchell, Margaretta K. *Recollections: Ten Women of Photography.* New York: Viking Press, 1979, pp. 120–139. 18 illus.

OBITUARIES, MEMORIAL TRIBUTES

Hammett, Kingsley. "Laura Gilpin Dies at 88." *Santa Fe New Mexican*, November 30, 1979.

"Obituaries." *Santa Fe New Mexican*, November 30, 1979.

"Top Photographer Laura Gilpin Dies." *Albuquerque Tribune*, November 30, 1979.

Nuckols, Carol. "Noted Photographer Laura Gilpin Dies." *Fort Worth Star-Telegram*, December 1, 1979.

"Laura Gilpin, 88, Studied Navajos in Her Photographs for 40 Years." *New York Times*, December 1, 1979.

Marvel, Bill. "Landscape Photographer Laura Gilpin Dies at 88." *Dallas Times Herald*, December 1, 1979.

Hall, Rosanna. "Laura Gilpin 'In Harmony' with Work." *Santa Fe New Mexican*, December 1, 1979.

Beerer, Pamela. "Laura Gilpin Dies at Age 88." *Albuquerque Journal*, December 1, 1979.

*"Laura Gilpin: Her Work Lives On." *Santa Fe New Mexican*, December 2, 1979. 5 illus.

"Laura Gilpin." *Santa Fe New Mexican*, December 3, 1979.

*"The Christmases of Laura Gilpin." *Santa Fe Reporter*, December 6, 1979. 10 illus.

Clift, William. "Remembering Laura Gilpin." *Santa Fe Reporter*, December 6, 1979.

Cooke, Regina. "Southwestern Photographer Laura Gilpin Dies." *Taos News*, December 13, 1979.

Additional Photographs Published

*Coke, Van Deren. "New Mexico and Photography." *New Mexico Magazine* 57 (April 1979): 35, *Campo Santo.*

*Morrison, Phylis. *Spider's Games: A Book for Beginning Weavers.* Seattle: University of Washington Press, 1979, p. 64, *Navajo Weaver and Child.*

*New Orleans Museum of Art. *Diverse Images: Photographs from the New Orleans Museum of Art.* Garden City, N.J.: Amphoto Press, 1979, p. 93, *Sunlight and Shadow.*

*Santa Fe Concert Association brochure, 43rd Season, 1979–1980, cover, *Snow Coral.*

*Spivey, Richard. *Maria.* Flagstaff, Ariz.: Northland Press, 1979. 13 illus.

*Witkin, Lee D. *A Ten Year Salute: A Selection of Photographs in Celebration, The Witkin Gallery, 1969–1979.* Danbury, N.H.: Addison House, 1979, p. 153, *White Iris.*

1980

Exhibitions

ONE-PERSON

June 4–August 22: New York, N.Y. Witkin Gallery. *Laura Gilpin.* REVIEW: Raynor, Vivien. "Art: The Photographs of Laura Gilpin Shown." *New York Times*, June 20, 1980.

October 9–19: Santa Fe, N.M. Sweeney Center. *Laura Gilpin, Photographer.* REVIEWS: *"Gilpin's Humanity Endures in Photos." *Santa Fe New Mexican*, October 8, 1980, *Navajo Woman, Child and Lambs.* § *Bienvenu, John. "Laura Gilpin Never Knew How Good She Was." *Santa Fe Reporter*, October 9, 1980, *Monument Valley.*

November 6–December 31: Phoenix, Ariz. Arizona Bank Galleria. *Laura Gilpin: Platinum Prints.*

GROUP

January 1–February 17: Knoxville, Tenn. Dulin Gallery of Art. *Recollections: Ten Women of Photography.* 20 prints.

January 26–February 24: Wichita, Kans. Wichita State

University. Ulrich Museum of Art. *The Great West: Real/Ideal.* 3 prints, illus. in cat.

March 1–April 15: Grand Rapids, Mich. Art Museum. *Recollections: Ten Women of Photography.* 20 prints.

March 15–April 13: Wausau, Wis. Woodson Art Museum. *The Great West: Real/Ideal.* 3 prints, illus. in cat.

May 1–June 15: Northhampton, Mass. Smith College Museum of Art. *Recollections: Ten Women of Photography.* 20 prints.

May 3–June 1: Billings, Mont. Yellowstone Art Center. *The Great West: Real/Ideal.* 3 prints, illus. in cat.

June 21–July 20: Bowling Green, Ky. Western Kentucky University. Ivan Wilson Center for Fine Arts. *The Great West: Real/Ideal.* 3 prints, illus. in cat.

July 1–August 15: Port Washington, N.Y. Port Washington Public Library. *Recollections: Ten Women of Photography.* 20 prints.

August 9–September 7: Saskatoon, Saskatchewan, Canada. Mendel Art Gallery. *The Great West: Real/Ideal.* 3 prints, illus. in cat.

September 1–October 19: Oxford, Ohio. Miami University Art Museum. *Recollections: Ten Women of Photography.* 20 prints.

September 5–October 12: Phoenix, Ariz. Art Museum. *Visitors to Arizona, 1846 to 1980.* 1 print, illus. in cat.

September 27–October 26: Cedar Falls, Iowa. University of Northern Iowa. College of Humanities and Fine Arts. *The Great West: Real/Ideal.* 3 prints, illus. in cat.

October 19–November 30: Tucson, Ariz. Museum of Art. *Visitors to Arizona, 1846 to 1980.* 1 print, illus. in cat.

November 1–December 15: Kansas City, Mo. Nelson-Atkins Museum of Art. *Recollections: Ten Women of Photography.* 20 prints.

November 15–December 14: Rockville, Md. Montgomery College. *The Great West: Real/Ideal.* 3 prints, illus. in cat.

Publications

ABOUT LAURA GILPIN

*Mezey, Phil. "Classic Visions from the Southwest." *Darkroom Photography* 2 (January–February 1980): 30–34. 5 illus.

"Gilpin Collection Includes Thousands of Photos." *Houston Chronicle,* February 16, 1980.

*Powell, Lawrence Clark. "Letter from the Southwest." *Westways* 72 (March 1980): 20–23, 84. 2 illus.

"Gilpin Photos Are Given New Home." *Albuquerque Journal,* March 2, 1980.

*Nuckols, Carol. "The Remarkable Gilpin." *Fort Worth Star-Telegram,* March 30, 1980. 2 illus.

*"Laura Gilpin Festival Poster." *Santa Fe New Mexican,* May 11, 1980, *Storm over La Bajada.*

*"Festival Posters on Sale." *Santa Fe New Mexican,* June 18, 1980, *Storm over La Bajada.*

*"Gilpin Gift." *Santa Fe New Mexican,* August 20, 1980, *Georgia O'Keeffe.*

*Whelen, Richard. "Are Women Better Photographers Than Men?" *Art News* 79 (October 1980): 85, *Red Rock Trading Post.*

*Sandweiss, Marni. "Laura Gilpin's Indians: An Enduring Image." *Four Winds* 1 (Autumn 1980): 52–63. 11 illus.

"Photography Show Opens with Movie about Gilpin." *Los Alamos Monitor,* December 4, 1980.

Additional Photographs Published

*Briggs, Charles L. *The Wood Carvers of Cordova, New Mexico.* Knoxville: University of Tennessee Press, 1980, p. 95, *George Lopez.*

*Frost, Hunter S. *Art, Artifacts, Architecture: Fountain Valley School.* Colorado Springs: Tiverton Press, 1980. 6 illus.

*Nelson, Mary Carroll. *The Legendary Artists of Taos.* New York: Watson-Guptill Publications, 1980. 5 illus.

1981

Exhibitions

ONE-PERSON

December 6–?: Santa Fe, N.M. The Loft. [*Photographs by Laura Gilpin*]. REVIEW: "New Santa Fe Gallery Presents Gilpin Photos." *Santa Fe New Mexican,* December 4, 1981.

GROUP

January 1–February 15: Utica, N.Y. Munson-Williams-Proctor Institute. *Recollections: Ten Women of Photography.* 20 prints.

January 10–February 8: Havre, Mont. Northern Montana State College. *The Great West: Real/Ideal.* 3 prints, illus. in cat.

February 28–March 29: Lubbock, Tex. Texas Tech University. Museum. *The Great West: Real/Ideal.* 3 prints, illus. in cat.

March 1–April 15: Charleston, S.C. Gibbes Art Gallery. *Recollections: Ten Women of Photography.* 20 prints.

April 18–May 17: Wenatchee, Wash. Wenatchee Valley College. *The Great West: Real/Ideal.* 3 prints, illus. in cat.

May 1–June 15: Little Rock, Ark. Arkansas Art Center. *Recollections: Ten Women of Photography.* 20 prints.

May 2–July 5: Oakland, Calif. The Oakland Museum. *American Photographers and the National Parks*. 6 prints, illus. in cat.

June 6–July 5: Chattanooga, Tenn. Hunter Museum of Art. *The Great West: Real/Ideal*. 3 prints, illus. in cat.

July 1–August 15: New Orleans, La. Museum of Art. *Recollections: Ten Women of Photography*. 20 prints.

July 25–August 23: Wichita Falls, Tex. Museum and Art Center. *The Great West: Real/Ideal*. 3 prints, illus. in cat.

September 1–October 18: Oakland, Calif. Mills College Art Gallery. *Recollections: Ten Women of Photography*. 20 prints.

September 8–October 2: St. Louis, Mo. University of Missouri. Gallery 210. *A Decade of Collecting: Master Photographs from St. Louis Private Collections*. 1 print.

September 12–October 11: Ardmore, Okla. Charles E. Goddard Center. *The Great West: Real/Ideal*. 3 prints, illus. in cat.

September 19–November 15: Washington, D.C. Corcoran Gallery of Art. *American Photographers and the National Parks*. 6 prints, illus. in cat.

October 31–December 6: Miami, Fla. Miami Dade Community College, North Campus. *The Great West: Real/Ideal*. 3 prints, illus. in cat.

November 1–December 15: Washington, D.C. Corcoran Gallery of Art. *Recollections: Ten Women of Photography*. 20 prints.

December 7–February 3, 1982: New York, N.Y. New York Public Library. *American Photographers and the National Parks*. 6 prints, illus. in cat.

Publications

ABOUT LAURA GILPIN

Hall, Rosanna. "New Art Gifts to Museum Add Splendor to Collection." *Santa Fe New Mexican*, January 11, 1981.

*Crossley, Mimi. "Images of Life." *Houston Post*, January 11, 1981.

*Pitts, Terence R. "The Early Work of Laura Gilpin, 1917–1932." *Center for Creative Photography*, Research Series, no. 13 (April 1981): 7–37. 24 illus.

*Duty, Michael. "Laura Gilpin, 1891–1979: As Timeless as the Lands & People." *Southwest Art* 10 (April 1981): 66–71. 11 illus.

Additional Photographs Published

*Cahn, Robert. *American Photographers and the National Parks*. New York: Viking Press, 1981. 3 illus.

*Education Development Center, Inc. "Treaty Rights and Dual Status: Who Owes What to Native Americans?"

In *The American Experiment: E Pluribus Unum*. Newton, Mass., 1981, cover, *Francis Nakai and Family*.

*Faunce, Hilda. *Desert Wife*. Lincoln: University of Nebraska Press, 1981, [cover design from a photograph by LG].

*Porter, Andrew J., et al. *American Literature*. Lexington, Mass.: Ginn and Company, 1981, p. 9, *Taos Ovens*.

*Pyle, Ernie. "Trading Post Days." *Santa Fe Reporter*, November 18, 1981, *Red Rock Trading Post*.

1982

Exhibitions

GROUP

January 10–February 25: Evanston, Ill. Northwestern University. Mary and Leigh Block Gallery. *Recollections: Ten Women of Photography*. 20 prints.

February 28–April 24: Chicago, Ill. Chicago Historical Society. *American Photographers and the National Parks*. 6 prints, illus. in cat.

March 13–April 24: Palm Beach, Fla. Society of Four Arts. *Recollections: Ten Women of Photography*. 20 prints.

May 17–June 27: Austin, Tex. Laguna Gloria Art Museum. *Recollections: Ten Women of Photography*. 20 prints.

May 27–July 11: Fort Worth, Tex. Amon Carter Museum. *American Photographers and the National Parks*. 6 prints, illus. in cat.

July 10–November 14: Denver, Colo. Art Museum. *Selections from the Strauss Photography Collection*. 1 print, illus. in cat.

July 24–September 26: Pittsburgh, Pa. Carnegie Institute, Museum of Art. *American Photographers and the National Parks*. 6 prints, illus. in cat.

August 1–September 15: Salt Lake City, Utah. Art Center. *Recollections: Ten Women of Photography*. 20 prints.

October 1–31: Lincoln, Nebr. Sheldon Memorial Art Gallery. *Ranchos de Taos: An Exploration in Photographic Style*. 1 print. REVIEW: Deats, Suzanne. "A Singular Source of Inspiration." *Santa Fe Reporter*, December 29, 1982.

October 17–December 5: Minneapolis, Minn. Institute of Arts. *American Photographers and the National Parks*. 6 prints, illus. in cat.

December–January 8, 1983: Santa Fe, N.M. Madonna House. *Madonna: Visions and Revisions*. REVIEW: Warren Jill. *Santa Fe New Mexican*, December 17, 1982.

December 17–February 27, 1983: Santa Fe, N.M. Museum of New Mexico, Fine Arts Museum. *Ranchos de Taos: An Exploration in Photographic Style*. 1 print.

Publications

ABOUT LAURA GILPIN

*Norwood, Vera. "The Photographer and the Naturalist: Laura Gilpin and Mary Austin in the Southwest." *Journal of American Culture* 5 (Summer 1982): 1–28. 16 illus.

*"Laura Gilpin." In *Contemporary Photographers*. New York: St. Martin's Press, 1982, p. 284, *Gertrude Käsebier*.

*Asbury, Dana. "How They Work: 3 Master Printers and Their Assistants." *Popular Photography* 89 (December 1982): 82–83, 157. 2 illus.

Additional Photographs Published

**The Indian Calendar 1983*. New York: E. P. Dutton, 1982. 2 illus.

**Las Barrancas*. Jacona, Santa Fe, New Mexico. New York: Sotheby Parke Bernet International Realty Corp., 1982. 7 illus.

*Sandweiss, Martha A. *Masterworks of American Photography: The Amon Carter Museum Collection*. Birmingham, Ala.: Oxmoor House, 1982. 9 illus.

*Time-Life. *Photography Year 1982*. Alexandria, Va.: Time-Life Books, 1982, p. 56, *Bryce Canyon National Park, Utah*.

1983

Exhibitions

GROUP

January 8–March 6: Denver, Colo. Art Museum. *American Photographers and the National Parks*. 6 prints, illus. in cat.

April 2–May 7: Colorado Springs, Colo. Fine Arts Center. *Ranchos de Taos: An Exploration in Photographic Style*. 1 print.

April 7–June 12: Poughkeepsie, N.Y. Vassar College Art Gallery. *Photo-Collecting at Vassar: 100 Years +10*. 1 print, illus. in cat.

April 7–June 26: Los Angeles, Calif. County Museum of Art. *American Photographers and the National Parks*. 6 prints, illus. in cat.

May 27–July 10: Fort Worth, Tex. Amon Carter Museum. *Ranchos de Taos: An Exploration in Photographic Style*. 1 print.

Publications

ABOUT LAURA GILPIN

*McKay, Douglas R. *Asylum of the Gilded Pill*. Denver: State Historical Society of Colorado, 1983, pp. 103, 145, 172. [3] illus.

Macmillan Biographical Encyclopedia of Photographic Artists & Innovators. New York: Macmillan Publishing Co., 1983, p. 231, *Navajo Ethel Kellerwood* [sic].

Additional Photographs Published

*Enyeart, James L., et al. "Non-destructive Elemental Analysis of Photographic Paper and Emulsions by X-ray Flourescence Spectroscopy." *History of Photography* 7 (April–June 1983): 106, *Temple of Kukulcan*.

Christian Science Monitor, July 25, 1983, *Casa Blanca, Canyon de Chelly*.

*Bunting, Bainbridge. *John Gaw Meem, Southwestern Architect*. Albuquerque: University of New Mexico Press, 1983. 9 illus.

*Davis, Douglas, ed. *Photography as a Fine Art*. New York: E. P. Dutton, 1983, p. 111, *Scissors, String & Two Books*.

*Frampton, Hollis. *Circles of Confusion: Film, Photography, Video Texts, 1968–1980*. Rochester, N.Y.: Visual Studies Workshop, 1983, p. 52, *Steps of the Castillo*.

*Sherman, John. *Santa Fe: A Pictorial History*. Norfolk, Va.: Donning Co., 1983, p. 163, *Mary Cabot Wheelwright*.

1984

Exhibitions

GROUP

July 10–August 17: New York, N.Y. Whitney Museum of American Art, Downtown Branch. *The Feminine Gaze: Women Depicted by Women, 1900–1930*. 1 print, illus. in cat.

September 7–October 31: Stamford, Conn. Whitney Museum of American Art, Fairfield County Branch. *The Feminine Gaze: Women Depicted by Women, 1900–1930*. 1 print, illus in cat.

Publications

ABOUT LAURA GILPIN

*Sandweiss, Marni. "Laura Gilpin '09." *Baldwin Echoes* 50 (Winter 1984): 10–11. 5 illus.

*Connor, Linda. "[Comments on Landscape Photography at Esalen Arts Symposium, Photography 1982, at Big Sur, California, November 7–12, 1982]." *Aperture*, no. 93 (Winter 1984), p. 50, *Summer Hogan Interior*.

Engel, Mary. "N.M. Conference to Focus on Women Writers, Artists." *Albuquerque Journal*, March 26, 1984.

*International Center of Photography. "Laura Gilpin." In *Encyclopedia of Photography*. New York: Crown Publishers, 1984, pp. 227–228, *Canyon de Chelly, Spider Rock*.

*Peterson, Susan. *Lucy M. Lewis: American Indian Potter.*
Tokyo: Kodansha International, 1984, pp. 24, 41, 202,
207; pls. 49, 50, 52.
*Rosenblum, Naomi. *A World History of Photography.* New
York: Abbeville Press, 1984, frontispiece, pp. 304,
337, 419. 2 illus.

Additional Photographs Published

*Jussim, Estelle. "The Manifold Shapes of Time and Light:
Tucson's Center for Creative Photography." *Arizona
Highways* 60 (January 1984): 2, *Navajos by Firelight.*
*"The Center for Creative Photography, University of
Arizona at Tucson." *Creative Camera*, no. 230 (February
1984), p. 1263, *A Child's Portrait.*

*Jackson, John B. *Discovering the Vernacular Landscape.*
New Haven: Yale University Press, 1984, p. xiii, *Rio
Grande Valley North of Santa Fe.*

1985

Publications

ABOUT LAURA GILPIN

Sandweiss, Martha Ann. "Laura Gilpin (1891–1979): Photographer of the American Southwest." Ph.D. diss.,
Yale University, 1985.

Notes

ABBREVIATIONS

ACM   Amon Carter Museum
BP   Brenda Putnam
EF   Elizabeth Forster
GK   Gertrude Käsebier
LG   Laura Gilpin
LGACM   Laura Gilpin Collection, Amon Carter
    Museum
WF   Walter Frese
WG   Walter Goodwin

Introduction: Laura Gilpin and the American Southwest (pages 11, 12)

1. *The Pueblos: A Camera Chronicle* (New York: Hastings House, 1941); *Temples in Yucatan: A Camera Chronicle of Chichen Itza* (New York: Duell, Sloan & Pearce, 1949); *The Enduring Navaho* (Austin: University of Texas Press, 1968). Gilpin rejected the spelling "Navajo" because she thought it suggested the corrupting influence of Spanish culture. However, because that is the spelling now used by the Navajo Tribe I have used it throughout this text, except in direct quotations where it would be inappropriate.

2. See, for example: John Mack Faragher, *Men and Women on the Overland Trail* (New Haven: Yale University Press, 1979); Annette Kolodny, *The Land Before Her: Fantasy and Experience of the American Frontiers, 1630–1860* (Chapel Hill and London: University of North Carolina Press, 1984); Sandra Myres, *Westering Women and the Frontier Experience, 1890–1915* (Albuquerque: University of New Mexico Press, 1982); Lillian Schlissel, *Women's Diaries of the Westward Journey* (New York: Schocken Books, 1982).

3. Kolodny makes a persuasive argument for the differences between men's and women's literary responses to the western landscape in *The Land Before Her*.

4. Laura Gilpin (LG), "Why I Live in New Mexico," TS, [1957], Laura Gilpin Collection, Amon Carter Museum (LGACM).

5. LG, "Foreword," in Mary Hunt Kahlenberg and Anthony Berlant, *The Navaho Blanket* (Los Angeles: Los Angeles County Museum of Art, 1972), p. 5.

6. LG, interview with Alicia Wille, [Santa Fe, 1977], TS, pp. 13, 3, 21; transcript on deposit in LGACM.

Discovering Photography, 1891–1916 (pages 13–32)

1. William Gilpin, *Notes on Colorado* (London: Witherby and Co., 1870), p. 10. Gilpin's birth date is given in numerous oral interviews and corroborated in her United States passport, issued March 20, 1922; see also LG, audio interview with Margaret Schoonover, tape 1, March 25, 1979, ACM; LG, audio interview with Mitchell A. Wilder, May 11, 1978, transcript, p. 10, ACM.

2. "Williams-Miller Family Genealogy" (photocopy of MS), Emma Miller Gilpin Family Genealogy File, LGACM; Schoonover interview, tape 1; "Death of Bernard Gilpin" (newspaper clipping, n.s., n.d.), Gilpin Family Genealogy File, LGACM; Gilpin Family Photographic Album, Collection of Kenneth Gilpin, Jr., Kentmere, Va.; LG, video interview with Arthur Ollman and Rosella Stern, March 1976, tape 5, copy on deposit at ACM; LG to Susan Allen, April 9, 1979 [all correspondence to or from Laura Gilpin cited in these notes can be found in LGACM, unless otherwise stated]; Wilder interview, p. 10.

3. Mrs. Jack Owen to LG, February 15, 1972; W. P. Gaskill to Mess. L. Gammon and Co., October 21, 1886; "Ranche Ramblings," *Denver Daily News*, April 20, 1884 (TS copy), LGACM.

4. J. E. Payne, "Cattle Raising on the Plains," in *The Plains of Colorado* (Fort Collins, Col.: Experiment Station, 1904), p. 8; Ora Brooks Peake, *The Range Cattle Industry* (Glendale: Arthur H. Clark Co., 1937), p. 273; LG to Mrs. Jack Owen, January 25, 1972.

5.   Owen to LG, February 15, 1972; Wilder interview, p. 10; see also unattributed inscription on verso of William Henry Jackson photograph "Brand of 1/2 Ranch" in the collection of the ACM (accession #78.83/23). Jackson's second wife, Emilie Painter, was a cousin of Frank Gilpin through her mother, Louisa Gilpin Painter; see LG to Gilbert Campbell, January 17, 1969; Beaumont Newhall and Diana E. Edkins, *William Henry Jackson* (Dobbs Ferry, N.Y.: Morgan and Morgan, Inc., in cooperation with the Amon Carter Museum, 1974), p. 141; Clarence S. Jackson, "My Recollections of William Gilpin," *Colorado Magazine* 26 (July 1949): 236–237. Laura Gilpin donated her annotated set of the Jackson photographs of the Horse Creek Ranch to the ACM in 1978 (accession #78.83/1–78.83/29).

6.   "Williams-Miller Family Genealogy"; *St. Louis Directory 1860* (St. Louis: R.V. Kennedy and Co., 1860), p. 359; "Memo Re: Robert H. Miller & Sons," Milan Hughston to the author, May 23, 1984, ACM; LG, audio interview with the author, September 1979, transcript, III, p. 5. ACM; Emma Miller to Fanny [Osborne], February 1, 1885.

7.   Emma Miller to Fanny [Osborne], February 1, 1885, and n.d., [ca. 1885].

8.   Frank Gilpin to Emma Miller, August 26, 1887.

9.   "Miller Family Genealogy," TS, Emma Miller Gilpin Family Genealogy File, LGACM. For information on the social climate of Colorado Springs, see Marshall Sprague, *Newport in the Rockies: The Life and Good Times of Colorado Springs* (Denver: Sage Books, 1961); and Marshall Sprague, *One Hundred Plus: A Centennial Story of Colorado Springs* (Colorado Springs: Colorado Springs Centennial Inc. [1971]).

10.   Schoonover interview, tape 2, March 29, 1979; LG, audio interview with the author, September 1979, tape 2, side 1; LG to Marshall Sprague, July 15, 1955.

11.   *Colorado Springs Directory 1896*; Bernard Gilpin to Emma Miller Gilpin, March 26, 1896; Marjorie Lambert, interview with the author, Santa Fe, February 3, 1981, notes on deposit at ACM; LG, audio interview with the author, tape 2; Mary M. Davis to the author, January 17, 1984, ACM [all correspondence to the author is on file at ACM]; Sargent & Rohrabacher, *Fortunes of a Decade* (Colorado Springs: *Colorado Springs Evening Telegraph*, 1900), p. 111.

12.   LG, interview with the author, tape 2. LG's Report Card (1905–1907) from the Baldwin School in Bryn Mawr, Pa., lists her prior school as the San Louis [Luis] School, which was the successor to the Ferris School. For Laura's friendship with Anne Parrish, see Schoonover

interview, tape 2. For further information on Palmer, see Robert Athearn, *Rebel of the Rockies: A History of the Denver and Rio Grande Western Railroad* (New Haven: Yale University Press, 1962). LG, quoted in Peggy James, "Laura Gilpin, Photographer," *Colorado Springs* 2 (March–April 1978): 18; Ollman and Stern interview, tape 2.

13.   "Francis Gilpin, Jr.," informational file, Alumni Records Office, Yale University, New Haven, Conn.; Sargent & Rohrabacher, *Fortunes of a Decade*, p. 111; Emma Miller Gilpin to Mrs. Peabody, November 6, 1902; Wilder interview, p. 10; LG, interview with the author, tape 2.

14.   Wilder interview, p. 10; Schoonover interview, tape 2; Margaretta Mitchell, *Recollections: Ten Women of Photography* (New York: Viking, 1979), p. 120.

15.   Schoonover interview, tape 2; Mitchell, *Recollections*, p. 120. Some of these snapshots are in a photographic album in the collection of Kenneth Gilpin, Jr., Kentmere, Va. [The author grew up in St. Louis, where the Igorots' reputed taste for dog meat was the subject of a story often recounted by her great-aunt, Regina Strauss, and grandmother, Elsie Glik, who attended the fair as children.] LG, film interview, filmed by Amon Carter Museum crew, Santa Fe, September 1979, tape reel 10, ACM.

16.   Schoonover interview, tape 2; Mitchell, *Recollections*, p. 120. Käsebier's portrait of Laura's brother, Francis, is in the collection of Kenneth Gilpin, Jr., Kentmere, Va. The best source of information of Käsebier is William Inness Homer, *A Pictorial Heritage: The Photographs of Gertrude Käsebier* (Wilmington: Delaware Art Museum, 1979).

17.   *The Baldwin Annual (1905–1906)* (Bryn Mawr: Baldwin School, 1906), library, Baldwin School, Bryn Mawr, Pa.; LG, Report Card, archives, Baldwin School; LG, interview with the author, tape 2.

18.   *Baldwin Annual (1905–1906)*, p. 94; LG, Report Card; *Baldwin Annual (1906–1907)*, pp. 10, 76, 81; Jane L. Brownell to Emma Miller Gilpin, March 25, 1907.

19.   Lee Sylvester to the author, September 9, 1981; LG, interview with the author, tape 2, and transcript, I, p. 1.

20.   Edith Brann, interview with the author, Colorado Springs, February 27, 1981, ACM; Helen Jackson interview with the author, Colorado Springs, February 25, 1981, ACM; Schoonover interview, tape 2; Wilder interview, p. 15; Mitchell, *Recollections*, p. 120; Ollman and Stern interview, tape 1.

21.   Schoonover interview, tape 2. For information about Louis Persinger, see "Louis Persinger," *Who's Who in America* (Chicago: Marquis–Who's Who, 1966–1967), p. 1661. Edith Brann interview.

22. Schoonover interview, tape 2; Geraldine Ostrove to the author, October 19, 1982. This letter from Ostrove, library director of the New England Conservatory of Music, indicates that Laura Gilpin was enrolled as a student in the 1911–12 school year; however, addresses and postmarks on the letters Gilpin received indicate that she was actually living in Boston and enrolled in the school during the 1910–11 school year.

23. Ostrove to the author, October 19, 1982. Those who studied music before taking up photography include Clarence White, Ansel Adams, and Paul Caponigro; see Maynard Pressley White, Jr., "Clarence H. White: A Personal Portrait" (Ph.D. diss., University of Delaware, 1975), p. 13; Liliane de Cock, ed., with a foreword by Minor White, *Ansel Adams* (Hastings-on-Hudson, N.Y.: Morgan and Morgan, Inc., 1972), "Foreword"; Paul Caponigro, *The Wise Silence: Photographs by Paul Caponigro*, essay by Marianne Fulton, preface by Paul Caponigro (Boston: New York Graphic Society, 1983), pp. 9–10, 174–175. LG, "Historic Architecture Photography: The Southwest," *Complete Photographer* 6 (July 20, 1942): 1989.

24. Katherine Foote to LG, March 15, 1911; Schoonover interview, tape 2; LG, interview with the author, tape 2; Colorado Springs directories, 1900–1911. Photographs of the ranch are in Gilpin Album 1, n.p., LGACM. See LG, interviews published in Mitchell, *Recollections*, p. 122; and Paul Hill and Thomas Cooper, *Dialogue with Photography* (New York: Farrar, Straus, Giroux, 1979), p. 286.

25. LG, interview with the author, tape 2.

26. "Society Girl Raises 400 Turkeys," *Denver Republic*, January 9, 1913.

27. Laura Gilpin's Autochromes are in the collection of the Amon Carter Museum (accession numbers 79.146/1– 79.146/51), as are a collection of Autochromes by her contemporary Karl Struss. Relatively few early American Autochromes have been reproduced; for examples, see Naomi Rosenblum, *A World History of Photography* (New York: Abbeville Press, 1984), pp. 292–295; see also a published portfolio of Struss's Autochromes, *The Dawn of Color* (joint publication of Stephen White Gallery, Los Angeles and PPS. Galerie F. C. Grundlach, Hamburg [1982]). The information that the still life of peaches was made on the Figure 4 Ranch with locally grown peaches is from Ollman and Stern interview, tape 1; this picture was selected as the frontispiece for Rosenblum, *A World History of Photography*. The Käsebier print is reproduced in Homer, *A Pictorial Tradition*, plate 19.

28. LG, interview with the author, transcript, III, p. 5.

29. LG, interview with the author, tape 2; Schoonover interview, tape 1; "Statement of Laura Gilpin in Account with Frank Gilpin," [1945], LGACM.

30. LG, interview with the author, transcript, I, p. 1; Wilder interview, p. 11; Mitchell; *Recollections*, p. 121. "Our Competitions," *American Photography* 10 (July 1916): 397, notes that Gilpin's photograph *Cloister at San Diego Exposition* won an honorable mention in the May 1916 competition; the photograph was later reproduced in *American Photography* 11 (September 1917): 518.

31. LG, interview with Margaretta Mitchell, Santa Fe, 1977, transcript, p. 11, LGACM, later edited for inclusion in Mitchell's book *Recollections*; Rosemary Nusbaum, *Tierra Dulce: Reminiscences from the Jesse Nusbaum Papers* (Santa Fe: Sunstone Press, 1980), p. 53; Edna Robertson, *Gerald Cassidy, 1869–1934* (Santa Fe: Museum of New Mexico, 1977), p. 5; *Official Catalogue of the Department of Fine Arts Panama Pacific International Exposition* (San Francisco: Wahlgreen Co., 1915), p. 242; "Photography at the Panama Pacific," *Camera Craft* 20 (March 1913): 133; "Pictorial Photography at Our Coming Esposition," *Camera Craft* 20 (December 1913): 578.

32. An extensive file of letters from Anne Simon to Laura Gilpin is included in LGACM; reference to Gilpin's previous connection to Simon is in Schoonover interview, tape 2. [Joyce Kilmer], "Anne Simon's Diary a Strange Soul Record," *New York Times*, November 26, 1916, magazine section; "In Memoriam," reprint from *Poet Lore* (Winter 1916), LGACM.

33. Schoonover interview, tape 2. Anne Simon to LG, September 27, December 25, 1915; April 10, 27, 1916; September 21, 27, 1915.

34. [Kilmer], "Simon's Diary"; [Otto T. Simon], *The Message of Anne Simon* (Boston: Richard G. Badger, Gorham Press, 1920), p. 49. Simon's husband, Otto, wrote three books of messages he claimed to have received from his wife after her death.

35. [Kilmer], "Simon's Diary."

36. Schoonover interview, tape 2. "Mrs. Otto Torney Simon, Pianist, Dies Suddenly," *Colorado Springs Gazette*, August 6, 1916; "Musician Passes Away," *Colorado Springs Evening Gazette*, August 7, 1916. Seventeen Autochromes made on Laura's trip to the Grand Canyon are in LGACM; *A Glimpse of the Canyon* won second prize in *American Photography*'s advanced monthly competition; see "Our Competitions," *American Photography* 10 (November 1916): 632; it was reproduced in the same issue on p. 615 and thus became Gilpin's first published photograph. Gilpin filed this journal entry (the journal itself does not survive) with Anne Simon's letters, MS [no title], August 10, [1916].

37. Mitchell, *Recollections*, p. 21; Schoonover interview, tape 2; Wilder interview, p. 12.

38.   Schoonover interview, tape 2; Patricia Trenton and Peter Hassrick, *The Rocky Mountains: A Vision for Artists in the Nineteenth Century* (Norman: University of Oklahoma Press, 1983), pp. 312–314; Schoonover interview, tape 3, n.d., 1979.

39.   LG, interview with the author, transcript, II, p. 12.

40.   Otto T. Simon to LG, September 26, 1916; Brenda Putnam [BP] to LG, August 23, September 28, 1916.

Becoming an Artist, 1916–1918 (pages 24–32)

1.   BP to LG, September 18, 28, 1916.

2.   "'Uncle Tom's Cabin' Author Is Placed in Hall of Fame," *Denver Post*, June 24, 1925; "Herbert Putnam," *Who Was Who in America* (Chicago: Marquis – Who's Who, 1960), III, 705; "Brenda Putnam," [photocopy of biographical catalogue entry], [n.p., n.d.], Brenda Putnam Clippings File, LGACM; "Sculptor Finds Charms of Babyhood Irresistable: Highways and Byways of Life Furnish Her Tiny Models," *Sun*, May 5, 1922, Brenda Putnam Clippings File, LGACM; "Brenda Putnam . . . Creator of Beauty," *Beautiful Florida* 6 (May 1930): 6.

3.   BP to LG, September 28, 1916. Accurate class lists and enrollment figures for the Clarence H. White School have not been found. The most complete enrollment record seems to be a typescript list of names, arranged by classes, located in the Clarence H. White Collection, The Art Museum, Princeton University. This typescript indicates that forty-five women and fourteen men studied at White's school in 1916–1917, a figure that may include students from his Canaan, Connecticut, summer school. The list, however, was compiled some years later from an incomplete class list and Laura Gilpin's name is not included. A Clarence White photograph of the class of 1917, currently in the Amon Carter Museum Collection (accession number 79.148/1), shows Gilpin with seven other women and two men. A scrapbook of work by the class of 1917, presented by them to White, is signed by nine women and four men ("1917 Class Scrapbook," Clarence H. White Collection). White expressed his own ideas about women and photography in "Photography as a Profession for Women," *News-Bulletin of the Bureau of Vocational Information* 2 (April 1, 1924): n.p. Helen Ferris and Virginia Moore, "Girls Who Did," [newspaper clipping], [n.p., n.d.], Brenda Putnam Clippings File, LGACM.

4.   BP to LG, June 13, September 8, 1917.

5.   LG to John Collier, Jr., May 26, 1950; Wilder interview, pp. 26–27; BP to LG, March 5, 1927.

6.   "History of the School," TS, and *The Clarence H. White School of Photography List of Students, 1915–16* (brochure), p. 15, Clarence H. White Collection, The Art Museum, Princeton University. No comprehensive history of the Clarence H. White School exists, and it has received only slight attention even in the key biographical studies of White, perhaps because White's involvement with the school postdated his period of greatest photographic activity; see Maynard Pressley White, Jr., "Clarence H. White: A Personal Portrait" (Ph.D. diss., University of Delaware, 1975), and *Clarence White* (Millerton, N.Y.: Aperture, 1979); Peter C. Bunnell, "The Significance of the Photography of Clarence Hudson White (1871–1925) in the Development of Expressive Photography" (Master's thesis, Ohio University, 1961); William Inness Homer, *Alfred Stieglitz and the American Photo-Secession* (Boston: New York Graphic Society, 1983). The best brief critical analysis of the school and its program is in Bonnie Yochelson, "Clarence H. White Reconsidered: An Alternative to the Modernist Aesthetic of Straight Photography," *Studies in Visual Communication* 9 (Fall 1983): 26–44.

7.   "A New School of Photography," *Platinum Print* 1 (August 1914): 12.

8.   There is an extensive body of work on Stieglitz; see particularly the following works, all of which include bibliographies: Sarah Greenough and Juan Hamilton, *Alfred Stieglitz: Photographs and Writings* (Washington, D.C.: National Gallery of Art, 1983); William Inness Homer, *Alfred Stieglitz and the American Avant-Garde* (Boston: New York Graphic Society, 1977); Homer, *Stieglitz and the Photo-Secession*; Weston J. Naef, *The Collection of Alfred Stieglitz: Fifty Pioneers of Photography* (New York: Metropolitan Museum of Art, 1978).

9.   For biographical information on White, see the works by his grandson Maynard Pressley White, Jr., Peter Bunnell, and William Homer, listed above.

10.   This secession from the Photo-Secession has been given relatively little attention by photographic historians; the best discussion of the movement is in Yochelson, "Clarence H. White Reconsidered." *Platinum Print: A Journal of Photographic Expression* changed its title to *Photo = Graphic Art*, in order to emphasize the connection between photography and the other graphic arts, with vol. 3, no. 1 (June 1916). The journal ceased publication with vol. 3, no. 2 (October 1917). This last issue indicates that the journal was then "the official journal of the Pictorial Photographers of America." The Pictorial Photographers of America published annual reports in 1917 and 1918 and in 1920 began publication of an annual called *Pictorial Photography in America*, which was published in 1920, 1921, 1922, 1926, and 1929. In December 1928, the PPA began

publication of a monthly photographic periodical, *Light and Shade*. The PPA was founded on November 15, 1915, in a meeting at the office of Dr. Charles Jaeger, the husband of photographer Doris Ulmann. The group's first formal meeting was on January 15, 1916, the date usually given for the inception of the group; see White, "Clarence H. White," p. 228. The Art Center was an alliance of the following organizations: Art Alliance of America, Art Directors Club, American Institute of Graphic Arts, New York Society of Craftsmen, Society of Illustrators, The Stowaways, and Pictorial Photographers of America; see Amasa Day Chafee, "The Pictorial Photographers of America," *Pictorial Photography in America 1922* (New York: Pictorial Photographers of America, 1922), p. 95.

11.   Edward R. Dickson, "Expressions in Type," *Platinum Print* 1 (November 1914): 11; "Editorially Expressed," *Platinum Print* 1 (December 1913): 9.

12.   See Edward R. Dickson, "Pictorial Photographers of America: Its Work and Aim," *Photo=Graphic Art* 3 (October 1917): 18; "Editorially Expressed: Our Camera Clubs and Their Opportunities," *Platinum Print* 1 (November 1914): 3.

13.   Arthur Wesley Dow, *Composition* (Boston: J. M. Bowles, 1899); Frederick C. Moffatt, *Arthur Wesley Dow (1857–1922)* (Washington, D.C.: National Collection of Fine Arts, 1977); "Program Notes," *Pictorial Photography in America, Volume 4* (New York: Pictorial Photographers of America, 1926), n.p.

14.   *Clarence H. White School of Photography*, brochure [n.p., n.d.], [New York, ca. 1922–1923], LGACM; Arthur Wesley Dow, "Painting with Light," *Pictorial Photography in America 1921* (New York: Pictorial Photographers of America, 1921), p. 5; *An Exhibition of Photographs by Laura Gilpin, August 1–15, 1921*, brochure, (Colorado Springs: Broadmoor Art Academy, 1921).

15.   Moffatt, *Arthur Wesley Dow*, p. 82; *Clarence H. White School of Photography*, brochure; the brochure notes: "The method of instruction used is the 'project method.' Each student on entering the school begins at once to use the camera and is set to work on a definitely graded series of technical and practical problems, which he is to perform under individual guidance and instruction."

16.   *Clarence H. White School of Photography*, catalogue brochure (1915), Clarence H. White Collection, The Art Museum, Princeton University. No catalogue was printed for the 1916–17 school year, although another publication indicates that the course of instruction would be the same as that outlined in the brochure for the previous year; see *Clarence H. White School of Photography List of Students 1915–16*.

17.   LG to Milton Meltzer, June 20, 1977; Wilder interview, p. 13.

18.   White, "Clarence H. White" pp. 192, 67; Walter Hervey, "Clarence H. White," *Pictorial Photography in America, Volume 4*. Ralph Steiner, who went on to a distinguished career in advertising photography and cinematography following his work with White in 1921–1922, recalled his teacher as "a rather simple person . . . and so generally kind that he had no desire to lead students in any direction except toward (vaguely) ART"; Margaret Bourke-White recalled him as a "great teacher"; and Alvin Langdon Coburn thought him "unselfish and lovable." See White, "Clarence H. White" p. 191; Margaret Bourke-White, *Portrait of Myself* (New York: Simon and Schuster, 1963), p. 29; Alvin Langdon Coburn, *Men of Mark* (London: Duckworth & Co., 1913), pp. 28–29. White is one of only five Americans included in Coburn's book of artists and literary figures.

19.   Wilder interview, p. 13.

20.   Daryl Rubenstein, *Max Weber: A Catalogue Raisonne of His Graphic Work* (Chicago: University of Chicago Press, 1980); Greenough and Hamilton, *Alfred Stieglitz*, p. 17.

21.   White, "Clarence H. White," p. 177; Max Weber, *Essays on Art* (New York: Printed by William Edwin Rudge, 1916), pp. 58, 55, 57; (these essays were based on the lectures he delivered at the Clarence H. White School).

22.   Hill and Cooper, *Dialogue with Photography*, p. 284; undated typescripts of lesson plans are included in the Clarence H. White Collection, The Art Museum, Princeton University.

23.   Max Weber, "The Filling of Space," *Platinum Print* 1 (December 1913): 6.

24.   For information on Coburn's early efforts at abstract photography, see Beaumont Newhall, *The History of Photography from 1839 to the Present Day*, 4th ed. (New York: Museum of Modern Art, 1978), pp. 161–162; and Jean S. Tucker, *Light Abstractions* (St. Louis: University of Missouri –St. Louis, 1980), pp. 9–10. Alvin Langdon Coburn, "The Future of Pictorial Photography," in *Photograms of the Year, 1916*, ed. F. J. Mortimer (London: Hazell, Watson and Viney, 1916), p. 23. M[ax?] W[eber?], "Design," *Photo=Graphic Art* 3 (June 1916): 8.

25.   *Camera Work* 48 (October 1916) and 49/50 (June 1917); Newhall, *History of Photography*, p. 174; Yochelson, "Clarence H. White Reconsidered," p. 30. See Paul Strand's pointed comments to the students of the Clarence White School in 1923: "The Art Motive in Photography," in *Photography in Print: Writings from 1816 to the Present*,

ed. Vicki Goldberg (New York: Simon and Schuster, 1981), pp. 276–287. Stieglitz wrote of White after he opened his school: "His photography went to the devil. His pupils – women – half-baked dilettantes – not a single real talent" (quoted in Weston Naef, *The Collection of Alfred Stieglitz*, p. 482).

26.   Mary White to Clarence White, n.d. [1916], Clarence H. White Collection, The Art Museum, Princeton University; Hill and Cooper, *Dialogue with Photography*, pp. 284, 291.

27.   Paul L. Anderson's ideas on photographic composition are best expressed in his books: *The Fine Art of Photography* (Philadelphia: J. B. Lippincott Co., 1919) and *Pictorial Photography: Its Principles and Practices* (Philadelphia: J. B. Lippincott Co., 1917); Paul Anderson to LG, August 12, 1940; *Clarence H. White School of Photography, 1915* (brochure), Clarence H. White Collection, The Art Museum, Princeton University.

28.   John Hafey and Tom Shillea, *The Platinum Print* (Rochester: Graphic Arts Research Center, Rochester Institute of Technology, 1979), p. 6; Ollman and Stern interview, tape 1; Paul Strand to LG, June 29, 1932; LG to Charles Robinson, November 27, 1932; Naomi Rosenblum to LG, January 1, 1978. The date for the halt in production of platinum paper is cited in Hafey and Shillea, p. 13; this book also offers evidence of the resurgence of interest in the platinum printing process.

29.   Frederic Ayres Johnson to LG, March 27, 1917; Schoonover interview, tape 3; Peter Henry Emerson, *Pictures of East Anglian Life* (London: Sampson, Low, Marston, Searle, and Rivington, 1888); *Camera Work* 1–50 (January 1903–June 1917).

30.   BP to LG, December 7, 1922; Alice [Shinn?] to LG, May 16, 1917.

31.   For the effects of the war on photographers, see *Photo = Graphic Art* 3 (October 1917); Louis F. Boucher, "Pictorial Photography in New Jersey," in *Pictorial Photography in America, 1920* (New York: Pictorial Photographers of America, 1920), p. 8; Dwight A. Davis, "Pictorial Photography in Massachusetts," in *Pictorial Photography in America, 1920*, p. 10. For the effects of the war on the Clarence White School, see White, "Clarence H. White," p. 227.

32.   Ollman and Stern interview, tape 1; Karl Struss to the author, June 23, 1980; LG to John Collier, Jr., May 26, 1950.

33.   For reproductions of similar views by Coburn and Struss made around the same time, see Newhall, *History of Photography*, p. 160; and Homer, *Alfred Stieglitz and the Photo-Secession*, p. 153.

34.   *Spring Exhibition, Perkins Hall*, brochure (Colorado Springs: Colorado Springs Art Society, 1917); *An Exhibition of Pictorial Photography by American Artists*, brochure, (Minneapolis: Minneapolis Institute of Arts, 1917). The Minneapolis show also traveled to Milwaukee, Chicago, and St. Louis (see Appendix). *Photo = Graphic Art* 3 (October 1917): [7]; Paul Anderson to LG, April 25, 1918; Anderson, *The Fine Art of Photography*, p. 168.

35.   See Plate 5, a scene of Washington Square with a figure shoveling snow carefully painted out of the negative, and Plate 9, a photograph of Brenda Putnam carving a memorial statue to Anne Simon with several "windows" drawn onto the negative.

36.   LG to John Collier, Jr., May 26, 1950.

37.   Wille interview, p. 4; Ollman and Stern interview, tape 1.

38.   White, "Clarence H. White," p. 189; C. P. Russell, "Artistic Settings for Photographers," *Printers' Ink Monthly* (January 1920), p. 51.

39.   *The Prairie* is part of a series of prints made to illustrate Eliza Morgan Swift's poem "On the Prairie"; Wille interview, p. 4; Wilder interview, p. 35.

Establishing a Career, 1918–1930 (pages 33–50)

1.   Biographical information about Betsy Forster and her family comes chiefly from her great-nephew Gerald Richardson, interview with the author, Santa Fe, January 29, 1981; and her niece Elizabeth Richardson, interview with the author, Albuquerque, August 18, 1982, notes on deposit at ACM. See also "Elizabeth Forster Dies after Illness," *New Mexican*, January 3, 1972; Gerald Shorb to the author, September 28, 1982; Rudolf A. Clemen, Jr., to the author, June 14, 1983; Karen Marczynski to the author, May 9, 1983.

2.   Emma Miller Gilpin to Elizabeth Forster [EF], September 1918.

3.   Marczynski to the author, May 9, 1983; see, for example, EF to LG, May 6, 1922.

4.   Mitchell interview, p. 3.

5.   Persis Wood, interview with the author, Colorado Springs, February 26, 1981; Marka Stewart, interview with the author, Colorado Springs, February 26, 1981; Edith Brann, interview with the author, Colorado Springs, February 27, 1981 (notes on deposit at ACM). "Gilpin Rites Will Be Held Saturday," *Colorado Springs Gazette*, July 9, 1943; "Mrs. Francis Gilpin Prominent Resident for Years

Here, Dies," [clipping from unidentified Colorado Springs newspaper, August 1927], LGACM; Barbara Jaeger, interview with the author, Colorado Springs, February 26, 1981; "Emma Miller Gilpin Condolence Letters," folder, LGACM; see Agnes Shober to LG, n.d. [ca. August 1927].

6. "Francis Gilpin, Jr.," in *History of the Class of Nineteen Hundred and Nineteen, Sheffield Scientific School, Yale University* ed. Raymond D. Savageau (New Haven: Published for the 1919S Class/Book Committee by the Class Secretaries Bureau, 1919), p. 118; "Francis Gilpin, Jr.," informational file, Alumni Records Office, Yale University, information courtesy William S. Reese.

7. *Summer Exhibition* (Colorado Springs: Colorado Springs Art Society, 1919); several Nova Scotia pictures are in LGACM (see ACM accession numbers 79.129/1–4).

8. Percy Hagerman, "Notes on the History of the Broadmoor Art Academy and the Colorado Springs Fine Arts Center, 1919–1945," TS, Library, Colorado Springs Fine Arts Center, Colorado Springs; Moffatt, *Arthur Wesley Dow*, p. 91; Wilder interview, p. 16. See also the catalogues of the Broadmoor Art Academy, published at least eleven times between 1920 and 1932. Laura Gilpin designed, illustrated, and oversaw the production of these brochures (see Appendix). C. P. DaCosta Andrade to LG, May 19, 1921; "Statement, Photographic Department, Broadmoor Art Academy, April–September 15, 1921," LGACM. *The Bulletin of the Alumni, Clarence H. White School of Photography*, Spring and Summer Number (June 1921), p. [2], LGACM.

9. A record of her sitters can be found in "Laura Gilpin Collection–Catalogue of Negatives," ACM; LG to EF, January 23, 1921; Wille interview, p. 17. The portrait *Charles Eaton* was exhibited in Denmark in 1920 and Baltimore in 1921; see exhibition catalogues: *Kobenhavns Fotografiske Amator-Klubs Jubilaeums: Udstilling, 1895–1920* (Copenhagen, 1920); and *Photographic Guild of Baltimore, Exhibition of the Nineteen Hundred and Twenty One Portfolio* (Baltimore: Peabody Gallery, 1921). Gilpin's 61-print show at the Broadmoor Art Academy in August 1921 included several portraits; see exhibition checklist: "An Exhibition of Photographs by Laura Gilpin, Greenhouse Gallery" (Colorado Springs: Broadmoor Art Academy, 1921).

10. *Kobenhavns Fotografiske Amator-Klubs Jubilaeums: London Salon of Photography, Catalogue of the International Exhibition* (London, 1920); "An Exhibition of Photographs by Laura Gilpin, Greenhouse Gallery" (1921); "Gilpin Art Photographs at Museum," *New Mexican*, October 15, 1921; M.R.F. Valle, "Art Notes," *Rocky Mountain News*, November 6, 1921; [George William Eggers], "The Art of Laura Gilpin," *Allied Arts* 2 (December 1921):

xvii. Gilpin acknowledged the truth of Eggers's comments by arranging for the simultaneous exhibition of work by Käsebier and David Octavius Hill, a photographer much admired by White.

11. John Wanamaker to LG, February 18, 1921; *London Salon of Photography, Catalogue of the International Exhibition* (London, 1921).

12. "Miss Gilpin Finds Inspiration in Art Museum of New Mexicans," *Colorado Springs Gazette*, July 4, 1920. For information on the history of the Museum of New Mexico, see the special anniversary issue of *El Palacio* 90 (1984); Beatrice Chauvenet, *Hewett and Friends: A Biography of Santa Fe's Vibrant Era* (Santa Fe: Museum of New Mexico Press, 1983); Arrell Morgan Gibson, *The Santa Fe and Taos Colonies: Age of the Muses, 1900–1942* (Norman: University of Oklahoma Press, 1983).

13. Schoonover interview, tape 3; LG to Emma Miller Gilpin, April 30, 1922; LG passport, issued March 20, 1922.

14. LG to EF, April 25, 1922; Hill and Cooper, *Dialogue with Photography*, p. 285.

15. Gilpin's letters from Europe are collected in a typescript journal, designated here as "Europe Journal," that is now in LGACM; see "Europe Journal," [ca. May 8, 1922]; BP to LG, October 27, 1922.

16. EF to LG, May 6, 1922; LG to Emma Miller Gilpin, n.d. [May 1922].

17. "Europe Journal," n.d. [June 1922], and [ca. May 8, 1922]; Wilder interview, transcript of tape 4, p. 1.

18. "Europe Journal," May 23, 1922.

19. Ibid., May 8, 23, 1922.

20. Ibid., September 11, 19, 1922.

21. Ibid., May 8, June 17, July 14, 1922.

22. Ibid., August 11, 1922. Gilpin scorned the use of the "miniature" 35mm camera for most of her life, but this first one held out the promise of novelty. She wrote home, "I have a number of these tiny negatives that may work up into something real!" "European Journal," August 11, July 21, 1922; LG, conversation with the author, Santa Fe, September 1979.

23. "European Journal," September 22, 1922.

24. Mary Sauter, "Laura Gilpin's Work," *Camera Craft* 29 (September 1922): 419.

25. See Appendix for 1923 exhibits; "International Camera Salon at the Art Centre," *New York Evening World*, May 29, 1923. This picture was later exhibited under the title *Spirit of the Prairie*.

26. *The Nutrition School Camp, Colorado Springs, Colorado* [Colorado Springs: Glockner Sanatorium, 1923]; *Winning Health in the Pikes Peak Region: Colorado Springs–Manitou* (Colorado Springs: Chamber of Commerce, 1923); "Health Book Finest Ever Issued Here," [Colorado Springs newspaper, 1923], unidentified clipping, LGACM.

27. LG, *Some Thoughts on Portraiture*, [Colorado Springs: printed for the author, 1923].

28. Ibid.; Gertrude Käsebier [GK] to LG, September 1, 1923.

29. Frank Gilpin to LG, December 22, 1923.

30. "[Mention of Gilpin exhibition]," *New York Herald*, January 20, 1924; "Skillful Photography," *New York Sun*, January 18, 1924.

31. LG, interview with the author, p. 8; Hill and Cooper, *Dialogue with Photography*, pp. 284, 285; Alfred Stieglitz to LG, January 22, 1924.

32. Paul Strand to LG, January 29, 1924.

33. Alfred Stieglitz, "A Plea for Art Photography in America," *Photographic Mosaics* 28 (1892): 135–137; rep. in Peter Bunnell, *A Photographic Vision: Pictorial Photography, 1889–1923* (Salt Lake City: Peregrine Smith, Inc., 1980). See Sarah Greenough, "Alfred Stieglitz and 'The Idea Photography,'" in Greenough and Hamilton, *Alfred Stieglitz, Photographs and Writings*, pp. 11–32.

34. Edward R. Dickson, "Notes on Pictorial Photography," *Platinum Print* 1 (March 1914): 6. The PPA publications devoted considerable space to discussions of the "New School" of photography. In the 1929 annual *Pictorial Photography in America* (New York: Pictorial Photographers of America, 1929), Frank Crowninshield commented on the decline of sentimentality and storytelling in photography and described the new style: "American photographers are being touched by so-called Modernism; by a new-found interest in our stark and skyscraper civilization. More and more they are yielding to the severity of cubes; to sharply opposed effects of shadow and light; to the Picasso-like quality which we everywhere see reflected in the life about us" (Foreword). In reviewing the PPA's third international photographic salon of 1929, PPA President Ira Martin praised the jurors for liberally accepting "glossy prints" ("Photographic Art in America: The P.P.A. Third International," *Light and Shade* 1 (May 1929): 9).

35. "Statement by Pictorialists," in *Principles of Pictorial Photography*, ed. John Wallace Gillies (New York: Falk Publishing Co., 1923), rep. in Bunnell, *Photographic Vision*, p. 206.

36. Ralph Steiner to LG, October 22, 1924.

37. For biographical information about Käsebier, see Homer, *Pictorial Heritage*; for Käsebier's own theories about photographic portraiture, see Gertrude Käsebier, "Studies in Portraiture," *Photographic Times* 30 (June 1898): 269–272.

38. Rebecca D. Symes, "Early Childhood and the Frontier," in Homer, *A Pictorial Heritage*, pp. 9–12; Homer, "Marriage, Art School, and Beginnings in Photography," in *A Pictorial Heritage*, p. 12.

39. GK to LG, October 28, 1924; September 1, 1923.

40. GK to LG, June 14, 1919; October 28, 1924; July 7, 1926.

41. BP to LG, August 22, 1923; June 25, 1926.

42. GK to LG, August 26, 1921; August 3, February 27, 1925.

43. GK to LG, December 15, 1924; August 3, 1925; July 7, 1926.

44. GK to LG, January 16, 1923.

45. Clarence White to LG, June 14, November 1, 1921; June 10, 1924. Walter Hervey to LG, December 29, 1921. Jane Felix White to LG, August 21, 1925.

46. While in New York in the fall of 1925, Laura became involved in the preparation of a memorial book of White's work as the chairman of a committee appointed by the Clarence White School Alumni Association, a close-knit group of photographers whose previous publications included two volumes of reproductions of work by the school's current and former students: *Camera Pictures* (New York: Alumni Association Clarence H. White School of Photography, 1924); *Camera Pictures* (New York: Alumni Association Clarence H. White School of Photography, 1925). Serving on the committee with her were Bernard Horne and Doris Ulmann. Laura approached Frederic Goudy about the typesetting and printing of the project and wrote a letter soliciting funds and advanced subscriptions from friends of the school. The project was complicated, however, when the PPA decided that *they* wanted to do a memorial volume in honor of White (Antoinette Hervey to LG, January 22, 1926). The issue became muddled in personal politics and Laura, who had returned to Colorado Springs in December, finally resigned her position as chairman of the alumni committee in March 1926 (LG to Stella Simon, March 15, 1926), pleading the exigencies of distance but actually glad to be done with the whole project. She made prints from some of White's negatives, which she had borrowed from his widow, in case they were needed for the PPA's book (LG to Walter Hervey, May 11, 1926). Eventually, the Alumni Association resigned their interest in the project and the

PPA brought out not a special book but a special volume of their 1926 *Annual* dedicated to Clarence White.

47. Jane Felix White to LG, January 6, 1926. Jerald Maddox to the author, telephone conversation, June 27, 1984. As one of the key sets of White's photographs, the Library of Congress prints became the basis for the Clarence White memorial exhibition shown at the Art Center in the spring of 1926. Estelle Jussim, *Slave to Beauty: The Eccentric and Controversial Career of F. Holland Day, Photographer, Publisher, Aesthete* (Boston: David R. Godine, 1981), p. 209. Gilpin commented on her role in placing Käsebier prints in the Library of Congress collection in the Wilder interview, p. 12.

48. Gilpin commented on her meeting with Bauer in a radio interview with station KVOR, January 28, 1939 (transcript in LGACM). BP to LG, May 12, 1925 (complete portfolio of the Bauer portraits in LGACM).

49. Emma Miller Gilpin to LG, November 29, 1925.

50. Brenda Putnam kept a journal, which she presented to Gilpin in typescript form after the conclusion of the trip; all details of the trip are from this source (BP Log), now in LGACM.

51. BP Log, pp. 12–14.

52. Ibid., p. 12; Willa Cather, *The Professor's House* (1925; reprint, New York: Vintage Books, 1973), p. 201.

53. BP Log, p. 14. Calvin Tomkins, *Paul Strand: Sixty Years of Photographs* (Millerton, N.Y.: Aperture, 1976), pp. 23, 150, 151; Paul Strand, *Paul Strand: A Retrospective Monograph, the Years 1915–46* (Millerton, N.Y.: Aperture, 1971), p. 98. See the reproductions of the Mesa Verde pictures in *The Pueblos: A Camera Chronicle*.

54. Alice Boughton to LG, August 21, 1929; Cather, *Professor's House*, p. 226.

55. BP Log, pp. 20, 23. Florence Curtis Graybill and Victor Boesen, *Edward Sheriff Curtis: Visions of a Vanishing Race* (New York: Thomas Y. Crowell, 1976), p. 13; Frederick Monsen, "Picturing Indians with the Camera," *Photo-Era* 25 (October 1910): 165; "Kirk Munroe," *Who Was Who in America* (Chicago: Marquis–Who's Who, 1968), I, 380.

56. BP Log, pp. 27, 33–35.

57. Mildred Adams, "A Worker in Light," *Woman Citizen* 54 (March 1926): 11.

58. *Photographs of the Southwest by Laura Gilpin,* four photogravures issued in folder: *Laguna Mission* (1925), *Mesa Verde National Park* (1925), *Arab of the American Desert* (1926), *Hymn to the Sun* (1926) [Colorado Springs, 1927]. LG to Mary Stewart, October 5, 1928.

59. "Gilpin Publishing Co. A Common Law Trust" (stock certificate); LG, *The Pikes Peak Region: Reproductions from a Series of Photographs by Laura Gilpin* (Colorado Springs: The Gilpin Publishing Co., 1926).

60. Ollman and Stern interview, tape 4; *The Rio Grande,* p. vii.

61. LG, "Type Designs," in "A Printer's Reader: Your First Reminder," large-format brochure and calendar ([Colorado Springs: Dentan Publishing Co.], February 1930).

62. *Pikes Peak Region,* n.p.

63. BP to LG, June 25, 1926; Horace Mitchell to LG, January 19, 1927.

64. BP to LG, March 23, May 15, 1927.

65. LG, *The Mesa Verde National Park: Reproductions from a Series of Photographs by Laura Gilpin* (Colorado Springs: The Gilpin Publishing Co., 1927).

66. This theme is implicit in Mary Austin's *The Land of Journey's Ending* (New York and London: Century, 1924). See also the writings collected in Keith Sagar, ed., *D. H. Lawrence and New Mexico* (Salt Lake City: Gibbs M. Smith, 1982); and Marta Weigle and Kyle Fiore, eds., *Santa Fe and Taos: The Writer's Era* (Santa Fe, Ancient City Press, 1982). *Mesa Verde National Park,* n.p.

67. "Mrs. Francis Gilpin Prominent Resident for Years Here, Dies," [Colorado Springs newspaper, n.d.], LGACM.

68. Vera Cook Salomonsky to Frank Gilpin, March 24, May 22, 1926. F. Gilpin, Inc., "Corporation Income Tax Return for Calendar Year 1929," copy on deposit in files of the Colorado Springs Fine Arts Center; photocopy available at ACM; copies of his 1930 and 1931 tax returns available in the same places. "Second Annual Exhibition of Fine Arts," [Denver newspaper, December 11, 192?], clipping on deposit in files of the Colorado Springs Fine Arts Center.

69. BP to LG, January 10, 1927; *Furniture by Francis Gilpin,* brochure, n.d.; "Laura Gilpin Collection–Catalogue of Negatives," ACM. Frank Gilpin to Warren Sparks, December 14, 1928. F. Gilpin, Inc., "Corporation Income Tax Return for 1929." Eugenie Shonnard to Frank Gilpin, October 18, 1929. "Francis Gilpin's Creations in Woodwork Masterpieces Much as Painting or Sonata," [Colorado Springs newspaper, n.d.], clipping in files of the Colorado Springs Fine Arts Center. "Mahogany from Home 400 Years Old Brought Here," [Colorado Springs newspaper, n.d.], clipping in files of the Colorado Springs Fine Arts Center; Black & Yates, Inc., to Schmeig-Hungate & Kotzian, Inc., July 17, 1930. The highboy was built for

the Stewart family of Colorado Springs. They later gave it to Laura Gilpin, who kept it as one of her most prized possessions and bequeathed it to the Colorado Springs Fine Arts Center.

70. *Cragmor, Colorado Springs, Colorado*, 16-pp. illustrated booklet [Colorado Springs: Dentan Printing Co., 1925]; *San Luis School, Boarding Department, Colorado Springs, Colorado*, 12-pp. illustrated brochure [Colorado Springs, 1928]. Gilpin also continued to do the annual illustrated brochures for the Broadmoor Art Academy.

71. LG to Arthur Fisher, February 10, 1926, Fisher Architectural Records Collection, Western History Department, Denver Public Library. LG, "Historic Architecture Photography: The Southwest," *Complete Photographer* 6, (July 20, 1942): 1987.

72. See *Colorado Springs Day Nursery*, 36-pp. illustrated brochure (Colorado Springs: Dentan Printing Company, 1924). Arthur Fisher to LG, February 11, 1926, Fisher Architectural Records Collection. The Fishers' set of Gilpin's prints is in the photography collection of the Colorado Historical Society.

73. LG to Arthur Fisher, September 1927, Fisher Architectural Records Collection.

74. *A Monograph of the Work of William E. Fisher, Arthur A. Fisher, Architects*, with a foreword by George William Eggers (Colorado Springs: Dentan Printing Co., 1929).

75. See Appendix for 1929 exhibitions; "The Cup Competition," *Light and Shade* 2 (October 1929): 7. Ira W. Martin, "Photographic Art in America: The P.P.A. Third International," *Light and Shade* 1 (May 1929): 6, 7, 9, and "Salon Policies," *Light and Shade* 2 (April 1930): 6, 7, 10. LG, "The Third International Salon of the Pictorial Photographers of America in Answer to Mr. Haz," [1929 or 1930], TS, p. 3. See also Jean S. Tucker, *Group f.64* (St. Louis: University of Missouri–St. Louis, 1978).

76. Milwaukee Art Institute *Bulletin* 3 (March 1930): 6; see Appendix; *Honolulu Star-Bulletin*, March 8, 1930; Lucile E. Morehouse, "Pictorial Photography Exhibit Includes Three Noted Artists," *Indianapolis Sunday Star*, June 8, 1930. "Certificate of Membership, Royal Photographic Society of Great Britain," May 12, 1930; H. H. Blacklock to LG, May 13, 1930.

77. Laura already had a large group of prints in the Library of Congress collection. In 1917 she had deposited a copyright copy of *The Prelude*, a photograph that featured Putnam's daughter Brenda as a pianist in a trio, and since then had submitted more then eighty prints to the library for copyright purposes (Eric Zengoto to the author, n.d. [April 1981], ACM). BP to LG, April 21, 1930; Herbert

Putnam to LG, May 12, 1930; BP to LG, April 25, 1930. An undated [1930] letter from Putnam to LG indicates the Library of Congress was keeping only ten prints, a fact contradicted in Putnam's subsequent letter of May 12, 1930. Linn Blanchard to LG, May 7, 1930, confirms that the library actually purchased sixteen photographs.

Meeting the Navajo, 1930–1933 (pages 51–58)

1. David Vestal, "Laura Gilpin: Photographer of the Southwest," *Popular Photography* 80 (February 1977): 132. Numerous fine arts photographers, including Alfred Stieglitz, had experimented with lantern slides. Although Laura was probably unaware of it, photographer and anthropologist Frederick Monsen had toured the country with lantern-slide lectures on southwestern archaeology and anthropology in the 1910s; see *The Frederick Monsen Lecture*, illustrated brochure, (n.p., n.d.), photocopy in the photographer's file, ACM.

2. LG, [Introduction to "Denizens of the Desert"], TS, LGACM.

3. *The Enduring Navaho*, p. v.

4. Ibid.

5. LG, interview with Eleanor Caponigro, Santa Fe, 1979, transcript, p. 14.

6. BP to LG, November 16, 1931. "Report of the Nursing Committee," *Eastern Association on Indian Affairs, Inc. Annual Report* [New York, 1932], p. 11; this report and other association records are in the American Association on Indian Affairs (AAIA) Collection at Princeton University Library. Elizabeth Richardson interview.

7. *Enduring Navaho*, p. 23. For information on Navajo life during the 1930s, see Clyde Kluckhohn and Dorothea Leighton, *The Navaho* (Cambridge: Harvard University Press, 1946); and Ruth Underhill, *The Navajos* (1956; rev. ed., Norman: University of Oklahoma Press, 1967). An excellent bibliography on the subject is Peter Iverson, *The Navajos: A Critical Bibliography* (Bloomington: University of Indiana Press, 1976).

8. *National Association on Indian Affairs, Inc. Annual Report* [New York, ca. 1933], p. [1].

9. *Observations on Indian Health Problems and Facilities*, Public Health Bulletin No. 23 (Washington, D.C.: U.S. Treasury Department Public Health Service, 1936), pp. 18–19; Margaret McKittrick, "Nursing Situation," *Eastern Association on Indian Affairs Annual Report* [New York, 1929], pp. 20–23; "Report of the Nursing Committee," p. 11.

10. Information on Elizabeth Forster's experiences in Red Rock is drawn from her typescript "Denizens of the Desert," a compilation of letters describing her work, now on deposit at ACM; the typescript is currently being prepared for publication by this author. A description of Forster's scouting trip is in EF to Emily [Stuart], October 10, 1931, in "Denizens." "Report of the Nursing Committee," p. 11. See also the following letters in "Denizens": EF to LG, November 7, 1931; EF to Helen, November 15, 1931; EF to Emily [Stuart], December 3, 1931; EF to LG, February 27, 1932.

11. Gerald Richardson interview.

12. EF to Mrs. [Margaret McKittrick] Burge, November 7, 1932, AAIA Collection.

13. *Enduring Navaho*, p. 24.

14. EF to Mrs. [Margaret McKittrick] Burge, November 7, 1932.

15. Irene Clurman, "Lively Laura Gilpin Preparing Another Southwest Chronicle," *Denver Rocky Mountain News*, November 16, 1975. LG, interview with Jon Burris, November 1977, transcript, p. 11, on deposit at ACM.

16. Christopher M. Lyman, *The Vanishing Race and Other Illusions: Photographs of Indians by Edward S. Curtis* (New York: Pantheon Books in association with the Smithsonian Institution Press, 1982), pp. 65–70; Frederick I. Monsen, "Picturing Indians with the Camera," *Photo-Era* 25 (October 1910): 166.

17. *Enduring Navaho*, p. 23.

18. Ibid., p. 31.

19. Ibid., p. 24; G. Herbert Taylor, ed., *My Favorite Photograph and Why* (New York: Dodge Publishing Co., 1937), p. 34.

20. Fred Jim, interview with the author, Shiprock, September 1981.

21. *Enduring Navaho*, p. 218.

22. EF to Mrs. Moris [Margaret McKittrick] Burge, n.d. [ca. April 15, 1933], AAIA Collection. Margaret McKittrick Burge to Oliver La Farge, March 15, 1933, AAIA Collection; Margaret McKittrick Burge, "New Mexico Association on Indian Affairs," [minutes of meeting, March 14, 1933], AAIA Collection. "Northern Navaho Agency Annual Statistical Report for 1932," [Federal Record Center microcopy 1011, roll 93, "Superintendents' Annual Narrative and Statistical Reports from Field Jurisdictions of the Bureau of Indian Affairs, 1907–1938"], p. 3. See the following letters in the AAIA Collection: Margaret McKittrick Burge to Oliver La Farge, March 15, 1933; Margaret

McKittrick Burge to Inky, April 17, 1933; Oliver La Farge to Miss A. E. White, April 19, 1933; Oliver La Farge to John Collier, April 24, 1933. See also "Minutes of a Meeting of the New Mexico Association on Indian Affairs, October 30, 1933," TS, New Mexico Association on Indian Affairs Collection, New Mexico State Records Center and Archives.

23. *Enduring Navaho*, p. v. Francis Nakai to Oliver La Farge, June 18, 1933, AAIA Collection.

24. *Enduring Navaho*, p. 54.

25. Numerous books document the visual record compiled by Farm Security Administration photographers. In particular, see F. Jack Hurley, *Portrait of a Decade: Roy Stryker and the Development of Documentary Photography in the Thirties* (Baton Rouge: University of Louisiana Press, 1972); Roy Emerson Stryker and Nancy Wood, *In This Proud Land: America 1935–1943 As Seen in the F. S. A. Photographs* (Greenwich: New York Graphic Society, 1973); Penelope Dixon, *Photographers of the Farm Security Administration: An Annotated Bibliography* (New York: Garland, 1983).

26. See, for example, Elizabeth Compton Hegemann, *Navaho Trading Days* (Albuquerque: University of New Mexico Press, 1963); Franc Johnson Newcomb, *Navaho Neighbors* (Norman: University of Oklahoma Press, 1966); Frances Gillmor and Louisa Wade Wetherill, *Traders to the Navahos: The Story of the Wetherills of Kayenta* (1934; rpt., Albuquerque: University of New Mexico Press, 1953). Gladys Reicherd, an anthropologist who spent summers on the Navajo reservation in the early 1930s, also compiled a snapshot record of Navajo life; see her book *Spider Woman: A Story of Navaho Weavers and Chanters* (New York: Macmillan Company, 1934). Although women wrote a great many of the memoirs about life on the Navajo reservation during the 1930s, they did not have a monopoly on the field; for an example of carefully posed and highly sentimentalized photographs by a male observer, see James DeLancey Verplanck, *A Country of Shepherds* (Boston: Ruth Hill, 1934).

27. Doris Ulmann, *The Appalachian Photographs of Doris Ulmann*, with a remembrance by John Jacob Niles and preface by Jonathan William (Penland, N.C.: The Jargon Society, 1971). I am also grateful to Mrs. John Jacob Niles, Lexington, Kentucky, for permitting me to see her large collection of Ulmann prints.

The Depression Years, 1931–1941 (pages 59–69)

1. LG, "Fellowship Application Form, John Simon Guggenheim Memorial Foundation," 1947; LG noted here

that during the early 1930s she could do her "landscape and other work for exhibition purposes only between commercial jobs." LG to H. H. Blacklock, October 26, 1934; LG to Ira Martin, February 26, 1935.

2. F. Gilpin, Inc., "Corporation Income Tax Return for Calendar Year 1931," Colorado Springs Fine Arts Center Files; LG to Gladys Willis, May 18, 1932; LG to Edgar McMeehan, May 4, 1932.

3. Frank Gilpin to LG, August 12, 1932.

4. BP to LG, February 5, March 18, February 25, March 18, 1931; LG to Charles Duell, October 9, 1947.

5. "Laura Gilpin's Southwest Photos Delight Scientists," *Santa Fe New Mexican*, [1931], Gilpin Scrapbook I, LGACM; LG, *Pictorial Lantern Slides of the Southwest*, brochure [Colorado Springs, 1932].

6. LG, *Pictorial Lantern Slides*; LG to Alden Donelly, February 16, 1932; Jesse Nusbaum to LG, February 26, 1932; LG to Margaret Alexander, January 31, 1948. Bertram Glover, *Lantern Slides* (London: British Periodicals, 1928), in Gilpin Library at ACM. Several boxed sets of slides are in LGACM.

7. LG, *Pictorial Lantern Slides*; LG to Catherine Grey, January 22, 1936.

8. LG to Jesse Nusbaum, January 12, 1932; BP to LG, March 18, 1932.

9. Ollman and Stern interview, tape 6; LG to T. A. Willard, November 30, 1932; LG to Calvin Wheat, March 17, 1932; Schoonover interview, tape 3; Hazel and F. Martin Brown interview with the author, Colorado Springs, February 27, 1981; LG to Sylvanus Morley, June 14, 1932; [LG], "Heat and Humidity as Photographic Problems Met by Laura Gilpin," *Mallinkrodt Photo Bulletin*, no. 52 [St. Louis, ca. 1946–7].

10. LG, "Historic Architecture Photography: The Southwest," *Complete Photographer* 6 (July 20, 1942): 1992–1993; Brown interview.

11. Schoonover interview, tape 3.

12. LG, [typescript label attached to ACM accession number 79.145/60].

13. LG to T. A. Willard, November 30, 1932; LG to Henry Luce, May 31, 1932; LG to Eleanor Treacy, June 29, 1932; Henry Luce to LG, August 30, 1932. F. H. Douglas, "Laura Gilpin Photographs of Chichen Itza Shown," *Rocky Mountain News*, December 10, 1933; "The Taylor Museum for Southwestern Studies: An Exhibit of Photographs of the Mayan Ruins at Chichen Itza, Yucatan, Executed by Laura Gilpin," checklist [ca. 1933]; LG to

Clyde Fisher, December 19, 1933; "Paleontologist to Pursue Homo Sapiens' Trail Back to Pre-Pleistocene Times," *Santa Fe New Mexican*, September 19, 1932. Herbert Putnam to LG, January 27, February 26, May 16, 24, 1934; Laura also sold a set of Yucatán prints to the Cranbrook Art Institute in Michigan (LG to Ira Martin, April 6, 1935); LG to Herbert Putnam, April 14, 1934.

14. LG to Margaret Carrington, September 20, 1932; Ollman and Stern interview, tape 6; Wilder interview, I, 3.

15. BP to LG, November 6, 1932. A variant of the Gish portrait printed on Gevaluxe paper, inscribed and signed by Lillian Gish, hung in Laura Gilpin's studio during the late 1970s; Lillian Gish interview with the author, New York City, May 27, 1981. Prints and negatives from the following Central City Opera House productions are in LGACM: *The Merry Widow* (1933), *Othello* (1934), *Central City Nights* (1935), *Gondoliers* (1936), *Ruy Blas* (n.d.).

16. LG to Arthur Fisher, August 8, 1932.

17. BP to LG, December 22, 1927; August 23, 1931; May 11, 1932. "Brenda Putnam Sums Up Things," *New York Sun*, February 16, 1933; [unidentified clipping], *Art Digest*, March 15, 1935, Brenda Putnam File, LGACM; the piece was purchased for the Norton Gallery and School of Art in West Palm Beach, Florida, in 1946 and remains in that collection.

18. BP to LG, October 14, 1933; EF, [Activities, 1933–1942], MS.

19. LG, *Pictorial Lantern Slides of the Southwest*, brochure advertising slide rental [Colorado Springs: 1934]; see Invitation (February 17, [1933]) to a lecture by LG called "The Mayan Architecture of Yucatan," sponsored by the Service Bureau, Inc., Gilpin Scrapbook I; LG to Ira Martin, February 26, 1935.

20. [LG], *Friendfield Turkeys, Woodland Park, Colorado*, brochure [1935].

21. Wilder interview, IV, 7.

22. Edith Brann interview; Marka Stewart interview with the author, Colorado Springs, February 26, 1981.

23. EF, [Activities, 1933–1942].

24. "Colorado Springs Fine Arts Center," *Architectural Forum* 65 (July 1936): 11–20; for information on Meem, see Bainbridge Bunting, *John Gaw Meem, Southwest Architect* (Albuquerque: University of New Mexico Press, 1983). Ernest Knee interview with the author, Santa Fe, January 31, 1981; Ansel Adams interview with Therese Heyman, Carmel, California, March 24, 1980, transcript on deposit at ACM. LG to Register of Copyrights, March

19, 1937. George Kubler interview with the author, New Haven, June 1, 1981; George Kubler, *Religious Architecture of New Mexico* (Colorado Springs: Taylor Museum, 1940); dated negatives for the Taylor Museum project and for Gilpin's documentation of Meem's buildings at the University of New Mexico are in LGACM. See the Appendix for the 1936–1938 exhibition brochures.

25.   EF, [Activities, 1933–1942]; Irene Fisher, "Somebody Told Me," *Albuquerque Tribune*, October 20, 1936; Wilder interview, IV, 7.

26.   EF, [Activities]; BP to LG, March 31, April 8, 1940; Elizabeth Richardson interview.

27.   LG to Mr. Schweitzer, September 19, 1939; Aileen Nusbaum to LG, July 6, 1939; "Minutes of a Meeting of the Board of Trustees, March 8, 1939," Colorado Springs Fine Arts Center Records.

28.   BP to LG, April 26, 1940; William H. Cowles to LG, March 15, 21, 25, 1940; LG to William H. Cowles, July 16, 1940; LG to Paul Anderson, August 7, 1940; Paul Anderson to LG, August 12, 1940.

29.   LG, "Colorado Springs Fine Arts Center Opens Department of Photography. March Fifteenth," TS; LG to Percy Hagerman, March 13, 1940; LG to Paul Anderson, August 7, 1940.

30.   Walter Frese (WF) to LG, August 29, September 20, 1940; Carley Smalley to LG, June 8, 1941; LG to WF, September 7, 1940; BP to LG, December 28, 1940.

31.   LG to WF, March 15, May 7, 1941; WF to LG, April 29, 1941; *Pueblos*, p. 5.

32.   LG to WF, August 2, September 30, December 9, 1941; WF to LG, June 5, 1942.

33.   *Pueblos*, p. 7. Upon seeing the classical statue *Apollo Belvedere*, painter Benjamin West is said to have remarked, "By God, a Mohawk" (see Bernard DeVoto, *Across the Wide Missouri* [1947; rpt., Boston: Houghton Mifflin Co., 1975], p. 318). In his book *Letters and Notes on the Manners, Customs, and Condition of the North American Indian* (1841; rpt., New York: Dover Publications, 1973), I, p. 16, George Catlin commented that the American Indians "afforded models equal to those from which the Grecian sculptors transferred to the marble such inimitable grace and beauty." Alfred Jacob Miller found the Indians he met in 1837 "equal in form and grace (if not superior) to the finest beau ideal ever dreamed of by the Greeks" and recommended the American West to tourists tired of the well-trod landscape of Egypt or Greece (Marvin C. Ross, ed., *The West of Alfred Jacob Miller* [1951; rev. ed., Norman: University of Oklahoma Press, 1968], pp. 64, 59). Harriet Monroe, "In Texas and New Mexico," *Poetry* (September

1920) p. 328. D. H. Lawrence, "The Dance of the Sprouting Corn," in *Mornings in Mexico* (1927; rpt., Salt Lake City: Gibbs M. Smith Inc., 1982), p. 126.

34.   Cather, *Professor's House*, p. 219; *Pueblos*, pp. 38, 106; Mary Austin, *Taos Pueblo*, photographed by Ansel Easton Adams and described by Mary Austin (San Francisco: 1930).

35.   Austin, *Land of Journey's Ending*, p. 63; *Pueblos*, p. 23; Cather, *Professor's House*, p. 242.

36.   *Pueblos*, p. 30.

37.   Ibid., pp. 123, 124; Mary Austin, *Earth Horizon* (New York: Literary Guild, 1932), p. 268. This is also a pervasive theme in the southwestern writings of Mabel Dodge Luhan; see, especially, *Winter in Taos* (Denver: Sage Books Inc., 1935).

38.   LG to WF, February 3, 1941; *Pueblos*, p. 4.

39.   LG to WF, March 15, 1941.

40.   *Pueblos*, pp. 42, 86.

41.   John Collier, Jr., "Laura Gilpin: Western Photographer," *New Mexico Quarterly* (Winter 1950–1951), p. 489.

42.   *Pueblos*, pp. 110, 107.

43.   Ibid., p. 124.

To Wichita, to Yucatán, and along the Rio Grande, 1942–1949 (pages 70–85)

1.   LG to WF, January 17, February 20, 1942; WF to LG, February 25, 1942; LG to WF, March 17, 1942.

2.   LG to WF, January 30, 1942; LG to Tom Maloney, February 9, 1942; LG to Francis Gilpin, Jr., January 21, 1942.

3.   LG to Francis Gilpin, Jr., January 21, 1942; BP to LG, n.d. [ca. April 1942]; LG to E. R. Bennett, June 7, 1942.

4.   LG, "Statement of Transactions, 317 Cheyenne Road, Colo. Springs," MS, [1942]; "War Production Board Preference Rating Certificate," [August 1942]; LG to Charlotte Muret, November 17, 1942; LG, interview with the author, p. 8.

5.   LG to WF, January 30, 1942; LG to Tom Maloney, February 9, 1942; Tom Maloney to LG, February 23, 1942; LG to Tom Maloney, March 22, 1942; Hill and Cooper, *Dialogue with Photography*, p. 288; LG, interview with the author, II, p. 6.

6.   LG to Isabel Herdle, February 23, 1942.

7. LG to Herbert Stabler, March 12, 1942; LG to Clyde Fisher, March 16, 1942. LG to Willard Morgan, April 28, 1942.

8. BP to LG, August 13, 1942.

9. LG to Alexius Forster, April 27, 1943; EF, [Activities, 1933–1942].

10. LG to Charlotte Muret, November 17, 1942; LG, interview with the author, p. 9.

11. Francis Gilpin, "Last Will and Testament," November 6, 1942.

12. LG to Victor Hungerford, January 24, 1943; Victor Hungerford to LG, January 7, 28, 1943; "County of El Paso. State of Colorado Docket File G-480."

13. Jack Wecker telephone interview with Beth Taylor Muskat, April 10, 1980, notes on deposit at ACM; George Findlay, "Rate or Job Change," April 10, 1942; Ollman and Stern interview, tape 5; LG, interview with Jon Burris, p. 17.

14. LG, interview with the author, II, p. 5; LG to Willard Morgan, September 9, 1943; Ollman and Stern interview, tape 5; Wille interview, p. 4; LG to Lee Witkin, July 3, 1972.

15. An album of photographs showing Gilpin at work in the Boeing plant is in LGACM; Lillian Gish to LG, February 8, 1943.

16. LG to Willard Morgan, September 9, 1943.

17. Hill and Cooper, *Dialogue with Photography*, p. 284; Burris interview, p. 4.

18. Wilder interview, p. 44; Ollman and Stern interview, tape 5.

19. LG to Mr. Divinia, n.d. [ca. May 1943].

20. Wilder interview, p. 22; *Fortune* 31 (May 1945): 133; LG, interview with ACM film crew, September 1979, tape 21; the photograph was exhibited in photographic salons in Wichita and St. Louis (see Milan Hughston, "Laura Gilpin: A Chronological Bibliography," TS, ACM Library).

21. Burris interview, p. 4.

22. "Gilpin Rites Will Be Held Saturday," *Colorado Springs Gazette*, July 9, 1943; LG to W. L. Hyde, May 28, 1948.

23. Dave Page to LG, March 15, 1944; Krehbiel, Page & Gilpin, Co., "United States Partnership Return of Income, 1944"; the company grossed just over $3,000 in 1944.

24. LG to Alexius Forster, April 27, 1943; Anne Parrish

Titzell to LG, January 28, 1944; LG to Douglas McKay, March 25, 1978; EF to LG, May 14, 1944.

25. Dr. Paul Draper to J. Donald Haney, March 16, 1945.

26. Jack Wecker, phone conversation with Beth Taylor Muskat; LG, "Fellowship Application Form, John Simon Guggenheim Memorial Foundation," 1947; Fanny Robbins to LG, n.d.; Draper to Haney, March 16, 1945; Emily Stuart to LG, April 27, 1943; LG to Alexius Forster, December 9, 1944.

27. "Francis Gilpin, Jr.," informational file, Alumni Records Office, Yale University; Edna Gilpin to LG, n.d. [ca. September 1949].

28. BP to LG, August 28, 1944; LG, interview with the author, I, p. 1; Wilder interview, IV, p. 4; "Agreement between Laura Gilpin and Duell, Sloan & Pearce, Inc. for the Publication Book of: Photographic Book on Rio Grande," May 25, 1945; Marta Weigle, "Publishing in Santa Fe, 1915–40," *El Palacio* 90 (Anniversary issue, 1984): 11.

29. ["Interview with Laura Gilpin on the Rio Grande"], TS, [ca. 1949], p. 1 (hereafter referred to as RG interview).

30. LG to John Collier, Jr., May 26, 1950; RG interview, pp. 3, 2; LG to "Gentlemen" [Duell, Sloan & Pearce], February 14, 1946.

31. RG interview, p. 1; LG to Gordon Wilbur, May 25, 1951; LG to Willard Morgan, August 5, 1945.

32. LG to Wally Goodwin (WG), June 28, 1945; WG to LG, July 3, 1945.

33. RG interview, pp. 4–5; LG to WG, July 18, 1945. Charles Lummis, "Our Amateur Photographs," *Land of Sunshine* 2 (January 1895): 28. LG, "Historic Architecture Photography" p. 1990.

34. LG to WG, Oct. 2, 1945.

35. LG to Leon Daniel, October 9, 1945; "Statement of Borrower," October 1945; April 19, 1945; LG to WF, November 14, 1945.

36. Hill and Cooper, *Dialogue with Photography*; p. 289; LG, interview with the author, p. 7.

37. LG to Bishop Kennedy, June 27, 1945; LG to John Haney, August 23, 1945; Douglas McKay, *Asylum of the Gilded Pill: The Story of Cragmor Sanitorium* (Denver: State Historical Society of Colorado, 1983), p. 82; LG to L. L. Dentan, June 13, 1946.

38. See "Laura Gilpin Collection–Catalogue of Negatives," ACM; Mabel Dodge Luhan, *Taos and Its Artists* (New York: Duell, Sloan & Pearce, 1947); LG to the author, private conversation, Santa Fe, September 1979.

39. LG, "U.S. Individual Income Tax Return," 1947, 1949.

40. Sylvanus Morley to LG, January 30, 1946, November 28, 1946; LG to Leon Daniel, March 3, 1946.

41. LG to WF, November 9, 1947; Karl Ruppert to LG, October 21, 1946; Sylvanus Morley to LG, November 28, 1946; LG to WF, November 9, 1947.

42. LG to WF, March 14, 1948.

43. *Temples*, pp. 5, 110.

44. Ibid., p. 121; John Lloyd Stephens, *Incidents of Travel in Central America, Chiapas, and Yucatan . . .* (1841; new ed., New Brunswick: Rutgers University Press, 1949), I, 79.

45. *Temples*, pp. 110, [4]; Wilder interview, pp. 26–27; BP to LG, April 4, 1948.

46. William McNulty, "Laura Gilpin's Mayan Text Expertly Done," *Santa Fe New Mexican*, April 2, 1948; Paul Martin to LG, April 22, 1948; Earl Morris to LG, June 25, 1948; Clyde Fisher, ["Book Review"], *Natural History* 57 (June 1948): 247.

47. LG to WG, May 20, 1946; LG to Charles Duell, August 24, 1947.

48. LG to WG, August 24, September 14, 1947. Ansel Adams commented that Laura would have benefited from the help of a good picture editor, such as he had on most of his publications (see Ansel Adams, interview with Therese Heyman, p. 4).

49. LG to WG, January 29, February 26, July 8, 1949; October 10, 1947.

50. *The Rio Grande: River of Destiny* (New York: Duell, Sloan & Pearce, 1949), p. [v].

51. Paul Horgan, *Of America East and West: Selections from the Writings of Paul Horgan* (New York: Farrar Straus Giroux, 1984), p. 154; LG to Edna Bennett, December 12, 1956.

52. TS draft for "Laura Gilpin's Rio Grande Country," *U.S. Camera* 13 (February 1950): 44–47.

53. LG to Ed Hannigan, n.d. [1949]; Wilder interview, IV, pp. 11–12; LG, interview with the author, II, p. 7; RG interview, p. 4.

54. Anne Noggle interview with the author, Albuquerque, February 4, 1981; Wilder interview, p. 22.

55. For the background of nineteenth-century photography of the American West, see Robert Taft, *Photography and the American Scene* (New York: Macmillan Co., 1938); William Goetzmann, *Exploration and Empire: The Explorer and the Scientist in the Winning of the American West* (New York: Knopf, 1966); Weston J. Naef, with James N. Wood and Therese Heyman, *Era of Exploration: The Rise of Landscape Photography in the American West, 1860–1885* (New York: Albright-Knox Art Gallery and the Metropolitan Museum of Art, 1975); Peter E. Palmquist, with a foreword by Martha A. Sandweiss, *Carleton E. Watkins: Photographer of the American West* (Albuquerque: University of New Mexico Press, 1983).

56. Homer, *Pictorial Heritage*. Ulmann, *The Appalachian Photographs of Doris Ulmann*; *The Darkness and the Light: Photographs by Doris Ulmann* (Millerton, N.Y.: Aperture, 1974). Therese Thau Heyman, *Anne Brigman: Pictorial Photographer/Pagan/Member of the Photo-Secession* (Oakland: Oakland Museum, 1974). Barbara Morgan, with introduction by Peter Bunnell, *Barbara Morgan* (Hastings-on-Hudson, N.Y.: Morgan & Morgan in cooperation with the Amon Carter Museum, 1972).

57. *The Rio Grande*, pp. 4, 5, 9, 49, 104–106, 46, 70, 128.

58. Ibid., p. 236.

59. Ibid., pp. 132, 231, 90.

60. John Brinkerhoff Jackson, [book review], *Arizona Quarterly* 4 (Winter 1949): 368–370.

61. John Collier, Jr., "Laura Gilpin: Western Photographer," *New Mexico Quarterly* (Winter 1950–1951): 485, 491, 486.

62. BP to LG, March 30, 1951.

63. Paul Horgan to LG, November 19, 1949; Barbara Morgan to LG, January 8, 1950; Oliver La Farge, "That Picturesque Vital Artery, the Rio Grande," *New York Herald Tribune*, November 13, 1949.

64. LG to Tom Maloney, February 20, 1941; LG to Sylvanus Morley, July 13, 1948. The Rio Grande photographs were exhibited at the Colorado Springs Fine Arts Center, November 14–December 27, 1948; Museum of Fine Arts, Dallas, December 4, 1949–January 15, 1950; Santa Barbara Museum of Art, September 1950; Roswell Museum, February 4–March 4, 1951; photographs from the Yucatán and Rio Grande series were exhibited together at the Arts Club of Washington, February 18–March 9, 1951 (see Appendix). "1000 Attend Laura Gilpin Art Exhibit," *Rocky Mountain News*, November 15, 1948.

65. LG, "Fellowship Application Form, John Simon Guggenheim Memorial Foundation," 1947; LG to WG, April 2, 1948; LG to WF, March 25, 1948; LG to Nancy Newhall, May 19, 1948.

66. LG to WF, September 21, 1948.

67. EF to E. T. Hagberg, n.d. [1948].

68. *Quiet Triumph: Forty Years with the Indian Arts Fund, Santa Fe* (Fort Worth: Amon Carter Museum with the Cooperation of the School of American Research, 1966); ["Chronology of the Indian Arts Fund"], TS, pp. 21, 23, in the collection of the School of American Research, Santa Fe; Betty Toulouse, interview with the author, Santa Fe, February 3, 1981; Ann Nolan Clark, "From Basement to Basement," TS, 1965, in the collection of the School of American Research, Santa Fe.

69. [?] to LG, November 8, 1948.

Back to the Navajo, 1950–1968 (pages 86–98)

1. LG to WF, January 17, 1942; WF to LG, May 22, 1942; LG to Sam Sloan, April 20, 1944.

2. LG to WG, December 3, 1947.

3. Charles A. Pearce to LG, January 27, February 10, 1950; LG to Pearce, February 14, 1950; "Tentative Outline for Book on the Navahos," March 11, 1950.

4. LG to WG and Pearce, March 28, 1950.

5. "Agreement between Laura Gilpin and Duell, Sloan & Pearce, Inc. for the Publication of Navaho Book," April 20, 1950; LG to WG and Pearce, March 28, 1950.

6. LG to WG, May 11 [1952?]; "Laura Gilpin Collection – Catalogue of Negatives," ACM.

7. LG to WG, May 7, 1950.

8. LG to Clyde Kluckhohn, September 9, 1950; LG to WG, September 22, 1950.

9. LG to Kluckhohn, May 30, 1951; LG, "U.S. Individual Income Tax Return, 1951"; LG to Pearce, October 14, 1951.

10. LG to Pearce, October 14, 1951.

11. Leonard McCombe, *Navaho Means People*, photographs by Leonard McCombe, text by Evon Z. Vogt and Clyde Kluckhohn (Cambridge: Harvard University Press, 1951); LG to Kluckhohn, February 12, 1952; LG to Pearce, January 28, 1952.

12. LG to Jack Snow, August 18, 1951.

13. LG to John Peckham, October 27, 1952; "Laura Gilpin Collection – Catalogue of Negatives"; LG, [Wenner-Gren grant request statement], TS, February 1952; LG to Beaumont Newhall, February 12, 1952; Marjorie Lambert to Paul Fejos, February 19, 1952.

14. LG to Alfred Orsini, November 30, 1952; LG to Dex-tone Press, March 31, 1952; LG to Pearce, January 28, 1952, May 4, 1953.

15. LG to Pearce, May 4, 1953; Beverly Gile, interview with the author, Santa Fe, February 5, 1981.

16. LG to Darlene Bekkedal, April 16, 1955.

17. LG to Walter Paepke, December 7, 1953. *Enduring Navaho*, pp. 29, 247; however, according to Edith Kennedy, a trader's wife in Red Rock, the baby Laura photographed in 1954 was actually the nephew of the boy she had photographed earlier (Edith Kennedy, interview with the author, Red Rock, September 10, 1982).

18. LG to Pearce and Charles Duell, January 25, 1954; LG, "Possible Titles," TS, n.d. [January 1954].

19. Pearce and Charles Duell to LG, February 5, 1954; LG to Pearce and Duell, February 8, 1954; Duell to LG, February 10, 1954; LG to Mitchell A. Wilder, February 15, 1954.

20. LG to Savoie Lottinville, February 14, 19, March 12, 1954; Lottinville to LG, March 12, 1954.

21. LG to Lottinville, March 31, 1954; LG to Duell, April 16, 1954.

22. LG to Lottinville, March 23, 1954; LG to Duell, April 16, 1954; LG to WF, June 26, 1954; *Enduring Navaho*, p. 10.

23. *Enduring Navaho*, pp. 68–72.

24. Ibid., p. 32.

25. Ibid., pp. 76–78.

26. LG to Laura Carpenter, July 15, 1955.

27. Lucille Minnick to LG, October 13, 1955; Lucy Wing to LG, October 13, 1955; Olwen Lloyd to LG, July 11, 1955; LG to Katherine Lee, September 1, 1955; Laura Carpenter to LG, October 8, 1955; LG to Carol Preston, September 4, 1955; Margaret Speer to LG, October 7, 1955; "Arts Club of Washington," calendar, April 1955; Beaumont Newhall to LG, December 2, 1955; LG to Roberta [?], December 5, 1955; LG to Wilder, May 6, 1956; LG to Mary Abbott, December 20, 1955.

28. First National Bank of Santa Fe, Note, December 7, 1955; Anne Parrish Titzell to LG, December 15, 1955. What they actually purchased was half of a house. In the mid-1970s, with financial help from a cousin, Laura was able to purchase the remaining portion of the structure and remodel the building as a one-family house.

29. LG to Mary Abbott, December 20, 1955; Abbott to LG, January 9, 1956; LG to Wilder, February 6, 1956. "Mitchell Armitage Wilder," TS résumé, AMC files; "Mitchell Armitage Wilder," *Who's Who in the South and*

Southwest, 11th ed. (Chicago: Marquis – Who's Who, [1969]), p. 1089. *The West: A Portfolio of Photographs* (Colorado Springs: Colorado Springs Fine Arts Center, 1953).

30.   LG, "U.S. Individual Income Tax Return, 1957"; "Laura Gilpin Collection – Catalogue of Negatives"; LG to Nancy Newhall, May 30, 1957.

31.   *Enduring Navaho*, pp. 112–120.

32.   LG to Margaret and Nathaniel Owings, June 25, 1959.

33.   LG to Imogen Cunningham, May 31, 1959; Beaumont Newhall, "The Aspen Photo Conference," TS, October 30, 1951, LGACM; *Enduring Navaho*, p. ix.

34.   LG, "U.S. Individual Income Tax Return, 1960." "Laura Gilpin Collection – Catalogue of Negatives"; LG to Elizabeth Gordon, June 12, 28, 1960; see also the article by LG, "The Austerity of the Desert Pervades Her Home and Work," *House Beautiful* 105 (April 1963): 144, 145, 198; LG to John Gaw Meem, February 20, 1961; LG to Willard Morgan, July 21, 1960[1961]; LG to EF, December 25, 1960; LG to Ansel Adams, August 26, 1961.

35.   EF to Emily Stuart, n.d. [ca. December 1960], December 28, 1960; Marjorie Batchelder McPharlin to Emily Stuart, January 21, 1961.

36.   Tony and Juanita Peña, interview with the author, San Ildefonso Pueblo, March 1, 1984; Richard Rudisill, interview with the author, Santa Fe, February 4, 1981.

37.   "Laura Gilpin Collection – Catalogue of Negatives." Gilpin replaced Kenneth Chapman as chairman of the Indian Arts Fund in October 1957; see *IAF Chronology* (Santa Fe: Indian Arts Fund, Inc. [1962]), on deposit at the School of American Research, Santa Fe. LG, "U.S. Individual Income Tax Return, 1962."

38.   LG to Willard Morgan, May 18, 1963; Frank Wardlaw to LG, May 20, 1963; LG to Wardlaw, June 1, 1963.

39.   LG to Mitchell A. Wilder, April 28, February 14, 1964.

40.   LG to Wardlaw, April 16, 1964; LG to Emily Stuart, April 27, 1964.

41.   *Enduring Navaho*, p. 248.

42.   LG, "Receipts," MS appended to "U.S. Individual Income Tax Return, 1966"; LG to Billie Norton, January 20, 1966; LG to Wardlaw, April 9, 1966; Burris interview, p. 6.

43.   Elinor Gregg to LG, September 5, 1966; for information on Gregg and her nursing career, see Elinor D. Gregg, *The Indians and the Nurse* (Norman: University of Oklahoma Press, 1965).

44.   Frederick Dockstader to LG, citation, April 20, 1967.

45.   LG to Wardlaw, October 31, January 22, 1967; LG to Beaumont Newhall, April 7, 1967; LG to Wilder, April 13, 1967; LG to Dr. Lewis Overton, June 17, 1967.

46.   LG to Wardlaw, November 2, 1968.

The Enduring Navaho, *1968 (pages 99–104)*

1.   *Enduring Navaho*, p. v; LG to Frank Wardlaw, January 22, 1967.

2.   LG to Barbara Spielman, November 15, 1967, January 31, [1968]; *Enduring Navaho*, p. vii.

3.   *Enduring Navaho*, p. 3.

4.   Ibid., p. 20.

5.   LG to Frank Wardlaw, June 17, 1967.

6.   *Enduring Navaho*, p. 250.

7.   Peter James Iverson, "The Evolving Navaho Nation: Continuity within Change" (Ph.D. dissertation, University of Wisconsin, 1975).

8.   *Pueblos*, p. 124; *Enduring Navaho*, p. 250.

9.   *Enduring Navaho*, pp. 106, 178.

10.   LG to Myron Berman, June 16, 1972.

11.   *Enduring Navaho*, pp. 23, 73, 246, 182, 248, 20, 157; LG, "Foreword," in Mary Hunt Kahlenberg and Anthony Berlant, *The Navaho Blanket* (Los Angeles: Los Angeles County Museum of Art, 1972), p. 5.

12.   LG to Mitchell A. Wilder, April 16, 1956; John Collier, Jr., to the author, June 23, 1982, ACM.

13.   LG, "Journal of Quotations I Want to Keep," loose-leaf notebook, n.p.

14.   *Enduring Navaho*, p. 250; LG, "Journal," n.p.

15.   LG, "Journal," n.p.; Dorothea Leighton and Clyde Kluckhohn wrote: ". . . the Navaho, though decidedly an individualist in some ways, is essentially group-minded. . . . To accept authority over his fellows or to take initiative in any obvious fashion has for the Navaho the psychological meaning of separating him from the social group to which he looks for both support and regulation." (*Children of the People: The Navaho Individual and his Develpoment* [Cambridge, Mass.: Harvard University Press, 1947], p. 107).

16. Dean Krakel to LG, April 1, 1969; Ansel Adams to LG, December 22, 1968 (courtesy the Trustees of the Ansel Adams Publishing Rights Trust, all rights reserved); Paul Strand to LG, August 19, 1969.

17. Ned Hatathli to LG, November 20, 1968; Editha Watson, "Book Review," *Navaho Times*, January 9, 1969; LG to Johnnie Yazzie, January 10, 1973.

Finished in Beauty, 1969–1979 (pages 105–114)

1. LG to Wilder, September 23, 1968; Beverly Gile, interview with the author, Santa Fe, February 5, 1981; Marjorie Lambert, interview with the author, February 3, 1981; BP to LG, January 10, 1963, January 8, 1968.

2. Lee Udall to LG, September 12, 1969; LG, "U.S. Individual Income Tax Return, 1968"; "U.S. Individual Income Tax Return, 1969"; LG to Nathan Resnick, October 3, 1969; LG to Ferrell Heady, January 18, 1970; LG to John Durrie, February 11, 1970.

3. "President's Citation for Laura Gilpin, Doctor of Humane Letters, University of New Mexico," [June 1970]; this citation was written by photohistorian Richard Rudisill.

4. LG to Wilder, September 18, 1971; LG, "Fellowship Application Form, John Simon Guggenheim Memorial Foundation," [1970]; LG to Ansel Adams, September 21, 1970.

5. LG to Van Deren Coke, August 17, 1971.

6. LG to Wilder, September 18, 1971; Anne Noggle, interview with the author; LG to Wardlaw, October 31, 1971.

7. "Certificate of Death, State of New Mexico" [for Elizabeth Forster], January 1, 1972; "Elizabeth Forster Dies after Illness," *New Mexican*, January 3, 1972; LG's typescript copy for the text is in LGACM.

8. Emily Stuart to LG, April 15, 1972.

9. LG to Ned Hatathli, January 30, 1972.

10. LG, "Journal," n.p.; Wille interview, p. 21; LG to Wardlaw, January 25, 1972; LG to WF, January 25, 1972.

11. Richard Rudisill, interview with the author, Santa Fe, February 4, 1981; Burris interview, p. 2.

12. Douglas Schwartz to LG, March 26, 1972; Frank Koski to LG, April 19, 1972; LG to Lee Witkin, May 15, 1972; LG to Ned Hatathli, March 13, 1972.

13. Dave and Corky Jones, interview with the author, Santa Fe, January 29, 1981; LG to Lee Witkin, July 3, 1972.

14. Peggy James, "Laura Gilpin Photographer," *Colorado Springs* 2 (March–April 1978): 26; Audrie Bobb, interview with the author, Santa Fe, January 29, 1981.

15. LG to Ansel Adams, May 14, 1973; Lee Witkin to LG, January 8, 1974.

16. William Clift, "Remembering: Laura Gilpin," *Santa Fe Reporter*, December 6, 1979; Ollman and Stern interview, tape 2; Rudisill interview.

17. *Laura Gilpin Retrospective* (Santa Fe: Museum of New Mexico, 1974); Manual Ortiz to LG, November 12, 1975; Noggle and Rudisill interviews.

18. Ansel Adams in *Laura Gilpin Retrospective*, p. 4; the catalogue also includes statements by Anne Noggle, Paul Strand, and Beaumont Newhall. Andrea Davis, "Through a Lens, from the Heart," *Santa Fe Reporter*, February 27, 1975.

19. Peggy Pond Church, interview with the author, Santa Fe, February 2, 1981; Desmond O'Hara to LG, telegram, October 19, 1975. Brenda Putnam bequeathed $1,000 to Gilpin (Roger Katen to LG, May 14, 1976).

20. LG to Carol Rachlin, January 19, 1976.

21. Clift, "Remembering: Laura Gilpin."

22. LG, interview with Eleanor Caponigro, pp. 1–2.

23. Ibid., pp. 6, 8, 7.

24. Ibid., p. 11.

25. LG to Imogen Cunningham, April 17, 1976; Imogen Cunningham to LG, April 25, 1976; LG to Helen Johnston, October 6, 1976.

26. Rosanna Hall, "Laura Gilpin: A Lifetime of Photography," *Santa Fe New Mexican*, July 1, 1976; LG to Dan Berley, June 18, 1976; LG to Robin Cronin, July 14, 1976; LG to Gordon Ray, June 15, 1976.

27. Anne Hillerman, "Governor's First Excellence Awards Given 6 N M Artists," *Santa Fe New Mexican*, October 7, 1974; Richard D. Lamm, "Executive Order" granting "Governor's Award in the Arts and Humanities" to LG, September 9, 1977; Lloyd E. Worner to LG, March 21, 1979.

28. Lambert interview; Noggle interview.

29. Wille interview, p. 3; LG to Michelle Mertz, April 13, 1977; Wilder interview, IV, p. 5; LG to Gloria Steinem, August 24, 1974.

30. Peggy Pond Church interview; C. F. Bieber, interview with the author, Santa Fe, January 30, 1981; Lambert interview; Ansel Adams, interview with Therese Heyman, p. 5; Bobb interview.

31. Many of these interviews have been collected at ACM, including copies of audio, video, or film interviews by the Center for Creative Photography (1977), Arthur Ollman and Rosella Stern (1976), Gretel Erlich (1978), Amon Carter Museum (1978 and 1979), and Margaret Schoonover (1979); ACM also has typescripts of oral interviews by Jon Burris (1977), Alicia Wille (1977), Margaretta Mitchell (1977), Eleanor Caponigro (1979), the author (1979), and others.

32. Ansel Adams, interview with Therese Heyman, p. 3.

33. Austin, *Land of Journey's Ending*, p. 438.

34. John Collier, Jr., to the author, July 23, 1982.

35. Dave and Corky Jones interview.

36. This is a common theme in women's accounts of their westward journeys; see, for example, Nannie T. Alderson and Helena Huntington Smith, *A Bride Goes West* (1942; rpr., Lincoln: University of Nebraska Press, 1969); a fine fictional rendering of this idea is in Wallace Stegner, *Angle of Repose* (1971; rpr., New York: Fawcett Crest Books, 1978).

37. Anita Da, interview with the author, San Ildefonso Pueblo, January 27, 1981; Rain Parrish, interview with the author, Santa Fe, February 4, 1981. Da indicated that the timing of Laura's arrival at San Ildefonso Pueblo in the early 1920s was the key to her acceptance there. Parrish, a Navajo working as curator of the Wheelright Museum, indicated that Laura was accepted by the Navajo near Red Rock because she first came in the 1930s when few outsiders were either curious or willing to help.

38. Elinor Gregg to LG, September 5, 1966.

39. [Michael Duty], "News Release: Laura Gilpin Collection," [May 14, 1978], ACM files; the film crew included the author and William Howze from the Amon Carter Museum; Richard Rudisill, personal communication to the author, November 1984.

40. "Obituaries," *Santa Fe New Mexican*, November 30, 1979.

41. *Enduring Navaho*, p. 240.

Index

In this index, photographs in the text are indicated by an italic page number i.e., *46*. References to plates are shown as follows: plate 12. Notes are indicated by page number followed by a colon and the number of the note, i.e., 316:2. All photographs by Laura Gilpin are listed under Photographs by Laura Gilpin. All books, brochures, pamphlets and portfolios by Laura Gilpin are listed under Books, brochures, pamphlets and portfolios.

This book, designed by Eleanor Morris Caponigro,
was set in Monotype Bembo at Meriden-Stinehour, Lunenburg, Vermont,
printed on Mohawk Superfine paper at Meriden-Stinehour, Meriden, Connecticut,
and bound in Scholco cloth at
Publishers Book Bindery, Long Island City, New York.
The monogram on the binding was designed for Laura Gilpin by Warren Chappell.